THE NATURE OF HUMAN

This book provides an overview of the approaches of leading scholars to understanding the nature of creativity, its measurement, its investigation, its development, and its importance to society. The authors are the 24 psychological scientists who are most frequently cited in the four major textbooks on creativity, and they can thus be considered among the most eminent living scholars in the field. Each author discusses how they define creativity, the kinds of questions they have addressed, theories they have proposed, and a description of their research and the most interesting empirical results it has produced. The chapters represent a wide range of substantive and methodological emphases, including psychometric, cognitive, expertise-based, developmental, neuropsychological, cultural, systems, and group-difference approaches. *The Nature of Human Creativity* brings together an incredible diversity of viewpoints, helping students and researchers to see the points of consensus as well as the differences in contemporary perspectives.

ROBERT J. STERNBERG is Professor of Human Development at Cornell University and Honorary Professor of Psychology at the University of Heidelberg. Formerly, he was IBM Professor of Psychology and Education at Yale University. His PhD is from Stanford, and he has thirteen honorary doctorates. He has won the Grawemeyer Award in psychology and both the William James and James McKeen Cattell Awards from the Association for Psychological Science as well as more than two dozen other major awards and is a member of the National Academy of Education and the American Academy of Arts and Sciences. He is a past president of the American Psychological Association and the Federation of Associations in Behavioral and Brain Sciences. He is among the most cited psychologists in the world, with over 142,000 citations and an h-index of 185.

JAMES C. KAUFMAN is Professor of Educational Psychology at the University of Connecticut. He is the author or editor of more than 300 papers and 40 books, including *Creativity 101* (2nd ed., 2016) and *The Cambridge Handbook of Creativity* (with Robert J. Sternberg; 2010). He co-created the "The Four-C Model of Creativity" (with Ronald A. Beghetto) and conducted the study that spawned the Sylvia Plath effect. He is a past president of Division 10 (Society for Psychology of Aesthetics, Creativity, and the Arts) of the American Psychological Association (APA) and is the president of the American Creativity Association. Professor Kaufman has won many awards, including Mensa's research award, the Torrance Award from the National Association for Gifted Children, and APA's Berlyne, Arnheim, and Farnsworth Awards. He cofounded two major journals *(Psychology of Aesthetics, Creativity, and the Arts* and *Psychology of Popular Media Culture)* and currently co-edits the *International Journal of Creativity and Problem Solving.*

THE NATURE OF HUMAN CREATIVITY

EDITED BY

ROBERT J. STERNBERG AND JAMES C. KAUFMAN

CAMBRIDGE
UNIVERSITY PRESS

CAMBRIDGE
UNIVERSITY PRESS

University Printing House, Cambridge CB2 8BS, United Kingdom

One Liberty Plaza, 20th Floor, New York, NY 10006, USA

477 Williamstown Road, Port Melbourne, VIC 3207, Australia

314–321, 3rd Floor, Plot 3, Splendor Forum, Jasola District Centre, New Delhi - 110025, India

79 Anson Road, #06–04/06, Singapore 079906

Cambridge University Press is part of the University of Cambridge.

It furthers the University's mission by disseminating knowledge in the pursuit of education, learning, and research at the highest international levels of excellence.

www.cambridge.org
Information on this title: www.cambridge.org/9781107199811
DOI: 10.1017/9781108185936

First published 2018

Printed in the United Kingdom by Clays, St Ives plc

A catalogue record for this publication is available from the British Library

Library of Congress Cataloging-in-Publication data
Names: Sternberg, Robert J., editor. | Kaufman, James C., editor.
Title: The nature of human creativity / edited by Robert J. Sternberg, James C. Kaufman.
Description: New York : Cambridge University Press, 2018.
Identifiers: LCCN 2017058260 | ISBN 9781107199811 (hardback)
Subjects: LCSH: Creative ability.
Classification: LCC BF408 .N3548 2018 | DDC 153.3/5 – dc23
LC record available at https://lccn.loc.gov/2017058260

ISBN 978-1-107-19981-1 Hardback
ISBN 978-1-316-64902-2 Paperback

Contents

Figures

Tables

Contributors

TERESA M. AMABILE Harvard Business School

JOHN BAER Rider University

RONALD A. BEGHETTO University of Connecticut

ARTHUR CROPLEY University of Hamburg

MIHALYI CSIKSZENTMIHALYI Claremont Graduate School

SAMANTHA ELLIOTT University of Oklahoma

GREGORY J. FEIST San Jose State University

ADRIAN FURNHAM University College, London

HOWARD GARDNER Harvard University

TERRI GOSLIN-JONES Saybrook University

BETH A. HENNESSEY Wellesley College

JAMES C. KAUFMAN University of Connecticut

TODD LUBART University of Paris Sorbonne City

ROBERT MARTIN University of Oklahoma

TRISTAN MCINTOSH University of Oklahoma

MICHAEL D. MUMFORD University of Oklahoma

JONATHAN A. PLUCKER Johns Hopkins University

RONI REITER-PALMON University of Nebraska at Omaha

JOSEPH S. RENZULLI University of Connecticut

RUTH RICHARDS Saybrook University

MARK A. RUNCO University of Georgia

SANDRA W. RUSS Case Western Reserve University

R. KEITH SAWYER University of North Carolina, Chapel Hill

PAUL J. SILVIA University of North Carolina at Greensboro

DEAN KEITH SIMONTON University of California, Davis

ROBERT J. STERNBERG Cornell University

THOMAS B. WARD University of Alabama, Tuscaloosa

ROBERT W. WEISBERG Temple University

EMILY WEINSTEIN Harvard University

Foreword

Mihaly Csikszentmihalyi

It is a daunting task to introduce such a magisterial collection written by some of the best scholars on the volume's topic – the elusive and alluring subject of creativity. Writing this foreword is indeed quite a responsibility, as well as being a greatly valued honor. My first article in this area of study was published just over half a century ago, in 1966, as a co-author to my thesis advisor, Jacob W. Getzels. It was entitled "Portrait of the Artist as an Explorer" and appeared in a now defunct journal called *Trans-Action*. Those were years when few psychologists studied creativity, and few schools offered serious programs of study on the topic.

Much has changed since. The arms race between the West and the Soviet Bloc halfway through the last century was at several points focused on the question of which country would be first to launch a vehicle into space, then who would reach the moon first with a human crew, and then who would get close enough to the farthest planets in our solar system to take good pictures of their surfaces.

All of these highly charged political projects needed a great deal of creativity to be completed – from the development of fuels to that of metals that could resist the heat caused by friction at reentry, to the provision of psychologically healthy environments during the long weeks of life under monotonous routines in cramped spaces. The demand for creative solutions to these unprecedented challenges had, as an unintended and unforeseen result, the effect of creating a market for creativity research in psychology. One of the earliest investigators of this topic, J. P. Guilford, was a fighter plane pilot in World War II and developed the first tests of "divergent thinking," which turned out to be good measures of a creative disposition.

From those days in the early 1950s onward, scholarly interest in the creative process has grown by leaps and bounds. It is not my task in this foreword to rehearse all the stages of the progress in this domain, except to say that, in my opinion, it has been a great ride. But I don't want to spend these lines rehearsing the past, exciting as it has been. Instead, let me comment on the future, and specifically on the future foreshadowed by the contributions to this volume.

The Physiology of Creativity

Although the neurological issues involved in the creative process are an important part of the puzzle, we have made remarkably little headway so far in identifying specific brain areas, or neural pathways, that might be involved in the production of creative ideas – despite the fact that this had been the focus of research by the first modern investigator of creativity, the Italian physician Cesare Lombroso, who, in 1891, published a treatise entitled *The Man of Genius*, which is one of the first attempts to apply modern science to an understanding of creativity. (As is widely known, the good doctor came to the conclusion that creative thinking and mental disorders seem to co-occur at high rates of frequency and tend to appear more frequently in some kinship genealogies than in others, suggesting a strong genetic component to creativity – an issue that has been reappearing in the literature ever since, down to our days.) The neurophysiological approach is unlikely to disappear soon, or ever, from understanding this process; and the chapters in this collection dealing with this issue remind us of the state of the art in this important domain.

The Sociocultural Context

But whether creative ideas appear and become adopted does not depend entirely on what happens within the individual's mind. History has shown that in certain places, at certain times, creativity reaches unprecedented levels, and then it dies out. In Western cultures, creativity blossomed in Egypt, in Greece, in Italy, and then in several European countries – some breaking boundaries in art, or in architecture, or in literature, or in religion, or in science, and sometimes in all of these domains at once. The most credible explanation for these spurts in the development of culture is that the environmental conditions – the economic, religious, social, political, and educational institutions of society – are sometimes well equipped to encourage and support new ideas and their implementation, thereby bestowing recognition and appreciation on the individuals proposing the novelty, and it is these conditions that explain the fact that for many centuries before the current era, so many novel works of art were produced on the tiny island of Milos between 15,000 and 150 BCE, or how Athens became a center of art much later, or Florence between roughly 1400 and 1550, or Paris in the nineteenth century.

In the present volume, the examination of the sociocultural context is not a central issue, but its effects are often implied in the analysis. Of course, it is impossible for a single volume to do full justice to every relevant perspective, and this should leave ample opportunities for scholars to include this important, and sorely neglected, viewpoint in future works.

Education

The educational perspective has been of long-standing interest to educational scholars, and its importance is well represented in this volume.

For a long time, educational research has been focused on *convergent thinking*, or the traditional patterns of repetition and memorization that for centuries constituted the backbone of scholastic learning. My maternal grandfather in his late seventies would often wake up from his afternoon naps screaming and flailing – his recurrent nightmare being that of having to pass his high school graduation exams that included the memorization of 8,000 lines from the Odyssey, in the original Greek.

I also remember how I learned one of the basic laws of solid geometry, by memorizing a short ditty, which in Hungarian went as follows: *Minden vizbe mártott test, a sújából annyit veszt, amennyi az által, kiszoritott viz súja*. This ditty in English means "Every object placed in water, will lose as much of its weight, as the weight of the water it displaces." These were memorable learning experiences illustrating convergent thinking. But few teachers, and then often against official educational policy, took the trouble of encouraging divergent thinking in their students.

One example of the latter would be László Rátz, a mathematics teacher in the Lutheran high school of Budapest, active between the two world wars. First, he tacked a page to the classroom wall on which a complex mathematical equation had been written. Then he challenged his students to provide the best proof for the equation within the next thirty days. Some of the students rose to the challenge; among them were Leo Szilárd, Eugene Wigner, Edward Teller, and John von Neumann. Their solution to the problems posed by their teacher were passed along among the students, and after a while, mimeographed copies of the proposed solutions could be bought at newsstands in Budapest. Just one of his students became a Nobel Prize winner in science, but at least half a dozen of them became leaders in their discipline. In the speech he gave when accepting his Nobel Prize, Eugene Wigner reminisced about his teacher with the following words:

"There were many superb teachers at the Lutheran gymnasium. But the greatest was my mathematics teacher László Rátz. Rátz was known not only throughout our gymnasium but also by the church and government hierarchy and among many of the teachers in the country schools. I still keep a photograph of Rátz in my workroom because he had every quality of a miraculous teacher: He loved teaching. He knew the subject and how to kindle interest in it. He imparted the very deepest understanding. Many gymnasium teachers had great skill, but no one could evoke the beauty of the subject like Rátz. Rátz cared deeply about mathematics as a discipline. He took special care to find his better students and to inspire them. Rátz felt so privileged to tutor a phenomenon like [John] von Neumann that he refused any money for it. Who could know that this precocious ten-year-old would someday become a great mathematician? Somehow Rátz knew. And he discovered it very quickly. Rátz was just as nice to me and nearly as devoted as he was to Neumann. Rátz was the only gymnasium teacher to invite me into his home. There were no private lessons. But Rátz lent me many well-chosen books, which I read thoroughly and made sure to return in good condition."

Teachers like Rátz are probably rare in each generation. But their example can be followed and should become a model for every educator: love what you are teaching, love whom you are teaching, and help them to become as good scholars in the discipline as they can be.

Leadership and Business

Throughout history, leaders of society and commerce had to keep their eyes open for new ways to do their business. If they did not, chances were good that they would miss important opportunities and mismanage their jobs. It is true that great empires have thrived on stability and tradition: the Egyptian, the Macedonian, and the empires of Asia for long periods actively discouraged novelty. In the long run, however, no nation and no economic enterprise can prosper without building novelty into its fund of knowledge. Nowadays, creativity, governance, and the economy are so intertwined that it is difficult to imagine being successful in one of these areas without also having developed the other two to a healthy degree.

The study of creativity in the workplace, intensely pursued at the State University of New York at Buffalo, is well represented in this volume by Teresa Amabile's chapter (Chapter 1), as well as by several others. Creativity in governance, or politics, is still a largely unexplored area, even though statesmen clearly differ in their ability to perceive, value, and implement good new ideas. This again is an area where young scholars could make important new contributions.

Creativity and the Life-span

If I have an area of specialty in psychology, it must be life-span psychology, because that is what I learned in grad school and have taught ever since. That does not mean I know much about the life-span, but it does say that when I am looking at what people think, feel, and do, I tend to look at it from the point of view of changes from birth to death. And this perspective is quite useful also in the understanding – or, at least, in the description – of creativity.

It has often been said that whereas all children are creative, very few adults are. There is some truth in this saying, although it really refers only to small c (everyday) creativity; in fact, exactly the opposite is true for Big C creativity, which is what most people are really interested in. We attribute creativity to children because they often come up with observations and statements that to an adult seem original – when in fact they are unusual due to the children's lack of understanding and express superficial connections between things they do not understand but want to know more about.

Sometimes these insights lead to interesting, almost poetic insights, but this is rarely the child's intent. In this sense, each child recapitulates the development of human understanding: our ancestors similarly created colorful myths to explain how the world was created, how the first man and woman started life, what makes the world go round – myths that can be called creative in that they give us psychological sustenance but that are not true in the sense their claims are usually made. When we took our son Mark to the beach for the first time, as we approached the shores of Lake Michigan, his eyes opened wide, as with a trembling finger he pointed to some of the bathers walking out of the lake to their blankets and beach umbrellas. "Look!" Mark whispered. "Water people!" It was a lovely figure of speech, but Mark did not mean to be poetic; he was just expressing surprise that there were people, apparently, who lived in the lake and only occasionally ventured ashore.

Schooling soon tames such personal attempts at understanding and channels a child's knowledge in the grooves that past thinkers have carved. This, of course, is why humanity has been so successful on this planet. When Sir Isaac Newton was asked how he had been able to see so much further into the nature of stars and galaxies than anyone else, he is said to have answered, "If I have seen further, it is because I was standing on the shoulders of giants." Of course, one must first want to see. But how far one can see depends on the availability of tall giants with broad shoulders. The danger to be avoided is to encourage only the convergent thinking based on what others have seen and ignore the new insights discovered by adventurous seekers.

Evolution and the Future of the Species

Which brings us to the last perspective that makes creativity such an important subject: it is not just about *now*; it is mainly about the future. The human condition in its present state is nothing to write home about. We have truly evolved in many wonderful ways these past few thousand years, yet, in many ways, we have not used the powers we acquired wisely. When longbows were perfected in England in the fourteenth century, many people in Europe came to believe that this new weapon would usher in the end of the world. Thoughtful people nowadays are worried that nuclear devices, made possible by the greatest scientific creativity of our species, will be the means of our demise. This state of affairs suggests that the most important creative breakthroughs we ought to look forward to might not be in the domain of armaments and warfare but rather in the domain of peaceful coexistence. What can we do to nurture in children an understanding that the world is a complex and fragile place and that its continued existence rests in their hands and in those of the generations yet to come? How can we recognize and implement new ideas in the area of mutual tolerance, of cooperative behavior? These are the kinds of questions that need to be answered for our species to survive. The present volume is an important step in our ability to answer them.

Preface

Creativity is the only way human beings and our society can make any pretense of "moving forward." Creativity has brought us all the major inventions and discoveries of humankind, and it is what has made possible all major contributions in art, music, architecture, literature, science, and many other fields. Without creativity, you're not reading these words – there would have been no printing press or personal computer; the fields of psychology, education, and business would never have developed as academic fields; and our esteemed contributors would not have become renowned scholars with so much to contribute to a discussion of the field.

It is not only at the level of societal progress that creativity has an impact. It plays a key role in our everyday lives. We use our creativity whenever we face new challenges, solve problems, or try to improve the immediate world around us. It is a key ability that helps us express, distract, and entertain ourselves or others. Not everyone can be a creative genius, of course, but anyone can be creative in some way.

Creativity is usually defined as the ability to make contributions that are both novel and task appropriate, often with an added component such as being high quality, surprising, or useful. Beyond this definition, many theories of creativity attempt to account for what it is that makes people creative. Many of these theories have been reviewed in Sternberg (1988, 1999) and Kaufman and Sternberg (2006, 2010, forthcoming).

When the field of human creativity got started, at least as a field in psychological science, it was largely an offshoot of the field of intelligence (Guilford, 1950, 1967, 1968). In Guilford's structure-of-intellect model, creativity (or divergent thinking) was one of several processes of intelligence. Today, however, the fields of human creativity and human intelligence, although related, have become distinct entities. Compendia on intelligence (e.g., Sternberg, 1985a, 2014; Sternberg and Kaufman, 2011) today say relatively little about creativity. Compendia on creativity (Kaufman and Sternberg, 2006, 2010, forthcoming) may say more about intelligence, but only as a related factor and not as a construct that encompasses creativity. Similarly, teaching for critical thinking can be viewed as including both analytical and creative thinking (see, e.g., Baron and Sternberg, 1987; Sternberg, 1985b). But teaching for creative thinking, which used to be somewhat of a specialized field (e.g., Covington et al., 1974; DeBono, 1973), has gone mainstream (see Beghetto, Kaufman, and Baer, 2014; Gregerson, Snyder, and Kaufman, 2013; Sternberg and Kaufman, forthcoming; Sternberg and Williams, 1996), and efforts to teach for creativity are widespread and international.

There are many different approaches to creativity. As is true in any field, many of these approaches are driven by the very most eminent scholars in the field. This book represents a collection of essays by those very people, as selected by objective means.

Many edited books have chapters chosen on the basis of editors' implicit theories of who matters in the field (or on the basis of the editors' friendships and collaborations). That was not the approach in selecting authors for this volume. In particular, we reviewed everyone cited in four major contemporary volumes on creativity: *Creativity 101*, 2nd ed. (Kaufman, 2016), *The Cambridge Handbook of Creativity* (Kaufman and Sternberg, 2010), *Explaining Creativity*, 2nd ed. (Sawyer, 2012), and *Creativity*, 2nd ed. (Runco, 2014). These books formed the basis for how we chose authors for this volume.

All four books were written for use as textbooks in courses on creativity or related processes such as innovation or insight (Sternberg and Davidson, 1982, 1983). With the assistance of Paul Joseph Barnett, we computed a combined tally of the living authors most frequently cited in these four texts. The resulting list comprises some of the top contemporary contributors to the field of creativity, as determined by textbook citations. We chose the twenty-four top-cited individuals, and amazingly, all of them agreed to write for the book. They comprise the sole (or, in some cases, senior) authors of this book, plus the author of the foreword.

Of course, there are other reasonable ways to choose the top contributors to the field of creativity; but we believe that our procedures produced a set of many of the most eminent scholars in the field. The authors represent a diverse group, ranging widely in their approaches to creativity, in their backgrounds and training, and in the kinds of theories they have produced and data they have collected.

We asked each invitee to write a chapter addressing as many of the following questions as possible, not necessarily in the order given:

1   What is creativity?
2   How is creativity best understood?
3   How is creativity best measured?
4   How is creativity best investigated?
5   What are some of the most interesting empirical results from your own research?
6   What are the sources of individual and group differences in creativity?
7   How is creativity best developed?
8   What are the most important questions about creativity that future research on creativity should address?
9   What is, and what should be, the role of creativity in society?
10 What would you like to be your lasting contribution to the field of creativity?

Authors also were invited to address any other questions that they believed would be of interest to readers.

Although there are a number of books on creativity, few of them explore in a systematic way the range of questions that we posed to our authors, including whether creativity is even a single thing or many things (Sternberg, 2005) and whether it is the same across cultures (Niu and Sternberg, 2003). The book thus comprises some of the most distinguished contributors to the field answering a range of questions that perhaps no other book addresses. The book is not a handbook; authors were not asked to represent a whole field of study. Rather, they were asked to focus on their own work and how it relates to the work of others. A separate handbook will be published shortly by Cambridge University Press (Kaufman and Sternberg, forthcoming).

The main goal of this book is to provide a broad overview of approaches of the leading scholars in the field to understanding the nature of creativity, its measurement, its investigation, its development, and its importance to society. The intended audience for this book is psychologists, cognitive scientists, educators, sociologists, and students in any field interested in creativity. This book is, in a sense, a companion to another book, *The Nature of Human Intelligence* (Sternberg, forthcoming), which used a similar method to choose authors to write on human intelligence.

We believe that there are several reasons to produce this volume at the current time.

First, the book highlights the diversity in points of view of the top scholars in the field. Some scholars still believe that creativity is largely what is measured by tests such as the Torrance Tests. But in this list, we have psychologists representing an extremely wide range of perspectives: cognitive, clinical, cultural, developmental, educational, organizational, personality, psychometric, social, and more. The book thus represents highly diverse views on creativity and shows that although there are some points of consensus about creativity, there are still many differences in perspective.

Second, many of the individuals who write about creativity (especially in the popular press) know little about it, at least from a scientific point of view. It is a field that invites almost anyone who views himself or herself as an expert to propose ideas and suggestions with little or no scientific basis. Sometimes popular experts espouse views that have been specifically disproven as best practice. It can be difficult to pick up a popular magazine without some expert telling you how to improve your creativity. Chances are that the expert has done no research in the field. All of the contributors to this book are top scientists, so the book will help set the field straight in terms of the science of creativity.

Third, a book such as this one can be used as a supplementary text in a course on creativity. Although an instructor might want to use a traditional textbook (e.g., Kaufman, Sawyer, or Runco) as a main volume, an advantage of this book is that the student will be able to learn from the originators of the key contemporary ideas in the field how they think about their work and the field. (An alternative supplement is our *The Cambridge Handbook of Creativity*, 2nd ed. [Kaufman and Sternberg, forthcoming], although the handbook is quite a bit longer than the present volume.)

Fourth, this book is being published exactly thirty years since the edited Sternberg (1988) book on *The Nature of Creativity* was published. That book was similar in goal, but authors for that book were not chosen in a quantifiable or systematic way. Given the rapid rate of progress in the field, that book is obviously out of date. This volume shows just how far the field has progressed since 1988.

Finally, many of the existing textbooks that cover creativity – introductory psychology textbooks, developmental psychology textbooks, educational psychology textbooks, and so on – represent the field of creativity as it existed at the end (or, in some cases, even the middle) of the twentieth century. Many of them are quite out of date. The average textbook may cover early pioneers, such as Guilford or Torrance, but has little to say of the major contributions of the last several decades. We hope that this volume will offer textbook authors an authoritative and up-to-date basis for updating their texts.

REFERENCES

Amabile, T. (1996). *Creativity in context: Update to "The social psychology of creativity."* Boulder, CO: Westview Press.

Baron, J. B., and Sternberg, R. J. (Eds.). (1987). *Teaching thinking skills: Theory and practice.* New York: Freeman.

Beghetto, R. A., Kaufman, J. C., and Baer, J. (2014). *Teaching for creativity in the Common Core classroom.* New York: Teachers College Press.

Covington, M. V., Crutchfield, R. S., Davies, L., and Olton, R. M. (1974). *The productive thinking program: A course in learning to think.* Columbus, OH: Merrill.

Csikszentmihalyi, M. (1997). *Creativity: Flow and the psychology of discovery and invention.* New York: Harper Perennial.

(2013). *Creativity: The psychology of discovery and invention.* New York: Harper Perennial.

DeBono, E. (1973). *CoRT thinking.* Blanford, UK: Direct Educational Services.

Gardner, H. (2011). *Creating minds.* New York: Basic Books.

Gregerson, M., Snyder, H., and Kaufman, J. C. (Eds.). (2013). *Teaching creatively and teaching creativity.* New York: Springer Science.

Guilford, J. P. (1950). Creativity. *American Psychologist,* 5, 444–454.

(1967). *The nature of human intelligence.* New York: McGraw-Hill.

(1968). *Creativity, intelligence and their educational implications.* San Diego, CA: EDITS/Knapp.

Kaufman, J. C. (2016). *Creativity 101.* 2nd ed. New York: Springer.

Kaufman, J. C., and Sternberg, R. J. (Eds.). (2006). *The international handbook of creativity.* New York: Cambridge University Press.

(Eds.). (2010). *The Cambridge handbook of creativity.* New York: Cambridge University Press.

(Eds.). (forthcoming). *The Cambridge handbook of creativity.* 2nd ed. New York: Cambridge University Press.

Niu, W., and Sternberg, R. J. (2003). Societal and school influences on student creativity: The case of China. *Psychology in the Schools,* 40(1), 103–114.

Runco, M. A. (2014). *Creativity: Theories and themes: Research, development, and practice.* 2nd ed. Cambridge, MA: Academic Press.

Sawyer, K. (2012). *Explaining creativity: The science of human innovation.* 2nd ed. New York: Oxford University Press.

Sternberg, R. J. (Ed.). (1985a). *Human abilities: An information-processing approach.* San Francisco: Freeman.

(1985b). Teaching critical thinking, Part 1: Are we making critical mistakes? *Phi Delta Kappan,* 67, 194–198.

(1988). *The nature of creativity.* New York: Cambridge University Press.

(1999). *Handbook of creativity.* New York: Cambridge University Press.

(2005). Creativity or creativities? *International Journal of Human Computer Studies*, 63, 370–382.

(2014). *Advances in the psychology of human intelligence*. Vol. 4. New York: Psychology Press.

(forthcoming). Improving people's creativity. In *The Cambridge handbook of creativity*, 2nd ed., edited by J. C. Kaufman and R. J. Sternberg. New York: Cambridge University Press.

(forthcoming). *The nature of human intelligence*. New York: Cambridge University Press.

Sternberg, R. J., and Davidson, J. E. (1982). The mind of the puzzler. *Psychology Today*, 16, 37–44.

(1983). Insight in the gifted. *Educational Psychologist*, 18, 51–57.

Sternberg, R. J., and Kaufman, S. B. (Eds.). (2011). *Cambridge handbook of intelligence*. New York: Cambridge University Press.

Sternberg, R. J., and Lubart, T. I. (1995). *Defying the crowd: Cultivating creativity in a culture of conformity*. New York: Free Press.

Sternberg, R. J., and Williams, W. M. (1996). *How to develop student creativity*. Alexandria, VA: Association for Supervision and Curriculum Development.

CHAPTER I

Creativity and the Labor of Love

Teresa M. Amabile

Every advance in the history of humankind has resulted from creativity, the production of new, appropriate ideas. Take the laser, which is a powerful, intensely focused beam of light. Lasers have become ubiquitous and crucial tools in our global society, with applications in everyday life ranging from printers and security systems to pointers and barcode scanners, as well as applications in medicine, dentistry, communications, industry, and nuclear fusion. The invention of lasers is generally traced to a paper outlining the basic principles of lasers in the December 1958 issue of *Physical Review* coauthored by Arthur Schawlow and Charles Towne ("Infrared and Optical Masers"), one of the accomplishments for which Schawlow received the 1981 Nobel Prize in Physics. Yet dozens of other scientists contributed to the knowledge required to develop the laser technologies of today. A different scientist, Theodore Maiman, built the first working laser in 1960, and another, Gordon Gould, was eventually awarded patent rights to the laser in 1988.

What Is Creativity (and Who Is Creative)?

Like many others in the field (e.g., Stein, 1975; Sternberg and Lubart, 1999), I define creativity as the production of ideas that are not only novel – different from previous ideas in some way – but also appropriate: useful, valuable, correct, or somehow fitting to the purpose that the individual creator intends. In physics, an idea cannot be considered creative unless it works, unless it can eventually be proven; for this reason, the "appropriate" aspect of creativity means "correct" in mathematics and science. But in other domains – the arts, for example – appropriateness is quite a different thing. There, work is generally considered creative if it is both novel and expressive of something, evoking a reaction (or range of reactions) in observers that the artist intended.

Unlike others in the field (e.g., Gardner, 1993; Gruber, 1982), I do not make the assumption that creativity is the sole province of geniuses – extraordinary people who receive wide recognition for having changed a field in some notable way. Like James Kaufman (Kaufman & Beghetto, 2009) and other scholars, I hold that levels of creativity exist within all domains of human activity – essentially, a continuum from the ordinary, everyday creativity such as the dentist (or parent) who figured out that children will be calmer during dental exams if they can wear fun sunglasses to protect their eyes from the bright light (often called "little c creativity"); through the moderate ("medium c") creativity of Maiman, who was able to build the first laser; to the breakthrough ("Big C") creativity of Schawlow, who articulated the scientific principles upon which all laser inventions were eventually built. Yet Schawlow, who won the Nobel Prize, never became as famous as his Nobel Prize–winning contemporary at Stanford University, the scientist Linus Pauling. Maiman was twice nominated for, but never received, the Nobel Prize, placing him lower than Schawlow on the "fame ladder." And, to my knowledge, no one has considered nominating the person who came up with the sunglass-dentistry idea for a Nobel Prize. Yet all of these people produced novel and appropriate ideas. All were creative.

The Labor of Love Aspect

In a 1982 interview, shortly after he accepted the Nobel Prize, Schawlow was asked what he thought made the difference between highly creative scientists and those who were notably less creative. The interviewer wondered if the secret lay with innate talent, intelligence, or training. Schawlow replied, "The labor of love aspect is important. The most successful scientists often are not the most talented. But they are the ones who are impelled by curiosity. They've got to know what the answer is" (Schawlow, 1982, p. 42). A few years earlier, I had become intrigued by the motivation that stems from curiosity, what Albert Einstein referred to as "the enjoyment of seeing and searching" (Einstein, 1949, p. 19). Edward Deci, Mark Lepper, and other psychological researchers called this *intrinsic motivation*: the drive to engage in a task because it is interesting, enjoyable, challenging, or satisfying in and of itself (e.g., Deci, 1971; Lepper, Greene, and Nisbett, 1973; White, 1959). Deci and Lepper had demonstrated what was, at the time, an astonishing phenomenon: when people (adults and children) do an activity that they were initially interested in, under conditions where they have been promised a reward for doing the activity, they become less interested in doing it later on, when the reward is no longer available. In other words, intrinsic motivation can be undermined by extrinsic reward (reward offered by someone else); subsequent research by these and other psychologists showed that other extrinsic motivators (like expected evaluation) and extrinsic constraints (like deadlines) can have similar effects.

Reading Einstein's autobiographical description of how his love and exploration of science had been dampened by the "coercion and sense of duty" (p. 19) that he experienced as a schoolboy, and finding similar stories in the autobiographies, diaries, and letters of other highly creative people, I wondered if an intrinsic (versus extrinsic) motivational state could have an effect not only on subsequent interest but also on current creativity. For this reason, I set out to develop a social psychology of creativity, an understanding of the effects of factors in the social environment, such as promised reward and expected evaluation, on an individual's ability to produce creative work on a particular activity at a particular point in time. I began by designing a series of simple controlled experiments, in which some participants would be randomly assigned to do a creativity task under an extrinsic constraint or extrinsic motivator, while others would do the same task under identical conditions – but without the extrinsic constraint or motivator.

Measuring Creativity

First, however, I had to find a good way to measure the creativity of the work that participants in my experiments would produce. At the time (the mid-1970s), creativity was assessed in most psychological studies through standardized creativity tests (e.g., Torrance, 1966) that were designed to identify gifted and talented children and adults. However, my experiments required creativity measures that would be relatively unaffected by the sort of large individual differences that the creativity tests had been designed to reveal. Instead, these studies required measures that would be relatively insensitive to traitlike skill differences in a population of ordinary children or adults but, instead, could reveal temporary fluctuations in creativity arising from different motivational states. For this reason, I developed a new measure, which I dubbed the *consensual assessment technique* (CAT) *for creativity* (Amabile, 1982a).

In the CAT, a small number of people (usually, three to eight) familiar with a domain give their own independent assessments of the level of creativity of each of a set of products in that domain that were made by participants in a study. The tasks used in my experimental studies did not require any degree of special skill beyond the level that ordinary people would be expected to have. For example, I might have the people participating in a study all create paper collages out of a standard set of materials, such as white poster board, a container of glue, and colorful pieces of paper, bits of yarn, and fabric scraps. Regardless of their experimental condition (say, expected evaluation versus no evaluation expected), all participants would receive an identical set of materials and would be given the same amount of time. After the experiment concluded, artists or people familiar with collage art would be recruited to make the assessments of creativity. Working independently, and without knowing that different collages had been produced under different experimental conditions, they would each view the collages in a different random order. Then, working under instructions to rate the collages relative to one another on creativity, using their own subjective definition of creativity in that domain (so that their ratings would not simply reflect the experimenter's view of creativity), these judges would rate each collage on a Likert scale, for example, a 1–7 or 0–40 scale.

The assumption underlying the CAT is that, although even experts might have difficulty articulating the qualities that lead them to rate one collage as more creative than another (and they do; see Amabile, 1982a, 1983a), they can nonetheless identify different levels of creativity in the products, and moreover, they can generally agree with other experts. To the extent that they do agree, these ratings can be considered valid measures of creativity. In fact, across a wide range of products, including collages, poems, stories, and small structures, judges using the CAT generally give ratings that show good interjudge agreement (Amabile, 1982a, 1983a, 1983b, 1996; Amabile and Mueller, 2008). As a result, judge ratings can be averaged to form an overall measure of creativity for each product.

Experiments on How the Immediate Social Environment Affects Creativity

The first of my studies, done as a field experiment, was quite simple (Amabile, 1982b). (It was the first study I conducted, but not the first published.) I invited a number of children living in an apartment complex to one of two "art parties" in the community center; the invitations were given out randomly. In the both of these parties, the children received name tags that each had a unique number, enjoyed some snacks, and played a few art-oriented games. Then, as the final "game," they were given the collage activity. Each child received an identical set of colorful origami papers in a variety of sizes and shapes (each set arranged identically), a standard-size piece of white poster board, and a container of glue. They were all asked to use the materials to make a "silly" collage.

The only difference between the two art parties lay in the instructions given by the experimenter (the "host" of the party) before the collage activity. At the first party, the experimenter told the children that, after the collage activity and before they went home, there would be a raffle for three prizes, and that everybody had the same chance to win one of the prizes. The experimenter then showed them the prizes – three quite attractive toys – and a fishbowl that had slips of paper inside, each with a number corresponding to a number on a child's name tag. Thus, the children at the first party believed that there was no connection between the collage activity (or any of the art activities) and the end-of-party raffle; this was the control condition. In the second party, the experimenter told the children that, at the conclusion of the collage activity, she and her two helpers (two other adults) would judge the collages and award a first prize to the best, a second prize to the next best, and a third prize to the third best. Thus, the children at the second party believed that they were competing for rewards and made their collages under that belief. This was the experimental condition, where the manipulation consisted of three extrinsic motivators combined into one: competition, expected evaluation, and reward. (In this party, like the first one, the prizes were eventually raffled off, so as not to undermine the confidence of any children. The experimenter told the partygoers that the collages were all so good that the adults simply couldn't decide on the best three.)

Subsequently, the CAT was used to produce creativity scores. The collages were arranged gallery-style on the walls of a conference room, and local artists were recruited to come in, individually, to rate the collages on creativity – using their own subjective definitions of creativity. The ratings showed a high degree of reliability (0.77 for the seven artist-judges), and so they were averaged to produce a mean creativity score for each collage. Analysis of these scores revealed that the children in the competitive reward condition had produced collages that were rated significantly lower in creativity. This study provided support for the *intrinsic motivation hypothesis of creativity*: people will be more creative when they are motivated primarily by the interest, enjoyment, satisfaction, and challenge of the work itself – and not by extrinsic motivators or constraints.

A series of experiments in the 1970s, 1980s, and 1990s, by myself, my students and colleagues, and others, demonstrated that creativity can be undermined in both children and adults by a number of extrinsic motivators and constraints: expected evaluation (Amabile, 1979; Hennessey, 1989), expected reward for doing the activity (Amabile, Goldfarb, and Brackfield, 1990; Amabile, Hennessey, and Grossman, 1986; Hennessey, 1989), surveillance while working (Amabile, Goldfarb, and Brackfield, 1990), competition (Amabile, 1982b), and constrained choice in materials to use (Amabile and Gitomer, 1984). In many of these studies, measures of intrinsic motivation correlated highly with measures of creativity. Moreover, quite direct evidence of motivational state as the mechanism emerged from a study that didn't actually introduce a specific extrinsic constraint or motivator (Amabile, 1985). In this experiment, simply focusing on extrinsic reasons for being a writer (like getting rich and becoming famous) versus intrinsic reasons (like enjoying playing with words and getting pleasure out of something good you have written) led to lower levels of creativity in creative writers (Amabile, 1985). Given this strong empirical support, I eventually began referring to the *intrinsic motivation principle of creativity*. I consider this to be the main discovery of my creativity research.

Nonexperimental Studies of the Social Environment and Creativity

Despite the utility of well-controlled experiments for pinpointing the causal effects of particular factors in the social environment on intrinsic motivation and creativity, there are clear limitations to experimental studies. The social-environmental manipulations, such as being told that your experimental session is being watched through a one-way mirror, are often quite artificial. The tasks, such as making a collage or writing a haiku poem, are much shorter than the potentially creative activities that most people do in everyday life. Most importantly, perhaps, the participants in these experiments have little invested in the activities they do in the laboratory. After a while, I became enormously curious about whether the social factors I had chosen to manipulate in the laboratory bore any correspondence to factors that influence the creativity of people who are trying to produce novel, appropriate solutions to problems every day in their work. To answer this question, I found it necessary to move out of the laboratory and beyond the experimental method.

Before I describe my own nonexperimental research, I want to highlight some very different, and highly influential, nonexperimental research on the social psychology of creativity that Dean K. Simonton began publishing around the same time (in the mid-1970s). Although we have since become friends, he and I did not know each other at that time and, indeed, were initially unaware of each other's work. In painstaking archival research of widely recognized creative individuals using historiometric methods, Simonton published a series of important papers on larger socio-cultural-political influences on creativity, such as the presence of competitors in one's field in the same generation (1977a); social reinforcements (1977a); role-model availability (1975, 1977b); formal education (1976); father's status (1976); political fragmentation (1975); imperial instability (1975); political instability (1975); war (1975, 1976, 1977a); internal political disturbances (1977a); and cultural persecution (1975). If we were photographers, Simonton and I could have been said to use lenses of quite different focal lengths. While his snapshots of the social psychology of creativity were wide, panoramic views of broad influences on the output of historical luminaries, mine were close-ups of ordinary people producing modestly creative work that would likely never become well known. His subjects, who were known by reputation to thousands, even millions, of others, were long dead. Mine, who would be known by few outside their own personal circles, were quite alive – and willing to talk to me.

I began my foray into real-world creativity with a series of interviews with R&D scientists at a number of companies, in collaboration with Stanley Gryskiewicz at the Center for Creative Leadership (Amabile and Gryskiewicz, 1987). Using a critical incident technique for data collection, we asked these scientists to describe in detail two significant events from their work experience: one that exemplified a high level of creativity and one that exemplified a low level of creativity. Our first finding was a general one, concerning the content of the stories. Despite common wisdom that high-level performance is all about the people, these interviewees talked in much greater detail about the social environments – the work environments – surrounding these events than about the talents and personal characteristics of the individuals involved. In a broad sense, this pattern validates the importance of the social psychology of creativity.

Some of the specific aspects of the work environment that emerged as differentiators between the highly creative and the less creative events echoed the independent variables that my colleagues and I (or other researchers) had manipulated in experimental studies. But others had not been examined experimentally and, indeed, would likely be very difficult to study in a controlled experiment. In order to investigate systematically the extent to which the work environment factors identified in the interviews did, indeed, play a role in the level of creativity produced by R&D projects, I developed a survey instrument called KEYS® to capture employees' self-perceptions of their work environment and used it in a validation study within a large high-tech firm (Amabile, Conti, Coon, Lazenby, and

Herron, 1996). KEYS® has two work environment dimensions, one called *stimulants to creativity* (comprising six scales) and one called *obstacles to creativity* (comprising two scales).

In phase 1 of this study, my colleagues and I asked a group of mid-level R&D managers in this firm to independently nominate the highest-creativity project and the lowest-creativity project with which they had been involved over the past three years, from among all projects where creativity was both possible and desirable. We then asked them to complete two KEYS® surveys, one describing the work environment of the high-creativity project and the other describing the work environment of the low-creativity project. Not surprisingly, the survey results showed significant differences on all eight dimensions of the work environment. The high-creativity projects were rated significantly higher on the six stimulants to creativity, and the low-creativity projects were rated significantly higher on the two obstacles to creativity. In phase 2, we used a modified version of the CAT to obtain independent assessments of the creativity of the projects that had been nominated in phase 1. For this, we asked a group of scientific and technical experts in the firm, who had not been involved in phase 1, to rate the creativity of the outcome of each of the nominated projects (skipping those with which they were unfamiliar).

For phase 3, we selected only those projects that had been reliably rated by the phase 2 experts as high or low in creativity. We then asked every person who had been a member of those project teams (unless they had participated in phase 1) to complete a KEYS® survey about the work environment of that particular project – and only that project. They had no idea that the project had been rated as high or low on creativity. Our aim was to see if the people who had worked on the projects that were later rated as highly creative perceived the work environments of their projects differently from the people who had work on the projects later rated as low in creativity – in the same directions as participants in phase 1. They did. In both phase 1 and phase 3, the high-creativity projects were rated significantly higher on several work environment stimulants to creativity:

- Freedom: Autonomy (or a low level of constraint) in deciding what work to do or how to do it; a sense of control over one's work.
- Challenging work: A sense of having to work hard on challenging and important projects.
- Sufficient resources: Access to appropriate resources, including funds, materials, facilities, and information. (Note: Although there was a

significant difference on this dimension in phase 1, there was none in phase 3.)

- Work group supports: A diversely skilled work group in which people communicate well, are open to new ideas, constructively challenge each other's work, trust and help each other, and feel committed to the work they are doing.
- Supervisory encouragement: A supervisor who serves as a good work model, sets goals appropriately, supports the work group, values individual contributions, and shows confidence in the work group.
- Organizational encouragement: An organizational culture that encourages creativity through the fair, constructive judgment of ideas, reward and recognition for creative work, mechanisms for developing new ideas, an active flow of ideas, and a shared vision of what the organization is trying to do.

In contrast, the low-creativity projects were rated significantly higher on work environment obstacles to creativity:

- Organizational impediments: An organizational culture that impedes creativity through internal political problems, harsh evaluation of new ideas, destructive internal competition, an avoidance of risk, and an overemphasis on the status quo.
- Workload pressure: Extreme time pressures, unrealistic expectations for productivity, and distractions from creative work. (Note: Although there was a significant difference on this dimension in phase 1, there was none in phase 3.)

Notice that, although several of the factors identified in the organizational impediments dimension (or the opposite of the organizational stimulant "freedom") are similar to those we had studied experimentally – such as evaluation, competition, and constrained autonomy – one factor identified in the organizational encouragement dimension is surprising in light of the experimental findings: reward. Organizational environments where people know that creative work is recognized and rewarded are more conducive to creative outputs than those that have no such rewards. As we delved deeper into these findings, and considered them in light of some surprising experimental findings (Amabile, Hennessey, and Grossman, 1986; Hennessey, Amabile, and Martinage, 1989; Hennessey and Zbikowski, 1993), we developed the concept of *motivational synergy* (Amabile, 1993). When people start out with high levels of intrinsic motivation to do an activity, rewards for doing the activity that are presented in a way that supports their feelings of competence or allows them to become more deeply involved in the activity will not undermine intrinsic motivation and creativity. Rather, those rewards will act as synergistic extrinsic motivators, combining in a positive way with intrinsic motivation, and supporting creativity.

The Diary Study

Although the findings of the KEYS® survey study revealed new elements of the social environment that can have important influences on creativity, it didn't tell us much about how people actually experience those work environments, day by day, while they are trying to be creative in their work. To put it bluntly, they revealed little about the *psychology* of the social psychology of creativity. In order to delve deeply into people's everyday psychological experience of doing creative work inside organizations, my collaborators and I carried out a multiyear study that involved collecting daily electronic diaries from 238 professionals as they were working on twenty-six important innovation projects inside seven different companies in three different industries.

Our aim was to get detailed information, in real time, about events unfolding in the work environment and the ways in which those events influence people's psychological experience – their perceptions of the work environment, their motivation, and their emotions. And, using separate measures of our participants' work, we wanted to see if psychological experience predicted creativity and other important dimensions of performance. Because we emailed the diary form to each participant each day of the project they were doing, we ended up with a treasure trove of data: nearly 12,000 individual diary entries. Each entry had Likert-scale ratings of the person's perceptions, motivation, and emotions that day, as well as a detailed description of one event that stood out in the person's mind from the work day. (Participants had not been told of our particular interest in creativity.) For measures of creativity, we analyzed the event descriptions for reports of coming up with a new idea or solving a complex problem. We also obtained measures of creativity and other dimensions of performance from our participants' supervisors and close colleagues.

The results of the diary study were consistent with, but went well beyond, the results from prior experimental and nonexperimental studies. The first major discovery was that psychological experience does predict creativity. In one set of analyses, we found that positive emotion on a given day not only predicted creative thinking on that day but also predicted creative thinking the next day (Amabile, Barsade, Mueller, and Staw, 2005). In another study, we found that perceptions of leader support in the work environment predicted creativity (Amabile, Schatzel, Moneta, and Kramer, 2004). And, in keeping with earlier studies, we found that intrinsic motivation predicted creativity (Amabile and Kramer, 2011).

The second discovery of the diary study arose from the very microscopic view that the daily diaries afforded of the events unfolding in the work environment and the participants' psychological experience. We made this discovery by systematically categorizing and looking for patterns in all events reported on the days that participants reported their most positive psychological experiences – the most positive emotions and perceptions of the work environment, and the strongest intrinsic motivation. Of all the events that occurred on those "best days," the single most prominent, by far, was simply making progress in meaningful work. As long as people found meaning in the work – that is, as long as they felt it contributed to something that they valued – any sense of forward movement in the work could lead to notably more positive emotions and perceptions, and stronger intrinsic motivation, than they experienced on days without a progress event. We call this *the progress principle*, and we found that it applies even to seemingly trivial progress, or *small wins* (Amabile and Kramer, 2011). In fact, in general, 28 percent of seemingly small events can have a strong impact on people's emotions the day they happen.

Unfortunately, there is a downside to the progress principle: Of all the events that occurred on people's "worst days" (in terms of their psychological experience), the single most prominent, by far, was having a setback in the work – the opposite of progress. And the negative effect of setback events on psychological experience was three to four times stronger than the positive effect of progress events. This last finding fits well with a broader phenomenon in psychology and related fields that, when it comes to psychological reactions to a wide variety of events, "bad is stronger than good" (Baumeister, Bratslavsky, Finkenauer, and Vohs, 2001).

The Dynamic Componential Model of Creativity

Without theoretical models that attempt to make sense of them, a body of empirical research findings on a given topic – even a large body of findings – remains just that. The findings have limited utility for igniting further research or guiding how people behave in the world. Recently, my colleague Michael Pratt and I developed a theory that builds on my prior theoretical models of creativity (Amabile, 1983a, 1983b, 1988, 1996) but incorporates more recent findings, including those that I have just described and research by many others in the field (Amabile and Pratt, 2016). This *dynamic componential model of creativity and innovation in organizations* is *componential* because it includes the four components that are essential for an individual (or a team of individuals working closely together) to produce creative work on any given task. Three of these components are internal to the individual: (1) skills in the task domain (knowledge and technical skill in the area in which the individual is working); (2) creativity-relevant processes (personality characteristics, ways of thinking, and ways of working that are conducive to producing novel ideas); and (3) task motivation (intrinsic and synergistic extrinsic motivation for the particular task). The fourth component is external to the individual: the social environment in which the individual is working; in organizations, this is the work environment within which the individual is located. The model is focused specifically on creativity *in organizations* because that is the primary environment in which I have focused my work over the past thirty years. It is a model of *creativity and innovation* because innovation is the implementation of creative ideas within an organization. And it is *dynamic* because it describes the ways in which psychological experience and creative performance influence each other through a series of feedback loops – and how both can be influenced by the social environment.

According to this model, all three internal components are necessary for creativity, and the external environment must be at least somewhat conducive. The model also specifies that the three internal components are differentially important at different stages of the creative process. Intrinsic motivation is particularly important as people are embarking on a creative task because intrinsic motivation leads to deeper engagement in the task; the more deeply people think about the problem, the more likely they are to undertake it with an open, flexible mindset. As people move along in the creative process, preparing to come up with ideas by gathering information about the problem, skills in the task domain are important, and synergistic extrinsic motivation can help people persevere in learning whatever new skills and knowledge they may need. At the next stage, actually generating ideas, high levels of creativity-relevant processes and intrinsic motivation can lead to broader exploration and, as a result, more ideas and a higher level of novelty in those ideas. Finally, when the time comes to select, validate, and communicate ideas, skills in the task domain and synergistic extrinsic motivation again become important – primarily, by ensuring that the selected idea is not only novel but also appropriate.

In organizations, managers at all levels, from the CEO down to an individual's immediate supervisor, exert a strong influence on the work environment; coworkers also play a role. To the extent that managers set challenging goals in meaningful work; grant as much autonomy as possible in meeting the goals; provide sufficient resources and time; recognize, reward, and foster open communication about new ideas; and view failure as a learning opportunity, the people who work for those managers will make creative progress in their work. To the extent that people make creative progress in their work, and to the extent that they receive support and encouragement from managers and coworkers, their psychological states will be more positive, further fostering creativity. Virtuous cycles can ensue. Unfortunately, to the extent that work environments are unconducive to creativity, and supports for people and their work progress are lacking, creativity is likely to suffer. Vicious cycles can emerge.

A Concluding Thought on the Power of Creativity

I started this chapter by saying that all human progress depends on creativity, and I stand by that claim. Yet it's also true that creativity is responsible for much evil in the history of humanity. Like the laser envisioned all those years ago by Arthur Schawlow, creativity can be powerful, and can be pointed in harmful directions as well as beneficial ones. We must realize that creativity, defined as producing novel ideas appropriate toward some goal, is amoral. The goal can just as easily be evil as good. It is only by combining creative capacities, strong passions, and conducive environments with equally strong moral values that we will be able to harness the power of creativity for the good of humanity and not its destruction.

REFERENCES

Amabile, T. M. (1979). Effects of external evaluation on artistic creativity. *Journal of Personality and Social Psychology*, 37, 221–233.

(1982a). Social psychology of creativity: A consensual assessment technique. *Journal of Personality and Social Psychology*, 43, 997–1013.

(1982b). Children's artistic creativity: Detrimental effects of competition in a field setting. *Personality and Social Psychology Bulletin*, 8, 573–578.

(1983a). Social psychology of creativity: A componential conceptualization. *Journal of Personality and Social Psychology*, 45, 357–377.

(1983b). *The social psychology of creativity*. New York: Springer.

(1985). Motivation and creativity: Effects of motivational orientation on creative writing. *Journal of Personality and Social Psychology*, 48, 393–399.

(1988). A model of creativity and innovation in organizations. Vol. 10 of *Research in organizational behavior*, edited by B. M. Staw and L. L. Cummings, 123–167. Greenwich, CT: JAI Press.

(1993). Motivational synergy: Toward new conceptualizations of intrinsic and extrinsic motivation in the workplace. *Human Resource Management Review*, 3, 185–201.

(1996). *Creativity in context: Update to the social psychology of creativity*. Boulder, CO: Westview Press.

Amabile, T. M., Barsade, S. G., Mueller, J. S., and Staw, B. M. (2005). Affect and creativity at work. *Administrative Science Quarterly*, 50, 367–403.

Amabile, T. M., Conti, R., Coon, H., Lazenby, J., and Herron, M. (1996). Assessing the work environment for creativity. *Academy of Management Journal*, 39, 1154–1184.

Amabile, T. M., and Gitomer, J. (1984). Children's artistic creativity: Effects of choice in task materials. *Personality and Social Psychology Bulletin*, 10, 209–215.

Amabile, T. M., Goldfarb, P., and Brackfield, S. C. (1990). Social influences on creativity: Evaluation, coaction, and surveillance. *Creativity Research Journal*, 3, 6–21.

Amabile, T. M., and Gryskiewicz, S. S. (1987). *Creativity in the R&D laboratory*. Technical Report 30. Greensboro, NC: Center for Creative Leadership.

Amabile, T. M., Hennessey, B. A., and Grossman, B. S. (1986). Social influences on creativity: The effects of contracted-for reward. *Journal of Personality and Social Psychology*, 50, 14–23.

Amabile, T. M., and Kramer, S. J. (2011). *The progress principle: Using small wins to ignite joy, engagement, and creativity at work*. Boston: Harvard Business Review Press.

Amabile, T. M., and Mueller, J. S. (2008). Studying creativity, its processes, and its antecedents: An exploration of the componential theory of creativity. In *Handbook of organizational creativity*, edited by J. Zhou and C. E. Shalley, 33–64. New York: Lawrence Erlbaum Associates.

Amabile, T. M., and Pratt, M. G. (2016). The dynamic componential model of creativity and innovation in organizations: Making progress, making meaning. *Research in Organizational Behavior*, 36, 157–183. doi:10.1016/j.riob.2016.10.001

Amabile, T. M., Schatzel, E. A., Moneta, G. B., and Kramer, S. J. (2004). Leader behaviors and the work environment for creativity: Perceived leader support. *The Leadership Quarterly*, 15(1), 5–32.

Baumeister, R. F., Bratslavsky, E., Finkenauer, C., and Vohs, K. D. (2001). Bad is stronger than good. *Review of General Psychology*, 5(4), 323–370.

Deci, E. (1971). Effects of externally mediated rewards on intrinsic motivation. *Journal of Personality and Social Psychology*, 18, 105–115.

Einstein, A. (1949). Autobiography. In *Albert Einstein: Philosopher-scientist*, edited by P. Schilpp. Evanston, IL: Library of Living Philosophers.

Gardner, H. (1993). *Creating minds*. New York: Basic Books.

Gruber, H. E. (1982). *Darwin on man.* 2nd ed. Chicago: University of Chicago Press.

Hennessey, B. A. (1989). The effect of extrinsic constraints on children's creativity while using a computer. *Creativity Research Journal,* 2, 151–168.

Hennessey, B. A., Amabile, T. M., and Martinage, M. (1989). Immunizing children against the negative effects of reward. *Contemporary Educational Psychology,* 14, 212–227.

Hennessey, B. A., and Zbikowski, S. (1993). Immunizing children against the negative effects of reward: A further examination of intrinsic motivation training techniques. *Creativity Research Journal,* 6, 297–308.

Kaufman, J. C., & Beghetto, R. A. (2009). Beyond big and little: The four C model of creativity. *Review of General Psychology,* 13(1), 1–12.

Lepper, M., Greene, D., and Nisbett, R. (1973). Undermining children's intrinsic interest with extrinsic rewards: A test of the "overjustification" hypothesis. *Journal of Personality and Social Psychology,* 28, 129–137.

Schawlow, A. L. (1982). Going for the gaps [Interview]. *Stanford Magazine,* Fall, p. 42.

Schawlow, A. L., and Townes, C. H. (1958). Infrared and optical masers. *Physical Review,* 112(6), 1940–1949.

Simonton, D. K. (1975). Sociocultural context of individual creativity: A transhistorical time-series analysis. *Journal of Personality and Social Psychology,* 32, 1119–1133.

(1976). Biographical determinants of achieved eminence: A multivariate approach to the Cox data. *Journal of Personality and Social Psychology,* 33, 218–226.

(1977a). Creative productivity, age, and stress: A biographical time-series analysis of 10 classical composers. *Journal of Personality and Social Psychology,* 35, 791–804.

(1977b). Eminence, creativity, and geographic marginality: A recursive structural equation model. *Journal of Personality and Social Psychology,* 35, 805–816.

Stein, M. I. (1974). *Stimulating creativity.* Vol. 1. New York: Academic Press.

Sternberg, R. J., and Lubart, T. I. (1999). The concept of creativity: Prospects and paradigms. In *Handbook of creativity,* vol. 1, edited by R. J. Sternberg, 3–15. New York: Cambridge University Press.

Torrance, E. P. (1966). *The Torrance tests of creative thinking: Norms-technical manual.* Lexington, MA: Personal Press.

White, R. (1959). Motivation reconsidered: The concept of competence. *Psychological Review,* 66, 297–323.

CHAPTER 2

The Trouble with "Creativity"

John Baer

As a creativity trainer I assumed creativity was domain general and that I was teaching techniques that would enable students to be more creative in whatever they did. When as a creativity researcher I tried to prove that, however, the evidence eventually forced me to accept the domain specificity of creativity and to understand what domain specificity implies for creativity training, as well as for creativity research, theory, and assessment. Because the content of creative products and the processes that produce those artifacts vary so much by domain, the term "creativity" has little meaning as a general concept. Understanding that what we lump together as "creativity" is a thin abstraction that tells us little about actual creativity will result in better creativity research, theory, training, and assessment.

More than anything else, my creativity research has focused on the question of whether the skills, approaches, dispositions, heuristics, talents, and any other factors that might underlie creativity are domain general or domain specific. That was not where my work in creativity started, however, nor where I thought it would lead. I've always been interested in creativity – Who isn't? – but my involvement in the *research* side of creativity grew, unexpectedly, out of the creativity training was doing decades ago using the CPS model.

CPS is an all-purpose approach to solving challenging problems that originated in the work of Alex Osborn (1953), the advertising executive who invented brainstorming. CPS can be used to solve tough problems of any kind. It was great fun, it seemed to work well (Baer, 1988), and I enjoyed teaching it.

Then I read Howard Gardner's (1983) seminal book on multiple intelligences theory, *Frames of Mind*. I was more interested in creativity than intelligence, but if what Gardner was saying about the modularity of intelligence was true, might it not also be true of creativity? A modular creativity would threaten the underpinnings of CPS, because if creativity varies from domain to domain – if the skills underlying creativity in the visual arts and

16

creativity in writing and creativity in math or science are different from and essentially independent of each other – then how could CPS training work across all domains? I decided to test this idea.

A research design to test the modularity of creativity seemed obvious. I would simply assess participants' creativity in different fields and then show (as I hypothesized) that (1) there was considerable overlap and that (2) creativity in one area predicted creativity in other areas. If the same people tended to be creative in many domains – if tasks X and Y came from different "intelligences" as defined by Gardner and there was a substantial correlation between creativity in X and creativity in Y – then it would show that creativity was not modular. As Ivcevic (2007) nicely summarized this idea years later:

> Domain generality would be supported by high intercorrelations among different creative behaviors . . . while domain specificity would be supported by relatively low correlations among different behaviors. (p. 272)

This test of domain generality/domain specificity – looking for intercorrelations across domains – is precisely the test that critics claim multiple intelligences theory, which argues for modularity in intelligence, has failed. In 1994 the Board of Scientific Affairs of the American Psychological Association (APA) established a Task Force to produce "an authoritative report" (Neisser et al., 1996, p. 77) on what is actually known about intelligence. The Task Force concluded that "subtests measuring different abilities tend to be positively correlated: people who score high on one such subtest are likely to be above average on others as well" and that psychometric evidence suggested "a hierarchy of factors with g at the apex" (p. 78).

This was exactly how I (and probably most people in the field of creativity theory; see, e.g., Amabile, 1983) thought of creativity. There were certainly domain-based differences, but there was also a large, domain-transcending core to creativity. My goal was to prove this, using the same approach that defenders of g used in arguing against multiple intelligences. Having demonstrated the domain generality of creativity (as I assumed my study would do), I might next assess the creativity, in different domains, of participants in CPS workshops before and after training. This, I trusted, would show that CPS boosted creativity across domains.

As I envisioned this program of research, however, I quickly hit a roadblock: How to assess creativity in different domains? I was interested in measuring actual creative performance. All of the Ps in the 4P Model (Rhodes, 1961, 1987) might be part of creativity, but three of these Ps (person, process, and press) are really there in the service of the fourth, product.

A press (environment) that supports creativity, a thinking process (or any other kind of process, such as the CPS model) that leads to creativity, and a personality that is conducive to creativity are creativity-relevant only if they tend to be associated with creative performances or products. If an environment, process, or personality was no more likely than chance to produce creative outcomes, then by definition it would not be associated with creativity. I therefore was interested in creative products or performances, even though my goal was related to a creative process (CPS).

Most of the available measures of creativity tended to focus on creative processes or personality traits, and they all had an even more significant drawback: They assumed domain generality. For example, the Torrance Tests, which were by far the most widely used creativity assessments available, assumed domain generality, despite the fact that they came in two versions, figural and verbal (Kaufman, Plucker, and Baer, 2008; Torrance and Presbury, 1984). As Plucker (1998) argued:

> No assumption is made that performance is specific only to the task or content area addressed in a particular divergent-thinking test. Even the creation of figural and verbal versions of the TTCT is not an acknowledgment of the possibility that creativity is content general. (p. 179)

All other major creativity tests had the same problem.

Luckily, 1983 also marked the publication of Amabile's game-changing *The Social Psychology of Creativity*, in which she introduced the consensual assessment technique (CAT). The CAT has been called the "gold standard" of creativity assessment (Carson, 2006) because its validity is rooted in actual creative performance and is determined in the same way that creativity is discerned in the "real world": via the consensus of experts in the domain. Nobel Prizes, Academy and Screen Actors Guild Awards, the Pulitzer and Booker Prizes, the Breakthrough Prizes, and many other major awards are decided by experts in the field in question. One might wonder how else could such honorees be chosen: by applying a rubric designed by psychologists? Hardly. How does one tell if a work of art or a scientific theory or a musical composition is a work of genius? Other than asking people who should know – the experts in the domain – there really aren't any good options. Experts may change their decisions (and their criteria) over time, of course, but at any moment in time, it is the consensus of experts in a field that determines what work is creative and what is pedestrian. The CAT works essentially the same way.

And there was one more feature of the CAT that made it perfect for the studies I wanted to do. Not only is the CAT probably the best available measure of creativity; it is also (unlike every other major test of creativity available at the time) noncommittal about the question of domain generality v. domain specificity. CAT assessments are based on specific tasks, such as writing a poem or a story or making a collage (the three most widely used tasks, although many others have also been used). Whether the creativity ratings obtained with the CAT are simply valid assessments of creativity in the domain of the task (such as poetry or art) or of creativity more generally is something the CAT neither assumes nor predicts. These are open empirical questions that the CAT takes no stance on. Some researchers (e.g., Amabile herself; Amabile, 1983, 1996) have interpreted CAT scores without reference to domain, assuming that the specific tasks used would not influence a study's outcome, while others have used them only to assess creativity in specific domains (e.g., Baer, 1991, 1994, 1996).

The results of these studies were consistent, both in my research and the work of others. As Plucker (1998) noted, "the conclusions of researchers using the CAT are almost always that creativity is predominantly task or content specific" (p. 181). The across-domain correlations have been vanishingly small. These studies have provided no evidence of domain generality; on the contrary, they have consistently supported domain specificity.

My initial studies therefore led me to reverse my predictions for later studies as it became increasingly clear that the data simply didn't leave much room for theories of domain-general creativity. Unlike intelligence, in which intercorrelations among assessments in different domains have shown a significant overlap, creativity was showing itself to be quite domain specific. In fact, the size of the domains was even smaller (making the number of relevant domains considerably larger) than Gardner's eight intelligences. Creativity, research showed, was much more like expertise (which is very domain specific) than intelligence (in which there is substantial evidence for *g*). I've reviewed all of this work, both mine and others', in Baer (2016) and will only present the results from three representative papers here (Baer, 1991, 1994, 1996). In all three of these (as well as many others that preceded and followed these three) all artifacts were judged using the CAT. Details of the measures employed in each domain can be found in the original papers.

The 1991 paper discussed four studies using participants of different ages. Participants in one group of studies were eighth-grade students who created four artifacts: writing a poem, writing a story, creating an interesting mathematical equation, and writing an interesting math word problem. The within-domain tasks (poetry- and story-writing in the verbal domain; inventing interesting math equations and writing interesting math

Table 2.1 *Intercorrelations among creativity ratings (raw scores)*

Task	Poetry	Story	Word problem	Equation
Poetry	–	0.23	0.31*	−0.14
Story	–	–	0.20	−0.03
Word problem	–	–	–	−0.20

* $p < 0.05$

word problems in the math domain) were designed to be quite different from each other even though they nominally fell in the same domain. As Tables 2.1 and 2.2 show, cross-domain correlations were low, and even tasks within the same larger domain showed little evidence that they were rooted in the same sets of skills.

The other three studies reported in the 1991 paper had similar outcomes using participants of different ages: second-grade students, fourth-grade students, and adults. The cross-domain correlations were low in all groups, including a second testing of the fourth-grade students a year later as fifth graders. (This year-later testing was not done with the other groups.) The only statistically significant correlations between creativity ratings in that study were between scores obtained on the same task in fourth and fifth grades. The same students who were more creative on a given task in fourth grade tended to be more creative on that task in fifth grade, indicating a consistency of creative performance within a domain over time.

But what about creativity training, the question that got me started in creativity research? In the 1994 study I trained students in the experimental group using standard divergent thinking exercises (a major component of CPS training) using a variety of topics. All the divergent thinking activities were of a verbal nature. I trained the control group in ways of solving mathematical word problems with no divergent thinking activities.

Table 2.2 *Intercorrelations among creativity ratings; variance attributable to IQ removed*

Task	Poetry	Story	Word problem	Equation
Poetry	–	−0.01	0.19	−0.14
Story	–	–	0.05	0.07
Word problem	–	–	–	−0.45*

* $p < 0.05$

All subjects were then given five tasks: telling stories, writing stories, writing poems, writing mathematical word problems, and making collages. Experts evaluated the creativity of each product. The divergent thinking groups scored significantly higher than controls on the storytelling, story-writing, and poetry-writing tasks. The lack of correlations among scores on the five tasks, however, suggests that several task-specific factors, rather than one general factor, led to observed group differences. This is consistent with previous research using subjects untrained in divergent thinking in showing that divergent thinking is not a general trait (Baer, 1994, p. 35).

The divergent thinking training appeared to have an effect, but not a general effect:

> Although divergent thinking does not appear to be either a single skill or a distinct set of skills widely applicable within broad cognitive domains . . . what is commonly referred to as divergent thinking may describe a large constellation of skills, each influencing creative performance on different tasks. (p. 43)

The 1996 study was a different kind of training study. Rather than teaching divergent thinking skills in what might be called a shot-gun approach, I targeted the training by using only a very narrow range of content for the exercises. The participants were seventy-nine seventh-grade students in the experimental group and a matched group of control students in the same school. Random selection determined groups. The experimental group students were trained over several sessions using only poetry-relevant divergent thinking exercises. Both groups later wrote both poems and stories. These were rated for creativity using the CAT by experts who worked independently and who did not know who had had the training sessions and who had not been trained. The students with the poetry-relevant divergent thinking training wrote more creative poems than the control group, but their short stories were no more creative than those of untrained subjects.

Even divergent thinking, I discovered, is very domain specific. The training made a clear difference, but only in areas that matched the training. This is similar to efforts to increase cognitive skills through training. It can be done, but the effect is very narrow with little or no transfer. Wishful thinking that practicing one kind of cognitive skill will result in across-the-board cognitive improvements probably accounts for the recent popularity of brain-training programs like Luminosity, Jungle Memory, and CogniFit (Day, 2013), even though there is no evidence supporting such cross-domain transfer (Katsnelson, 2010; Owen et al., 2010; Redick et al., 2013; Thompson et al., 2013). Divergent thinking training seemed to follow the same pattern: significant effects, but only on tasks similar to those used in training, with little or no impact even on different kinds of tasks within the same larger domain. The need for fairly extreme domain specificity to assess the effects of creativity training echoes what Pretz and McCollum (2014) wrote about the need for extremely domain-specific analyses: "Perhaps prior studies of domain-specific creativity were not specific enough" (p. 233).

Other researchers have conducted similar studies and have also found very limited cross-domain correlations (e.g., Han, 2003; Han and Marvin, 2002; Runco, 1987, 1989; Ruscio, Whitney, and Amabile, 1998). A convergence of research results by a diverse group of researchers is important, of course. It is especially so when it comes from researchers trying to prove you wrong, as happened in a large 1996 study by Conti, Coon, and Amabile that combined the results of three previously reported studies with overlapping participants (ninety young adults enrolled in an Introductory Psychology course).

Conti, Coon, and Amabile's (1996) participants completed a total of four story-writing tasks and three art activities. Conti, Coon, and Amabile predicted positive cross-domain correlations, in contrast to the prediction of domain-specificity theory. (Recall Ivcevic's [2007] formulation: "domain specificity would be supported by relatively low correlations among different behaviors"; p. 272.) Conti, Coon, and Amabile made these predictions, in fact, in direct response to my research:

> In contrast to recent proposals by Baer (1991, 1993, 1994), the componential model predicts that because there are cross-task skills that contribute to creativity, creativity measures will be positively correlated across different tasks and situations. (p. 386)

There were a total of thirteen cross-domain correlations in Conti, Coon, and Amabile's study, and there was simply no evidence of domain generality in these correlations at all. Of the thirteen correlations of this kind, *none* – not one of the thirteen – was statistically significant. Even mean scores from the seven tasks in the two domains – the mean of the four writing tasks and the mean of the three art tasks – did not produce a statistically significant result. (As both domain specificity and domain generality predict, the within-domain correlations were strong and statistically significant, but this outcome is irrelevant to the generality/specificity question.)

Amabile, the CAT's creator, has argued for both domain-specific and domain-general factors in creative performance (Amabile, 1983, 1996). Her research, however, actually supports domain specificity rather powerfully

(Conti, Coon, and Amabile, 1996). But that was clearly not her intention in creating the CAT. She has maintained that the CAT itself is neutral on the question of specificity/generality and can be used, in exactly the way I proposed, to test for domain generality and domain specificity (as she did in the study just reviewed). Domain generality theorists have acknowledged that divergent thinking tests like the Torrance Tests assume domain generality, but have suggested that the CAT, in turn, assumes domain specificity (e.g., Plucker, 1998). As Amabile herself has argued, however, that is simply untrue. In fact, in much of her research with the CAT, Amabile (1983, 1996) herself has treated CAT scores as general measures of creativity, not measures of creativity in a particular domain.

Depending on one's measurement goals and theoretical stance, one might think of the CAT as either a domain-general or a domain-specific test – or at least one could, until research showed, consistently, that the CAT could only measure creativity in the specific domain from which the artifacts being judged are drawn, because that is the only kind of creativity there is. To the extent that domain specificity is true, *all* tests of creativity are necessarily domain specific, regardless of their intent or their claims, because there is simply no domain-general factor to measure; all one can measure is creativity in the domain(s) included in the test. By including tasks from a variety of domains, one might create a test that measures creativity in several domains, but that would be, at best, a multiple-domain test, not a domain-general test of creativity.

Which brings me back to the Torrance Tests, which come in two versions, figural and verbal. The choice of which to use is simply a matter of convenience or suitability to the sample, because both are offered as domain-general tests (Plucker, 1998). These tests assume domain generality, but they have nonetheless provided evidence for domain specificity. They have done this in two ways: (1) by proving to be two independent and essentially uncorrelated measures, and (2) by evidencing mutually contradictory results in validation studies.

(1) According to one of his closest collaborators, Torrance himself found that the figural and verbal Torrance Tests were measuring two very different sets of skills.

> Responses to the verbal and figural forms of the TTCT are not only expressed in two different modalities ... but they are also measures of different cognitive abilities. In fact, Torrance (1990) found very little correlation ($r = .06$) between performance on the verbal and figural tests. (Cramond, Matthews-Morgan, Bandalos, and Zuo, 2005, pp. 283–284)

It's rather hard to argue that two tests are measuring the same construct if their shared variance totals less than one-half of 1 percent, is it not? This is exactly the approach I used when I hoped to find domain generality in creative performance, and it is exactly the approach that the Board of Scientific Affairs of the APA's Task Force on Intelligence (Neisser et al., 1996) used as a primary way to show that intelligence has a significant domain-general component. Domain generality failed that test using CAT measures, as described above. And domain generality also failed that test using the two most widely employed divergent thinking tests. Plucker (1998) has argued that "[p]erformance assessments produce evidence of task specificity, and creativity checklists and other traditional assessments suggest that creativity is content general" (p. 180), but even these most traditional of all creativity assessments – the Torrance Tests of Creative Thinking – have provided strong evidence for domain specificity. By offering two versions of the Torrance Tests – even though they may have been intended to measure a single, domain-general set of abilities – the Torrance Tests have in fact allowed an unexpected test of domain generality. That test, conducted by Torrance himself, failed to find evidence of domain generality (with a correlation of just 0.06). As Sawyer (2012) concluded, "Different tests, each designed to measure creativity, often aren't correlated with one another, thus failing to demonstrate convergent validity" (p. 61).

(2) Validation studies of the Torrance Tests have received mixed reviews over the years. Many have concluded, as did Kogan (1983), Wallach, (1970), Anastasi (1982), and Crockenberg (1972) many years ago and as many reviewers have done more recently (Baer, 1993, 2011a, 2011b; Sawyer, 2012; Simonton, 2007; Sternberg, 1985), that no domain-general divergent thinking test has been validated as predictive of creativity. One common criticism of studies that have claimed to show validity of the Torrance Tests revolves around the kinds of criterion variables Torrance used as indicators of creativity, such as changing religious affiliation or subscribing to a professional journal. (On what basis might one conclude that things like changing religious affiliation or subscribing to a professional journal evidence creativity? There is no clear answer.) And then there is the problem that all of these indicators are based on self-report, which brings in another source of validity concerns. Crockenberg (1972) argued that "given the creativity criteria used ... [the results of these studies] should not be taken too seriously" (p. 35) and Sternberg (1985) argued that "such tests capture, at best, only the most trivial aspects of creativity" (p. 618). More recently Sawyer (2012) pointed out that Guilford himself admitted that divergent thinking tests don't correlate highly with real-world creative output, adding

that "although there remain some dissenters, most psychologists now agree that DT tests don't predict creative ability" (p. 51).

Despite these problems, validation studies of the Torrance Tests offer some unexpected (and unsought) evidence of domain specificity of divergent thinking. Plucker (1999) chose to reanalyze data from the Torrance validation study that provided the "most compelling" evidence for validity of the Torrance Tests, arguing that "[a]ny analysis of this topic should begin with this seminal study" (p. 104). Two hundred students took the Torrance Tests every year in grades 1–6. Torrance then used these divergent thinking test scores to predict a variety of self-reported criterion measures. As noted above, there has been much dispute about the validity of the criterion measures Torrance used, but Plucker's paper was interesting because he determined that in his reanalysis of Torrance's longitudinal data, one of the two Torrance Tests that subjects had taken did positively predict later self-reported creative performance – but the other did not. The difference in the predictive ability of the two Torrance Tests is telling, and Plucker couldn't explain why one of the Torrance Tests – the Verbal Test – predicted creativity while the other Torrance Test – the Figural Test – did not without resorting to domain specificity:

> The importance of verbal DT relative to figural DT may be due to a linguistic bias in the adult creative achievement checklists. For example, if a majority of the creative achievements required a high degree of linguistic talent, as opposed to spatial talent or problem solving talents, the verbal DT tests would be expected to have a significantly higher correlation to these types of achievement than other forms of DT. (Plucker, 1999, p. 110)

Exactly. Domain-specificity theory predicts that different measures of creativity rooted in different domains will predict creative performance *only in their respective domains*.

Domain generality theorists like Lubart and Guignard (2004) (who argued that "performance-based evaluations provide results favoring a domain-specific view"; p. 53) and Plucker (1998) agree that performance assessments routinely support domain specificity. They claim that creativity checklists provide evidence of domain generality, however. Do they?

Plucker (1998) cited a study by Runco (1987) that used students' self-reported levels of creativity in seven performance domains:

> Runco (1987) compared students' creativity checklist responses to quality ratings of the students' creativity (scored using a technique not unlike the CAT). The students' checklist scores provided evidence of content generality, and the quality ratings suggested content specificity. (p. 181)

So self-reported creativity by these students suggested domain generality, but their actual creative performance argued for domain specificity. Which kind of measure should we trust? (This is reminiscent of the Marx brothers' line from *Duck Soup*, "who are you going to trust, me or your lying eyes?")

There have been two excellent reviews of self-report creativity checklists in recent years, and it seems that the best one can say about such checklists is that they *might* have *limited* validity, especially some of the newest checklists, *but only when used to make very low-stakes decisions*. When Reiter-Palmon, Robinson, Kaufman, and Santo (2012) reviewed several frequently used self-report measures of creativity, they urged cautioned:

> These results suggest that although self-perceptions of creativity may provide some information about creativity, researchers should be cautious when using this measure as a criterion. (p. 107)

But when Silvia, Wigert, Reiter-Palmon, and Kaufman (2012) reviewed "four new and promising [creativity self-report] scales" (p. 19), they concluded that, although most such reviews "end on a grim note" (p. 31), the four new scales were more promising, at least if used only for low-stakes assessment.

These are hardly ringing endorsements, and because most of the creativity-checklist research that has been cited to support domain generality did not use the four "new and promising" scales, what self-reported creativity checklists can tell us about domain generality or domain specificity is probably quite limited.

As Sawyer (2012) concluded in his textbook *Explaining Creativity*, "[a] wide range of studies has shown that much of creative ability is domain-specific" (p. 60). Is there any domain generality at all? Probably. In our APT model of creativity, Kaufman and I proposed a hierarchy with some, possibly minor, domain-general factors (such as intelligence) and several levels of increasingly domain-specific factors that do most of the creativity heavy lifting (Baer and Kaufman, 2005; Kaufman and Baer, 2004).

Does this mean that CPS, which is where I started my creativity research journey, should be abandoned? Not at all. But it means that we must recognize that CPS (and divergent thinking skills, which are integral to CPS) will work differently (and require different training and practice) in different domains. Consider this parallel: We recognize that acquiring expertise generally requires practice and/or study, but we don't assume that the kinds of practice or study that lead to expertise in music will lead to expertise in cosmology. Expertise is very domain specific. So is creativity.

Confused (and often unrecognized) assumptions of domain generality, which are unfortunately common, have made it more difficult to understand creativity and have led to a plethora of conflicting and impossible-to-replicate results. For example, consider the relationship (or lack of relationship) between creativity and mental illness. Much ink has been spilled in this dispute going back many decades, but we now know that the presence or absence of such a linkage, as well as its degree where it exists, depends on the domain in question.

> The rate and intensity of adulthood symptoms vary according to the particular domains in which creative genius is expressed . . . geniuses in the natural sciences tend to be more mentally healthy than in the social sciences; geniuses in the social sciences, more so than those in the humanities; and geniuses in the humanities, more so than those in the arts. (Simonton, 2010, pp. 226–228)

Assuming domain generality made the truth about the creativity-mental illness connection impossible to see. Only a domain-specific orientation made it possible to undercover the truth.

Does this make studying and training creativity less exciting? Probably. Believing that one's students will become more creative in everything they do is a more satisfying theory for teaching CPS. But it makes creativity training even more essential (and more time consuming) when one realizes that it must be done not once and for all, but domain by domain. Ditto for creativity research and theory. Believing that one's theory is about all of creativity is more motivating than understanding that one's theory will probably only work in some domains (and will need to be tested in each). But assuming domain generality has a serious danger: It means one's research probably won't withstand replication when tried in other domains.

In some ways the root of the domain-specificity problem goes back to a dispute in philosophy at least as old as Plato and Aristotle. Are forms – abstract ideas like "beauty," "quality," and "goodness" – real, with an existence outside our minds? Would these abstractions be part of the world whether or not humans ever noticed them? Or are such concepts simply words that have no objective correlate, no independent existence, in the real world? Would there exist such a thing as "beauty" in the world even if no one ever noticed it, or is "beauty" a human invention? Nominalists argued that we must "avoid the temptation . . . of assuming that the ontological structure of the world matches the structure of our thoughts" (Kronman, 2016, p. 347).

There are times when it is helpful to use the term "creativity" to describe, collectively, a set of things from diverse domains. (I won't venture a definition beyond noting that novelty and appropriateness, as defined by the domain in question, seem to be key ingredients.) But the usefulness of the concept "creativity" does not mean that there actually exists in the world something that corresponds to what we intend when we use this term. The abstractions "beauty," "quality," and "goodness" can also be useful terms, but most of us can use them without losing sight of the fact that these are actually collections of things that are, in their actual manifestations, quite varied and for the most part unrelated. Beauty, quality, and goodness are all things that matter to us, but they are not things that are readily amenable either to research or to training – *except* research and training that focuses on beauty, quality, or goodness *in specific domains*.

We need a more nominalist understanding of "creativity," one that recognizes that the actual ideas and things we describe as creative – and the processes that yield those creative ideas and artifacts – are for the most part unrelated unless those things and ideas come from the same domain.

It is those domain-specific manifestations and domain-specific processes that we should be studying and training.

REFERENCES

Amabile, T. M. (1982). Social psychology of creativity: A consensual assessment technique. *Journal of Personality and Social Psychology*, 43, 997–1013.
  (1983). *The social psychology of creativity*. New York: Springer.
  (1996). *Creativity in context: Update to the social psychology of creativity*. Boulder, CO: Westview.
Anastasi, A. (1982). *Psychological testing*. New York: Macmillan.
Baer, J. M. (1988). Long-term effects of creativity training with middle-school students. *Journal of Early Adolescence*, 8, 183–193.
  (1991). Generality of creativity across performance domains. *Creativity Research Journal*, 4, 23–39.
  (1993). *Creativity and divergent thinking: A task-specific approach*. Hillsdale, NJ: Lawrence Erlbaum Associates.
  (1994). Divergent thinking is not a general trait: A multi-domain training experiment. *Creativity Research Journal*, 7, 35–46.
  (1996). The effects of task-specific divergent-thinking training. *Journal of Creative Behavior*, 30, 183–187.
  (2011a). Four (more) arguments against the Torrance Tests. *Psychology of Aesthetics, Creativity, and the Arts*, 5, 316–317.
  (2011b). How divergent thinking tests mislead us: Are the Torrance Tests still relevant in the 21st century? *Psychology of Aesthetics, Creativity, and the Arts*, 5, 309–313.

(2016). *Domain specificity of creativity*. San Diego, CA: Academic Press/Elsevier.

Baer, J., and Kaufman, J. C. (2005). Bridging generality and specificity: The Amusement Park Theoretical (APT) model of creativity. *Roeper Review*, 27, 158–163.

Carson, S. H. (2006). Creativity and mental illness. Invitational Panel Discussion Hosted by Yale's Mind Matters Consortium, New Haven, CT, April 19.

Conti, R., Coon, H., and Amabile, T. M. (1996). Evidence to support the componential model of creativity: Secondary analyses of three studies. *Creativity Research Journal*, 9, 385–389.

Cramond, B., Matthews-Morgan, J., Bandalos, D., and Zuo, L. (2005). A report on the 40-year follow-up of the Torrance Tests of creative thinking. *Gifted Child Quarterly*, 49, 283–291.

Crockenberg, S. B. (1972). Creativity tests: A boon or boondoggle for education? *Review of Educational Research*, 42, 27–45.

Day, E. (2013). Online brain-training: Does it really work? *The Guardian*, April 20. www.theguardian.com/science/2013/apr/21/brain-training-online-neuroscience-elizabeth-day.

Gardner, H. (1983). *Frames of mind: The theory of multiple intelligences*. New York: Basic Books.

Han, K. S. (2003). Domain specificity of creativity in young children: How quantitative and qualitative data support it. *Journal of Creative Behavior*, 37, 117–142.

Han, K. S., and Marvin, C. (2002). Multiple creativeness? Investigating domain-specificity of creativity in young children. *Gifted Child Quarterly*, 46, 98–109.

Ivcevic, Z. (2007). Artistic and everyday creativity: An act-frequency approach. *Journal of Creative Behavior*, 41, 271–290.

Katsnelson, A. (2010). No gain from brain training. *Nature News*, 464(7292), 1111.

Kaufman, J. C., and Baer, J. (2004). The Amusement Park Theoretical (APT) model of creativity. *Korean Journal of Thinking and Problem Solving*, 14(2), 15–25.

Kaufman, J. C., Plucker, J. A., and Baer, J. (2008). *Essentials of creativity assessment*. New York: John Wiley.

Kogan, N. (1983). Stylistic variation in childhood and adolescence: Creativity, metaphor, and cognitive styles. In *Handbook of child psychology: Vol. 3. Cognitive development*, 4th ed., edited by P. H. Mussen, 628–706. New York: John Wiley.

Kronman, A. T. (2016). *Confessions of a born-again pagan*. New Haven, CT: Yale University Press.

Lubart, T., and Guignard, J.-H. (2004). The generality-specificity of creativity: A multi-variant approach. In R. J. Sternberg, E. L. Grigorenko, and J. L. Singer (Eds.), *Creativity: From potential to realization* (pp. 43–56). Washington, DC: American Psychological Association.

Neisser, U., Boodoo, G., Bouchard, T. J., Boykin, A. W., Brody, N., Ceci, S. J., Halpern, D. F., Loehlin, J. C., Perloff, R., Sternberg, R. J., and Urbina, S. (1996). Intelligence: Knowns and unknowns. *American Psychologist*, 51, 77–101.

Osborn, A. F. (1953). *Applied imagination*. New York: Charles Scribner's Sons.

Owen, A. M., Hampshire, A., Grahn, J. A., Stenton, R., Dajani, S., Burns, A. S., Howard, R. G., and Ballard, C. G. (2010). Putting brain training to the test. *Nature*, 465(7299), 775–778.

Plucker, J. A. (1998). Beware of simple conclusions: The case for the content generality of creativity. *Creativity Research Journal*, 11, 179–182.

(1999). Is the proof in the pudding? Reanalyses of Torrance's (1958 to present) longitudinal data. *Creativity Research Journal*, 12, 103–114.

Pretz, J. E., and McCollum, V. A. (2014). Self-perceptions of creativity do not always reflect actual creative performance. *Psychology of Aesthetics, Creativity, and the Arts*, 8, 227.

Redick, T. S., Shipstead, Z., Harrison, T. L., Hicks, K. L., Fried, D. E., Hambrick, D. Z., Kane, M. J., and Engle, R. W. (2013). No evidence of intelligence improvement after working memory training: A randomized, placebo-controlled study. *Journal of Experimental Psychology: General*, 142(2), 359.

Reiter-Palmon, R., Robinson, E., Kaufman, J., and Santo, J. (2012). Evaluation of self-perceptions of creativity: Is it a useful criterion? *Creativity Research Journal*, 24, 107–114.

Rhodes, M. (1961). An analysis of creativity. *The Phi Delta Kappan*, 42(7), 305–310.

(1987). An analysis of creativity. In *Frontiers of creativity research: Beyond the basics*, 216–222. Buffalo, NY: Bearly.

Runco, M. A. (1987). The generality of creative performance in gifted and nongifted children. *Gifted Child Quarterly*, 331, 121–125.

(1989). The creativity of children's art. *Child Study Journal*, 19, 177–190.

Ruscio, J., Whitney, D. M., and Amabile, T. M. (1998). Looking inside the fishbowl of creativity: Verbal and behavioral predictors of creative performance. *Creativity Research Journal*, 11, 243–263.

Sawyer, K. (2012). *Explaining creativity: The science of human innovation*. 2nd ed. Oxford: Oxford University Press.

Silvia, P. J., Wigert, B., Reiter-Palmon, R., and Kaufman, J. C. (2012). Assessing creativity with self-report scales: A review and empirical evaluation. *Psychology of Aesthetics, Creativity, and the Arts*, 6, 19–34.

Simonton, D. K. (2007). Creative life cycles in literature: Poets versus novelists or conceptualists versus experimentalists? *Psychology of Aesthetics, Creativity, and the Arts*, 1, 133–139.

(2010). So you want to become a creative genius? You must be crazy! In *The dark side of creativity*, edited by D. Cropley, J. Kaufmann, A. Cropley, and M. Runco, 218–234. New York: Cambridge University Press.

Sternberg, R. J. (1985). Implicit theories of intelligence, creativity, and wisdom. *Journal of Personality and Social Psychology*, 49, 607–627.

Thompson, T. W., Waskom, M. L., Garel, K. L. A., Cardenas-Iniguez, C., Reynolds, G. O., Winter, R., Chang, P., Pollard, K., Lala, N., Alvarez, G. A., and Gabrieli, J. D. E. (2013). Failure of working memory training to enhance cognition or intelligence. *PloS One*, 8(5), e63614. www.plosone.org/article/info%3Adoi%2F10.1371%2Fjournal.pone.0063614.

Torrance, E. P. (1974). *Torrance Tests of creative thinking: Norms-technical manual.* Lexington, MA: Ginn.

    (1990). *The Torrance Tests of creative thinking: Norms-technical manual.* Bensenville, IL: Scholastic Testing Service.

Torrance, E. P., and Presbury, J. (1984). The criteria of success used in 242 recent experimental studies of creativity. *Creative Child and Adult Quarterly*, 9, 238–243.

Wallach, M. A. (1970). Creativity. In *Carmichael's handbook of child psychology*, vol. 1, 3rd ed., edited by P. H. Mussen, 1211–1272. New York: John Wiley.

CHAPTER 3

Do We Choose Our Scholarly Paths or Do They Choose Us?

My Reflections on Exploring the Nature of Creativity in Educational Settings

Ronald A. Beghetto

> Whenever I think of the past, it brings back so many memories.
> – Steven Wright

Steven Wright's humorous observation is an apt description of what happens whenever I reflect on my scholarly journey. It brings back a lot of memories. Some of them, however, stand out more than others. Reflecting on those memories has raised the following question: How much of our scholarly path do we choose versus how much of our path is chosen for us by our prior, formative experiences?

In answering this question, I would argue that the journey of a scholar is a sustained creative endeavor. And like any sustained creative endeavor, it represents a *developmental teleology* (Anderson, 1987; Beghetto, forthcoming-a; Peirce, 1931/1965). The journey is not driven by a predetermined end. Rather, it is aimed at resolving unsettling questions and experiences with ends that take shape and change along the way. Our past experiences, therefore, help form the choices we make and the scholarly paths we take. And, at the same time, our paths have an emergent feature to them with surprising twists and turns along the way.

In what follows, I reflect on my journey in the field of creativity studies by way of a few key experiences that have influenced the trajectory of my work. I also discuss how the choices I made resulted in new questions and directions for me to pursue. When discussing my prior experiences, I do so in relation to the themes I have pursued in my work (and not, necessarily, in chronological order).

"Creativity Is Dead"

As an untenured assistant professor of education at the University of Oregon, I had a department head who came very close to dissuading me from pursuing creativity as a line of research. In one of my early annual review meetings with him, he asked: "So, what *exactly* is your scholarly signature?" This was a fair question, because my interests spanned across many topics, including: creativity, educational evaluation of school reform initiatives, teacher development, learning, and instructional change.

I told him I was most interested in studying creativity in educational settings, both because I already had done some work in the area and because I saw it as a unifying theme that could connect the dots across my various interests.

He responded by saying, "Creativity is dead."

Perhaps seeing that I was a bit taken aback by his response, he provided an illustration. He walked over to his bookshelf and took down a recent conference program from the American Educational Research Association (AERA).[1] He sat down next to me, opened the program so we could both see the pages, and *slowly* read aloud sections from the massive index of topics and special interests groups. He would pause and repeat each of the reoccurring topics, none of which included creativity. After what seemed like an eternity, he tossed the program on the table and said, "See, creativity is dead in education." He then explained that if I wanted to increase my chances of attaining tenure I better get on track with something more "mainstream" in the field of educational research.

My well-intended[2] department head's admonition about studying creativity was an unsettling experience for me. But this wasn't the first time I heard dismissive comments about creativity. As a graduate student, some of my professors and fellow graduate students were often quick to note that, outside of gifted education, no one really understood or cared much about creativity in education. I was therefore used to people being dismissive of creativity. But this was the first time I had been told that studying creativity might impede my chances of obtaining tenure.

When I later shared this story during a round table discussion at a meeting of the AERA. Jane Piirto, who was one of the people at the table, leaned forward and informed me, "If you believe that, you're dead." She told me to stop wringing my hands and, instead, put them to work in continued pursuit of my intellectual passion in creativity. I honestly do not know if I

---

1 AERA is the premier educational research conference for researchers who study education and educationally related phenomena.
2 It is worth noting that after I started publishing more in the area of Creativity, my Department Head quickly became one of my biggest supporters (e.g., sharing creativity-related information he came across and directing other people to me who were also interested in the topic).

would have continued studying creativity if Jane hadn't put that challenge to me.

Why Doesn't Creativity Matter?

The 2004 paper that Jonathan Plucker, Gayle Dow and I published in *Educational Psychologist* (Plucker, Beghetto, and Dow, 2004) provided much needed terra firma for me in the early days of my journey. That paper was a long time in the making and working on it really helped me clarify the role that creativity could play in education. Jonathan and I started initial work on it when I was still a graduate student.

We both had experiences with education colleagues who viewed creativity as a nontopic. And the irony was not lost on me when my fellow graduate students and professors who held strong constructivist perspectives on learning[3] failed to see the connection between creativity and learning.

Jonathan and I often mused that perhaps the problem among our colleagues and other educational researchers was that the construct of creativity was surrounded by myths, which likely were perpetuated by a fuzzy or incomplete understanding of creativity (see Sternberg and Lubart, 1999). Moreover, we wondered whether this fuzziness extended to authors who use the term "creativity" in their published articles. We therefore endeavored to explore whether and how authors defined the term.

With Gayle Dow, we examined the use of the term "creativity" in a sample of ninety published articles. To help ensure that we were examining articles that were focused on creativity, we selected articles only if the term "creativity" was used in the title. We found that of the ninety selected articles, only 38 percent actually provided an explicit definition of the term and 21 percent provided no definition. In articles that never provided a definition of the term, authors mentioned *creativity* an average of thirty-two times and two articles included the term more than one hundred times without defining it.

Based on our analysis, we proposed the following synthesized definition of creativity:

> Creativity is the interaction among *aptitude, process, and environment* by which an individual or group produces a *perceptible product* that is both *novel and useful* as defined within a *social context*. (p. 90)

---

3 Constructivist and student-centered perspective on learning typically have their basis in the writings of scholars (such as Jean Piaget, Lev Vygotsky, John Dewey, Maxine Green) who have also written about the connection between creativity and learning.

We encouraged educators to adopt this definition as it might help them recognize smaller-c levels of creativity in education settings (e.g., a fourth-grade science project could be considered creative in the *social context* of a school science fair, even though it may not be viewed as creative in other contexts).

In a related publication (Plucker and Beghetto, 2004), Jonathan and I built on our definition and asserted that creativity might be thought of as having both domain specific and domain-general features (cf. Baer and Kaufman, 2005). We attempted to illustrate how taking an extreme perspective on either end of the domain-general versus domain-specific continuum could result in superficiality on the domain-general end and fixedness on the other end (which we viewed as particularly problematic in educational settings).

"Why Not Call It Mini-c?"

Following the publication of the 2004 *Educational Psychologist* piece, I continued to wrestle with the paradoxical disconnect I was seeing in how my education colleagues and students were espousing a constructivist perspective on learning (which typically had a basis in the work of Piaget and Vygotsky), yet didn't recognize the connection with creativity.

I did not view this disconnect as a deficit on the part of my colleagues and students, but rather as a failure in boundary spanning between the creativity and educational literature. Indeed, as I immersed myself deeper in the creativity literature, I became aware of several fellow travelers who explicitly recognized the connection between creativity and learning, including the importance of acknowledging more subjective forms of creativity (e.g., Cohen, 1989; Guilford, 1950; Moran and John-Steiner, 2003; Runco, 1996). I thereby endeavored to build on these conceptions of creativity to further clarify the connection between creativity and learning.

As fate would have it, the same AERA conference that Jane Piirto threw down the pursue-your-intellectual-passion-in-creativity gauntlet, I met James Kaufman. Quite the fortuitous conference! We later connected by phone and I shared with him some of my thinking on the importance of highlighting the intrapersonal as well as the interpersonal aspects of creativity, the need to clarify the connection between creativity and related perspectives on learning, the importance of recognizing subjective accounts of creativity, and how this confluence of ideas had a grip on my thinking.

James and I talked for quite a while on that day and generated many ideas. Our conversation centered on the problem of the two big categories of creativity (i.e., little c and Big C), not being inclusive enough to properly account for the aspect of creativity that I was awkwardly calling "subscript-c." I recall James asking, "Why not call it mini-c?"

This led to the publication of our 2007 paper, *Toward a Broader Conception of Creativity: A Case for Mini-C Creativity* (Beghetto and Kaufman, 2007). In that paper, we defined mini-c creativity as "the novel and personally meaningful interpretation of experiences, actions, and events" (p. 73). James and I continued to collaborate on the mini-c concept and eventually expanded our views into what became the *four-C model of creativity* (Kaufman and Beghetto, 2009), where we introduced the category of *Pro C* creativity. Pro C creativity represents professional-level creative accomplishments that have progressed beyond little c creativity but have not yet attained (and may never attain) the legendary status of Big C creativity (Kaufman and Beghetto, 2009). The Pro C category helped us further broaden the categories of creativity.

James became a key collaborator and we published quite a bit on the four-C model of creativity in an effort to help illustrate how determinations of creativity can range from the immediate inner eye of the creator to the future eyes of critics and connoisseurs who stand in judgment of creative contributions. This line of work continues to serve as an important pathway in my scholarly journey and applied work (e.g., helping me make the construct of creativity more accessible to teachers, students, and educational leaders).

"Either/or"

The concepts of mini-c and little c creativity have generally been well received among many of my education colleagues and students of education. At the end of the day, however, many continue to remind me that education is primarily about promoting academic learning. Consequently, even teachers who value supporting students' creative potential, may feel caught between trying to support student creativity on one hand and promote academic learning on the other. This can result in teachers feeling as though they must choose between *either* supporting creativity *or* promoting academic learning (Beghetto, 2007a).

I recognize this feeling from my own prior teaching experiences. Before becoming a professor, I was a classroom teacher. My first teaching assignment was teaching eighth grade. Because of an influx of students, I was asked to teach a section of every subject area,[4] including co-teaching two mini-courses (one on salsa making with the school counselor and the other on rock-climbing with the special education teacher).

I tried my best to approach my teaching creatively. Given the sheer amount of academic content that needed to be covered, I often felt like I was being pulled in opposing directions. I soon felt myself drifting toward an instructional approach that made it more and more difficult to make room for creativity in my classroom.

Around that same time, I was asked by a small group of students to serve as the coach for their afterschool Odyssey of the Mind (OM) team.[5] The OM program required me to approach teaching in a different way. Specifically, I was not allowed to guide them through the steps of solving problems. Rather, I was required to play more of a supportive role as they tried to come up with their own solutions to various ill-defined problems and challenges.

As a result, I observed deeper levels of student engagement, interest, and understanding than was otherwise noted in my regular classroom. I was impressed, but not clear how to make the connection to my everyday teaching of academic subject matter. I ultimately viewed creativity and academic learning as somewhat competing goals, but based on my OM experience had a hunch that they could be complementary goals.

When I later became a professor of teacher education, I was therefore interested in exploring how educators might view nurturing creativity and supporting academic learning as compatible (rather than competing) goals. My initial explorations into this line of work started with prospective teachers. I was interested in exploring how they conceptualized the relationship between creativity and academic learning.

I found, for instance, that prospective teachers tended to view creativity and academic learning as representing two different and sometimes opposing vectors (Beghetto, 2007b, 2008). Moreover, even those prospective teachers who recognized the value in exploring students' unexpected and potentially creative ideas often still harbored concerns that pursuing those ideas would disrupt the academic lesson they prepared (Beghetto, 2007b).

---

4 Teaching every subject to eighth graders was particularly challenging given that my preparation was focused on high school language arts! At the time, you could be hired out of your grade area and concentration if you were granted a type of "emergency certification" (which provided time to complete any required certification courses).

5 Odyssey of the Mind (OM) is "an international educational program that provides creative problem-solving opportunities for students from kindergarten through college." www.odysseyofthemind .com/learn_more.php.

This is a common concern, even among experienced teachers (Kennedy, 2005).

I also found that prospective teachers tended to believe that there was a specific grade level (i.e., typically an elementary grade) when teachers should start emphasizing the memorization of academic facts instead of focusing on encouraging students' creative imagination (Beghetto, 2008). When I explored the justifications that prospective teachers used for this either/or belief, I was able to classify their reasons into two major categories.

The first category is what I call the *memorization-as-foundation justification*, which refers to a belief that students need a foundation of facts prior to being able to think creatively. This view is, at least in spirit, aligned with what creativity researchers have long maintained about the interdependent role of knowledge and creativity (e.g., Guilford, 1950; Vygotsky, 1964/2004). The problem with this view, however, is that it is used to justify the deferral of nurturing creativity to some later date, rather than recognizing that the creative imagination can aid learning (Vygotsky, 1964/2004).

The second category that serves as a basis for either/or beliefs is what I called the *memorization-as-time-to-get-serious justification* (Beghetto, 2008). This justification is a bit more fatalistic, as it signifies a belief that creativity is a frivolous educational pursuit. It is used to justify the idea that at some point students need to leave creativity behind in order to get down to the serious business of memorizing academic facts so they are ready for the rigors of later schooling and the world of work.

Creative Learning

At the crux of the "either/or" perspective is a view that creativity and learning are separate. I have therefore endeavored to clarify a "both/and" approach that might help prospective and practicing teachers recognize the complementary relationship between nurturing creativity and supporting students' academic learning. My efforts in this area have been aimed at understanding and clarifying how other scholars have conceptualized this relationship, including what is meant by the term, "creative learning."

More specifically, I have attempted to establish a theoretical basis for the concept of creative learning (Beghetto, 2016a, 2016b, 2016c) as well as explore the empirical link between creativity and academic learning (Gadja, Karwowski, and Beghetto, 2016; Gadja, Beghetto, and Karwowski, 2017).

In my paper, *Creative Learning: A Fresh Look* (Beghetto, 2016c), for instance, I reviewed various conceptions of the relationship between creativity and learning. In that paper, I discuss how these conceptions run the gamut from viewing creativity and learning as independent (creativity | learning) and incompatible (creativity ≠ learning) to bi-directional (creativity → learning; learning → creativity) and interdependent (creativity ←→ learning). I also note how some scholars, such as Guilford (1967), have gone as far as to claim "creativity and learning are much the same phenomenon" (p. 307).

Working from the interdependent (both/and) perspective, I introduced a new model of creative learning with empirically testable assertions. In that paper, I defined creative learning as the "combination of intra-psychological and inter-psychological processes that result in new and personally meaningful understandings for oneself and others" (p. 4). The process model of creative learning that I introduce in the paper is based on this definition and outlines the interdependent relationship between creativity and learning. Specifically, the model endeavors to clarify the creative processes at play in the development of students' personal understanding and, in turn, how the sharing of those personal understandings can result in creative contributions to the learning of others.

In addition to outlining an empirically testable model of creative learning, I have also explored the empirical relationship between creativity and learning. In a 2016 meta-analysis with Aleksandra Gadja and Maciej Karwowski, for instance, we examined the relationship between measures of creativity and academic learning across 120 studies. We found a positive, albeit modest relationship ($r = 0.22$). We also found that this relationship was stable across cross-sections of time, but that more objective measures (e.g., standardized tests) and different types of measures (e.g., verbal versus figural tests of creativity) served as significant moderators of this relationship.

In a subsequent study (Gajda, Beghetto, and Karwowski, 2017), we explored teacher and student behaviors in classrooms that were classified as having a positive, negative, and null relationship between creativity and academic learning. We were particularly interested in exploring the interpsychological aspect of creative learning (as outlined in Beghetto, 2016c), which included teacher and student interactions during whole-group, class discussions. The challenge in doing this type of study is that it requires a blended and more dynamic methodological approach that enables researchers to display and interpret what would otherwise be ephemeral patterns of interaction (e.g., Beghetto, 2017a; Tanggaard and Beghetto, 2015).

Consequently, an additional goal of that paper was to demonstrate the potential value of blending more static, quantitative analysis with more dynamic analytic techniques that allowed for the display and interpretation of different patterns of interaction in the classroom. In doing so we were able to document some interesting patterns of interaction across classroom types, including more extended and exploratory interactions in a classroom classified as having a positive association between creativity and learning; more directive and rapidly closing patterns of interaction in a classroom with a negative relationship, and the lack of exploration, development, and refinement of students' ideas in a classroom with a null relationship between creativity and learning (Gajda, Beghetto, and Karwowski, 2017).

Rethinking Self-Beliefs

In addition to examining the relationship between creativity and learning, I have also been interested in understanding what factors might promote students' expression of creative thought and action in educational settings. My experiences with my Odyssey of the Mind (OM) team, once again, played a formative role in how I have approached this topic.

Indeed, one of the most unsettling aspects of my OM experience was the fact that the same students, in the same classroom, with the same teacher were somehow able to generate multiple creative ideas at 3:30 PM (during Odyssey of the Mind time), but not during our regular class time (a few hours earlier). What really stood out to me was the confidence those students had in their ideas *and* how they were able to turn those ideas into creative outcomes.

This experience helped shape my interest in understanding the nature of students' creative beliefs and how those beliefs might influence creative behavior. My colleagues and I have made some headway in this area (e.g., Beghetto, 2006; Beghetto and Karwowski, 2017; Kaufman and Beghetto, 2013; Kaufman, Beghetto, and Watson, 2015), particularly with respect to conceptualizing the important role that self-beliefs can play in the development of creative potential (Beghetto, 2010; Kaufman and Beghetto, 2013).

The empirical results from this line of work, however, have not yielded much more than modest associations between beliefs and performance (for a review, see Beghetto and Karwowski, 2017). This has been a humbling experience for me and has prompted me to rethink my work in this area. A serious limitation I have come to recognize is the way I have previously conceptualized and measured student beliefs (e.g., Beghetto, 2006), which lacks the sensitivity to adequately account for the various personal, situational, and task-specific factors at play. I have therefore been working on developing more dynamic, comprehensive, situationally specific, and micro-longitudinal conceptualizations and measures (Beghetto, 2017a; Beghetto and Karwowski, 2017, forthcoming).

"You're No John Keats"

The flipside of what my students seemed to experience on the OM team is creative suppression. Creative suppression can take many forms (from overt to more subtle and unintentional) and has been another key area of interest in my work. As with the other topics, this one has its basis in a few formative experiences.

One comes from my childhood. I can still vividly recall several instances when extended family members openly mocked my father, who was a jeweler and inventor (with several patents), as he shared prototypes of solutions to everyday problems. The jeering comments and cruel laughter of those family members had a chilling effect on him. He eventually stopped sharing his ideas and prototypes with anyone beyond my immediate family.

Another comes from when I was an undergraduate. My poetry professor was impressed by a poem I wrote for extra credit on an exam. He asked me to share all the poems I'd ever written and he'd give me feedback. When I stopped by a couple weeks later to get his feedback, he informed me that my Oeuvre was basically "a pile of saccharine bullshit" adding, "You're no John Keats" (my favorite poet at the time).

My professor was, of course, correct. I was no John Keats, not even close. And much of what I gave him was, in retrospect, embarrassingly terrible. His feedback served as a critical blow for my budding identity as an aspiring poet. I set the poetry pen down that day and haven't picked it up since. To be fair to my professor, I knew he didn't pull punches when it came to honest feedback and that's what I was looking for from him. I also knew other aspiring poets from my class who received similar feedback from him, yet they didn't stop writing. So why did I?

I have attempted to address this question by exploring what factors might explain why some people give up on pursuing a creative aspiration following negative performance outcomes whereas others do not, a phenomenon I call *creative mortification* (Beghetto, 2013a, 2014; Beghetto and Dilley, 2016). My work in this area has indicated that if people experience the emotion of shame – coupled with a belief that they cannot improve – then they will be more likely to experience creative mortification (Beghetto, 2013a, 2014; Beghetto and Dilley, 2016).

In addition to creative mortification, I have been interested in understanding more subtle and inadvertent forms of creative suppression, what

I "call killing ideas softly" (Beghetto, 2013a). This form of suppression can occur when teachers habitually ask students known-answer questions and then dismiss student responses that do not match what the teachers expect to hear (Beghetto, 2016b). In such cases, school success becomes more akin to a game of "intellectual hide-and-seek" (Beghetto, 2007) instead of an opportunity to share and receive feedback on one's unique ideas and insights.

This pattern of classroom talk can reproduce itself in students who later go on to become classroom teachers (Beghetto, 2010, 2013a). I have therefore developed and incorporated simulations into my courses to help prospective and practicing teachers become aware of moments when they inadvertently (or intentionally) suppress potentially creative ideas. They are then given an opportunity to revisit these moments and try out more supportive ways of responding to unexpected student ideas (Beghetto, 2013b).

What Is Creative Teaching?

The final theme I'd like to highlight is my work on creative teaching. Of all the themes I have explored, this one is perhaps most central to my own professional identity. My interest in this topic has its roots in my former experiences as a classroom teacher and I have cultivated this interest over the years in my research and applied work with prospective and practicing teachers. It is also the work I most enjoy doing as it is filled with so much potential, even though it is an area that is not well understood by teachers or well developed in the creativity literature.

Building on prior work on the scholarship of teaching (Shulman, 1987) and previous efforts aimed at distinguishing two types of creative teaching (e.g., Jeffrey and Craft, 2004), I have endeavored to clarify three forms of creative teaching (Beghetto, 2013a; Beghetto, 2017c): teaching *for* creativity, teaching *with* creativity, and teaching *about* creativity. Each of these forms of creative teaching has different pedagogical aims and draws on different types of pedagogical knowledge.

Consequently, knowing how to teach students to be creative in the context of learning math is not only different from teaching them to be creative in different subject areas, but also different from knowing how to teach math creatively, which is also different from knowing how to teach about creativity in mathematics. In a recent chapter on the topic (Beghetto, forthcoming-b), I reviewed my and others' prior work on these three forms of teaching, outlined directions for future research, and provided some initial ideas for how researchers might measure each of these forms of creative teaching.

In addition to outlining different forms of creative teaching, I have been working on ways that teachers can incorporate insights from creativity research to help young people (and themselves) respond productively to the uncertainty of ill-defined and complex challenges (Beghetto, 2016a, 2017b, 2017c). This includes developing what I call "legacy projects," which allow students to partner with external experts and put their academic learning to creative use by addressing problems that making a meaningful and lasting contribution (Beghetto, 2017b, 2017c).

This line of work is increasingly becoming my focus as it further clarifies the connection between learning and creativity. It also pushes creative thought and action beyond the walls of the classroom in a positive and productive way. Moreover, the outcomes of these efforts are – at least in the eyes of teachers, administrators, and other school-related stakeholders – much more persuasive than statistical effect sizes, because they meet the interocular traumatic test: They hit you right between the eyes.

To Be Continued

My journey in the field of creativity studies, while clearly influenced by several prior experiences, has never ceased to intrigue and, at times, surprise me. Although it seems true one can make the most sense of such a journey in retrospect, something that has been clear to me every step of the way has been the kindness and support of fellow travelers (thank you, Jane Piirto!) and the fortune of being able to collaborate with so many great colleagues along the way – especially, in those critical and somewhat fragile early years (thank you, Jonathan Plucker and James Kaufman!).

Even as interest in creativity continues to grow, the field remains rather small in terms of the number of active scholars. But it is great in terms of opportunities to work on intriguing and ever-emerging questions on the nature of human creativity. I am glad that I was somehow able to find my way on this path – and look forward to where it will continue to take me.

REFERENCES

Anderson, D. R. (1987). *Creativity and the philosophy of C. S. Peirce*. Hingham, MA: Kluwer.

Baer, J., and Kaufman, J. C. (2005). Bridging generality and specificity: The Amusement Park Theoretical (APT) model of creativity. *Roeper Review*, 27, 158–163.

Beghetto, R. A. (2006). Creative self-efficacy: Correlates in middle and secondary students. *Creativity Research Journal*, 18, 447–457.

(2007a). Ideational code-switching: Walking the talk about supporting student creativity in the classroom. *Roeper Review*, 29, 265–270.

(2007b). Does creativity have a place in classroom discussions? Prospective teachers' response preferences. *Thinking Skills and Creativity*, 2, 1–9.

(2008). Prospective teachers' beliefs about imaginative thinking in K–12 schooling. *Thinking Skills and Creativity*, 3, 134–142

(2010). Creativity in the classroom. In *Handbook of creativity*, edited by J. C. Kaufman, and R. J. Sternberg, 191–205. New York: Cambridge University Press.

(2013a). *Killing ideas softly? The promise and perils of creativity in the classroom*. Charlotte, NC: Information Age.

(2013b). Nurturing creativity in the micromoments of the classroom. In *Creatively gifted students are not like other gifted students: Research, theory, and practice*, edited by K. H. Kim, J. C. Kaufman, J. Baer, B. Sriramen, and L. Skidmore, 3–15. Rotterdam, Netherlands: Sense.

(2014). Creative mortification: An initial exploration. *Psychology of Aesthetics, Creativity, and the Arts*, 8, 266–276.

(2016a). Leveraging micro-opportunities to address macroproblems: Toward an unshakeable sense of possibility thinking. In *Creative intelligence in the 21st century: Grappling with enormous problems and huge opportunities*, edited by D. Ambrose and R. J. Sternberg, 159–174. Rotterdam, Netherlands: Sense.

(2016b). Learning as a creative act. In *Modern curriculum for gifted and advanced learners*, edited by T. Kettler, 111–127. Waco, TX: Prufrock.

(2016c). Creative learning: A fresh look. *Journal of Cognitive Education and Psychology*, 15, 6–23.

(2017a). Creative openings in the social interactions of teaching. *Creativity: Theories-Research-Applications*, 3, 261–273.

(2017b). Legacy projects: Helping young people respond productively to the challenges of a changing world. *Roeper Review*, 39, 1–4.

(2017c). Creativity in teaching. In *Cambridge handbook of creativity across different domains*, edited by J. C. Kaufman, J. Baer, and V. P. Glăveanu, 549–564. New York: Cambridge University Press.

(forthcoming-a). Abductive reasoning and the genesis of new ideas: Charles S. Peirce. In *The creativity reader*, edited by V. Glăveanu. Oxford: Oxford University Press.

(Forthcoming-b). *What if? Unleashing the power of complex challenges in teaching and learning*. Alexandria, VA: ASCD.

Beghetto, R. A., and Dilley, A. E. (2016). Creative aspirations or pipe dreams? Toward understanding creative mortification in children and adolescents. *New Directions for Child and Adolescent Development*, 151, 85–95.

Beghetto, R. A., and Karwowski, M. (2017). Untangling creative self-beliefs. In *The creative self*, edited by M. Karwowski and J. C. Kaufman, 3–22. Boston: Academic Press.

Beghetto, R. A., and Karwowski, M. (forthcoming). Unfreezing creativity in classrooms: Toward a more dynamic approach. In *Dynamic perspectives on creativity*, edited by R. A. Beghetto and G. Corazza. Switzerland: Springer.

Beghetto, R. A., and Kaufman, J. C. (2007). Toward a broader conception of creativity: A case for mini-c creativity. *Psychology of Aesthetics, Creativity, and the Arts*, 1, 73–79.

Cohen, L. M. (1989). A continuum of adaptive creative behaviors. *Creativity Research Journal*, 2, 169–183.

Gajda, A., Beghetto, R. A., and Karwowski, M. (2017). Exploring creative learning in the classroom: A multi-method approach. *Thinking Skills and Creativity*, 24, 250–267.

Gajda, A., Karwowski, M., and Beghetto, R. A. (2016). Creativity and school achievement: A meta-analysis. *Journal of Educational Psychology*, 109, 269–299.

Guilford, J. P. (1950). Creativity. *American Psychologist*, 5, 444–454.

——— (1967). Creativity and learning. In *Brain function: Vol. IV. Brain function and learning*, edited by D. B. Lindsley and A. A. Lumsdaine, 307–326. Los Angeles: University of California Press.

Jeffrey, B., and Craft, A. (2004). Teaching creatively and teaching for creativity: Distinctions and relationships. *Educational Studies*, 30, 77–87.

Kaufman, J. C., and Beghetto, R. A. (2009). Beyond big and little: The four C model of creativity. *Review of General Psychology*, 13, 1–12.

——— (2013). In praise of Clark Kent: Creative metacognition and the importance of teaching kids when (not) to be creative. *Roeper Review*, 35, 155–165.

Kaufman, J. C., Beghetto, R. A, and Watson, C. (2015). Creative metacognition and self-ratings of creative performance: A 4-C perspective. *Learning and Individual Difference*, 51, 394–399.

Kennedy, M. (2005). *Inside teaching: How classroom life undermines reform*. Cambridge, MA: Harvard University Press.

Moran, S., and John-Steiner, V. (2003). Creativity in the making: Vygotsky's contemporary contribution to the dialectic of development and creativity. In *Creativity and development*, edited by R. K. Sawyer, V. John-Steiner, S. Moran, R. J. Sternberg, D. H. Feldman, J. Nakamura, 61–90. New York: Oxford University Press.

Peirce, C. S. (1931/1965). *Collected papers of Charles Sanders Peirce*, edited by C. Hartshorne and P. Weiss, vol. 6. Cambridge, MA: Harvard University Press.

Plucker, J. A., and Beghetto, R. A. (2004). Why creativity is domain general, why it looks domain specific, and why the distinction does not matter. In *Creativity: From potential to realization*, edited by R. J. Sternberg, E. L. Grigorenko, and J. L. Singer, 153–167. Washington, DC: American Psychological Association.

Plucker, J., Beghetto, R. A., and Dow, G. (2004). Why isn't creativity more important to educational psychologists? Potential, pitfalls, and future directions in creativity research. *Educational Psychologist*, 39, 83–96.

Runco, M. A. (1996). Personal creativity: Definition and developmental issues. *New Directions in Child Development*, 72, 3–30.

Shulman, L. S. (1987). Knowledge and teaching: Foundations of the new reform. *Harvard Educational Review*, 57, 1–22.

Sternberg, R. J., and Lubart, T. I. (1999). The concept of creativity: Prospects and paradigms. In *Handbook of creativity*, edited by R. J. Sternberg, 3–15. New York: Cambridge University Press.

Tanggaard, L., and Beghetto, R. A. (2015). Ideational pathways: Toward a new approach for studying the life of ideas. *Creativity: Theories-Research-Applications*, 2, 129–144

Vygotsky, L. S. (1967/2004). Imagination and creativity in childhood. Translated by M. E. Sharpe Inc. *Journal of Russian and East European Psychology*, 42, 7–97.

CHAPTER 4

Bringing Creativity down to Earth
A Long Labor Lost?

Arthur Cropley

The Task

The discussion of creativity has been dogged since antiquity by widespread acceptance that it involves "some divine principle" (Tsanoff, 1949, p. 2), and is beyond human understanding. The Sputnik shock, when the then Soviet Union successfully launched the first artificial earth satellite, propelled the discussion along a new pathway. Creativity was suddenly no longer seen as confined to artists, a view that I had previously unquestioningly accepted, but as also involving engineers, industrialists, politicians, even soldiers. It was hailed as not just an aesthetic or even spiritual phenomenon, but as a means of achieving peace, stability, prosperity, justice, good health, and general well-being, and there were calls in the United States and the Western world for its systematic promotion in schools and universities. Sputnik I may only be a small piece of history nowadays, but I still have vivid memories of watching it moving slowly across the night sky of my native Australia on October 4, 1957, and of having a strong feeling that the world would never be the same again. I had the good fortune of entering graduate school at the University of Alberta a few years later, and my PhD supervisor, Dr. Charles Anderson, who provided inspirational leadership throughout my doctoral studies, urged me to concentrate on the hot new field of creativity. I accepted the task he assigned me, and have no regrets.

Although sixty years have passed since Sputnik I, the linking of creativity with higher powers and the arts is still alive and widely accepted: For example, it is said to enable humans "to connect with the eternal" (Hunter, 2012, p. 27). Some people go so far as to reject the idea of any connection to practical matters: Albrecht (2016, p. 177) cited a teacher participating in her research who argued that producing anything, even artworks, *blocked* her creativity and that it is the process of "following my inner voice" which constitutes creativity. Rothman (2014) complained about what he called "creativity creep," arguing that: "If you're really creative, really imaginative, *you don't have to make things.* You just have to live, observe, think, and feel" [emphasis added]. Where this leads in educational psychology was eloquently illustrated by Kawenski (1991, p. 263). In a design class, her students' "romantic notions led them to believe that creative thinking consisted of just letting their minds waft about dreamily, *waiting for the muse to strike them*" [emphasis added]. Disputing that creativity results from the Muse's kiss (effortless creativity) is the task I have been working on for more than fifty years. I call this "bringing creativity down to Earth" (Cropley, 2016).

Bringing creativity down to Earth does not mean denying the existence of sublime achievements or denigrating special talent, as Rocavert (2016) recently complained, any more than treating intelligence as a normal human quality means denying the special position of acclaimed people such as Albert Einstein or Stephen Hawking. However, as Guilford (1987) pointed out, historically speaking only about two in every million people reach extraordinarily high levels of achievement. Thus, although intensive study of the sublime creativity of eminent people is thoroughly worth doing and may well involve learning a great deal, it unfortunately involves almost nobody, and certainly not schoolchildren, scarcely any of whom are already, or ever will be, included in the two in a million. Approaching fifty years ago, Nicholls (1972, p. 717) put the matter plainly when he proposed studying creativity as a "normally distributed trait," and called for a focus on the "ordinary" 99.9998 percent. My endeavor has been to bring creativity down to Earth, but to do this without commoditizing it and reducing it to "fast food creativity" (A. J. Cropley and Cropley, 2009, p. 15).

The Myths of Creativity

Along with other writers, I have argued (e.g., Cropley, 2012) that the study of creativity is dogged by "myths." These include: the myth of *inscrutability* (creativity is beyond human comprehension); the myth of *ineffability* (creativity cannot be described in words but only experienced in the form of beauty); the myth of *ineluctability* (creativity cannot be controlled – in educational terms, it cannot be encouraged, fostered, or trained). I have focused on (1) busting the myth that creativity is unknowable (e.g., Cropley, 2016); (2) breaking the nexus between creativity and the arts without denying that it is of central importance there (e.g., D. H. Cropley and Cropley, 2010a); (3) emphasizing the day-to-day usefulness of creativity not just in an abstract sense (e.g., promoting psychological health; Cropley, 1990) but also in a practical sense (e.g., promoting material welfare and comfort; Cropley, 2007); (4) emphasizing the importance of products (e.g., D. H. Cropley and Cropley, 2010a); (5) pointing out that creativity can have a "dark" side (e.g., D. H. Cropley, Cropley, Kaufman, and Runco, 2010; D. H. Cropley and Cropley, 2013); (6) focusing on education practice, both in general terms (Cropley, 1967a) and more specifically (D. H. Cropley and Cropley, 2000, 2010b).

Busting the Myth of Inscrutability: Knowing What Creativity Is

Creativity and Intelligence

My initial approach to creativity was based on the work of Getzels and Jackson (1962), whom I interpreted as regarding creativity as a separate ability from conventional intelligence or even competing with it. "Creativity" seemed too emotive and value-laden to be the label for the "new" ability, and in my earliest work I referred to "originality" (e.g., Cropley, 1965; Cropley and Anderson, 1966). However, I soon began using Guilford's then novel terminology, "divergent thinking" (Guilford, 1950). Subsequently, I succumbed to the allure of "creativity." The dominant issue in the early years was the relationship between the "new" ability (creativity) and the "old" one (intelligence). I found (Cropley, 1967a) that there were disproportionately large numbers of schoolchildren who scored high on both or low on both. Furthermore (Cropley, 1967b), schoolchildren high on both got the best school grades and university science majors high on both were selected for honors-level classes more frequently than their classmates who were high on intelligence alone, despite no differences in grades. An *oblique* factor rotation (Cropley, 1966) also showed that a factor defined by convergent thinking tests and a factor defined by the new divergent thinking tests correlated around 0.5. Thus, the two kinds of test measure something different, but also the same.

Various conceptualizations of this simultaneous sameness and difference exist (e.g., the threshold theory, the overlapping skills approach, the components model; see Cropley, 2001). I concluded that creativity and intelligence are best understand as *two patterns of application of a unified, general mental power* that underlies both kinds of test. I initially referred to the power as "creative intelligence" or "true giftedness" (Cropley, 1995, p. 99), but soon realized that these terms had been preempted by the already well-established concepts of "intelligence" and "giftedness." I began using the terms "divergent style" and "convergent style" to distinguish between the two (Cropley, 1967b; Cropley and Field, 1968). Subsequently, however,

I specifically argued (Cropley, 2006a) that creativity is not synonymous with the divergent style, but depends heavily on *convergent* thinking too. In fact, the essence of practical, productive, down-to-earth creativity lies in combining divergence and convergence.

I also concluded that it is possible to combine styles by switching backward and forward between them, although most people find this difficult. The style approach seems to attract little interest in educational discussions, but the idea of switching is well established in organizational psychology, with terms like "oscillation," "dynamic shifting," or mental "ambidexterity" being used to refer to it (D. H. Cropley and Cropley, 2015, p. 42). I still adhere to the style approach: Regardless of the level of cleverness, one style of thinking is to converge, another is to diverge. Furthermore, I believe that people (including teachers and students) can be taught to understand the difference between the two thinking styles, or "modes" as Wallach and Kogan (1965) called them, and to recognize when they are operating in the one or the other mode. They can also be taught how to diverge: Most people do not need to be taught to *converge*, as this is thrust upon them in home, school, and society (Cropley, 1973, 2006b).

Creativity Outside the Arts: Organizational Creativity

In recent years, I have extended my interest in down-to-earth creativity to encompass creativity in commercial organizations (e.g., D. H. Cropley and Cropley, 2015). Organizational creativity is subject to the "usefulness imperative" (p. 21), so that simply going beyond boundaries – commendable, perhaps, in aesthetic creativity – is not enough. In fact, David Cropley and I have argued (D. H. Cropley and Cropley, 2015, pp. 32ff.) that the key to understanding, and especially to evaluating, creativity and its products is the *intention* of the person generating the creativity. This may range from absolutely no intention at all of producing a concrete product of any kind and for any purpose (purely spiritual creativity in the sense of Rothman, see above) to generating novelty for the explicit purpose both of producing a product and of communicating it to other people; at its extreme, in the hope of obtaining material benefit. Consideration of the hope of gain introduces what might be called "demand-side" creativity, and has obvious links to Sternberg's investment model (e.g., Sternberg, Kaufman, and Pretz, 2002). Focusing on the motivation of the individual producing the product differs from the well-known four-C model (Kaufman and Beghetto, 2009), which emphasizes the properties of the product itself and its reception by the external world.

In my earlier thinking about creativity I had become aware that it involves "a bundle of paradoxes" (e.g., Cropley, 1997b, p. 8). The same phenomenon can be simultaneously good for creativity and also bad for it: an example is knowledge of a field. Broad knowledge fosters the production of numerous ideas (good for creativity), but also channels thinking along known lines (bad for it) (Cropley, 2006a). Confronted with this, David Cropley and I (e.g., D. H. Cropley and Cropley, 2008a) explored the well-known idea of "phases" in the creative process, extending Wallas's (1926) phase model by adding an initial phase of "preparation" and later phases of "communication" and "validation" (D. H. Cropley and Cropley, 2015, p. 137). In organizational creativity, the usefulness imperative means that getting the product into the hands of consumers (communication) and getting a positive reaction from them (validation) are absolutely vital. The apparent paradoxes arise from the fact that what is good for creativity is specific to a particular phase. For example, remaining open to a wide range of possible solutions is good in the phase of generation, but bad in the phase of verification, where the one true answer must be found.

Subsequently, on the basis of existing, well-established creativity theory (the 4Ps model), David and I (D. H. Cropley and Cropley, 2015, p. xv) worked out what we call the six "building blocks" of organizational creativity (Process; personal Motivation; personal Properties; personal Feelings; Product; Press), and realized that we could dichotomize these to yield contrasting poles: for example, divergent versus convergent processes, tolerance for ambiguity versus preference for closure, or willingness to go it alone versus urgent need for feedback from others. Ultimately (D. H. Cropley and Cropley, 2008a, 2015, p. 184), we mapped the contrasting poles of the building blocks onto the phases, and identified an orderly structure which is not paradoxical at all. On the basis of this systematic structuring of the relationship between phases and building blocks we developed what we call the innovation phase model (IPM) of organizational creativity.

This model has turned out to have practical usefulness we did not foresee at the time we began developing it. For example, it has led to the development of a tool for analyzing creativity in organizational settings: the Institutional Phase Assessment Instrument (IPAI) (see later discussion). D. H. Cropley (2010) used it as a framework for working out how to disrupt the malevolent creativity of terrorists (see later discussion). Soh Kaycheng (e.g., Soh, 2015) developed the Creativity Facilitating Teacher Index (CFTIndex), which provides a self-assessment by teachers of nine dimensions of their own teaching behavior. One of the CFTIndex's subscales has noticeably lower reliability and factorial validity than the other eight. When the nine subscales were mapped onto the seven phases of the IPM, it immediately became apparent that this rogue subscale refers to a mixture of two of the seven phases of the IPM, whereas each of the remaining subscales focuses on a single phase.

Breaking the Nexus with the Arts: Negative Creativity

Removing creativity's aura of other-worldly virtue by bringing it down to earth raises the issue of creativity whose products are not only *not* aesthetically pleasing, but are also clearly *not* admirable, or are even despicable. McLaren (1993) and James, Clark, and Cropanzo (1999) began a focused discussion of the "dark side" of creativity, or "negative" creativity. In its most general form, negative or dark creativity encompasses creativity with undesirable consequences, regardless of the intention of the creator or, indeed, possibly in direct contradiction of the intention of the creator. With colleagues (see D. H. Cropley, Cropley, Kaufman, and Runco, 2010), I have discussed, among other things, how people with good intentions can nonetheless apply their creativity to developing weapons of mass destruction, as in the Soviet Union (Zaitseva, 2010) or the United States (Hecht, 2010).

With, in particular, David Cropley, I have extended this discussion to encompass the special case of "malevolent" creativity (D. H. Cropley and Cropley, 2011a, 2013; D. H. Cropley, Kaufman, and Cropley, 2008, 2013). Malevolent creativity not only does harm, but this is its conscious purpose and its fundamental intention. The most striking contemporary manifestation of malevolent creativity is terrorism. D. H. Cropley, Kaufman, and Cropley (2008) worked out antiterrorism principles specifically derived from creativity theory and discussed the terrorists' problem of "creativity decay" (p. 109). In D. H. Cropley, Cropley, Kaufman, and Runco (2010), Hari (2010) discussed the application of defensive creativity to combating terrorism, and D. H. Cropley (2010) applied the IPM in order to develop proposals for accelerating creativity decay and disrupting the planning of large-scale atrocities.

Another domain in which malevolent creativity is seen is crime (e.g., D. H. Cropley and Cropley, 2013): useful and effective novelty is generated for the specific purpose of improving the benefits yielded by criminal behavior. This fusion is most obvious in areas such as fraud, but is also seen in some cases of theft or murder as well as in areas such as cybercrime, drug smuggling, people trafficking, or illegal exporting of high-tech products. Applying creativity theory to crime provides concepts for distinguishing between "resourceful" crime and, for example, sheer brutish antisocial aggressiveness. In making this link, my hope was to offer perspectives on crime that differ sharply from a focus on age, gender, race, or level of education. However, our work in this area has aroused little interest.

Busting the Myth of Ineffability: Saying What Creativity Is

The question now arises of what down-to-earth creativity creates if it is not works of sublime art inspired by unknowable higher powers. How do you recognize down-to-earth creativity when you see it? In my early writings (e.g., Cropley, 1967a), I recommended ignoring products, on the grounds that whether a product is creative or not is too heavily dependent upon social conventions, which differ, among other things, from social group to social group, from era to era, and from content domain to content domain. However, in more recent years I have realized that products are the core public manifestation of down-to-earth creativity. Creativity as a private experience – such as simply *being* creative or *feeling* creative without actually *doing* anything (Rothman, 2014), or "following my inner voice" (Albrecht, 2016, p. 177) – is now of no interest to me. I have gone so far as to refer to this as "onanistic" creativity.

In studying creative products, I have focused on what Burghardt (1997, p. 4) called "creativity with a *purpose*" [emphasis added]. Although it is clear that such creativity can lead to intangible products, such as new ways of conceptualizing the world (e.g., philosophy, mathematics) or tangible aesthetic products (e.g., in visual arts, performing arts, literature), what interests me is products in the form of "devices or systems that perform tasks or solve problems" (Horenstein, 2002, p. 2), especially practical, real-life problems. I often refer to such products as "solutions." Creative solutions are the result of what David Cropley and I call *functional* creativity (D. H. Cropley and Cropley, 2010a): creativity with the deliberate intention of producing something *useful* in a concrete sense – creativity with attitude.

The Key Properties of Functionally Creative Products

Initially, mainly in collaboration with David Cropley, I built on previous research on creative products (e.g., Taylor, 1975; Jackson and Messick, 1965; Besemer and O'Quin, 1987) to develop a "universal aesthetic of creativity" (D. H. Cropley and Cropley, 2008b, p. 155), and focused on four properties of a product which make it functionally creative. These are (1) *novelty* (the core of creativity); (2) *relevance and effectiveness* (the product refers to

a real issue and contributes to dealing with it or understanding it better);
(3) *elegance* (elegant products "delight" observers); (4) *genesis* (the product
opens up new ways of looking at known issues or draws attention to new
issues and gives hints on how to deal with them). These four properties are
reminiscent of the work of Altshuller (1988), Savransky (2000), and Sternberg, Kaufman, and Pretz (2002). However, these authors were discussing
the creative *process*, whereas in my work I have focused on the results of the
process – the *product*.

Although intuitively it is the sine qua non of any kind of creativity, novelty is insufficient on its own. It may involve no more than ignorance, reflex
nonconformity, lack of discipline, blind rejection of what already exists, or
simply letting yourself go. This is mere *pseudo-creativity*. Pseudo-creativity
can easily become self-indulgence or may involve a special kind of conformity to stereotypical "creative" patterns of behavior and be no more than
pretentiousness – pure onanistic creativity. Novelty production that goes
beyond mere ostentatious display of differentness and addresses a genuine
issue, but offers no realistic prospect of a solution because it has no relevance and effectiveness, is referred to as *quasi-creativity*. Thus, a combination of the first two criteria – *novelty*, on the one hand, and *relevance
and effectiveness*, on the other – is indispensable for functional creativity.
The addition of the remaining two criteria to a product – *elegance* and *genesis* – changes both the amount and also the kind of creativity. Novelty,
relevance and effectiveness, elegance, and genesis are seen in the sublime
works of celebrated creators such as Einstein or Stephen Hawking, or creative engineers such as Edison, to be sure, but also manifest themselves in
humbler products.

Busting the Myth of Ineluctability: Deliberately
Influencing Creativity

Creativity is neither inscrutable nor ineffable. The final step is to show that
it is not ineluctable: It is possible to work out (1) what people need to do
more of in order to be more creative, (2) communicate this to them in terms
they can understand (i.e., in a down-to-earth way), and (3) give them feedback on favorable and unfavorable aspects of their concrete behavior that
makes clear where and how they can act more creatively. It is also possible
to provide an environment, or *press*, as Rhodes (1961) put it, that encourages creative behavior. For example, in Cropley (2005) and A. J. Cropley
and Cropley (2009), I worked out guidelines for setting classroom tasks in
all disciplines in a way that "presses" for creativity. The guidelines focus on

four dimensions: (1) specificity of preparation for the task; (2) level of clarity of definition of the task; (3) degree of structure or formalization of the solution search; (4) level of predefinition of the solution. Broad and general preparation, low level of task definition, open forms of solution search, and discretion about what constitutes a solution provide press for processes like problem discovery, problem construction, or problem invention, on the one hand, and solution definition or self-evaluation, on the other. In terms of Sternberg's (2007) criteria, creative classroom press gives students the *opportunity* to work creatively, an *incentive* to do so, and a *reward* when they do it.

The Creative Solutions Diagnosis Scale (CSDS): Influencing Products

On the basis of the four rubrics of functional creativity outlined above (novelty; relevance and effectiveness; elegance; genesis), David Cropley and I went beyond press and constructed a scale for assessing the creativity of *products* (the Creative Solutions Diagnosis Scale; CSDS). Research on the psychometric properties of the CSDS (e.g., D. H. Cropley, Kaufman, and Cropley, 2011; D. H. Cropley and Kaufman, 2012) revealed that it measures not four but five separate dimensions or rubrics: (1) Relevance and Effectiveness; (2) Problematization; (3) Propulsion; (4) Elegance; (5) Genesis. "Relevance and Effectiveness," "Elegance," and "Genesis" have already been explained above. "Problematization" and "Propulsion" result from splitting "Novelty" into two components, on the one hand, the extent to which a product draws attention to shortcomings in what already exists (Problematization), and, on the other hand, the extent to which the product offers new ways of looking at such shortcomings (Propulsion). These two aspects of the novelty of products are reminiscent of problem recognition and definition in Torrance's (1963) early discussions of the creative process, or "problem construction" as Mumford et al. (1996, p. 63) put it. Each rubric is identified by a number of *indicators* (e.g., redirection, convincingness, germinality), and the indicators are specified by means of down-to-earth descriptors (e.g., "The product shows how to extend the known in a new direction," "The product is skillfully executed and well finished," or "The product suggests new ways of looking at existing problems").

Turning directly to education, we have developed an app based on the latest version of the CSDS to assist teachers in "diagnosing" the creativity of students' work or to promote self-assessment by students (see D. H. Cropley and Cropley, 2016). The app represents the implementation in the form of a simple electronic performance support system of the theoretical framework already explained and summarized above. On opening the app, the user (typically a teacher, although the CSDS can be used for self-rating) enters the name and e-mail of the person whose work is being assessed (typically a student), and the name of the product being assessed. Successive screens then present the twenty-one indicators of the CSDS, with a brief description of each indicator, and invite the user to rate the artifact (often an essay, but it could be any other work product), using a five-point Likert-type scale. A summary screen then shows the scores for each of the five factors listed above, both as the mean of each indicator, and as a percentage score. Finally, a detailed summary of the scores for indicators and factors is emailed to the user and, if this person is not the creator of the work product, to that person as well. The app includes a summary of the meaning of each factor and indicator, in order to assist the user to understand the scores.

The Institutional Phase Assessment Instrument (IPAI): Influencing Press

In the domain of organizational creativity, D. H. Cropley and Cropley (2010c, 2011b, 2012) and D. H. Cropley, Cropley, Chiera, and Kaufman (2013) developed the Innovation Phase Assessment Instrument (IPAI). This instrument is grounded in the theoretical framework represented by the IPM (see above). Each particular phase in the process of production of novelty that is relevant and effective, elegant, and genetic requires a particular form of each building block. For example, the phase of generation, requires divergent thinking, proactive motivation, innovative personal properties, and generative personal feelings, which lead to generation of novel products and are fostered by low demand in the work environment. By contrast, the phase of verification requires convergent processes, reactive motivation, adaptive personal properties, and conserving feelings, which lead to identifying a proven product and are fostered by high demand in the work environment. I refer to each building block as defining a "node" of each particular phase. For example, in the phase of generation there are six nodes: divergent *thinking*, proactive *motivation*, innovative *personal properties*, generative *feelings*, novel *products* and low *environmental press*. Since there are seven phases, each with six nodes, there are forty-two nodes in all.

The people filling out the IPAI are asked to rate their organization on each node by indicating whether statements about the organization are true or false; for example, "In this organization, right from the beginning managers state clear criteria for recognizing solutions." Each item has a response that, according to the model (D. H. Cropley and Cropley, 2012, p. 38), represents the *ideal* for a particular node. This is sometimes *true* (e.g., "Staff want their ideas to be subjected to external scrutiny"), and sometimes *false* (e.g., "Staff do not analyze their own work"). For example, for the node motivation in the phase of generation one item is, "In this organization staff prefer unambiguous information." According to the IPM, the motivation that favors innovation in the generation phase is *high tolerance for ambiguity*. Consequently, the answer to this item which indicates that the organization is favorable to creativity is *false*. The purpose of the IPAI is to *diagnose* the extent to which an organization is favorable or unfavorable for organizational creativity in each node, to show what characteristics make it favorable or unfavorable, and to make suggestions for improvement. Sternberg's (2016) work on organizational modifiability makes detailed down-to-earth suggestions on what such improvements could look like in universities.

Fostering Creativity in Education: Influencing Process

The building blocks of down-to-earth creativity outlined above are relevant to learning in school. In fact, there is now a concerted call for education to foster such psychological resources (e.g., Plucker, Beghetto, and Dow, 2004), but as Cropley (2012) concluded, little understanding of what is actually involved, or of how to promote them. Writers such as Hetland, Winner, Veenema, and Sheridan (2007, p. 6) and Sternberg (2007) argued that what is involved are not highly task-specific skills but more general "habits of mind." These habits of mind make creativity *transferable*. Once students have become accustomed to linking ideas from disparate fields or approaching the same idea from different perspectives, or have begun to enjoy the risk of trying a new approach or the feeling of being on the verge of something new, these processes and personal characteristics can become habitual and be transferred to other subject areas. In fact, they may be transferred without the person involved actually noticing.

Self-Evaluation

The question that now arises is what my efforts in the last fifty years have achieved. I have already argued that the CSDS can be applied to evaluating any kind of product. I also believe that the scale can be used for self-assessment. Thus, it seems appropriate to use it to assess my own contribution to the psychology of creativity. The self-ratings which follow do not refer to this chapter, but to the body of work summarized in the chapter.

1   Relevance and Effectiveness: My work has shown familiarity with existing knowledge in the area, and has made well-founded comments that are clearly presented in a thought-provoking way (even if you do not agree with me).
2   Problematization: My work has drawn attention to shortcomings of existing approaches.
3   Propulsion: My work has taken existing work in a new direction, for example, by linking it to down-to-earth issues. It has shown how what already exists could be improved (e.g., evaluation of classroom work products). It has shown what benefits would derive from the changes it suggests.
4   Elegance: My work has been presented in easily readable, well-organized reports over many years. It is well rounded and easily understandable. Its elements fit together harmoniously.
5   Genesis: My work has cast new light on issues I myself did not specifically foresee. Examples are the application of the IPM to test construction and combating terrorism (see above).

Overall, I would say that my half-century of effort has coincided with ever-increasing reference to creativity not only in educational circles but in many other fields such as industry or politics. However, the down-to-earth approach to creativity is by no means universally accepted. For example, Rocavert (2016) criticized the commoditization of creativity and complained that insufficient respect is being paid to great talent nowadays, while Clapp and Jiminez (2017, p. 8) argued that "creativity is not a capacity at all," and that seeing it as a capacity may inhibit "broad participation in creativity," since it implies that some people have more of it than others. These are ideas that are diametrically opposed to what I have spent my time saying. I also cannot see any evidence of real practical change in, for example, teachers' understanding of creativity or of what they are supposed to be doing in the classroom, or what children are there to learn. Much "creativity" talk is mere lip service or even cant. I can, however, see plentiful evidence of pseudo-creativity (mere or even stereotyped "nonconformity") and quasi-creativity (the confusing of free expression of uninformed ideas with creativity), and a disturbing countertendency in research publications toward focusing on reiterating the already known, thus avoiding pseudo-creativity and quasi-creativity by focusing on relevance and effectiveness, it is true, but at the cost of sacrificing generation of novelty because of the risk it brings of being wrong.

REFERENCES

Albrecht, N. J. (2016). Teachers teaching mindfulness with children: An interpretative phenomenological analysis. Unpublished doctoral dissertation, School of Education, Flinders University of South Australia. www.researchgate.net/publication/311376289.

Altshuller, G. S. (1988). *Creativity as an exact science*. New York: Gordon and Breach.

Besemer, S. P., and O'Quin, K. (1987). Creative product analysis: Testing a model by developing a judging instrument. In *Frontiers of creativity research: Beyond the basics*, edited by S. G. Isaksen 367–389. Buffalo, NY: Brady.

Burghardt, M. D. (1997). *Introduction to the engineering profession*. New York: HarperCollins.

Burkhardt, H. (1985). *Gleichheitswahn Parteienwahn* [Obsession with sameness]. Tübingen, Germany: Hohenrain.

Clapp, E. P., and Jiminez, R. L. (2017). Expanding opportunities for creative participation: A systems-based approach to creativity and creative problem solving in education. *International Journal of Creativity and Problem Solving*, 27, 5–20.

Cropley, A. J. (1965). Originality, intelligence and personality. Unpublished doctoral dissertation, Department of Educational Psychology, University of Alberta.

(1966). Creativity and intelligence. *British Journal of Educational Psychology*, 36, 259–266.

(1967a). *Creativity*. London: Longman.

(1967b). Divergent thinking and science specialists. *Nature*, 215, 671–672.

(1973). Creativity and culture. *Educational Trends*, 8, 19–27.

(1990). Creativity and mental health in everyday life. *Creativity Research Journal*, 3, 167–178.

(1995). Creative intelligence: A concept of true giftedness. In *Actualizing talent: A lifelong challenge*, edited by J. Freeman, P. Span, and H. Wagner, 99–114. London: Cassell.

(1997a). Fostering creativity in the classroom: General principles. In *The creativity research handbook*, edited by M. Runco, 83–114. Cresskill, NJ: Hampton Press.

(1997b). Creativity: A bundle of paradoxes. *Gifted and Talented International*, 12, 8–14.

(2001). *Creativity in education and learning*. London: Kogan Page.

(2005). *Problem-solving and creativity: Implications for classroom assessment*. Leicester, UK: British Psychological Society.

(2006a). In praise of convergent thinking. *Creativity Research Journal*, 18, 391–404.

(2006b). Creativity: A social approach. *Roeper Review*, 28(3), 125–130.

(2007). Functional creativity: A concept of socially-useful creativity. *Baltic Journal of Psychology*, 7, 26–38.

(2012). Creativity and education: An Australian perspective. *International Journal of Creativity and Problem Solving*, 22(1), 9–25.

(2016). The myths of heaven-sent creativity: Towards a perhaps less democratic but more down-to-earth understanding. *Creativity Research Journal*, 28, 238–246.

Cropley, A. J., and Anderson, C. C. (1966). Some correlates of originality. *Australian Journal of Psychology*, 18, 218–227.

Cropley, A. J., and Cropley, D. H. (2009). *Fostering creativity: A diagnostic approach for higher education and organizations*. Cresskill, NJ: Hampton Press.

Cropley, A. J., and Field, T. W. (1968). Intellectual style and high school science. *Nature*, 217, 1211–1212.

Cropley, D. H. (2010). Malevolent innovation: Opposing the dark side of creativity. In *The dark side of creativity*, edited by D. H. Cropley, A. J. Cropley, J. C. Kaufman, and M. A. Runco, 339–359. Cambridge: Cambridge University Press.

Cropley, D. H., and Cropley, A. J. (2000). Fostering creativity in engineering students. *High Ability Studies*, 11, 207–219.

(2008a). Resolving the paradoxes of creativity: An extended phase model. *Cambridge Journal of Education*, 38, 355–373.

(2008b). Elements of a universal aesthetic of creativity. *Psychology of Aesthetics, Creativity, and the Arts*, 3, 155–161.

(2010a). Functional creativity: "Products" and the generation of effective novelty. In *The Cambridge handbook of creativity*, edited by R. J. Sternberg, and J. C. Kaufman, 301–317. New York: Cambridge University Press.

(2010b). Recognizing and fostering creativity in design education. *International Journal of Technology and Design Education*, 20, 345–358.

(2010c). The innovative institutional environment: Theoretical insights from psychology. *Baltic Journal of Psychology*, 11, 73–87.

(2011a). Creativity and lawbreaking. *Creativity Research Journal*, 23, 313–320.

(2011b). Understanding value innovation in organizations: A psychological framework. *International Journal of Creativity and Problem Solving*, 21(1), 17–36.

(2012). A psychological taxonomy of organizational innovation: Resolving the paradoxes. *Creativity Research Journal*, 24, 29–40.

(2013). *Creativity and crime*. Cambridge: Cambridge University Press.

(2015). *The psychology of innovation in organizations*. Cambridge: Cambridge University Press.

(2016). Promoting creativity through assessment: A formative CAA tool for teachers. *Educational Technology*, 56(6), 17–24.

Cropley, D. H., Cropley, A. J., Chiera, B. A., and Kaufman, J. C. (2013). Diagnosing organizational innovation: Measuring the capacity for innovation. *Creativity Research Journal*, 25, 388–396.

Cropley, D. H., Cropley, A. J., Kaufman, J. C., and Runco, M. A. (Eds.). (2010). *The dark side of creativity*. Cambridge: Cambridge University Press.

Cropley, D. H., and Kaufman, J. C. (2012). Measuring functional creativity: Non-expert raters and the Creative Solution Diagnosis Scale. *Journal of Creative Behavior*, 46, 119–137.

Cropley, D. H., Kaufman, J. C., and Cropley, A. J. (2008). Malevolent creativity. *Creativity Research Journal*, 20, 105–115.

(2011). Measuring creativity for innovation management. *Journal of Technology Management and Innovation*, 6, 13–29.

(2013). Understanding malevolent creativity. In *Handbook of research on creativity*, edited by J. Chan and K. Thomas, 185–195. Northampton, MA: Edward Elgar.

Getzels, J. W., and Jackson, P. W. (1962). *Creativity and intelligence*. New York: John Wiley.

Guilford, J. P. (1950). Creativity. *American Psychologist*, 5, 444–454.

(1987). Creativity research: Past, present and future. In *Frontiers of creativity research: Beyond the basics*, edited by S. G. Isaksen, 33–65. Buffalo, NY: Bearly.

Hari, A. (2010). A systems engineering approach to counterterrorism. In *The dark side of creativity*, edited by D. H. Cropley, A. J. Cropley, J. C. Kaufman, and M. A. Runco, 329–328. Cambridge: Cambridge University Press.

Hassenstein, M. (1988). *Bausteine zu einer Naturgeschichte der Intelligenz* [Building blocks for a natural history of intelligence]. Stuttgart, Germany: Deutsche Verlags-Anstalt.

Hecht, D. K. (2010). Imagining the bomb: Robert Oppenheimer, nuclear weapons, and the assimilation of technological innovation. In *The dark side of creativity*, edited by D. H. Cropley, A. J. Cropley, J. C. Kaufman, and M. A. Runco, 72–90. Cambridge: Cambridge University Press.

Hetland, L., Winner, E., Veenema, S., and Sheridan, K. M. (2007). *Studio thinking: The real benefits of visual arts education*. New York: Teachers College Press.

Horenstein, M. N. (2002). *Design concepts for engineers*. 2nd ed. Upper Saddle River, NJ: Prentice Hall.

Hunter, A. G. (2012). *Spiritual hunger: Integrating myth and ritual into daily life*. Edinburgh: Einhorn Press.

Jackson, P. W., and Messick, S. (1965). The person, the product, and the response: Conceptual problems in the assessment of creativity. *Journal of Personality*, 33, 1122–1131.

James, K., Clark, K., and Cropanzano, R. (1999). Positive and negative creativity in groups, institutions, and organizations: A model and theoretical extension. *Creativity Research Journal*, 12, 211–227.

Kaufman, J. C., and Beghetto, R. A. (2009). Beyond big and little: The four C model of creativity. *Review of General Psychology*, 13, 1–12.

Kawenski, M. (1991). Encouraging creativity in design. *Journal of Creative Behavior*, 25(3), 263–266.

McLaren, R. B. (1993). The dark side of creativity. *Creativity Research Journal*, 6, 137–144.

Mumford, M. D., Baughman, W. A., Threlfall, K. V., Supinski, E. P., and
    Costanza, D. P. (1996). Process-based measures of creative problem-solving
    skills: I. Problem construction. *Creativity Research Journal*, 9, 63–76.
Nicholls, J. G. (1972). Creativity in the person who will never produce anything
    original and useful: The concept of creativity as a normally distributed trait.
    American Psychologist, 27, 717–727.
Plucker, J. A., Beghetto, R. A., and Dow, G. T. (2004). Why isn't creativity more
    important to educational psychologists? Potentials, pitfalls, and future direc-
    tions in creativity research. *Educational Psychologist*, 39(2), 83–96.
Rhodes, M. (1961). An analysis of creativity. *The Phi Delta Kappan*, 42, 305–310.
Rocavert, C. (2016). Democratizing creativity: How arts/philosophy can con-
    tribute to the question of arts bias. *Creativity Research Journal*, 28, 229–237.
Rothman, J. (2014). Creativity creep. *The New Yorker*, September 2. www.
    newyorker.com/books/joshua-rothman/creativity-creep.
Savransky, S. D. (2000). *Engineering of creativity*. Boca Raton, FL: CRC Press.
Soh, K. (2015). Creativity fostering teacher behaviour around the world: Anno-
    tations of studies using the CFTIndex. *Teacher Education and Development*,
    April 28. doi:10.1080/2331186X.2015.1034494.
Sternberg, R. J. (2007). Creativity as a habit. In *Creativity: A handbook for teachers*,
    edited by A.-G. Tan, 3–25. Singapore: World Scientific.
    (2016). *What universities can be*. Ithaca, NY: Cornell University Press.
Sternberg, R. J., Kaufman, J. C., and Pretz, J. E. (2002). *The creativity conundrum:
    A propulsion model of kinds of creative contributions*. New York: Psychology
    Press.
Taylor, I. A. (1975). An emerging view of creative actions. In *Perspectives in creativ-
    ity*, edited by I. A. Taylor und J. W. Getzels, 297–325. Chicago, IL: Aldine.
Torrance, E. P. (1963). *Education and the creative potential*. Minneapolis: University
    of Minnesota Press.
Tsanoff, R. (1949). *The ways of genius*. New York: Harper.
Wallach, M. M., and Kogan, N. (1965). *Modes of thinking in young children*. New
    York: Holt, Rinehart, and Winston.
Wallas, G. (1926). *The art of thought*. New York: Harcourt Brace.
Winner, E. (1985). *Invented worlds: The psychology of the arts*. Cambridge, MA:
    Harvard University Press.
Zaitseva, M. N. (2010). Subjugating the creative mind: The Soviet biological
    weapons program and the role of the state. In *The dark side of creativity*, edited
    by D. H. Cropley, A. J. Cropley, J. C. Kaufman, and M. A. Runco, 57–71.
    Cambridge: Cambridge University Press.

CHAPTER 5

In Search of the Creative Personality

Gregory J. Feist

On the cusp of adolescence, I became fascinated by the transformation of our house in Louisiana. My parents had decided to remodel and add on to our house rather than move. As it turns out, the contractors doing the work were not very competent, so my father – a psychology professor but who grew up in a small farming community in Kansas and who from a young age worked at whatever needed to be done – decided to complete the work himself. He had the help of some friends and even I chipped in a bit in whatever way I could. Within a year or so, we had a "new" house.

The transformation of our house from one thing to a different thing captured my imagination. The former garage was now a full bedroom and a carport now existed where none had existed. This newly arranged house started as a vision in my parents' imagination and ended up a new reality. I was captivated by the process of going from imagination and thought to actual creation. This fascination initially formed into an interest in architecture and until about seventeen I wanted to be an architect.

At seventeen, however, two things happened that would change my career trajectory away from architecture. First, my junior year in high school, I wrote a paper for my English class on creativity and its stages, mostly reviewing Graham Wallas's famous model (preparation, incubation, insight, and verification/elaboration) (Wallas, 1926). Second, I decided to study abroad (in Germany) my senior year of high school. During this year abroad my budding interest in philosophy and psychology took root. In addition to epistemology, I also became deeply intrigued by the philosophy of science. My host father was a physics teacher with many books in the philosophy of science, such as those by Popper (1959), Kuhn (1962), and Lakatos and Musgrave (1970). Little did I know that these three books just happened to be the three most seminal books of twentieth-century philosophy of science.

After intensively reading in philosophy and living in an environment that forced me to challenge my assumptions, one day right after my eighteenth birthday I had an epiphany – a crystallizing experience, as Howard Gardner (1993) would call it – that I wanted to be a professor of philosophy. I literally felt like a different person after this insight. I wanted to devote my life to understanding the big questions, like how do we know things and what is valid versus invalid knowledge. In essence, the philosophical question of the nature and acquisition of knowledge (epistemology) was simply a more abstract extension of my fascination with how new things, like houses and buildings, come about. Just as importantly, living in a different culture at a critical time in my intellectual and social development, I came to have multiple perspectives on the world and my assumptions – a quality that lends itself both to philosophical and metacognitive thinking (i.e., thinking about one's thinking).

Upon returning to the United States, I attended the university where my father taught psychology, McNeese State University in Louisiana. Although a philosophy major, my last semester there as a sophomore, I enrolled in my father's psychology course Theories of Personality, in which we read about all the major theories of personality from Freud, Jung, and Adler to Skinner and Bandura. I could never have predicted that within 20 years, I would co-author a textbook in Theories of Personality with my father! (Feist, Feist, and Roberts, 2018).

One last major developmental and career change occurred after two years of majoring in philosophy in college when I realized I would rather test my ideas empirically than simply have them and argue for them logically and rationally. I read enough philosophy to know this was the classic philosophical battle between rationalism and empiricism. Indeed, this desire to move beyond rationalism stemmed from reading Hume's *Enquiry Concerning Human Understanding* and Kant's famous *Critique of Pure Reason*. Evidence rather than logic and reason was what I was after, so I switched from philosophy to empirical psychology.

For me, the question of knowledge and its creation had really always been about creativity – how does *new* knowledge come into being and why are some people more than others likely to have such radically new ideas that change the world? That was what I was really interested in and what I wanted to spend my career trying to answer. While working on self concept research with personality psychologist Seymour Epstein at the University of Massachusetts, I learned about the groundbreaking work on personality and creativity at the University of California, Berkeley's Institute of Personality Assessment and Research (IPAR). For graduate school, my sights narrowed to Berkeley and IPAR.

Questions

There were two main events that forged the connection between creativity and personality in my mind: taking my father's course Theories of Personality while a sophomore in college and then being trained at Berkeley's IPAR. The connection between creativity and personality is a natural one because they both have at their core uniqueness and individual differences. Applied to creativity, the obvious question becomes "what unique qualities – whether they be cognitive styles, attitudes, developmental histories, motivational styles, or personality traits – make creative ideas more likely in some people compared to others?" Berkeley's IPAR at the time had a thirty-five-year tradition of examining this question with scientists, writers, mathematicians, architects, graduate students, and college students. In particular, Donald MacKinnon (1970; Hall and MacKinnon, 1969), Frank Barron (1955, 1957, 1963), Harrison Gough (1961; Gough and Woodworth, 1960), and Ravenna Helson (Helson and Crutchfield, 1970) had pioneered new assessment techniques, including the weekend-assessment, and had provided some important answers to the question of the creative personality.

Findings

My dissertation research had its origin in a decision-making seminar at Berkeley that was co-taught by Daniel Kahneman and Phil Tetlock. In addition to being inspired by Kahneman's humble brilliance, I was also inspired by Tetlock's work on a cognitive coding system called "integrative complexity," which involves coding text of any kind on its complexity, from simple, black-and-white thinking to highly complex and integrated thinking. I thought, what a great thing to apply to revolutionary scientific thinking! One ideal source of revolutionary thinking in science, I thought, would be the published acceptance speeches of winners of the Nobel Prize for physics, chemistry, or medicine. Because we wanted other psychological data, we decided against this historical analysis of texts. So for my dissertation, under the guidance of Gerald Mendelsohn and Phil Tetlock, I interviewed living eminent professors of physics, chemistry, and biology at major research universities throughout California – many of whom were members of the National Academy of Sciences. The interviews were semistructured around ten key questions, such as what they considered to be their best work and why, what role emotion and intuition play in their creative process, what accounts for success in science, and whether art and science are really conflicting cultures. I created creativity scores for each scientist via combined peer ratings of eminence and historical significance as well as their overall publication and citation numbers. In addition to transcribing and coding the recorded interviews for their complexity of thought (Feist, 1994), I also, after the fact, had blind (to their identity) raters assess the personality of each scientist using the California Q-sort technique of Jack Block. This led to one of the most important findings from the study: the most eminent and creative scientists were rated as higher on hostility and arrogance than were less eminent and creative scientists (Feist, 1993). A journalist picked up on this finding and after interviewing me for the piece, started with this line: "Greg Feist is a nice guy. Too bad for him" (implying I was too nice to make it big in science!).

My next main contribution came a few years later when I decided to take on the first meta-analysis of the empirical literature on creative personality in art and science (Feist, 1998). My own research and especially much that came from IPAR (as well as Cattell, Eysenck, and others) had accumulated to the point where a quantitative review of the literature was now possible (e.g., Cattell and Drevdahl, 1955; Domino, 1994; Eysenck, 1995; Mansfield and Busse, 1981). A big hurdle, however, was that from the 1950s to 1990s, many different personality inventories had been used with different assessed traits. I needed one overall personality taxonomy to classify traits. The Big Five system (Costa and McCrae, 1992) afforded me that. Most critically, there was a body of published research reporting the extent to which many of the classic inventories such as Cattell's 16 Personality Factor (16PF), Gough's California Psychological Inventory, and Eysenck's Personality Questionnaire related to the more five factors from the Big Five (e.g., Gerbing and Tuley, 1991; McCrae, 1991; McCrae, Costa, and Piedmont, 1993). Converting these scales to Big Five dimensions allowed me to examine quantitatively which personality dimensions were consistently associated with creative achievement in art and in science.

The main findings from this meta-analysis were that creative artists and scientists shared certain personality profiles, but differed on others. In general, openness to experience and low conscientiousness were the strongest associations with creativity in both art and science. Both creative groups were also relatively high on the confidence dimension of Extraversion, and on Eysenck's measure of psychoticism. In addition, creative artists more than creative scientists were unusually cold and aloof, independent, and norm-doubting.

Another of my studies worth discussing came from a collaboration with one of my intellectual heroes, Frank Barron, who in the late 1960s had moved from IPAR to University of California at Santa Cruz. He had been trying to follow up one of the very first studies at IPAR – the 1950 graduate students, most of whom were in the sciences (Barron, 1955). In the mid and late 1990s, we began a collaboration to find and reassess as many of the original eighty participants as we could. In 1950, those participants had gone through the patented and intense three-day live-in assessment technique, where a small group of ten students at a time would live at the Institute for three days. They took a large battery of psychological tests including personality, social, motivational, occupational, and intellectual assessments. They also took part in planned and informal social activities and were interviewed for their life histories by an esteemed group of assessors, including Erik Erikson, Donald MacKinnon, Harrison Gough, and Nevitt Sanford, who then rated their personalities, career potential, and originality. In addition to these staff ratings, the graduate advisors of each participant assessed the potential, intellect, and originality of their student. On average, these students were twenty-seven years old.

Forty-four years later we found as many of these former students, who were now an average age of seventy-two and at or near retirement (Feist and Barron, 2003). Because we had such a rich source of psychological data from 1950, as they began their careers, the key idea was to see how and to what extent various psychological qualities predicted creativity and career success. The major prediction was that personality traits would predict career success over and above intellectual factors and that is what we found. Specifically, personality traits of tolerance and psychological mindedness at age twenty-seven explained 20 percent more variance in lifetime creative achievement at age seventy-two than did ratings of potential and intellect. Moreover, we found that ratings of intellect made by the psychological staff at age twenty-seven were stronger predictors of lifetime creative achievement at age seventy-two than were scores on structured tests of intelligence at age twenty-even. (An interesting back story to this article is that it was rejected not once but twice by the journal that published the original results in 1950 and then went on to be awarded "article of the year" by the journal that published it.)

Functional Model of the Creative Personality

From these and other empirical findings on personality and creativity, I developed a "functional model" of the creative personality (Figure 5.1) (Feist, 1998, 2010). The essence of the model is that traits function to lower behavioral thresholds, that is, they make certain behaviors more

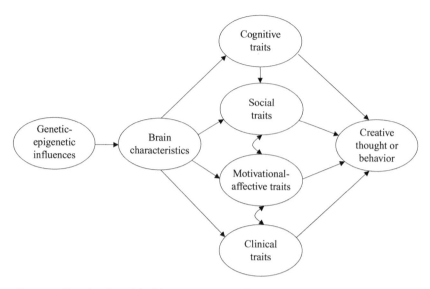

Figure 5.1 Functional model of the creative personality. From Feist (2010), reprinted with permission from Cambridge University Press

likely and others less likely. For example, for a person who is "anxious," his or her threshold for experiencing anxiety, worry, and distress is relatively low. They experience these states more frequently and more intensely than a nonanxious person. In addition, the model argues there are biological precursors to these personality traits such as genetic, epigenetic, and neurochemical influences that lower the thresholds of creative thought and behavior.

Applied to creativity, the trait of openness to experience is the most direct personality trait that lowers thresholds for creative ideas and behavior. To be a bit more precise, there are categories of traits that lower the threshold for creative thought and behavior, namely, cognitive, social, motivational-affective, and clinical. Cognitive traits most notably include openness to experience because the latter is the tendency to be imaginative, open, and flexible in one's thought and behavior. Social traits involve attitudes toward and interactions with other people, such as warmth or hostility, and introversion or extraversion. Motivational-affective traits are those involving movement toward and focus on goals, such as ambition, drive, intrinsic motivation, and persistence. Finally, clinical traits are those that may be dysfunctional in everyday life, such as depression, anxiety disorder, schizotypy, and bipolar disorder.

Creativity and Psychology of Science

Early in my career I was more and more compelled to merge two long-standing interests of mine, namely, the philosophy of science and creativity. Having read the work of main figures in the philosophy of science, especially Popper's (1959) *Logic of Scientific Discovery*, I became convinced that there was also a "psycho-logic of scientific discovery" and that psychology had a very important story to tell about how scientific ideas, knowledge, and discoveries come about. While I was working on my dissertation, two books were published that convinced me the time was ripe for the psychology of science to stand next to the philosophy, history, and sociology of science. These two books were *Scientific Genius: A Psychology of Science* by Dean Simonton (1988), and *Psychology of Science: Contributions to a Metascience* by Gholson, Shadish, Neimeyer, and Houts (1989). So inspired, I entitled my dissertation "The Psychology of Science: Personality, Cognitive, Motivational, and Working Styles of Eminent and Less Eminent Scientists" (Feist, 1991).

After my dissertation, I discovered another person interested in developing a psychology of science, Michael Gorman, and we published a review of the extant literature (Feist and Gorman, 1998). Soon thereafter, I began writing a book on the topic, but also decided to tackle a larger topic as well, namely, how did the human mind become capable of doing science (*The Psychology of Science and the Origins of the Scientific Mind*; Feist, 2006)? The book made two fundamental claims. First, there are psychological forces (developmental, cognitive, personality, social, and clinical) behind scientific thought and behavior, and psychologists have conducted enough research to begin to codify a full-fledged field of the "psychology of science." Second, scientific thought is not an inevitable outcome of the evolution of the human mind, but the building blocks of scientific thinking – observation, categorization, pattern recognition, hypothesis testing, cause and effect reasoning, and explanation/theory construction – are evolutionarily adapted cognitive mechanisms. In short, implicit and explicit scientific thinking is simply an extension of these evolved mechanisms. One outcome of the book was the development of a scientific society and biennial conferences on the psychology of science.

Measuring Scientific Creativity

Historically, publication and citation data have been widely used to measure scientific productivity or creativity (Feist, 1997; Simonton, 1988,

2004). Publication and citation data are highly positive correlated, but they are not one and the same. Borrowing from sociologists Cole and Cole (1973), I developed a 2 × 2 typology of scientific productivity with four categories: "prolific scientists" publish many papers and are highly cited; "mass producers" publish many papers but are not highly cited; "perfectionists" publish relatively few papers but are highly cited; and "silent" scientists produce few papers and are not cited frequently. In a sample of eminent scientists, the correlation between publication and citation outcomes was 0.52, meaning publication data explains about 25 percent of the variance in citation data (Feist, 1997).

Following up the assessment of scientific creativity, a graduate student (Maya Grosul) and I developed a more integrated and complex measure of scientific creativity (Grosul and Feist, 2014). In addition to publication and citation data, we took advantage of two more recent indices of scientific productivity, namely the h-index and Soler's creativity index (Soler, 2007). Hirsch (2005) developed the h-index, which is defined when an author of N articles has h number of articles cited at least h times. For example, if a scientist has published thirty-five articles and at least ten of those papers are cited at least ten times, her h-index is 10. In addition, Soler (2007) proposed a "creativity index" that is a sum of the citations plus the number of references cited by the paper and then normalized by dividing it by number of authors. Soler included references because he argued that creativity has two components: use of previous knowledge and creation of new knowledge. Use of previous knowledge is a measure of a paper's usefulness, whereas creation of new knowledge is a paper's originality. Usefulness and originality are commonly considered by creativity researchers to be the two core criteria for creativity (Amabile, 1996; Plucker and Renzulli, 1999; Runco, 2004; Sternberg, 1988). In short, the creativity index is high when a scientist has many more citations than references. This measure has two main advantages over pure citation counts: first, it devalues highly cited review papers because they generally do not provide much new knowledge; second, it devalues self-citations. Moreover, it was validated by the fact that between the three physicists with the highest creativity index two have won the Nobel Prize and the third won the Fields Medal (Dume, 2006). The index, however, does make some questionable assumptions such as the most creative papers have smaller ratios of references to citations and that citations are always a valid indicator of creativity.

Given the limits of any one measure and based on the psychometric principle that multiple measures of a construct increase its measured validity, Grosul and I then took these four measures of scientific

Table 5.1 *Definitions of individual and overall scientific creativity indices*

Measure of creativity	Definition
Productivity (P_i)	Total number of journal articles produced by a scientist across his/her entire career
Impact (C_i)	Total number of citations a scientist's work received over his or her entire career
h-index (h)	When a scientist of N articles has h number of publications cited at least h number of times, and the remaining published articles receive fewer than h citations
Soler's creativity index	Sum total of published articles, total number of citations for each article, total number of cited references in each article, divided by total number of authors of each article
Overall creativity score	Log-transformed, standardized, and equal weighted sum of P_i, C_i, h-index, and creativity index

Note: Adapted from Grosul and Feist (2014)

creativity (publications, citations, h-index, and creativity index) and log-transformed, standardized, and summed them, resulting in an "overall scientific creativity index" (see Table 5.1). We applied the overall creativity score to a sample of 145 full professors of physical, biological, and social science throughout the United States, and found that personality differences on openness to experience, conscientiousness, neuroticism, and psychoticism predicted overall creativity once demographic variables such as age and gender were held constant (Grosul and Feist, 2014).

Mental Health and Creativity

My most recent foray into creativity and personality has involved a large-scale study of world-class creative artists, writers, poets, actors, painters, physicists, chemists, psychologists, anthropologists, and technologists. We are examining the age-old question of whether there is any association between high levels of creativity and lifetime rates of mental illness (Feist, Dostal, and Kwan, 2017). We are testing this question by first obtaining ranks and lists of creative artists, scientists, and athletes who either died after 1950 or were born by 1980. We chose athletes as a comparison group to disentangle fame from creativity, on the assumption that they are famous but generally not creative (i.e., do not create novel and useful ideas or products), and therefore would provide a test of whether fame rather than creative achievement is associated with mental illness. Next, we looked for and obtained a published biography on the person's life. From an initial list of 776 people across 13 professions, we obtained usable digital biographies on 198 people (103 artists, 68 scientists, and 27 athletes). Biographies were first scanned for presence of 172 mental health key words (e.g., addict, Aspergers, bipolar, compulsive, depression, drug abuse, mania, neurotic, schizophrenia, schizotypal, suicide). If a paragraph contained any of these key words, a program selected it and these paragraphs were next evaluated by a graduate student on whether or not they applied to the creator in question. If not, the paragraph was ignored. If so, the paragraphs on each participant were then rated by a pair of trained and blind (creators names were redacted) undergraduate raters on the presence or absence of nineteen different mental illnesses using a three-point rating scale (0 = absent; 1 = probable; 2 = present):

Adjustment disorder
Alcoholism
Anxiety disorder
Autism spectrum disorder
Bipolar disorder
Conduct disorder
Depression/depressive disorders
Drug use/dependency
Eating disorder
Gambling disorder
Kleptomania
Obsessive compulsive disorder
Paraphilia
Personality disorder
Posttraumatic stress disorder
Schizophrenia
Sleep disorder
Somatic disorder
Suicide/suicide attempt
Synesthesia

As the primary outcome variable, we calculated a measure of lifetime prevalence for a disorder that combined "probable" and "present" ratings into a "yes" category and absent into a no category.

We found that artists had a mean of about two disorders over the course of their lifetime, whereas scientists and athletes had a mean of about one. Similarly, 83 percent of the creative artists suffered at least one disorder during their lifetime, whereas slightly less than 60 percent of the creative scientists and famous athletes did. Compared to the overall lifetime rate of the general public of 46 percent (Kessler et al., 2005) these rates are elevated, and creative artists are more likely to suffer from a psychological disorder than creative scientists or famous athletes. The four most common disorders experienced by both creative artists and scientists were depression, anxiety, alcoholism, and drug abuse. The answer to our question of whether world-class creativity is associated with mental illness seems to be a qualified yes. It is more true for artists than for scientists and it is not fame per se that is associated with creativity since athletes have fewer disorders than artists. To be fair, a comparison of world-class creative artists and less creative artists is needed to have confidence that artistic creativity per se is most clearly associated with mental illness. That analysis, however, cannot be made with biographies, because biographies are only written about the most creative artists.

Future Paths and Unanswered Questions

This chapter has attempted to provide a brief overview of my personal, empirical, and theoretical search for the creative personality in art and science. Writing about a career or life inevitably gives the impression of order and logical progression of events, but of course neither life nor profession is logical, inevitable, or predictable. I started with questions and curiosity, and most importantly fascination and desire to understand how new ideas come into existence. Have I found the creative personality? Sort of. Personally, I have spent now close to thirty-five years satisfying my curiosity about new ideas, new creations, and new knowledge. Empirically, I have spent close to thirty years conducting studies on the creative personality and the psychology of science. And most recently, I have begun to develop theoretical conceptual models and how personality is connected to creative thought and behavior.

An inevitable question then becomes: what comes first, personality or creativity? That is a difficult question to answer, but my hunch is personality comes first but that openness and creative thought and behavior ultimately work together in a mutual cycle of influence. We need to measure both things starting at a very young age and then continue to measure them over the course of the lifetime to get a better sense of which comes first. Along these lines, I recently returned from a trip to Dalian China on the invitation of Wen Liu. She and her graduate students have undertaken a wonderful series of studies into the early development of the creative personality in preschool-aged children (Liu and Lu, 2008). In an attempt to address the "chicken-egg" question of creativity and personality, we hope to begin collaborative studies in both the United States and China that measure the two constructs in young children with the intent of continuing to do so for years. By assessing both personality and creative thought and behavior at an early age, we believe we can shed light on their causal relationship.

REFERENCES

Amabile, T. (1996). *Creativity in context.* Boulder, CO: Westview.
    (1955). The disposition towards originality. *Journal of Abnormal and Social Psychology,* 51, 478–485.
    (1957). Originality in relation to personality and intellect. *Journal of Personality,* 25, 730–742.
    (1963). *Creativity and psychological health.* New York: Van Nostrand.
Cattell, R. B., and Drevdahl, J. E. (1955). A comparison of the personality profile (16PF) of eminent researchers with that of eminent teachers and administrators, and the general population. *British Journal of Psychology,* 46, 248–261.
Cole, J. R., and Cole, S. (1973). *Social stratification in science.* Chicago: University of Chicago University.
Costa, P. T., and McCrae, R. R. (1992). *NEO-PI professional manual.* Odessa, FL: Psychological Assessment Resources.
Domino, G. (1994). Assessment of creativity with the ACL: An empirical comparison of four scales. *Creativity Research Journal,* 7, 21–33.
Dume, B. (2006). Worlds most creative physicist revealed. http://physicsworld.com/cws/article/news/2006/aug/17/worlds-most-creative-physicist-revealed.
Eysenck, H. J. (1995). *Genius: The natural history of creativity.* Cambridge: Cambridge University Press.
Feist, G. J. (1991). The psychology of science: Personality, cognitive, motivational and working styles of eminent and less eminent scientists. Unpublished doctoral dissertation, University of California, Berkeley.
    (1993). A structural model of scientific eminence. *Psychological Science,* 4, 366–371.
    (1994). Personality and working style predictors of integrative complexity: A study of scientists' thinking about research and teaching. *Journal of Personality and Social Psychology,* 67, 474–484.
    (1997). Quantity, impact, and depth of research as influences on scientific eminence: Is quantity most important? *Creativity Research Journal,* 10, 325–335.
    (1998). A meta-analysis of the impact of personality on scientific and artistic creativity. *Personality and Social Psychological Review,* 2, 290–309.

(2006). *The psychology of science and the origins of the scientific mind.* New Haven, CT: Yale University Press.

(2010). The function of personality in creativity: The nature and nurture of creative personality. In *The Cambridge handbook of creativity*, edited by J. C. Kaufman and R. J. Sternberg, 113–130. New York: Cambridge University Press.

Feist, G. J., and Barron, F. (2003). Predicting creativity from early to late adulthood: Intellect, potential, and personality. *Journal of Research in Personality*, 37, 62–88.

Feist, G. J., Dostal, D., and Kwan, V. (2017). Testing the "mad-genius" myth: Lifetime rates of mental disorders of creative artists, creative scientists, and famous athletes. Unpublished manuscript.

Feist, G. J., and Gorman, M. E. (1998). Psychology of science: Review and integration of a nascent discipline. *Review of General Psychology*, 2, 3–47.

Feist, J., Feist, G. J., and Roberts, T. A. (2018). *Theories of personality* (9th edition). New York: McGraw-Hill.

Gardner, H. (1993). *Creating minds: An anatomy of creativity*. New York: Basic Books.

Gerbing, D. W., and Tuley, M. R. (1991). The 16PF related to the Five-Factor Model in personality: Multiple-indicator measurement versus a priori scales. *Multivariate Behavioral Research*, 26, 271–289.

Gholson, B., Shadish, W. R., Neimeyer, R. A., and Houts, A. C. (Eds.). (1989). *Psychology of science: Contributions to metascience*. Cambridge: Cambridge University Press.

Gough, H. G. (1961). A personality sketch of the creative research scientist. Paper presented at the fifth annual conference on Personnel and Industrial Research, University of California, Los Angeles, February.

Gough, H. G., and Woodworth, D. G. (1960). Stylistic variations among professional research scientists. *Journal of Psychology*, 49, 87–98.

Grosul, M., and Feist, G. J. (2014). The creative person in science. *Psychology of Aesthetics, Creativity, and the Arts*, 8, 30–43.

Hall, W. B., and MacKinnon, D. W. (1969). Personality inventory correlates of creativity among architects. *Journal of Applied Psychology*, 53, 322–326.

Helson, R., and Crutchfield, R. (1970). Mathematicians: The creative researcher and the average PhD. *Journal of Consulting and Clinical Psychology*, 34, 176–186.

Hirsch, J. E. (2005). An index to quantify an individual's scientific research output. *Proceedings of the National Academy of Sciences of the United States of America*, 46, 16569–16572.

Kessler, R. C., Berglund, P., Demler, O., Jin, R., Merikangas, K. R., and Walters, E. E. (2005). Lifetime prevalence and age-of-onset distributions of DSM-IV disorders in the National Comorbidity Survey Replication. *Archives of General Psychiatry*, 62(6), 593–602.

Kuhn, T. (1962). *The structure of scientific revolutions*. 2nd ed. Chicago: Chicago University Press.

Lakatos, I., and Musgrave, A. (Eds.). (1970). *Criticism and the growth of knowledge.* Cambridge: Cambridge University Press.

Liu, W., and Lu, Q. (2008). The study of structure of creative personality about preschool children aged 3 to 5. *Psychological Research*, 1.

MacKinnon, D. W. (1970). Creativity: A multi-faceted phenomenon. In *Creativity*, edited by J. Roslanksy, 19–32. Amsterdam: North-Holland.

Mansfield, R. S., and Busse, T. V. (1981). *The psychology of creativity and discovery: Scientists and their work.* Chicago: Nelson-Hall.

McCrae, R. R. (1991). The Five Factor Model and its assessment in clinical settings. *Journal of Personality Assessment*, 57, 399–414.

McCrae, R. R., Costa, P. T., and Piedmont, R. L. (1993). Folk concepts, natural language, and psychological constructs: The California Psychological Inventory and the Five-Factor Model. *Journal of Personality*, 61, 1–26.

Plucker, J. A., and Renzulli, J. S. (1999). Psychometric approaches to the study of human creativity. In *Handbook of creativity*, 3rd ed., edited by R. J. Sternberg, 35–62. Cambridge: Cambridge University Press.

Popper, K. (1959). *Logic of scientific discovery.* New York: Science Editions.

Runco, M. (2004). Everyone has creative potential. In *Creativity: From potential to realization*, edited by R. J. Sternberg, E. L. Grigorenko, and J. L. Singer, 21–30. Washington, DC: APA Books.

Simonton, D. K. (1988). *Scientific genius: A psychology of science.* Cambridge: Cambridge University Press.

(2004). *Creativity in science.* Cambridge: Cambridge University Press.

Soler, J. M. (2007). A rational indicator of scientific creativity. *Journal of Infometrics*, 1, 123–130.

Sternberg, R. J. (1988). A three-facet model of creativity. In *The nature of creativity*, edited by R. J. Sternberg, 125–147. Cambridge: Cambridge University Press.

Wallas, G. (1926). *The art of thought.* New York: Harcourt, Brace, and Jovanovich.

CHAPTER 6

From Fascination to Research
Progress and Problems in Creativity Research

Adrian Furnham

Introduction: A Personal Statement

Everyone has had the experience of enchantment and wonder in the face of works of great imagination and creativity. Much depends on your interests and values on "what turns you on." It may be poetry or painting, engineering or architecture, music or design. The sheer brilliance of the creator can literally take the breath away as one marvels at the genius of person who could produce such as masterpiece.

For me, the painting called *The Garden of Earthly Delights* is extraordinary. It was painted by *Hieronymus Bosch* around 1500 and could be called (very) early Surrealist art. When distressed, I turn to poetry for solace and reflection, preferring the more recent poets like Elliot, Kipling, and Rossetti. I can also regulate my moods with great music because I am eclectic in my tastes, choosing from Leonard Cohen to Sibelius (the great Finnish composer). I love architecture, especially art deco styles. I think we all have very different tastes in, and definitions of, great works we might call creative, and this is part of the problem for the researcher.

I do not think of myself as a very creative person but I do appreciate the great work of others. What follows is a sort of "stream-of-consciousness" essay as I reflect on my journey into the curious world of creativity research. I start off with the usual problems of definition and then move on to discuss three different but important personal influences on my interest and research on creativity. I then consider the all-important question for differential psychologists, namely, the relationship between creativity, personality, and intelligence.

I should note that I came to do research on creativity later in my life. I was warned against research in this area because of the difficulties of measuring creativity. Science begins with definition and classification or what my very first lecturer called, in the words of the time, "operationalization of the dependent variable." How do you define and measure creativity? The same problem faced those interested in personality and intelligence, but they seemed so much better at devising theories and tests than researchers interested in creativity. It was described by a colleague as "backwater" because of problems with both definition and measurement. But creativity is just too interesting a topic to ignore, so like many others before me I have been seduced into researching it. I have, like many academics been helped by talented and hard-working doctoral and masters students.

Distinctions and Definitions

Creative people go under different names such as: designer, entrepreneur, and inventor. I have always thought there are three dimensions to creative activity. These are three categorical dimensions not usually discussed in literature but which I think are important.

Intrinsic versus Extrinsic

Some people are paid to be creative; others do it for pure joy. The question is how people are rewarded for being creative and what difference it makes.

There is an extensive literature on the difference between the two different types of motivation. Over fifty years ago, a group of psychologists led by Herzberg were to develop a theory of great consequence. Two-factor theory states that there are certain factors in the workplace that cause *job satisfaction*, while a separate set of factors cause *dissatisfaction*.

Two-factor theory then distinguishes between: Motivating/Intrinsic Factors such as challenging work, recognition for one's achievement, being given responsibility, opportunity to do something meaningful, involvement in decision-making, and sense of importance to an organization. These together give positive satisfaction, arising from intrinsic conditions of the job itself, such as recognition, achievement, or personal growth.

Hygiene/Extrinsic Factors such as job security, salary, fringe benefits, work conditions, good pay, paid insurance, and vacations paradoxically do not give positive satisfaction or motivation, though dissatisfaction results from their absence. The term "hygiene" is used in the sense that these are maintenance factors. These are extrinsic to the work itself, and include aspects such as company policies, supervisory practices, or wages/salary.

Many professionals are *paid to be creative*; others find that some (leisure/unpaid) activity gives them an outlet for their "creative urges."

Often people in very serious, responsible, professional jobs like doctors, lawyers, even soldiers have "another life" where they indulge their creative instincts. This become an outlet for their "creative urges" and such a passion that at some point they quit their well paid jobs for a far less stable, predictable occupation as a "creative."

Many people think that commercial or entrepreneurial creativity (i.e., being paid for one's creativity) is somehow *less* creative (though possibly more useful) than people pursuing creativity for its own sake. Indeed, the history on invention suggests the opposite. The history of the clockwork radio is a good example. It is the story of an English amateur engineer who invented a radio that neither ran on electricity nor batteries.

There are reasons to believe that if one is paid to be creative (extrinsic motivation), the output drops in terms of quality and quantity. This touches the debate on money as a motivator (Pink, 2011) and the evidence that some extrinsic rewards, reduce intrinsic motivation. Indeed, this suggests an interesting project to examine changes on creative output as creators move from amateur to professional: from unpaid (or poorly paid) to well paid. It appears to be a question as yet unanswered in the creativity literature.

Certainly there is evidence that people employed in "creative agencies," high-tech or pharmaceutical companies feel rewarded by both intrinsic and extrinsic factors.

Adaptors versus Innovators

Some creative people take good ideas and work on them to make them better or more efficient. In some senses they "think inside the box" while innovators like to start with a "blank page" and "think outside the box."

Kirton (1976) has developed a theory of adaptors and innovators (A-I) who are seen as describing two qualitatively different and consistent individual approaches in preferences for different ways of solving problems. Kirton distinguished between style and level of creativity. Level of creativity is measured through evaluations of the quality of people's creative ideas or products. Style of creativity is supposed to capture the different approaches of adaptive creativity directed toward improvements within an existing framework, compared with innovative approaches directed toward basic change of the existing state of affairs.

However, individuals are not seen as being fixed at either end of the A-I continuum and when individuals depart from the behavior associated with their preferred style, this has been called coping behavior. It is argued that differences along the adaptive–innovative continuum should be unrelated to variations in the level of creative performance.

Some studies show that innovators obtain higher scores on measures of creativity (Kirton, 1976). Yet adaptors perceived creative products in their workplace as more logical, useful, and adequate than do innovators, while innovators perceived creative products as more original and transformational than do adaptors.

There has been much critique about Kirton's theory and measure but the distinction is an important one. Simple small changes to objects and processes can make a very big difference in how they are perceived and used. On the other hand, innovating a quite new and very different process is often considered the essence of creativity.

The academic question is differences in the quality and quantity of creative output of adaptors and innovators who are similar on other salient variables. This could reveal differences between artistic and scientific creativity (see below).

Head versus Heart

This is essentially about creativity in the arts and sciences. For more than sixty years, there has long been an interest in the different thinking styles of those in arts/humanities from those in sciences (Snow, 1959; Hudson, 1966). Hudson (1966) suggested that those with a bias toward convergent thinking moved toward the physical sciences, while those with a divergent thinking bias moved toward the humanities.

Indeed, there is an experimental literature which shows that the personality correlates of creativity in the arts are very different from those in the sciences. Researchers have tested the idea that personality and thinking style differences between arts and science students account for differences in creativity (Haller and Courvoisier, 2010). Indeed, I have worked in this area partly because of my own experience of an arts degree in divinity and history. Most of my colleague are science graduates and "hard scientists" at that. I am an arts student by training and inclination. I have always recognized, we are different in the way we approach questions and issues. Is this difference a function of personality, thinking style, or values?

Artists are significantly higher on Neuroticism than nonartists; lower on Extraversion than nonartists; higher on Openness than nonartists; lower on Agreeableness than nonartists; lower on Conscientiousness than nonartists, and higher on Psychoticism than nonartists. On the other hand, scientists are significantly higher on Intellect than nonscientists; lower on Neuroticism than nonscientists; higher on Conscientiousness than nonscientists. Also, "everyday creatives" are significantly higher on Extraversion and Agreeableness than are artists or scientists (Batey and Furnham, 2006).

It would be crude and simplistic to believe artistic creativity is all about emotions and the heart and scientific creativity all about ideas and the head. Many creative artists are highly educated, logical and skillful in the medium (painting, music) and many scientists are concerned with emotional responses. Yet the role of affect seems to play a very different role in creative artists and scientists.

However, this distinction does relate to a very important and well-established issue in creativity research, namely, convergent and divergent thinking. Convergent thinking involves a single, well-established answer to a problem. It emphasizes speed and accuracy, and focuses on recognizing the familiar, reapplying techniques, and accumulating stored information. The aim is to discover a single best answer that is either right or wrong. The solution that is derived at the end of the convergent thinking process is the best possible answer the majority of the time. Divergent thinking typically occurs in a spontaneous, unconstrained environment where as many creative ideas as possible are generated and evaluated. Multiple ideas and solutions are explored in a short amount of time, and unexpected connections and concepts are celebrated. Brainstorming is a celebration of divergent thinking.

Thus I am suggesting a partly new *research agenda*. It concerns three variables: whether creativity is influenced by type of reward (intrinsic-extrinsic), the personality/thinking style of the creative person (adaptor-innovator) and their training and type of work (art vs. science). I suspect each plays a part in the creative process and products that arise.

Three Influences on Me

My interest in creativity developed over the years. It owes much to experiences I had at three universities which shaped my research. They have led to rather different and tangentially related areas of research. In each instance, I found a different potential type of measure of creativity. In each case, my research was primarily concerned with relating these measures to standardized measures of personality and intelligence. I will briefly describe this research, its overall contribution, and whether and how I believe it should be continued.

Undergraduate Lectures and Practicals: The Discovery
of Art Judgement Tests

I grew up in South Africa and went to the University of Natal. I was extremely fortunate to have a brilliant teacher, Dr. Bruce Faulds, who dedicated his life to teaching. Every Wednesday for thirty weeks, we completed a psychometric test and analyzed the class and our individual results. Because of his interest in musical ability, he became interested in the measurement of art ability. Early researchers this century were interested in whether it is possible to determine whether one has artistic or musical ability. I remember completing two of these tests, which I have subsequently used in my research: the Meier and Seashore (1929) Art Judgement and Grave's (1948) Design Judgement tests.

The psychometrics of art judgment dates back more than nine decades, when Meier and Seashore (1929), after six years of research, published an "objective measure of art talent." This measure was designed to facilitate the identification of "promising art talents." They conceived art as a general ability complex (comprising more than twenty different but related traits). They regarded aesthetic or artistic judgment as a basic and indispensable component, which all gifted artists should possess in a highly developed manner. In essence it was a stable ability trait.

The test consists of pairs of pictures that differ in one feature. One of the pictures is "real" (corresponds to an original work of art and has been rated as such by experts of the arts); the other represents a simple variation of the original (complexity, harmony, golden ratio). Participants are given the task to identify the "better" (original) design/picture. There is a "correct" answer.

Although early studies have reported on the predictive and cross-cultural validity of Meier and Seashore's (1929) test, researchers expressed concern about its poor relationship to psychometric intelligence. Later, Meier presented a modification of this test, the Meier Art Judgement Test (Meier, 1940). The Meier art test kept the 100 most discriminating of the 125 original items of the Meier-Seashore. Of these, twenty-five were assigned double weight in scoring. Nevertheless, research on the Meier Art Judgement Test has been rather infrequent.

Another test developed in the same period was the Maitland Graves Design Judgement Test (Graves, 1948). This test involves showing participants ninety pictures, mostly but not exclusively in pairs, and asking them to indicate their preference. The figures are mainly abstract shapes and in black, white, and green and range from simple line-drawings to fairly elaborate shapes. For each pair of slides, there was always a correct answer that corresponded to the "better" design in the slide.

The Maitland Graves test has attracted wide attention to determine its validity. Some studies have been critical, arguing that test scores do not discriminate between artists and nonartists (Eysenck, 1970; Eysenck and Castle, 1971) – yet more recent studies (Uduehi, 1996) found that it did. On the other hand, critics have suggested that the test is now dated because of the changing view on aesthetic principles (Liu, 1990). Furthermore, Gotz and Gotz (1974) found that twenty-two different art experts (designers, painters, sculptors) had 0.92 agreements on choice of preferred design, albeit being critical of them.

Although very few scholars now retain an interest in art judgment tests, renewed attention to the relationships between creativity and art preferences may prove useful for the extant literature.

I remembered these (now old and obscure) tests well, and nearly twenty years later began using them in my research when looking at personality trait and intelligence correlates of creativity (Furnham, Zhang, and Chamorro-Premuzic, 2006). In various studies we have shown that personality traits, notably Psychoticism and Openness (Furnham, 1999; Furnham and Bachtiar, 2008), predict artistic creativity, which in turn may be related to various aesthetic experiences. Interestingly, however, scores on the Meier test were significantly predicted by personality (specifically the Big Five traits of Openness and Conscientiousness).

In one study we (Furnham and Rao, 2002) found that art judgment as measured by the Meier test was not significantly related to aesthetic judgments of Mondrians or Hirst (when we presented actual copies alongside systematically varied facsimiles). Later we (Furnham and Chamorro-Premuzic, 2004) found intelligence to be significantly associated with art judgment as measured by the Graves (1948) Abstract Art Design Test, but not with art interests/background/experience (as defined by the responses of a self-report scale designed by the authors). Furthermore, results showed that two personality traits, namely Conscientiousness (negatively) and Extraversion (positively), were significant predictors of art judgment. The clearest finding concerned the relationship between personality traits (notably Openness to Experience) and art interests. In several regressions, Openness was found to account for up to 33 percent of the variance in art experience.

There are very few people researching these old tests today and there appears to be no new tests like these which measure "good judgment" in art. Indeed the tests may be out-of-print. This may be because there is too little agreement about what constitutes good art, design, or painting although that is an interesting question in its own right,

Later, when I was giving a lecture in London, I befriended the great Hans Eysenck. He had done his PhD during the war on experimental aesthetics and was very interested in creativity. He introduced me to the Barron-Welsh Art Scale (Barron and Welsh, 1952) as a measure of creativity. This scale consists of eighty-six different black-and-white pictures arranged and numbered so that there are eight pictures per page. Participants are instructed to make quick, instinctive, dichotomous judgments about how much they like or dislike each picture. They are asked to fill in an "L" for "like" or a "D" for "dislike." This test requires no language skills, can be used on children and adults, is simple, and does not require extensive concentration (Welsh, 1987).

I have done a number of studies using this measure (Furnham, Batey, Booth, Patel, and Lozinskaya, 2011), which is quick and simple. I doubt, however, whether it is a very sensitive measure of creativity and always advocate that it be used in conjunction with other tests to give a more reliable and multidimensional assessment of creativity. Indeed there seems to be no clear distinction between tests of aesthetic judgment and "artistic" tests of creativity. I would imagine they are highly positively correlated but not certain this has been demonstrated.

All tests described here are about the judgment of pictures or designs. They are intriguing but clearly insufficient measures of creativity. More importantly they are about judgment rather that productivity. In other words, they speak nothing to the question of the difference between an artist and an art-critic which seems to be a missing discussion in the literature.

A Postgraduate Seminar: Convergent and Divergent Thinking

When I was at university in Scotland we had a visiting speaker named Liam Hudson. He was famous for a book called *Contrary Imaginations*. For more than sixty years, there has been an interest in the different thinking styles of those in arts/humanities from those in sciences (Snow, 1959). Hudson (1966) suggested that those with a bias toward convergent thinking moved toward the physical sciences, while those with a divergent thinking bias moved toward the humanities. The book's thesis attracted criticism but also replication and extension. For instance, Hartley and Greggs (1997) gave divergent thinking tests to four groups of students: pure arts, arts and social science, social science, and pure science. The hypothesis that divergent thinking would decline along the arts–science continuum found support in that arts students as a whole scored significantly higher than science students on the four tests.

There are many tests of convergent and divergent thinking. Some are "use of objects" where people have to list in a few minutes as many as possible "interesting and unusual" things that can be done with that object. There are usually two judgments: simple quantity (total number) but also quality (as measured by reliable judgments of "experts").

I have done a number of studies using divergent thinking as a measure of creativity. Furnham, Batey, Booth, Patel, and Lozinskaya (2011) found, in two studies, little difference in divergent thinking fluency between arts and science students, though the former showed less evidence of creativity than the latter. However, there is now much more interest in intellectual styles (cognitive, learning, teaching/thinking), their relationship to personality and intelligence, and how styles relate to career preference and success (Zhang, Sternberg, and Rayner, 2012).

I have been lucky to have among my friends, members of various psychological consultancies that logged the data they collected in assessment centers. Because employers often want to know about the creativity of potential managers they (Kaizen Ltd. of Bristol, England) decided to attempt to test it. They used a variation of the famous Consequences Test (Christensen, Merrifield, and Guilford, 1953). This test has been and is still a popular measure of DT (McCrae, Arenberg, and Costa, 1987; Silva, 2011). The test presents people with a statement like "What would happen if everyone went blind?" or "What would happen if we never needed to eat food again"? Participants write down all the consequences of that event and these are rated. Hargreaves (1927) and Guilford (1950, 1967) were among the first to operationalize creativity in terms of tests of DT. DT tests are most commonly quantitatively scored for the number of responses provided by the participant (fluency). They may be scored for statistical infrequency of response (originality) (Wallach and Kogan, 1965). DT responses may be scored for the number of categories included in a participant's answers or flexibility as well as scored for comprehensiveness of answer or elaboration (Torrance, 1974). An alternative to the quantitative-based approach involves the use of ratings of DT responses by judges. The most popular method employed has been the consensual assessment technique (Amabile, 1982; Hennessey and Amabile, 1988a, 1988b).

From early studies investigating incubation DT has been used as a potential for creativity (Vincent, Decker, and Mumford, 2002) though there remain skeptics about their ability to predict real-world creativity

(Zeng, Proctor, and Salvendy, 2011). The Consequences Test has been tested with regard to its divergent and convergent validity as well as its concurrent and predictive validity (Gelade, 1995; Vincent, Decker, and Mumford, 2002). The test has been used in various vocational settings to look at such issues as leadership skills and performance (Connelly et al., 2000).

In our studies we used various items from the Consequences Test where participants are given a specific time limit either per problem or for all problems. Responses as for other DT tests may be assessed quantitatively or qualitatively, which is usually done by consensual rating techniques, where a pool of expert and/or trained judges make a range of specific judgments with respect to issues like overall quality, originality, and realism as well as complexity, use of principles, or the number of positive versus negative outcomes. Perhaps the best-known scoring technique is that of Hennessey and Amabile (1988a, 1988b), who specified six principles (quality, original-ity, realism, time span, complexity, presence of positive and negative con-sequences) while others (i.e., Mumford, Marks, Connelly, Zaccaro, and Johnson, 1998) have added more.

In one study (Furnham and Crump, 2015), we had around 6,000 work-ing adults in the sample tested over a period of more than ten years. They completed a standard personality test and gave details about their work history. Those in retail and consulting scored highest and those in engi-neering and manufacturing lowest on two scores (fluency and original-ity) derived from the test. Implications and limitations of the study are considered.

There is no doubt in my mind that DT tests are part measures of creativ-ity in the sense that it is necessary but not sufficient to measure creativity as such. What is always surprising is the range and diversity of scores with some people really enjoying and excelling at the task with others struggling greatly with something which is difficult and unfamiliar. The important question is what precisely are these tests measuring.

A Friend's PhD Supervisor: Schizotypy and the Other Personality Disorders

When I was doing my doctorate at Oxford (DPhil), I briefly befriended a young American student who was studying creativity under the supervision of a prominent clinical psychologist, Gordon Claridge, who had studied with Hans Eysenck. He was particularly interested in schizotypy (Claridge, 1997, 2009; Claridge and Blakey, 2009). I then became aware of the work on Eysenck's concept of schizotypy linked to psychoticism. Later I became aware of Schizotypal Personality disorder. I then became interested in what might be called "the dark side of creativity."

The theory goes like this: there are common information-processing patterns in those with psychoticism and schizotypy. They seem unable to inhibit irrelevant information from entering consciousness. Hence unrelated ideas become interconnected and there is a widening of the associative horizons. Clearly both "creatives" and psychotics share the "ability" to produce more unusual associations between words and ideas compared with "normals." Also the data suggest that creatives have a high resting level of activation and are oversensitive to stimuli. However, with low levels of inhibition, the more they are stimulated the more their levels of arousal drop, favoring creative performance.

A number of studies have sought to look at personality correlates of highly creative people (Simonton, 2012) and various studies have demonstrated a relationship between creativity and schizotypy (Batey and Furnham, 2008). Studies have also been done looking at broad higher-order traits like Openness and Psychoticism, as well as narrower traits like hypomania (Acar and Runco, 2012; Batey and Furnham, 2006; Furnham, Batey, Anand, and Manfield, 2008).

In a meta-analysis of the relationship between creativity and schizotypy, Acar and Sen (2013) found a mean effect size of 0.07, based on forty-five studies which included 268 effect sizes. They looked at five possible moderators and found only the *schizotypy* significant. There was no effect for the different measures of schizotypy. The results from the meta-analysis suggested that positive-impulsive schizotypy related to Extraversion, but negative-disorganized schizotypy was not related to Introversion and it was the latter that was most closely related to creativity.

In various more recent studies, the measure of schizotypy I used was the Imaginative scale from the Hogan Development Survey been shown to be correlated with Divergent Thinking ($r = 0.17$, $N = 345$), suggesting that it is indeed a marker of creativity (Furnham, Crump, Batey, and Chamorro-Premuzic, 2009). I believe that one might use a schizotypy scale as a measure of proneness to creativity. Again we have a test which is probably in the necessary but not sufficient class: that is, it is a part measure of trait creativity.

I have been lucky to be exposed to these three different but related areas of creativity research. I retain an interest in the now very neglected art judgment tests but continue to pursue my work on DT and "the dark side of creativity." The latter area remains one of considerable debate: namely whether there is a link between "various forms of madness" and creativity.

Five Questions

For me, there remain some fundamental questions about research into creativity. They have provoked, and continue to provoke my interest in the topic:

1. The (operational) definition of (many different kinds of) creativity. I do not believe we should get "hung up" on definitions but equally I think we cannot ignore the problem. What constitutes a really creative product, be it a painting or a product? Clearly there is a dimension from low to high creativity but it is likely that we need various dimensions to measure it robustly. This needs a lot more work.
2. The (valid and reliable and multidimensional) measurement of creativity. This for me is the crucial issue that is holding researchers back from doing good research in the area. I have "played with" all sorts of tests that seem to be "linked to" creativity but I know of no robust and psychometrically valid tests of any sort that can be claimed to be a good measure. One that I have pursued is simply getting people to list the quality and quantity of creative activities that they take part in (Batey and Furnham, 2008). Inevitably a battery of psychometrically validated tests will be best.
3. Providing a good account of the process and mechanisms that accounts for how creativity occurs. It is all very well describing links between variables and recounting the life stories of famous people, but we need to explain the *neurological and behavioral process* that occurs to produce creativity of any sort. This is perhaps where developments in neuroscience will come in to their own. This will give us literally a picture or map of brain functioning during periods of creativity to give us some-understanding of the complex processes occurring when a person is "being creative." Too much of the work is descriptive rather than explanatory.
4. Providing good evidence that creativity is causally linked to salient and important life-outcome variables. The question here is the potential benefits and drawbacks of creativity. Do organizations benefit from hiring creative people? Is there any relationship between creativity and mental and physical health? When you ask senior business people if they want more "creative" people in their organization a vast majority

say yes. What I believe they really mean is innovative rather than creative people: innovating new products and processes being more difficult than coming up with the idea in the first place. Business people know that new ideas, products, and businesses processes are the keys to success but have little knowledge of the creativity literature, particularly of the "dark side" of creativity. There is an extensive, growing and disputed literature on the relationship between creativity and "madness" (Simonton, 2014a, 2014b, 2014c) which suggests there are often negative correlates of creativity. In is in this direction where my current interests are going.

5.   Overclaiming and misclaiming the importance and role of creativity. There are many claims about teaching people how to become creative. The question is how strong the evidence is for these and other claims. I have cynically claimed that there are various bogus models that so-called creativity trainers use, who all claim, with little or no evidence that both "everyone is creative" and that this latent creativity can be harnessed and released.

"First, there is the *muesli model*. People need to unblock their creativity. They are in some curious way creativity-constipated and unable to let go and express themselves. In this sense creativity courses may be seen as laxatives. Second, there is the *dominatrix model*. Here we are told to unleash our creativity. Somehow we have been bound up, tied down, physically constrained from that most natural and normal of tasks, namely being creative. So creativity courses are liberators. Third, there is the *arsonist model*. Creative consultants and trainers aim to spark ideas and light fires. They see people as dry tinder just waiting for the right moment. Their job is to find ways of facilitating fire-setting ideas. The courses are igniters. Fourth, there is the *kindergarten model*. The problem appears to be that we have all forgotten how to be playful. Playfulness is apparently not only a lot of fun but it is also very productive. So our trainer helps us regress to a time when we were happy and quite unabashed to draw pictures, sing songs, etc. These courses aim for rediscovery. Fifth, there is the *jail-liberator model*. The problem, you see, is that we have all been boxed in a sort of cognitive jail that has stopped us . . . wait for it . . . thinking outside the box! And here, our happy consultants throw open the doors of our prison and out pops our creative jack-in-the-box. The course delivers a release" (Furnham, 2008, p. 234).

The whole topic of whether creativity can be taught or trained is a difficult one and I remain a skeptic. Some people are (much) more creative than others. Just as I do not believe you can train intelligence (though one can teach knowledge and skills) and that personality changes over time do occur but are not strong, so I believe creativity is normally distributed and not particularly prone to change, though I accept there are ways of exploring and exploiting particular talents in individuals.

Conclusion

I say to students and people who ask my advice on vocational issues that you should follow your passions. Often students are pragmatic when it comes choosing a degree or a dissertation within the degree. I used to advise students *not* to choose creativity to research because it is too difficult to do well by the criteria of empirical psychology: but I have changed my mind. I believe creativity research is interesting, fun, and, just as important, rigorous. Equally one could argue that personal and organizational survival is dependent on creativity so the more we know about the topic the better.

Furthermore, I think with developments in behavioral genetics and neuroscience we are beginning to understand the mechanisms and processes involved in creative activity. The editors of this book are among the most gifted and important creativity researchers working today and this volume is a fine testament to state-of-the-art research in creativity.

REFERENCES

Acar, S., and Runco, M. A. (2012). Psychoticism and creativity. *Psychology of Aesthetics, Creativity, and the Arts*, 6, 341–350.

Acar, S., and Sen, S. (2013). A multilevel meta-analysis of the relationship between creativity and schizotypy. *Psychology of Aesthetics, Creativity, and the Arts*, 7, 214–228.

Amabile, T. M. (1982). Children's artistic creativity: Detrimental effects of competition in a field setting. *Personality and Social Psychology Bulletin*, 8, 573–578.

Barron F., and Welsh, G. S. (1952). Artistic perception as a possible factor in personality style: Its measurement by a figure preference test. *Journal of Psychology*, 33, 199–203.

Batey, M., and Furnham, A. (2006). Creativity, intelligence, and personality: A critical review of the scattered literature. *Genetic, Social, and General Psychology Monographs*, 132, 355–429.

(2008). The relationship between measures of creativity and schizotypy. *Personality and Individual Differences*, 45, 816–821.

Christensen, P. R., Merrifield, P. R., and Guilford, J. P. (1953). *Consequences from A-1*. Beverly Hills, CA: Sheridan Supply.

Claridge, G. (1997). *Schizotypy: Implications for illness and health*. Oxford: Oxford University Press.

(2009). Personality and psychosis. In *Handbook of personality*, edited by P. J. Corr and G. Matthews, 631–648. Cambridge: Cambridge University Press.

Claridge, G., and Blakey, S. (2009). Schizotypy and affective temperament: Relationships with divergent thinking and creativity styles. *Personality and Individual Differences*, 46, 820–826.

Connelly, M. S., Gilbert, J. A., Zaccaro, S. J., Threlfall, K. V., Marks, M. A., and Mumford, M. D. (2000). Exploring the relationship of leader skills and knowledge to leader performance. *Leadership Quarterly*, 11(1), 65–86.

Eysenck, H. J. (1970). Explanation and the concept of personality. In *Explanation in the behavioural sciences*, edited by R. Borger and F. Cioffi, 387–410. Cambridge: Cambridge University Press.

Eysenck, H. J., and Castle, M. (1971). Comparative study of artists and non artists on the Maitland Graves Design Judgement Tests. *Journal of Applied Psychology*, 55, 389–391.

Furnham, A. (1999). Personality and creativity, *Perceptual and Motor Skills*, 88, 407–408.

(2008). *Personality and intelligence at work*. London: Routledge.

Furnham, A., and Bachtiar, V. (2008). Personality and intelligence as predictors of creativity. *Personality and Individual Differences*, 45, 613–617.

Furnham, A., Batey, M., Anand, K., and Manfield, J. (2008). Personality, hypomania, intelligence and creativity. *Personality and Individual Differences*, 44, 1060–1069.

Furnham, A., Batey, M., Booth, T., Patel, V., and Lozinskaya, D. (2011). Individual difference predictors of creativity in art and science students. *Thinking Skills and Creativity*, 6, 114–121.

Furnham, A., and Chamorro-Premuzic, T. (2004). Personality traits, psychometric intelligence, and art judgement. *Personality and Individual Differences*, 36, 705–715.

Furnham, A., and Crump, J. (2013). The sensitive, imaginative, articulate art student and conservative, cool, numerate science student. *Learning and Individual Differences*, 25, 150–155.

(2014). A bright side, facet analysis of Schizotypal Personality Disorder. *Thinking Skills and Creativity*, 11, 42–47.

(2015). The creativity of people in different work sectors. *Business Creativity and the Creative Economy*, 1, 88–93.

Furnham, A., Crump, J., Batey, M., and Chamorro-Premuzic, T. (2009). Personality and ability predictors of the "consequences" test of divergent thinking in a large non-student sample. *Personality and Individual Differences*, 46, 536–540.

Furnham, A., and Rao, S. (2002). Personality and the aesthetics of composition: A study of Mondrian and Hirst. *North American Journal of Psychology*, 4, 233–242.

Furnham, A., Zhang, J., and Chamorro-Premuzic, T. (2006). The relationship between psychometric and self-estimated intelligence, creativity, personality, and academic achievement. *Cognition and Personality*, 25, 119–145.

Gelade, G. (1995). Creative style and divergent production. *Journal of Creative Behaviour*, 29(1), 36–53.

Gotz, K. O., and Gotz, K. (1974). The Maitland Graves Design Judgment Test judged by 22 experts. *Perceptual and Motor Skills*, 39, 261–262.

Graves, M. (1948). *Design Judgement Test*. San Antonio, TX: Psychological Corporation.

Guilford, J. P. (1950). Creativity. *American Psychologist*, 5, 444–454.

——— (1967). *The nature of human intelligence*. New York: McGraw-Hill.

Haller, C., and Courvoisier, D. (2010). Personality and thinking style in different creative domains. *Psychology of Aesthetics, Creativity, and the Arts*, 4, 146–160.

Hargreaves, H. L. (1927). The "faculty" of imagination: An enquiry concerning the existence of a general "faculty," or group factor, of imagination. *British Journal of Psychology Monograph Supplement*, 3, 1–74.

Hartley, J., and Greggs, M. A. (1997). Divergent thinking in arts and science student: Contrary imaginations at Keele revisited. *Studies in Higher Education*, 22, 93–97.

Hennessey, B. A., and Amabile, T. M. (1988a). The conditions of creativity. In *The nature of creativity*, edited by R. J. Sternberg. New York: Cambridge University Press.

——— (1988b). Storytelling: A method for assessing children's creativity. *Journal of Creative Behavior*, 22, 235–246.

Hudson, L. (1966). *Contrary imaginations*. London: Methuen.

Kirton, M. (1976). Adaptors and innovators: A description and measure. *Journal of Applied Psychology*, 61(5), 622–629.

Liu, F. (1990). Critique of three tests of aesthetic judgement. *Visual Arts Research*, 16, 90–94.

McCrae, R. R., Arenberg, D., and Costa, P. T. (1987). Declines in divergent thinking with age: Cross-sectional, longitudinal, and cross-sequential analyses. *Psychology and Aging*, 2, 130–136.

Meier, N. C. (1940). *The Meier Art Tests: I, Art Judgment*. Iowa City: Bureau of Educational Research and Service, University of Iowa.

Meier, N. C., and Seashore, C. E. (1929). *The Meier-Seashore Art Judgement Test*. Iowa City: Bureau of Educational Research, University of Iowa.

Mumford, M., Marks, M., Connelly, M., Zaccaro, S., and Johnson, J. (1998). Domain-based scoring in divergent-thinking tests. *Creativity Research Journal*, 11, 151–163.

Pink, D. H. (2011). *Drive: The surprising truth about what motivates us*. New York: Penguin.

Seashore, C. E. (1929). Meier-Seashore Art Judgement Test. *Science*, 69, 380.

Silvia, P. J. (2005). Emotional responses to art: From collation and arousal to cognition and emotion. *Review of General Psychology*, 9, 342–357.

Simonton, D. K. (2012). Taking the US Patent Office criteria seriously: A quantitative three-criterion creativity definition and its implications. *Creativity Research Journal*, 24(2–3), 97–106.

(2014a). Historiometric studies of genius. In *The Wiley handbook of genius*, edited by D. K. Simonton, 87–106. Oxford: John Wiley.

(2014b). The mad (creative) genius: What do we know after a century of historiometric research? In *Creativity and mental illness*, edited by J. C. Kaufman, 25–41. New York: Cambridge University Press.

(2014c). The mad-genius paradox: Can creative people be more mentally healthy and highly creative people more mentally ill? *Perspectives on Psychological Science*, 9, 470–480.

Snow, C. (1959). *The two cultures*. Cambridge: Cambridge University Press.

Torrance, E. P. (1974). *Torrance Tests of creative thinking: Norms and technical manual*. Bensenville, IL: Scholastic Testing Services.

Uduehi, J. (1996). A cross-cultural assessment of the Maitland Graves Design Judgement Test using IS and Nigerian subjects. *Visual Arts Research*, 21, 11–18.

Vincent, A. S., Decker, B. P., and Mumford, M. D. (2002). Divergent thinking, intelligence, and expertise: A test of alternative models. *Creativity Research Journal*, 14, 163–178.

Wallach, M. A., and Kogan, N. (1965). *Modes of thinking in young children: A study of the creativity-intelligence distinction*. New York: Holt, Rinehart, and Winston.

Welsh, G. S. (1987). *Manual for the Barron-Welsh Art Scale*. Redwood City, CA: Mind Garden.

Zeng, L., Proctor, R. W., and Salvendy, G. (2011). Can traditional divergent thinking tests be trusted in measuring and predicting real-world creativity? *Creativity Research Journal*, 23, 24–37.

Zhang, L. F., Sternberg, R. J., and Rayner, S. G. (Eds.). (2012). *Handbook of intellectual styles*. New York: Springer.

CHAPTER 7

Creativity
The View from Big C and the Introduction of Tiny c
Howard Gardner and Emily Weinstein

Howard

1961 onward. As a young student and scholar, I was very much involved in the arts – as a reasonably skilled pianist and sometime teacher of piano and as a regular attendee at performances and a visitor to museums. I also enjoyed reading about artists and artistry. When I began my doctoral studies, I had never taken a course in psychology per se. For whatever reasons, I already had the interests of a psychologist – though psychology more in the lay sense (personality, motivation, mental illness) than in the academic mode of experiments on rats, pigeons, and college sophomores.

1967. In my second year as a doctoral student, I wrote a long paper (fifty+ pages) on the psychological study of creativity. I thought that the paper had been long lost, but in preparing this chapter, I actually relocated it. What's interesting is that in the paper, I already express skepticism about the mainstream approach to creativity within psychology – the administration of "creativity tests" – as pioneered by J. P. Guilford, E. Paul Torrance, and Sarnoff Mednick. In terminology that my colleagues and I adopted subsequently, I was doubting the significance of "little c" creativity – at least for the issues in which I was interested. (If you looked at the photographs in my boyhood room, they were either family members or examples of "Big C" creativity – Albert Einstein, Ernest Hemingway, Winston Churchill.)

If you had asked me about creativity at the time, I suspect that I would have yoked creativity specifically to the arts and seen it as a trait that certain persons possessed. After all, I was a sometime art aficionado; I was a founding member of Project Zero, a research group focused on arts education that still exists! I was getting ready to write a thesis on the perception of style in the visual arts; and I was rolling up my sleeve to write my first scholarly book, *The Arts and Human Development* (Gardner, 1973). Yet whatever interest I had in creativity went underground for two decades, and when it reemerged some decades later, it had a quite different flavor.

1971. In my efforts to understand artistry, I embarked on a series of studies of artistic development in young people. I was convinced that Piaget's studies of cognitive development provided the best model for investigation, but I noted that, for Piaget, "full development as a *scientist*" was the normal end state of human beings. In counterpoint, I imagined a world in which "*participation in the artistic process*" was an alternative – and perhaps more universally applicable – end state for human beings.

In a parallel line of work, aimed at teasing out the nature and composition of artistic skills and understandings, I began to work with once normal individuals who had the misfortune of having suffered damage to the brain – via a stroke, trauma, or tumor. Virtually every working day, I found myself observing unusual patterns of performance. In the morning, at the Boston Veterans Administration Medical Center, I encountered brain-damaged patients who had lost the ability to use language but were still capable of musical performance and understanding; or individuals who lost their spatial understanding but could still read and write language. Then, in the afternoon, either at Project Zero or at a nearby public school, I would observe children who were skilled in one or another art form while being challenged in their school subjects; or conversely, young academic stars who could neither carry a tune nor a draw a straight line.

1981. Trying to make sense of these perplexing patterns of human performance (including impaired performances) and aided by a generous research grant from the Bernard Van Leer Foundation, I assembled a small research team. We combed the literature on human performance and human potential from a range of natural sciences (neuroscience, genetics) and social sciences (psychology, anthropology, educational research) in an effort to organize the current understanding of human cognitive capacities. And I eventually put forth a synthesis of this research in *Frames of Mind: The Theory of Multiple Intelligences* (Gardner, 1983).

As has become well known, though still controversial, I proposed that the notion of a single human intelligence – supposedly captured by psychometric instruments and by the statistic known as g – was inadequate; it did not encompass the range of human abilities as observed across cultures and across time. Instead, I posited the existence of a range of relatively independent computational capacities known as the "multiple intelligences." In addition to the linguistic and logical-mathematical intelligences that are prioritized by standard psychometric instruments

(Piaget was actually interested primarily in logical-mathematical intelligence), I proposed at least five more intelligences: musical, spatial, bodily, interpersonal, and intrapersonal. Later I added one more intelligence, the intelligence of the naturalist.

In postulating musical intelligence, it may appear that I was smuggling the arts into my intellectual arena. But in fact I argued that *any* intelligence may be used artistically but that no intelligence is explicitly artistic. To be specific, in writing this part of the essay, I am using linguistic intelligence, but have no pretense that the words and phrases are being used artistically. If, however, I were to employ alliteration or assonance or create poetic passages, then the "language intelligence" would be functioning artistically. Conversely when musical tones are used to signal that my laptop has been turned on or that it is time to wake up, then music is functioning in a pragmatic rather than in an artistic way. And, to choose an example from the interpersonal realm, if I shove other people to get onto a subway car, that's not interpersonal intelligence. But if I figure out how to placate a person who is making a disturbance on the subway, that is a manifestation of interpersonal intelligence.

1990. In an essay on creativity, I took an apparent detour to "MI theory" because it dominated my research agenda in the late 1970s and because its educational implications became a priority in the 1980s. As I interacted with readers and critics (some friendly, others less so), I was often asked about the implications of the theory for the understanding of creativity. The most frequently asked questions: Is creativity the same thing as intelligence? If there are several intelligences, are there also several creativities?

It's never quite clear how a question or an idea transmogrifies into a project or a book – and what happens, or does not happen, thereafter. (Now that's a promising topic for a student of creativity to investigate!) But in any event, I decided to study individuals who, from all evidence, were strong in a particular intelligence – to understand how each of their minds worked; and, to the extent possible, to determine the similarities and differences among these individuals.

Whom to study? After some reflection, I decided to study individuals of indisputably high creativity – ones about whom much information was available, and ones who lived at roughly the same historical time (so that one possible source of difference was "controlled for"). Also, it was important that I personally resonated to the individuals. And so, for example, I could have studied various musical composers (Bartok, Schoenberg, Duke

Ellington) but I elected to study the one whose music I preferred. Here's the final list:

Linguistic: T. S. Eliot
Logical-mathematical: Albert Einstein
Musical: Igor Stravinsky
Spatial: Pablo Picasso
Bodily Kinesthetic: Martha Graham
Interpersonal: Mahatma Gandhi
Intrapersonal: Sigmund Freud

In some ways, I was doing a standard work of biography, largely from a psychological perspective. But I also was self-consciously positioning myself between two already established approaches:

1. The historiometric approach, most associated with the work of Dean Keith Simonton (Simonton, 2004). Here one poses a question of interest and then seeks to answer the question by quantification – an approach made immeasurably more powerful by ready access to "big data." So if, for example, one wanted to know whether great creators invariably have high general intelligence (g), one could find or estimate the IQ scores of 500 creative individuals and see how they measure on this measure (that's what Lewis Terman and Catherine Cox did decades ago).
2. The single-case approach, most associated with the work of Howard Gruber (1981). Here one identifies a highly creative individual and then seeks to trace the emergence and full flowering of his or her work over the course of a lifetime. In Gruber's case, he focused on two individuals – Charles Darwin and Jean Piaget. Gruber's students and others working in that tradition have examined other specific creative lives in great detail.

Without quite realizing it at the time, I was taking a stand in favor of the importance of studying and understanding "Big C" Creativity. That is, I was positing that we can learn a great deal about creativity by focusing on indisputable exemplars – and perhaps understanding a Picasso or a Graham would help us understand more modest degrees of creativity (smaller Cs). I was also revisiting the skepticism first raised in my student paper twenty-five years earlier – namely, the unlikelihood that understanding "cocktail party" fluency (in three minutes, "how many uses can you think of for a paper clip"), would in any meaningful way illuminate the pinnacles of human creative achievement in which I was interested.

1993. My studies culminated in a lengthy book *Creating Minds*. The book was well received (in my experience, not always the case!) and it was also the one that I most enjoyed writing. That's because I am both bio-graphically – and historically – minded. This project gave me the license to comb through many written works and to enjoy many works of art (and science and politics). By and large the research was secondary, rather than primary; but in the case of dancer Martha Graham, I had great pleasure in looking at rare footage of her performances available in the library of Lincoln Center in New York City.

What are the headlines from that study? To begin with the question that animated the investigation, the creative individuals whom I studied were by and large strong in more than a single intelligence. For example, T. S. Eliot stood out both as a poet and a philosopher: indeed, he finished all the work needed to receive a doctorate in philosophy from Harvard University. Sigmund Freud was clearly a person of high IQ but stood out as well in terms of the personal intelligences. As far as I could determine, the subjects also had areas of weakness – for example, Freud had no under-standing of music; several of my subjects had been indifferent students. And indeed, only Igor Stravinsky emerged as competent across the range of intelligences – he could conceivably have been a lawyer, a musician, or an artistic impresario.

You can be very strong in an intelligence (for whatever reasons), and if you work hard at tasks that draw on that intelligence, you will become an expert in the relevant domains. But being an *expert* is different from being a *creative individual*. In the 1980s, I became convinced by the argument put forth by Mihaly Csikszentmihalyi (1988) – that creativity is not simply the property of a single individual. Creativity is better thought of as an interactive process – between an *individual* with one or more talents; an existing or emerging area of competence, which one calls a *domain;* and a set of individuals and institutions that allocate attention, resources, and rewards to certain "products" and not others – the so-called *field*.

Each of my creators went beyond sheer expertise. In each case, the *creator* gravitated toward an existing domain (physics, painting) which he or she proceeded to alter in significant ways; or ultimately founded a new *domain* of knowledge/expertise (psychoanalysis, modern dance); and sooner or later, the creator's work became appreciated by relevant persons and insti-tutions – by the *field*. What struck me was that creative individuals often combine skills and knowledge from more than one intelligence and put them together in ways that have little precedence. And so Sigmund Freud, trained as a scientist in neurology, applied those skills and ways of thinking to human unconscious processes; Einstein, a physicist with logical-mathematical skills, also drew on unusually powerful spatial skills; Eliot, a trained philosopher, captured ideas and controversies in blank verse. Put differently, creative individuals are characterized less by strength in one intelligence (the so-called expert), and more by the distinctive ways in which they combined two or more intelligences.

My study in comparative biography uncovered many intriguing findings. One might equally characterize them as "hypotheses" – to tweak an old adage, the plural of "case studies" is not "data." Here are some findings that caught my fancy:

Creative individuals are born in somewhat remote areas. But as soon as they can, they move to a big city, find other "young rebels," and make common cause with them.

The creators I studied came from bourgeois households. They were loved and supported by family, so long as they worked hard.

Creators find or create something that is anomalous. Instead of running away from it or reverting toward "standard operating procedure," these aspiring creators become intrigued and explore further and more deeply. (See my curiosity, noted earlier, about the trek from initial idea to finished work.)

The greater the anomaly, the more isolating the experience. And so creative individuals often feel that they are going mad; at such times, they especially need (and, when fortunate, receive) support from caring others.

Creative individuals gain from such support; and because they are often magnetic, charismatic personalities, other individuals like to be in their vicinity. But these supporters are often rejected when they are no longer useful – if you get too close to creative fire, you may get singed.

Consistent with this last point, creative individuals are dedicated fully to their work – so long as they remain active in the field. To paraphrase the poet W. B. Yeats, they prioritize "perfection of the work" over "perfection of the life." As individual personalities, in their relationship to other persons, they range from remote (Einstein) to sadistic (Picasso).

Whether or not they are personally extroverted or eager for publicity, they did what was needed to bring their work to the attention of others – or were fortunate enough to have someone else who served as their agent.

It takes about ten years to develop expertise in a new area. Perhaps confirming this rule of thumb, "my" creators developed new lines of work at approximately decade intervals.

As noted, these are all hypotheses, which remain to be tested by historiometric (or, if possible, experimental) means. And when I began to speak about them, individuals often cited counterexamples. These counterexamples were useful to me. As one example, the great philosopher Ludwig Wittgenstein was not born in a remote village; he grew up as a member of a Viennese family that was wealthy and well connected. A little research revealed that Wittgenstein left Vienna and went further and further afield – to a rural Austrian village, to Cambridge, England, to Ithaca, New York. Clearly, it was important to Wittgenstein to get away from his roots – and in this case, from a major metropolitan area to various remote outposts.

I am also chagrined that my list of creators was heavily skewed toward white males – Gandhi and Graham being the two exceptions. And so in subsequent writings, I have paid attention to other creative individuals – the writer Virginia Woolf, the activist Eleanor Roosevelt – and the movement leader Martin Luther King Jr. I also studied a creative individual from an earlier era – the great composer Mozart (Gardner, 1995, 1997).

2000. One of the rewards of a life of scholarship is that one is free to explore issues of interest, wherever one's curiosity leads. Two decades of interest in intelligence and creativity overlapped with an interest in the professions (the Good Work Project; Gardner, Csikszentmihalyi, and Damon, 2001); in ethics (the Good Project); and in the qualities of a good education (Gardner, 1999, 2011) and a large ongoing project on liberal arts and sciences in the twenty-first century.

Another of the rewards of the scholarly life is the opportunity to work with gifted young scholars, who critique and extend one's own work. Jin Li (1997) distinguished between two forms of creativity: In *vertical creativity*, the rules of the domain are quite strictly laid out and it is relatively straightforward to determine who is advancing the domain (think physics, think classical ballet); in *horizontal creativity*, the rules are much looser and participants are free to move about in various directions (think postmodern literary criticism, think contemporary painting). Mia Keinanen studied creative activity in a horizontal domain (modern dance). She found that, rather than learning at the feet of masters (so to speak), learning emerged as the product of regular intense interactions among peers (Keinanen and Gardner, 2004).

The twenty-first century: Three challenges. Using a terminology that I first heard from Mihaly Csikszentmihalyi, but that may have an earlier origin, I was clearly focused on Big C *creativity*. As noted, the mainstream of psychological research has alighted instead of "little c" creativity. While there's no agreed upon definition, this contrast has made its way into the literature.

Someone once asked Mihaly Csikszentmihalyi whether he himself was an example of Big C or little c creativity, and he quipped, "Well, I am middle C." Whether or not that self-characterization is correct, it's clear that we need a term to describe individuals and achievements that are significant, worth noting, but that do not in themselves change a field or domain. Kaufman and Beghetto (2009) propose "Pro C" to describe professional creativity – Pro C creators are highly accomplished professional experts who have not yet (and may not ever) reach eminent status, yet who surpass the "little c" designation. In biographies, one finds the names of persons who clearly aided the Big C creators (e.g., Louis Horst for Martha Graham, Wilhelm Fliess for Sigmund Freud, members of the Olympiad for Albert Einstein) but who we would not consider to be highly creative. To use a current yardstick, Big C creators occupy a great deal of space in Wikipedia; in contrast, middle c creators, if mentioned at all, have little space in Wikipedia, and that space tends to focus on the person's relation to the Big C creator.

To be sure, there are no hard-and-fast indices for the various font sizes of C. It is helpful to think of the four Cs as a continuum, with no sharp division between any two nodes. So, to use a well-known example, the composer Antonin Salieri was no Mozart: but on some criteria, he could qualify as a Big C, rather than a middle c creator.

Two other issues intersect in potentially intriguing ways with the size of font of the C.

My earlier work has deliberately focused on the single individual – if not the painter of lore holed up in his Bohemian attic, at least the clear-cut leader of a lab or a movement. What do we know about creativity that emanates from groups – what corporations often label as "Skunk Works"? Is group creativity different from individual creativity? And to take the strongly critical view, is individual creativity to some extent an illusion?

My studies all focused on individuals who did their work before the rise of computers, the Internet, the web, ubiquitous social media. Now these forms of communication, of thinking, are ambient and perhaps determinant. How does the era of The App Generation (Gardner and Davis, 2013) change the context of creativity for eminent creators? And how do youths' heavy uses of social media relate to creativity? When a youth posts a

Facebook entry or shares a snapchat photo or – perhaps most revealingly – tweets a response to some event, does this count as creativity at all? We propose to introduce a fourth "c" – tiny c – and to speculate about its relation to the larger fonts.

Emily

2017. To state the obvious: Howard's academic study of creativity began well before the digital era. *Creating Minds*, published in 1993, also predates smartphones and social-networking apps. In contrast, my own research focuses on the effects of digital media on users, especially young persons (Weinstein, 2014).

Today, daily digital media use is normative. Mobile phones are omnipresent and a majority of US-based adults own personal smartphones. Eighteen- to twenty-four-year-olds check their cellphones an average of *eighty-two times per day* (Deloitte, 2016). Most teens and adults also actively maintain accounts on multiple social-networking sites.

Social-networking sites are a Web 2.0 innovation – they exemplify social, participatory platforms designed to support user-generated content (O'Reilly, 2005). The early Internet (i.e., "Web 1.0") comprised relatively static websites created for passive consumption. With Web 2.0, networked citizens connect as content co-producers.

What are the consequences, for creativity, of a networked world? Earlier in this chapter, Howard outlines findings from his *Creating Minds* research. The core findings are almost certainly unchanged by digital technologies – that eminent creators combine two or more intelligences in distinctive ways is not a function of historical context. However, Howard also describes collection of observations that typify the life paths of exceptional creators. Social technologies fundamentally alter the context surrounding creative individuals; one might therefore wonder whether, and to what extent, the original observations apply in a digital age. For example:

> *Creative individuals are born in somewhat remote areas. But as soon as they can, they move to a big city, find other "young rebels" and make common cause with them.*

Enhanced connectivity is an obvious consequence of the Internet; social technologies change the nature of geographic isolation. Young creators can access the major works of their domains regardless of where they live. The Guggenheim's online collection includes nearly 1,700 works from more than 575 artists; from the Metropolitan Museum of Art, 400,000 works are available for free, high-resolution download; and the Smithsonian's searchable database provides digital records of more than 10 million works in its collection.

Young creators also easily unite with physically distant contemporaries. C. J. Pascoe (2013) writes about Clarissa, a seventeen-year-old aspiring writer who participates in a networked writing community called Faraway Lands. Clarissa connects with a cohort of peers who share her fantasy fiction passion:

> Online, [Clarissa] found a community of like-minded peers who shared her interests, and who collaboratively wrote stories and critiqued each other's work. Clarissa made great strides in her writing, engaging with it in ways that felt more authentic, and more motivating than her writing classes at school. (Ito et al., 2013, p. 6)

Clarissa's story presents an example of *connected learning*. Interest-driven and socially embedded, *connected learning* expands youths' opportunities for both education and participation in public life (Ito et al., 2013). Web 2.0 functionally supports affinity groups, which are often characterized by both high levels of peer support and extensive mentoring (Campbell et al., 2016).

While there is clearly less of an imperative to move to urban "creative centers," more than ever ambitious young persons do move to so-called creative cities. Indeed, in the United States, and perhaps elsewhere, the difference between urban attraction and life elsewhere is greater than before. And there is no evidence that online contact substitutes adequately for in-person contacts. As has been quipped frequently "Why do I travel long distances to conferences dedicated to the power of online learning and of virtual contacts?"

Expansive digital databases and connected learning opportunities ostensibly support little and middle c creativity. What is the consequence of new digital media (NDM) for Big C creativity? Will future eminent creators still tend to begin life in remote areas and then, as soon as they are able, move to cities in search of affinity groups? Or do the affordances of NDM obviate the need for urban relocation?

* The greater the anomaly, the more isolating the experience. And so creative individuals often feel that they are going mad; at such times, they especially need (and, when fortunate, receive) support from caring others.

Mobile technologies and social apps expand support networks in at least two ways. First, NDM enable "tele-cocoons." Existing close ties are accessible around the clock and across the globe. Caring others are always a phone call (or text message, e-mail, video call, tweet, snapchat, etc.) away. Mobile phones allow people to move through the world metaphorically surrounded by tele-cocoons of personal support (Habuchi, 2005). Social apps also facilitate relational connection: when actively used for support-seeking, social-networking sites activate ever-broadening networks of close and loose ties.

Second, NDM create opportunities for new forms of social support. Crisis Text Line, for example, provides "access to free, 24/7 support and information via the medium people already use and trust: text [messaging]." The text-based hotline enables immediate communication with trained volunteers. Online community groups and message boards also offer readily accessible social support. Functional barriers to connection are arguably lower than ever before. And yet, as Sherry Turkle (2011) cautions, technology can disrupt the quality of self-reflection and social connection, distracting from and diminishing the power of deep relationships.

Based on my interviews with networked youth, I find that teens do routinely use social apps in the service of supportive relational connections; however, digital interactions may also exacerbate feelings of disconnection, particularly when youth already feel vulnerable or isolated (Weinstein and Selman, 2016). Relational exchanges on social-networking sites often reflect or amplify existing social circumstances. While networked interactions can certainly comprise substantive communication, friends often demonstrate support through less personal interactions, such as "likes," "tags," and emoji-infused comments. Howard's creators received deep, sustained support from one or two key persons. How do contemporary creators fare when they require social support to sustain themselves and their work? What role do social technologies play in creators' supportive relationships?

Creative individuals are dedicated fully to their work – so long as they remain active in the field. To paraphrase the poet W. B. Yeats, they prioritize "perfection of the work" over "perfection of the life."

The App Generation is accustomed to life on-demand – immediate, efficient results across personal, relational, and professional domains (Gardner and Davis, 2013). Frequent job changes among young adults arguably reflect the app-mentality. A shared expectation of constant accessibility also generates pressure for rapid response, even when the quantity of digital communication becomes overwhelming (Weinstein and Selman,

2016). And so young adults check their cellphones on more than eighty occasions per day.

Perhaps unsurprisingly, media multitasking abounds and the average duration of concentrated, on-task focus is merely eight seconds as of 2015 (Microsoft, 2015). *There's an app for that, too!* To minimize digital distractions, one can download apps that functionally block access to designated sites for limited periods of time. Apps reflect the Zeitgeist of the digital era, which includes the perpetual struggle for attention amidst a backdrop of unprecedented distractions and endless possibilities. How do the conditions of networked life influence longer-term, sustained dedication among creators?

> * *Whether or not they were personally extroverted or eager for publicity, they did what was needed to bring their work to the attention of others – or had someone else who served as their agent.*

NDM open new pathways to fame (and shame), dissemination, and self-promotion. It is the age of micro-celebrity – "a self-presentation technique in which people view themselves as a public persona to be consumed by others, use strategic intimacy to appeal to followers, and regard their audience as fans" (Marwick, 2015, pp. 333–334). Social technologies transfer power in the attention economy: creators can sidestep traditional gatekeepers and disseminate their own works. At the same time, creative ideas are in competition with the expansive quantities of information that "trend" in and out of view on social apps. Criticisms leveled at anything innovative, sometimes vicious, can be very discouraging – there are advantages to working in splendid obscurity, as Einstein and Freud did.

In the age of self-publishing and rapid, low-cost circulation, how do different fields discern extraordinary ideas? And how do creators personally manage the opportunities for self-promotion amidst the realities of negative tweets and comments?

Toward "Tiny c"

Howard intentionally focuses on unambiguously exceptional creators. NDM fundamentally reshape the ecology and may alter creators' paths to extraordinary, Big C creativity. Social technologies also contribute new contexts for creativity – though more of the middle c, little c, and, we propose, tiny c varieties.

The creative potential of NDM is most often linked to the ways social media revolutionize massive collaboration. Peppler (2013) argues that online creations pose a challenge to traditional views of creativity. Remixing – the practice of directly integrating and building on others' digital works – muddies questions about authorship and novelty. Peppler also describes the issue of defining "the field" in online spaces. Inevitably, certain ideas receive disproportionate attention and circulation among online crowds. Yet the most shared ideas are not necessarily the most creative.

Still, the potential of NDM to efficiently harness collective intelligence is potentially game-changing if one ascribes to a *participatory* or *group* views of creativity – that is, the notion that collaboration, not the individual mind, underlies creativity (e.g., Sawyer, 2007; Clapp, 2016). Sawyer (2007), an early investigator of group creativity, argues that all significant innovations stem from invisible collaboration webs.

Skunk Works exemplify creative collaboration. Skunk Works traditionally refer to smaller units within larger organizations that are established (often off-site) to support radical innovation (Bennis and Biederman, 1998). With NDM, domain experts from across the globe are easily connected via ever-improving communication tools. Web 2.0 platforms such as Google Docs, Dropbox, videoconferencing, and online brainstorming boards facilitate remote collaboration. But do Skunk Works work as well without the odor – or is physical presence integral a group's creative chemistry?

Successful online collaborations exemplify what is possible with NDM, though not what is universal. For digital youth, social media creativity most often takes more ordinary forms: witty Instagram comments, playful Snapchat "masterpieces" (so-named by the platform), and clever, socially relevant tweets. The mass of these creative expressions falls below the threshold of little c creativity. (A traditional panel of judges assembled by Teresa Amabile and her colleagues is unlikely to identify the deluge of Snapchat masterpieces as *creative* – though peers with appropriate "app expertise" may be able to reach consensus.) Contemporary teens practice these tiny c forms of social media creativity throughout their daily lives.

Over the last several years, as I conducted interviews and focus groups with dozens of networked youth, I routinely met teens who self-identify as creators. These teens leverage social-networking sites in the service of creative expression. Fifteen-year-old Lily (all names are pseudonyms), for example, has a "meme account" that she uses to remix images with superimposed text; her goal is to produce and share original (novel) posts that will be judged by her peers as humorous, "relevant," and creative. She shares a recent example: a picture of someone who looks dramatically exasperated and Lily's added text, "When you're almost done washing dishes and a sibling comes and puts a spoon in the sink." The post was well received by Lily's followers, as indicated by the immediate influx of likes and comments. Lily is also a painter and shares photographs of her visual artworks through a separate social media account. Throughout the day, she and her friends maintain ongoing Snapchat exchanges of digitally edited images.

Social media provide Lily with a forum to share her offline creative works, as well as a new avenue for creative expression – both of which are common experiences across her peer group. Lily's creativity on social media may certainly escalate into little or middle c creativity; however the bulk of her social media creativity falls in the tiny c category – generated rapidly and forgotten quickly. As Lily's examples reflect, tiny c social media creativity is also often produced in an effort for social connection, rather than as a solitary creative endeavor. Kaufman and Beghetto (2009) propose "mini-c" related to "the genesis of creative expression" (p. 2). Their mini-c includes personally meaningful insights, as well as insights related to development and learning; our tiny c instead refers to digitally enabled creative interactions with and through apps. Kaufman and Beghetto put forth an implicit developmental sequence. In contrast, we impose our "four-C yardstick" in terms of the likelihood that specific ideas and products have or are likely to have significant impact on the domain and/or the field.

Does tiny c creativity go anywhere? Donning a developmental lens, Howard's studies of creators in early times suggest that a novelist is not likely born of tweets. However, when the passion to master (and perhaps tweak) a domain is already in place, NDM provide opportunities for creativity that range from tiny to more substantial. Clarissa (a fantasy fiction writer) and Lily (a painter and meme-creator) find new venues for creativity through social technologies. Clarissa then translates her networked creativity to the offline context when she applies to a writing camp (Pascoe, 2013). Creativity in digital spaces can certainly inspire ongoing work in other domains and contexts. The Harry Potter Alliance, for example, leverages fan fiction as a lens for civic issues in order to empower young creators as activists (Jenkins, 2015).

We began with a question about the consequence of NDM for creativity. The answer depends, in part, on one's view of the construct. Teresa Amabile (2013) describes the difference between Howard's categorical approach to creativity (identifying a few creative individuals) and her continuum approach (assuming people are generally "capable of some degree of creativity in some domain"). If one adopts the categorical view, it makes sense to ask how creative individuals are supported and constrained by life in a digital era. To this end, we describe how NDM shift creators' surrounding contexts in potentially meaningful ways, including the provision of unprecedented access to creative works, peer groups, social support, and avenues for self-promotion. If one adopts the continuum view, a more relevant question is whether creative expression on social apps encourages or delimits people's existing creative tendencies. We argue that everyday creative digital expressions – tweets, snaps, instas, status updates, and the like – reflect tiny c creativity. Whether or not tiny c creativity nudges the app generation toward more creative thinking overall – and we simply don't know whether it does – NDM sizably influence the context for contemporary creativity across domains.

REFERENCES

Amabile, T. M. (2013). Big C, little c, Howard, and me. In *Mind, work, and life: A Festschrift on the occasion of Howard Gardner's 70th birthday*, edited by M. Kornhaber and E. Winner, 5–22. Cambridge, MA: published via Amazon. Available for free at https://howardgardner01.files.wordpress.com/2012/06/festschrift-_-volumes-1-2-_-final.pdf.

Bennis, W., and Biederman, P. W. (1998). None of us is as smart as all of us [creative collaborations]. *Computer*, 31(3), 116–117.

Campbell, J., Aragon, C., Davis, K., Evans, S., Evans, A., and Randall, D. (2016). Thousands of positive reviews: Distributed mentoring in online fan communities. In *Proceedings of the 19th ACM Conference on Computer-Supported Cooperative Work and Social Computing*, 691–704. New York: ACM.

Clapp, E. P. (2016). *Participatory creativity: Introducing access and equity to the creative classroom*. New York: Routledge.

Csikszentmihaly, M. (1988). Society, culture, and person: A systems view of creativity. In *The nature of creativity*, edited by R. J. Sternberg, 325–339. New York: Cambridge University Press.

Deloitte (2016). 2016 Global mobile consumer survey: US edition. www2.deloitte.com/us/en/pages/technology-media-and-telecommunications/articles/global-mobile-consumer-survey-us-edition.html.

Gardner, H. (1973). *The arts and human development*. New York: John Wiley.

(1983). *Frames of mind: The theory of multiple intelligences*. New York: Basic Books.

(1993). *Creating minds: An anatomy of creativity seen through the lives of Freud, Einstein, Picasso, Stravinsky, Eliot, Graham, and Gandhi*. New York: Basic Books.

(1995). *Leading minds*. New York: Basic Books.

(1997). *Extraordinary minds*. New York: Basic Books.

(1999). *The disciplined mind*. New York: Simon and Schuster.

(2011). *Truth, beauty, and goodness reframed*. New York: Basic Books.

Gardner, H., Csikszentmihalyi, M., and Damon, W. (2001). *Good work: When excellence and ethics meet*. New York: Basic Books.

Gardner, H., and Davis, K. (2013). *The app generation: How today's youth navigate identity, intimacy, and imagination in a digital world*. New Haven, CT: Yale University Press.

Gruber, H. (1981). *Darwin on man*. Chicago: University of Chicago Press.

Habuchi, I. (2005). Accelerating reflexivity. In *Personal, portable, pedestrian: Mobile phones in Japanese life*, edited by M. Ito, D. Okabe, and M. Matsuda, 165–182. Cambridge, MA: MIT Press.

Ito, M., Gutierrez, K., Livingston, S., Penuel, B., Rhodes, J., Salen, K., Schor, J., Sefton-Green, J., and Watkins, S. C. (2013). *Connected learning: An agenda for research and design*. Irvine, CA: Digital Media and Learning Research Hub.

Jenkins, H. (2015). "Cultural acupuncture": Fan activism and the Harry Potter alliance. In *Popular media cultures*, 206–229. London: Palgrave Macmillan UK.

Kaufman, J. C., and Beghetto, R. A. (2009). Beyond big and little: The four c model of creativity. *Review of General Psychology*, 13(1), 1.

Keinanen, M., and Gardner, H. (2004) Vertical and horizontal mentoring for creativity. In *Creativity: From potential to realization*, edited by R. J. Sternberg, E. Grigerenko, and J. L. Singer, 169–193. Washington, DC: American Psychological Association.

Li, J. (1997). Creativity in horizontal and vertical domains. *Creativity Research Journal*, 10(2–3), 107–132.

Marwick, A. (2015). You may know me from YouTube: (Micro)-celebrity in social media. In *A companion to celebrity*, edited by P. D. Marshall and S. Redmond, 333–350. Hoboken, NJ: John Wiley.

Microsoft (2015). *Attention spans*. Consumer Insights Report. Microsoft Canada.

O'Reilly, T. (2005). What is Web 2.0 [Web log comment]. September 20. www.oreilly.com/pub/a/web2/archive/what-is-web-20.html.

Pascoe, C. J. (2013). Case study 1: Clarissa: Connecting interests with academic success. In *Connected learning: An agenda for research and design*, edited by M. Ito, K. Gutierrez, S. Livingston, B. Penuel, J. Rhodes, K. Salen, J. Schor, J. Sefton-Green, and S. C. Watkins, 10–11. Irvine, CA: Digital Media and Learning Research Hub.

Peppler, K. (2013). Social media and creativity. In *Routledge international handbook of children, adolescents, and media*, edited by D. Lemish, 193–200. New York: Routledge.

Sawyer, K. (2007). *Group genius: The creative power of collaboration*. New York: Basic Books.

Simonton, D. K. (2004). *Creativity and science*. New York: Cambridge University Press.

Turkle, S. (2011). *Alone together: Why we expect more from technology and less from each other*. New York: Basic books.

Weinstein, E. (2014). The personal is political on social media: Online civic expression patterns and pathways among civically engaged youth. *International Journal of Communication*, 8, 210–233.

Weinstein, E., and Selman, R. L. (2016). Digital stress: Adolescents' personal accounts. *New Media and Society*, 18(3), 391–409.

CHAPTER 8

I Never Intended to Become a Research Psychologist

Beth A. Hennessey

I never intended to become a research psychologist. In fact, as an under-graduate, I'd believed that psychology was a waste of time. I took only one college course on the subject, sneaking into a Child Development class despite not having the prerequisites. My ultimate goal in college was to prepare for a career as an elementary school teacher. After graduation, I worked as an apprentice at the Shady Hill School in Cambridge, Massachusetts, and earned my master's degree in elementary education. Then I traveled to Denver to teach in what was termed an Integrated Day class-room – an "open" environment that combined kindergarten, first grade, and second grade. Under this system, students stayed in my classroom for three years, and I was privileged to be able to witness the amazing developmental progression that happens as children mature from ages five to seven.

As I went on in teaching, however, I became more and more worried about my students' motivation and creativity – or better said, their lack thereof. As kindergartners, they were raring to go. Their imaginations ran wild. They were enthusiastic about almost anything I suggested and came up with fantastic solutions to problems. But many of those same children, by the time they finished second grade, had lost that willingness to take risks and try new things. I started worrying about what it was about my classroom, or classrooms in general, that slowly but surely was killing students' motivation and creativity.

Physically, my classroom looked like I was doing everything that I could to promote my children's interest and exploration. I had cozy reading areas and fabulous math manipulative materials. Children wrote and illustrated their own stories and constructed elaborate marble chutes that taught them about the physics of movement and acceleration. They experimented with batteries and bulbs, learned about circuits, built with hammers and nails. But something wasn't right. My students' love of learning, along with their creativity and imagination, were dying right before my eyes. So, with youthful optimism, I decided to go back to graduate school and figure things out. Now, more than thirty years later, I am still engaged in that investigative process – just as energized, maybe even more so, as when I started out. Moving back and forth between conducting experimental studies and constructing ever more detailed models and theories, my colleagues and I now have a great deal to offer educators interested in promoting the motivation and creativity of their students.

Decades of carefully conducted research have revealed a great deal about how teachers and the climates they create in their classrooms can impact student learning and motivation. Perhaps most important of all, we now recognize the pivotal role that motivation plays in learning. What I didn't realize when I was teaching young children but what I well understand now is that a classroom is far more than just the sum of its activity areas or materials. Like every teacher, I was sending subtle but powerful messages to my students about what kinds of learning and behavior I believed were important, valuable, and "good." If I were to go back and again teach in that school, the classroom routines, assignments, and activities I would put in place would look very different from what I did decades ago. And I would pay far more attention to my students' motivational orientation.

The Motivation/Creativity Connection

Educational and psychological theorists, myself included, generally distinguish between two types of motivation: intrinsic and extrinsic. Intrinsic motivation is the motivation to do something for its own sake. Children driven by intrinsic motivation engage in an activity because they really want to, for the sheer pleasure and enjoyment of the task itself. Extrinsic motivation, on the other hand, is the motivation to do something for some external goal, such as the receipt of a reward made contingent on task engagement, for example to receive a good grade or money. Cognitive psychologists have demonstrated that an intrinsically motivated state is characterized by deeply focused attention, enhanced cognitive functioning, and increased and persistent activity. Simply stated, intrinsic motivation leads to deeper thinking and better connected, more long-lasting learning (Flink, Boggiano, and Main, 1992; Gottfried, 1990; Hidi, 1990; Lepper and Cordova, 1992; McGraw and McCullers, 1979; Tobias, 1994), and for this reason, an intrinsically motivated orientation is something that every teacher at all grade levels must strive to engender in the classroom and in their students. My own primary interest in the motivation of students stems from the fact that intrinsic task interest is also directly tied to creativity of performance.

In graduate school, I studied under the direction of Teresa Amabile, one of the most influential creativity theorists and researchers of our time. Dr. Amabile's research and theorizing have made a particular impact in the areas of creativity, innovation, and entrepreneurship in the workplace (see Chapter 1 in this volume). Years ago, when I was studying with her, much of her attention was focused on educational settings. Central to that foundational work was Amabile's Intrinsic Motivation Principle of Creativity: for young and old alike, intrinsic motivation is conducive to creativity and extrinsic motivation is almost always detrimental (Amabile, 1996).

My own professional life has been dedicated to the question of how we can best structure classrooms so that they are optimally conducive to the development of student intrinsic motivation and creativity. In fact, while still a fledgling educator in Denver, I had already become convinced that a teacher's primary job was to develop and nurture students' creativity. Creativity is what moves civilizations forward; without creativity, we will never be able to solve this world's many, seemingly intractable problems. According to one recent estimate, 65 percent of children starting elementary school today will, in decades to come, find themselves employed in completely new job types that don't even yet exist (World Economic Forum, 2016). Now more than ever before, what is needed is a workforce equipped with the creative thinking skills and flexibility required to deal with the onslaught of disruptive change forecasted by economists and observers of industry and the business world. As a society, we have an obligation to prepare students for this reality. But perhaps equally importantly, the opportunity to exercise creativity brings joy and meaning to our lives.

Importantly, creativity extends far beyond musical performance, the visual arts, or theater and dance. Creativity is also at the heart of scientific study, medical practice, and computer coding. In fact, creativity is, or should be, at the core of most every occupation, avocation, or worthwhile endeavor. Despite the ubiquity of creativity, it is not at all an easy phenomenon to assess. Many researchers and theorists choose to focus on the creative process, but my own work operationalizes creativity in terms of the fruit of that process – the creative product. Although the steps leading up to the generation of a creative outcome are both fascinating and essential, on a practical level, it is much easier as a researcher to concentrate on the tangible outcomes of the creative process. Products can be compared, judged, and scrutinized. Creative processes, on the other hand, are ephemeral, very much internal phenomena that can only be inferred.

The model upon which my own research work and that of my colleagues is based says that there is a direct link between the motivational orientation brought by an individual to a task and their likelihood of creativity of performance on that task; and it is the environment, or at least certain aspects of the environment, that in large part determine that motivational orientation. Each of the studies with which I have been involved is built upon the premise that certain social and environmental characteristics (factors like how a teacher presents a project to students or how various classroom incentive systems are set up) can have a profound effect upon motivation. We have found that motivation is a delicate entity: It can be easily destroyed. That in itself is bad news. I'm sure every teacher and student would rather approach each day's work with excitement and an eagerness to learn. But what is even perhaps more disturbing is that, without intrinsic motivation, students won't perform to their potential. All aspects of their work will suffer – including their creativity.

Creativity in the Classroom

My training as a social psychologist reminds me that each of us is constantly being bombarded by all sorts of environmental influences that can serve to either promote or kill our intrinsic motivation and directly impact the quality of our performance. In a basic research paradigm, study participants who have been randomly assigned to either constraint or no-constraint conditions (e.g., expected reward or no reward) produce some sort of observable product that can be assessed for creativity. Their motivational orientation is also measured. Almost all of my empirical investigations have been carried out in actual classroom settings, rather than under more highly monitored laboratory conditions. Of course, there are important trade-offs here. Investigators gathering data in the field lose the ability to control many of the extraneous variables that might impact their study results. I've had to scrap more than one study when a well-meaning teacher mistakenly divulged to her students or their parents that their creativity was being measured. And I cannot count the times I've shown up at a school only to be told that, as it turns out, the children will not be available due to an unforeseen event such as a schoolwide assembly or the long-awaited hatching of the eggs in a classroom incubator. Investigators who choose to do their work in the field lose control on a number of levels: but for me, that loss is more than compensated for by the added validity that comes from gathering data in real-world settings.

The first empirical study I was involved in while still a novice graduate student serves as a concrete example of the kind of research I do (Amabile,

Hennessey, and Grossman, 1986, study 1). This investigation was carried out in a fourth-grade classroom with the goal of determining the effect of an expected reward on students' subsequent intrinsic task motivation and creativity of performance. Children were randomly assigned to a reward or a no-reward group and each met individually with me, the experimenter. The reward offered was the opportunity to play with an "instant" Polaroid camera. Children assigned to the reward condition signed a contract and promised to later tell a story in order to first have a chance to use the camera. Children in the no-reward condition were simply allowed to use the camera and then were presented with the storytelling instructions; there was no contingency established between the picture-taking activity and the creativity assessment task. Instead, the picture taking was presented along with the storytelling as one in a series of fun things to do.

For the storytelling procedure, the children were asked to tell a story into a tape recorder to accompany a set of illustrations in a book with no words (see Hennessey and Amabile, 1988). But how are investigators like myself to decide whether stories produced by study participants working under the expectation of reward are more or less creative than products made by persons in a control/no-reward condition? In my own work, the answer to this dilemma has been to rely on the consensual assessment of experts. In fact, consensual assessment has been employed in studies of creativity since the 1960s (see MacKinnon, 1962). Other early adopters of this methodology include Getzels and Csikszentmihalyi (1976), Helson and Crutchfield (1970), Kruglanski, Friedman, and Zeevi (1971), and MacKinnon (1962). But the popularity and refinement of this approach can, in large part, be credited to the work of Amabile (1982). In fact, in recent years, Amabile's consensual assessment technique, or CAT for short, has been termed by some as the "gold standard" of creativity assessment (Baer and McKool, 2009, 2014; Carson, 2006).

Although product creativity may be difficult to define, creativity is something that we recognize and agree upon when we see it. Hundreds of investigations employing this methodology have demonstrated that panels of independent expert raters, persons who have not had the opportunity to talk with one another or with the researcher about possible hallmarks of product creativity, are well equipped to make judgments about the creativity of products. More than thirty years of research have, in fact, clearly established that product creativity can be reliably and validly assessed based on the consensus of experts. Drawing from the work of Amabile (1996), the consensual assessment technique (CAT) is grounded on two complementary definitions of creativity. The underlying conceptual definition states that a product will be judged as creative to the extent that (1) it is both a novel and appropriate, useful, correct, or valuable response to an open-ended task; (2) the operational, or consensual, definition upon which the CAT is based makes it especially applicable to empirical research: a product or response is creative to the extent that appropriate observers agree it is creative. Appropriate observers are those familiar with the domain in which the product was created (Hennessey, Amabile, and Mueller, 2011).

The creativity "experts," the raters in this picture-taking investigation (Amabile, Hennessey, and Grossman, 1986), were elementary school teachers familiar with the kinds of products produced by children in this age group. The majority of these judges did not know one another, and they were not permitted to confer with one another prior to or during the rating process. Using seven-point scales and guided only by their own, subjective definitions of creativity, teacher-judges were asked to rate the stories relative to one another rather than against some abstract norm. In this investigation, as has been the case with every study with which I have been involved, interrater agreement was high. Results showed a highly statistically significant difference between groups – for example, with the stories told by children in the control/no-reward condition rated as significantly more creative than the stories told by children who had contracted to tell a story in order for the opportunity to use the camera. These differences could NOT be explained away by chance – something other than chance was operating here – namely, the classroom conditions under which the children were working. Correlational analyses went on to reveal a pattern suggesting a relation between intrinsic interest and creativity: Story creativity scores were significantly, positively correlated with measures of time spent with the target book during a subsequent free-play period. In other words, children who produced the more creative stories were far more likely to choose to revisit the picture book a second time. Moreover, when asked if the storytelling had felt more like work or like play, study participants were more likely to describe the task as work if they had been offered a reward for their participation and more likely to label it as play if no reward was offered.

Importantly, all children in this investigation had the chance to take pictures and tell a story. The only difference in the experience of the rewarded and nonrewarded children was their *perception* of the picture-taking task. For those children who looked at the opportunity to use the camera as a reward contingent on their promise to tell a story, intrinsic task motivation and creativity suffered. As it turns out, the promise of a reward is not the only extrinsic environmental constraint that has been found to undermine task motivation and creativity. Countless empirical studies, carried out by myself and others, reveal five "sure-fire" killers of intrinsic task motivation and creativity of performance. Expected reward, expected evaluation, time limits, surveillance, and competition have all been shown to kill intrinsic motivation and creativity. The most deleterious extrinsic constraint of them all may well be situations of competition, perhaps because competitions often combine aspects of each of the other "killers" – in competitions, a reward is at stake, performance is evaluated to determine who is the winner, time limits are imposed, and others are frequently watching (see Hennessey, 2004, 2013a, 2013b, 2017).

Expected reward, expected evaluation, time limits, surveillance, competition. Unbelievably, this list reads very much like the recipe for the typical classroom – a realization that has for decades deeply concerned me. In my own Denver classroom those many years ago, I thought I was doing my students a favor by instituting a variety of reward and evaluation systems. I believed I was motivating them to become more immersed in their work, to experiment and try new things. I now know better. After spending decades conducting studies demonstrating what teachers who value intrinsic task motivation and creativity must *not* do, I eventually came to the point where I wondered how I might turn this message around. I would like nothing better than to think that schools will change – that the emphasis on grades, standardized test scores, and competition will lessen and be replaced with opportunities for students of all ages to collaborate, take risks, experiment with ideas, and immerse themselves in difficult questions and problems that really interest them. But old habits die hard. If anything, US schools in the last two decades have seen an increased reliance on a one-size-fits-all curriculum (see Hennessey, 2015b).

Immunizing against the Negative Effects of Reward

Over time, I found myself asking whether, rather than change the harsh realities of the classroom, we might change how students react to those realities. In a series of three related investigations, my colleagues and I were guided by a medical metaphor. We decided to look at extrinsic constraints as a kind of germ or virus and wondered whether it might be possible to "immunize" children against the usually negative effects of extrinsic contraints on intrinsic motivation and creativity. Our goal was twofold: (1) to strengthen intrinsic motivation and (2) to provide antibodies (techniques) for fighting the negative effects of extrinsic motivation.

In the first of these research attempts (Hennessey, Amabile, and Martinage, 1989, study 1), elementary school students were randomly assigned to intrinsic motivation focus or control groups and met with an experimenter over two consecutive days for the purpose of viewing videos and engaging in directed discussion. The tapes shown to students in the intrinsic motivation focus condition depicted two eleven-year-olds talking with an adult about various aspects of their schoolwork. Scripts for this condition were constructed so as to help children focus on the intrinsically interesting, fun, and playful aspects of a task. Ways to make even the most routine assignment exciting were suggested, and participants were helped to distance themselves from socially imposed extrinsic constraints such as rewards or situations of competition. Tapes shown to students in the control condition featured the same two young actors talking about some of their favorite things, including foods, music groups, movies, and seasons.

Following this training procedure, all students met individually with a second adult for testing. As in the previous study described earlier, half of the children in each of the training conditions were told that they could take two pictures with an instant camera only if they promised to later tell a story for the experimenter. For children in the no-reward conditions, this picture taking was presented simply as the first in a series of "things to do." It was expected that only those participants who had been specifically instructed in ways to overcome the usual deleterious effects of extrinsic constraints would maintain baseline levels of intrinsic motivation and creativity in situations of expected reward (i.e., they would be immunized against the negative effects of extrinsic constraints). The data from this initial investigation not only confirmed these expectations but gave us reason to believe that our intervention had much more of an impact than we had expected. Intrinsic motivation-trained children tended to report higher levels of intrinsic motivation on a paper-and-pencil assessment than did children in the control (no-training) condition; in addition, we found that the offer of reward actually augmented the creativity of the trained group. This additive effect of intrinsic and extrinsic motivation was quite robust. In fact, the creativity of children who received intrinsic motivation training and expected a reward was significantly higher than that of any other design group.

In our initial discussion of these immunization study results, we hypothesized that children who entered the creativity testing situation after having undergone intrinsic motivation training would have a much more acute awareness of their own intrinsic interest in school-type tasks and their already positive feelings about the tasks they were doing would be heightened. In two follow-up investigations of our intrinsic motivation focus techniques (Hennessey, Amabile, and Martinage, 1989, study 2; Hennessey and Zbikowski, 1993), it was again the children who had received immunization training and who were expecting a reward who produced the most creative products. Yet, in these follow-up studies, the effect of training was far less dramatic. Taken together, the results of studies 2 and 3 indicate that we cannot expect that children exposed to our intrinsic motivation training and offered a reward for their performance will demonstrate unusually high levels of creativity. Nevertheless, we can expect that these children will be able to maintain baseline levels of intrinsic motivation and creativity under reward conditions.

Importantly, other researchers have piggybacked off of our original experimental paradigm and have reported somewhat parallel results (e.g., Gerrard, Poteat, and Ironsmith, 1996). Most recently, a study focused on the impact of creativity training on professional design engineers in the workplace (Burroughs, Dahl, Moreau, Chattopadhyay, and Gorn, 2011) showed that products produced when both training and rewards were provided were judged to be significantly more creative than products developed under any of the other experimental conditions. Yet in the absence of training, the expectation of reward undermined creative performance.

Storytelling

I remember in graduate school being worried that I would one day run out of interesting research ideas to explore. Now, my concerns are just the opposite. Will I live long enough to answer even a small fraction of the burning questions that continue to fuel my passion for research? Every study with which I have been involved has generated new and fascinating directions for further investigation. Moreover, as my research program has progressed, I have become more and more interested in the methods that my colleagues and I employ to investigate the issues that interest us. Take the storytelling task, for example. I based that test of children's verbal creativity on a literacy activity I had used in my own classroom in Denver. Now, many years later, not only does the storytelling task continue to serve my own research needs, but it also has been adopted by a wide variety of other investigators as well. Russ and colleagues frequently incorporate storytelling in their studies of pretend play (e.g., Fehr and Russ, 2016; Hoffman and Russ, 2012; Russ, Robins, and Christiano, 1999) and a variety of other investigators have adopted this methodology to explore everything from domain specificity (Han, 2003) to the relation between elaborated role play and creativity (Mottweiler and Taylor, 2014).

Exploring the Consensual Assessment Technique

In recent years, the mechanisms behind the consensual assessment of products have also come to capture my attention. For decades, my colleagues and I have been especially well served by the CAT. Without exception, each investigation employing the CAT with which I have been involved has yielded high levels of interrater reliability. But how is it that teacher-judges or other "experts," persons who neither receive training from experimenters nor confer with one another, consistently agree about the relative creativity of products? In an effort to explore the underpinnings of the consensual assessment process, I have carried out a variety of studies. In a series of four related investigations (Hennessey, 1994), I found that (1) judges were able to reliably assess not only the creativity of a finished product but also the creativity of the process that went into producing that product; (2) ratings of process and product creativity tend to be highly correlated; (3) information about the age of a creator can significantly affect judges' subjective assessments. A number of other researchers (see especially work carried out by Baer, Kaufman, and colleagues, e.g., Baer, Kaufman, and Gentile, 2004; Kaufman, Baer, Agars, and Loomis, 2010) have also taken a careful look at what it is that judges do when they are asked to assess the relative creativity of products. For me, one of the most exciting features of the CAT is that it has proven to be especially useful for studies of creativity across cultures. Because investigative paradigms employing the CAT focus on the production of real-world, tangible products that are rated by persons who share the cultural and societal background of the individuals doing the creating, a multiplicity of practical and theoretical problems and biases typically associated with cross-national investigations are avoided (see Hennessey, Kim, Guomin, and Sun, 2008).

Creativity across Cultures

Importantly, cross-cultural considerations of creativity are fraught with a number of methodological and theoretical challenges that reach far beyond the issue of how best to assess the creativity of products. Everything we think we understand about creativity and the creative process is socioculturally dependent. Creativity and culture are inextricably linked. In fact, in a 2014 chapter, my colleague Beth Altringer and I argued that creativity might best be viewed as an important vehicle for cultures to advance their purposes (Hennessey and Altringer, 2014). Conclusions about whether our own or others' ideas, artworks, or inventions are important, creative, and worthy of attention are very much based on cultural norms and values, as are the ways that individuals (or groups) are socialized to react to the imposition of extrinsic constraints such as rewards or evaluations. Creativity cannot be separated from the societal and cultural contexts in which it arises. Taking this view even further, a small group of theorists (e.g., Karkhurin, 2014) have recently argued that Western conceptions of creativity must be complemented with Eastern views that include considerations of authenticity, morality, aesthetics, and the quest to fit into the existing paradigms rather than an overarching need to break with tradition.

At long last, researchers and theorists are coming to the realization that the study of creativity without a consideration of culture is incomplete (at best). In my estimation, the majority of the more comprehensive and exciting contemporary investigations of the interface between creativity and culture have been carried out in workplace settings. But a few investigators and theorists, myself included, have also set their sights on classrooms. In my own research, I've begun to ask whether the infamous killers of motivation and creativity (reward, evaluation, time limits, surveillance, and competition) can be expected to have the same deleterious effects in classrooms in China, Saudi Arabia, or Turkey that they have in the United States or other Western nations (see Hennessey [2015a] for an exploration of Saudi classrooms). Isolated investigations comparing data gathered in the United States against data gathered in other nations are not nearly enough. What is needed is a comprehensive systems perspective incorporating a consideration of creative behavior at multiple levels of analysis. Creativity must be explored at the "little c" cultural level (e.g., the culture of the classroom or workplace), at the societal level, and at the "Big C" cultural level (i.e., culture writ large). The construction of such systems models is difficult and highly complex. My own first attempt at such model building incorporates a consideration of creative behavior, motivation, environment and culture (Hennessey, 2015a).

Trickle down

Importantly, in my mind, no amount of theorizing, model building, or methodological refinement is worth much of anything unless this work can be helped to trickle down in a meaningful way to educational stake holders: teachers, administrators, curriculum developers, policy makers, and parents. In the thirty-five years that I have been engaged in the research process, I have spoken with thousands of parents and educators about the undeniable link between intrinsic motivation and creativity of performance, as well as the killers of motivation that are routinely built into the school day. My audiences, most especially classroom teachers, nod their heads in agreement. They know in their heart of hearts that the research findings I present make sense, but they feel overwhelmed by the prospect of trying to fight an educational system that is both entrenched in tradition and increasingly driven by bureaucratic one-size-fits-all prescriptions. The major impetus behind the immunization studies was, in fact, the overwhelming and paralyzing sense of hopelessness that so many classroom teachers have expressed to me over the years. In my experience as a researcher, it has always been far easier to demonstrate how to kill intrinsic motivation and creativity than it has been to show how motivation and creative behavior might be maintained or even promoted. The immunization research allowed me to offer a concrete list of changes that did not necessitate sweeping curricular or policy reform–changes that teachers interested in preserving the intrinsic motivation and creativity of students could implement in their own classrooms.

In fact, throughout my research career, I have frequently made a conscious effort to step back to examine the real-world import of my research findings. I have repeatedly considered in conversations with educators and in my published writing what a classroom designed to promote student motivation and creativity would look like and have offered a number of practical suggestions as to how teachers might effect important and lasting change in their own classrooms (see Hennessey, 2004, 2013a, 2015b, 2017). In a nutshell, these recommendations boil down to the supreme importance of giving students the gift of time, ample time, to immerse themselves in seemingly intractable problems and challenges. Students of all ages need and deserve time and license to make mistakes, hit dead ends, and pick themselves up to try again. Students need time to persevere and to collaborate with one another. Students need time to learn to trust their intuitions even in the face of failure (see Hennessey, 2015b).

In many respects, my own research findings as well as those of many of my colleagues call for a return to the open-classroom model. The "open" terminology has traditionally been used to describe a student-centered classroom design made popular in the United States in the 1970s. This educational innovation originated in the British public elementary ("infant") schools after World War II and spread slowly to the United States. In the classic open-classroom environment, students moved freely and at their own pace from "station" to "station" – exploring reading skills, hands-on science experiments, mathematical manipulatives, and art materials. I was trained in this approach; but, unfortunately, like many other American teachers and administrators who set out to duplicate the highly successful British educational innovation, I concentrated almost entirely on the *visible* hallmarks of the open classroom, the physical trappings rather than instilling in my students an understanding of the fundamental importance of finding joy in learning, of taking intellectual risks, of identifying and then following one's passions, and of being driven by genuine curiosity rather than the promise of reward, the threat of evaluation, or the fear of making mistakes in front of one's peers.

To discount open classrooms as merely another ideological fad that has come and gone would negate the deeper message of the Open Education Movement. Children really do learn best when they are genuinely interested in and see the importance of what they are doing, and their creativity is dependent on this intrinsic interest as well. Educators did not get things exactly right in the 1970s. But their message rings as true today as it did some three or four decades ago.

REFERENCES

Amabile, T. M. (1982). The social psychology of creativity: A consensual assessment technique. *Journal of Personality and Social Psychology*, 43, 997–1013.
    (1996). *Creativity in context*. Boulder, CO: Westview.
Amabile, T. M., Hennessey, B. A., and Grossman, B. (1986). Social influences on creativity: The effects of contracted-for reward. *Journal of Personality and Social Psychology*, 50, 14–23.
Baer, J., Kaufman, J. C., and Gentile, C. A. (2004). Extension of consensual assessment technique to nonparallel creative products. *Creativity Research Journal*, 16, 113–117.
Baer, J. S., and McKool, S. (2009). Assessing creativity using the Consensual Assessment Technique. In C. Schreiner (Ed.), *Handbook of research on assessment technologies, methods, and applications in higher education* (pp. 65–77). Hershey, PA: IGI Global.
    (2014). The gold standard for assessing creativity. *International Journal of Quality Assurance in Engineering and Technology Education*, 3, 81–93.
Burroughs, J. E., Dahl, D. W., Moreau, P., Chattopadhyay, A., and Gorn, G. J. (2011). Facilitating and rewarding creativity during new product development. *Journal of Marketing*, 75, 53–67.
Carson, S. (2006). Creativity and mental illness. Invitational panel discussion hosted by Yale's Mind Matters Consortium, New Haven, CT, April 19.
Fehr, K. K., and Russ, S. W. (2016). Pretend play and creativity in preschool-age children: Association and brief intervention. *Psychology of Aesthetics, Creativity, and the Arts*, 10, 296–308.
Flink, C., Boggiano, A. K., and Main, D. S. (1992). Children's achievement-related behaviors: The role of extrinsic and intrinsic motivational orientations. In

Achievement and motivation: A social-developmental perspective, edited by A. K. Boggiano and T. S. Pittman, 189–214. New York: Cambridge University Press.

Gerrard, L. E., Poteat, G. M., and Ironsmith, M. (1996). Promoting children's creativity: Effects of competition, self-esteem and immunization. *Creativity Research Journal,* 9, 339–346.

Getzels, J. B., and Csikszentmihalyi, M. (1976). *The creative vision: A longitudinal study of problem finding in art.* New York: John Wiley.

Gottfried, A. E. (1990). Academic intrinsic motivation in young elementary children. *Journal of Educational Psychology,* 82, 525–538.

Han, K.-S. (2003). Domain-specificity of creativity in young children: How quantitative and qualitative data support it. *Journal of Creative Behavior,* 37, 117–142.

Helson, R., and Crutchfield, R. (1970). Mathematicians: The creative researcher and the average PhD. *Journal of Consulting and Clinical Psychology,* 34, 250–257.

Hennessey, B. A. (1994). The consensual assessment technique: An examination of the relationship between ratings of process and product creativity. *Creativity Research Journal,* 7, 193–208.

(2004). *Developing creativity in gifted children: The central importance of motivation and classroom climate.* NRCG/T Senior Scholar Series RM04202. Storrs, CT: National Research Center on the Gifted and Talented.

(2013a). Cultures of creativity: Nurturing creative mindsets across cultures – a toolbox for teachers. In *Cultures of creativity,* edited by D. Gauntlett and B. S. Thomsen. Billund, Denmark: The Lego Foundation. www.legofoundation.com/en-us/research/research-articles/.

(2013b). Motivation is everything. In *The creative imperative: School librarians and teachers cultivating curiosity together,* edited by J. Jones and L. Flint, 85–95. Santa Barbara, CA: Libraries Unlimited.

(2015a). Creative behavior, motivation, environment and culture: The building of a systems model. *Journal of Creative Behavior,* 49(3), 194–210.

(2015b). If I were secretary of education: A focus on intrinsic motivation and creativity in the classroom. *Psychology of Aesthetics, Creativity, and the Arts,* 9, 187–192.

(2017). Intrinsic motivation and creativity in the classroom: Have we come full circle? In *Nurturing creativity in the classroom,* 2nd ed., edited by R. A. Beghetto and J. C. Kaufman, 227–264. New York: Cambridge University Press.

Hennessey, B. A., and Altringer, B. A. (2014). Creativity across cultures. In *Creativity: Theory and practice from psychological perspectives* [in Swedish], edited by I. Carlsson and E. Hoff, 233–254. Stockholm: Liber.

Hennessey, B. A., and Amabile, T. M. (1988). Story-telling: A method for assessing children's creativity. *Journal of Creative Behavior,* 22, 235–246.

Hennessey, B. A., Amabile, T. M., and Martinage, M. (1989). Immunizing children against the negative effects of reward. *Contemporary Educational Psychology,* 14, 212–227.

Hennessey, B. A., Amabile, T. M., and Mueller J. S. (2011). Consensual assessment. In *Encyclopedia of creativity*, vol. 1, 2nd ed., edited by M. A. Runco and S. R. Pritzker, 253–260. San Diego, CA: Academic Press.

Hennessey, B. A., Kim, G., Guomin, Z., and Sun, W. (2008). A multi-cultural application of the consensual assessment technique. *International Journal of Creativity and Problem Solving*, 18, 87–100.

Hennessey, B. A., and Zbikowski, S. M. (1993). Immunizing children against the negative effects of reward: A further examination of intrinsic motivation training techniques. *Creativity Research Journal*, 6, 297–307.

Hidi, S. (1990). Interest and its contribution as a mental resource for learning. *Review of Educational Research*, 60, 549–571.

Hoffman, J., and Russ, S. (2012). Pretend play, creativity, and emotion regulation in children. *Psychology of Aesthetics, Creativity, and the Arts*, 6, 175–184.

Karkhurin, A. V. (2014). Creativity.4in1: Four-criterion construct of creativity. *Creativity Research Journal*, 26, 338–352.

Kaufman, J. C., Baer, J., Agars, M. D., and Loomis, D. (2010). Creativity stereotypes and the consensual assessment technique. *Creativity Research Journal*, 22, 200–205.

Kruglanski, A., Friedman, E., and Zeevi, G. (1971). The effects of extrinsic incentives on some qualitative aspects of task performance. *Journal of Personality*, 39, 606–617.

Lepper, M. R., and Cordova, D. T. (1992). A desire to be taught: Instructional consequences of intrinsic motivation. *Motivation and Emotion*, 16, 187–208.

MacKinnon, D. W. (1962). The nature and nurture of creative talent. *American Psychologist*, 17, 484–495.

McGraw, K. O., and McCullers, J. (1979). Evidence of a detrimental effect of extrinsic incentives on breaking a mental set. *Journal of Experimental Social Psychology*, 15, 285–294.

Mottweiler, C. M., and Taylor, M. (2014). Elaborated role play and creativity in preschool age children. *Psychology of Aesthetics, Creativity, and the Arts*, 8, 277–286.

Russ, S. W., Robins, A. L., and Christiano, B. A. (1999). Pretend play: Longitudinal prediction of creativity and affect in fantasy in children. *Creativity Research Journal*, 12, 129–139.

Tobias, S. (1994). Interest, prior knowledge and learning. *Review of Educational Research*, 64, 37–54.

World Economic Forum (2016). Executive summary: The future of jobs and skills. Retrieved from www3.weforum.org/docs/WEF_Future_of_Jobs.pdf.

CHAPTER 9

What Creativity Can Be, and What Creativity Can Do

James C. Kaufman

If I look back at my first two decades in creativity research, I think that much of what I have done and what I want to do centers around two primary questions that compose the title of this chapter: What can creativity be? What can creativity do? They are simple questions but each one forces us to rethink the basic parameters of how we consider creativity.

What Can Creativity Be?

When I first discovered creativity, I was a third-year graduate student with a summer to go through a long reading list. The books I devoured were broadly broken into two camps. Some discussed everyday creativity, touching on how our mind creates (Finke, Ward, and Smith, 1992), what social environments best align for creativity (Amabile, 1996), and how people can try to be more creative in their own lives (Sternberg and Lubart, 1995). Others sought to learn from creative geniuses (Csikszentmihalyi, 1997; Gardner, 1993; Simonton, 1994). Without ever articulating this dichotomy, I became interested in both aspects. Some of my early work examined eminent writers (Kaufman, 2001a, 2001b, 2003, 2005a; Kaufman and Baer, 2002b), whereas other studies looked at student writers (Baer, Kaufman, and Gentile, 2004; Kaufman, 2002; Kaufman, Gentile, and Baer, 2005).

As I began collaborating with Ron Beghetto, the eminent-everyday split (often called little-c and Big-C) felt too limiting. What happens to people just starting out? Someone designing her first scientific experiment or writing his first play would be called little-c by default because there was no other type of description. Even creativity researchers did not bother distinguishing between the nine-year-old playing with different colors, the neophyte college freshman drawing in his room, the aspiring artist showing her work in local coffee houses, and the young professional eking out a living by selling his paintings. They were all little-c, with Big-C reserved for Rembrandt or Van Gogh. Such a labeling issue may seem semantic, yet the implications were very real. Words impact how we think. If a teacher, parent, or friend is unconsciously accepting a "Monet-or-bust" mentality, then beginners get overly punished and young professionals are still lumped with amateurs.

We first proposed the idea of mini-c, or individual creativity (Beghetto and Kaufman, 2007, 2009), which represented the personally meaningful insights that inspired people. A mini-c idea might not be appreciated by others; it might not even be spoken aloud. But it matters. With appropriate mentorship, struggle, and understanding of one's strengths and weaknesses (Beghetto and Kaufman, 2013, 2014; Kaufman and Beghetto, 2013b), mini-c can be recognized by others. It is now little-c, the everyday creativity that is widely understood and studied.

Even with the new construct, we felt that something was missing. Big-C was for legends – the creators who end up studied in school or on postage stamps. What about everything that does not quite reach that level? Where do we put those who may be destined to be footnotes or even forgotten, yet whose creativity brings pleasure, gathers acclaim, and is considered impressive in their time? We thus proposed Pro-C, or expert-level creativity (Kaufman and Beghetto, 2009, 2013a; Kaufman, Beghetto, Baer, and Ivcevic, 2010).

The Four-C model of creativity has been widely adopted around the world; perhaps most gratifying has been seeing people expand their conceptions of what creativity can be. A child learning how to solve an algebraic proof or a retiree taking up the clarinet are creative, and it "counts." Debating the exact number of Cs or focusing on the gaps in the model (e.g., Beghetto and Kaufman, 2015) is beside the point; I don't care if there are 4 Cs or 400. The important thing, to me, is that nearly anyone can be creative.

One of my other areas of work reflects this interest in helping people find their voice. I can no longer count the number of students I have had sit in my office or classroom and insist that they are not creative. They have this self-doubt because they view creativity as being inherently artistic. Because they cannot draw, write, perform, or play music, they see themselves as uncreative. With John Baer, I have long been interested in highlighting how all domains can be creative (Kaufman and Baer, 2002a, 2004a, 2006). This line of research is often framed as the question of domain specificity versus domain generality – in other words, whether creativity can be expressed as a general trait or ability or whether being creative in one domain requires its own of requirements that differ from being creative in a different domain.

Can you legitimately call someone "creative," implying that she will be more creative than other people across most areas?

I find this particular debate less interesting, perhaps because over the last decade the field has converged in the middle. Our own theoretical contribution to this issue has been our Amusement Park Theory (Baer and Kaufman, 2005, 2017; Kaufman and Baer, 2004b, 2005, 2006). We begin with some initial requirements for creativity that are true for anything (enough intelligence and motivation, along with a tolerant environment). There are then general thematic areas, which are broad categories of interests that may draw someone's interest early in life. These are one way of trying to establish a structure of creativity, much the same way that intelligence theories propose a core set of cognitive processes and abilities. Yet intelligence theories argue that a truly smart person would excel at many (if not most) categories (which, depending on the theory, might include acquired knowledge, practical intelligence, planning ability, or bodily kinesthetic intelligence). In contrast, people are unlikely to succeed at too many different general thematic areas because of their discrepant focus.

I have done several self-report studies on this topic (Kaufman, 2006, 2012; Kaufman, Cole, and Baer, 2009; Kaufman et al., 2009) and found anywhere from four to nine areas. There is usually an everyday general thematic area, which entails the type of real-life creative actions that most of us can do. Other common areas are visual arts, creative writing, performance, and mathematics/science; sometimes, business, humor, sports, and academic scholarship have been included. Under each general thematic area are many different domains. Creative writing, for example, might include poetry, plays, fiction, and nonfiction (among others), whereas performance might encompass dancing, singing, acting, and many more. Under domains are microdomains, which are subspecialties. Poetry might have sonnet, haiku, free verse, quatrains, limericks, and many others.

In addition to offering a way of consider the basic structure of creativity, the Amusement Park Theory also tries to highlight domains or microdomains that might be overlooked. Perhaps the students who continue to insist they are not creative might change their mind if they see a creativity model that include their own areas of strength, whether money management or event planning or designing board games.

I continue to be interested in highlighting all of the different ways and areas that people can create. My work with David Cropley and colleagues focuses on how being evil might be a potential creative domain (Cropley, Kaufman, and Cropley, 2008; Cropley, Kaufman, White, and Chiera, 2014). Some of my work with current and former students has explored the role of intelligence, personality, and motivation in creativity (Avitia and Kaufman, 2014; Davis, Kaufman, and McClure, 2011; Kaufman, Pumaccahua, and Holt, 2013). With my wife, Allison, I've moved beyond people to focus on animal creativity (A. Kaufman and Kaufman, 2014; A. Kaufman, Butt, Colbert-White, and Kaufman, 2011; Kaufman and Kaufman, 2006). Yet in a broader sense, I have slowly been drawn to a different question: What can creativity do?

What Can Creativity Do?

Taking a step back to think about the actual worth of the construct you study (whether it is a protein, eighteenth-century poet, or ancient language) can feel strange. Everyone contributing to this book presumably thinks that creativity is important. It is a reasonable assumption that nearly everyone reading this book has a similar viewpoint. But the world does not.

My first job after graduate school was working for a big testing company. Relatively early in my employment, I thought I saw a way to measure creativity using a test we were already using. Excited, I burst into my boss's office and told him of how we might be about to assess creativity. His two-word response changed my life: "So what?"

My boss had not spent the last several years immersed in the glow of discovering the joys of creativity research. He faced innumerable possible constructs that our company measured, wanted to measure, or could measure. We were driven by the market, and no one was clamoring for a new creativity test. More importantly, if one looked at the field objectively, there was scant reason to motivate such a demand.

Schools and organizations tended to claim at least passive benevolence (regardless of their actual, more nuanced implicit beliefs). But creativity scholars – both then and now – tend to focus on what leads to creativity. This research can be in the form of examining the creative process or problem solving, looking at individual traits and abilities associated with higher creativity, or studying the environments that best nurture innovation. These are all incredibly important activities – please do not interpret what follows as any type of attack on this work. But there is little in these studies to convince a nonbeliever that creativity is worth investment. Most creativity studies use the construct as a dependent variable, or something to be predicted (Forgeard and Kaufman, 2016).

The other type of research, which is a much smaller percentage of our work, explores how creativity helps predict or enhance desired, positive outcomes. Are creative people happier or more productive? Do creative products sell better? Are creative organizations more productive? There are certainly many, many studies that suggest the answer is yes (for a review, see Kaufman, 2016). But there is not a compelling body of research to help support these ideas in the same way (for example) we have thoroughly investigated the creative problem-solving process or creative personality.

One of the positive outcomes I have become fascinated by over the last decade is social change and equity. My interest began with discussions with my colleague Gwyneth Boodoo about the concept of fairness. I then received a fortuitous invitation from Cecil Reynolds to write a chapter on nonbiased assessment (Kaufman, 2005b); he helped me distinguish different types of potential bias as I wrote and discovered the literature. In this chapter, I began exploring the idea of using creativity as a supplement to other criteria or assessments (I was certainly not the first to use this approach; see, e.g., Sternberg, 2008).

I also began conducting studies that examined gender and ethnic differences in creativity. In measures of creative performance, there were typically no differences (Kaufman, Baer, and Gentile, 2004; Kaufman, Niu, Sexton, and Cole, 2010; see also Baer and Kaufman, 2008). For self-reported creativity, African Americans were often higher than Caucasians (Kaufman, 2006; Ivcevic and Kaufman, 2013). We also found evidence, incidentally, that bisexuals rated their creativity higher than both heterosexuals and homosexuals (Ben-Zeev, Dennehy, and Kaufman, 2012).

The consistent thread to me was that a lot of underrepresented groups had a potential strength that was not being recognized. Creativity is largely absent on standardized tests (Kaufman, 2010; Sternberg and Kaufman, 2018) and IQ tests (Kaufman, 2015; Kaufman, Kaufman, and Lichtenberger, 2011), and even gifted programs which include creativity often do not measure it effectively (Kaufman, Plucker, and Russell, 2012; Luria, O'Brien, and Kaufman, 2016). I am definitely not the first to advocate for creativity to be included in admissions (Sternberg, 2010), nor do I think that the road ahead will be easy.

My hope, however, is to approach the issue from many different angles. Working with students and colleagues, I am trying to discuss this question of how creativity can be used for social good from angles of social justice, educational policy, technology, law, theater, and many other disparate fields.

It is easy to look at the world around us and feel discouraged. There are so many ways in which society seems to be regressing or ready to explode

130

or implode on itself. As I get older, I need my life's work to have meaning –
or at least to have the potential of having meaning. As much as I am still
interested in what creativity can be, I want to follow this question of what
creativity can do. If creativity can continue to evolve into a mechanism or
tool that can give voice and strength to others, then at least there is one
positive direction that the world will be moving toward.

REFERENCES

Amabile, T. M. (1996). *Creativity in context: Update to "The social psychology of creativity."* Boulder, CO: Westview Press.

Avitia, M. J., and Kaufman, J. C. (2014). Beyond g and c: The relationship of rated creativity to long-term storage and retrieval (glr). *Psychology of Aesthetics, Creativity, and the Arts*, 8, 293–302.

Baer, J., and Kaufman, J. C. (2005). Bridging generality and specificity: The Amusement Park Theoretical (APT) model of creativity. *Roeper Review*, 27, 158–163.

(2008). Gender differences in creativity. *Journal of Creative Behavior*, 42, 75–106.

(2017). The Amusement Park Theoretical model of creativity: An attempt to bridge the domain specificity/generality gap. In *Cambridge handbook of creativity across different domains*, edited by J. C. Kaufman, V. P. Glăveanu, and J. Baer (pp. 8–17). New York: Cambridge University Press.

Baer, J., Kaufman, J. C., and Gentile, C. A. (2004). Extension of the consensual assessment technique to nonparallel creative products. *Creativity Research Journal*, 16, 113–117.

Ben-Zeev, A., Dennehy, T. C., and Kaufman, J. C. (2012). Bisexual versus lesbian and heterosexual women's self-assessed creativity. *Journal of Bisexuality*, 12, 347–359.

Beghetto, R. A., and Kaufman, J. C. (2007). Toward a broader conception of creativity: A case for "mini-c" creativity. *Psychology of Aesthetics, Creativity, and the Arts*, 1, 13–79.

(2009). Intellectual estuaries: Connecting learning and creativity in programs of advanced academics. *Journal of Advanced Academics*, 20, 296–324.

(2013). Fundamentals of creativity. *Educational Leadership*, 70, 10–15.

(2014). Classroom contexts for creativity. *High Ability Studies*, 25, 53–69.

(2015). Promise and pitfalls in differentiating amongst the C's of creativity. *Creativity Research Journal*, 27, 240–241.

Cropley, D. H., Kaufman, J. C., and Cropley, A. J. (2008). Malevolent creativity: A functional model of creativity in terrorism and crime. *Creativity Research Journal*, 20, 105–115.

Cropley, D. H., Kaufman, J. C., White, A. E., and Chiera, B. A. (2014). Layperson perceptions of malevolent creativity: The good, the bad, and the ambiguous. *Psychology of Aesthetics, Creativity, and the Arts*, 8, 400–412.

Csikszentmihalyi, M. (1997). *Creativity: Flow and the psychology of discovery and invention*. New York: HarperCollins.

Davis, C. D., Kaufman, J. C., and McClure, F. H. (2011). Non-cognitive constructs and self-reported creativity by domain. *Journal of Creative Behavior*, 45, 188–202.

Finke, R. A., Ward, T. B., and Smith, S. M. (1992). *Creative cognition: Theory, research, and applications*. Cambridge, MA: MIT Press.

Forgeard, M. J. C., and Kaufman, J. C. (2016). Who cares about imagination, creativity, and innovation, and why? A review. *Psychology of Aesthetics, Creativity, and the Arts*, 10, 250–269.

Gardner, H. (1993). *Creating minds*. New York: Basic Books.

Ivcevic, Z., and Kaufman, J. C. (2013). The can and cannot do attitude: How self estimates of ability vary across ethnic and socioeconomic groups. *Learning and Individual Differences*, 27, 144–148.

Kaufman, A. B., Butt, A. B., Colbert-White, E. N., and Kaufman, J. C. (2011). Towards a neurobiological model of creativity in nonhuman animals. *Journal of Comparative Psychology*, 125, 255–272.

Kaufman, A. B., and Kaufman, J. C. (2014). Applying theoretical models on human creativity to animal studies. *Animal Behavior and Cognition*, 1, 77–89.

Kaufman, J. C. (2001a). Genius, lunatics, and poets: Mental illness in prize-winning authors. *Imagination, Cognition, and Personality*, 20, 305–314.

(2001b). The Sylvia Plath effect: Mental illness in eminent creative writers. *Journal of Creative Behavior*, 35, 37–50.

(2002). Narrative and paradigmatic thinking styles in creative writing and journalism students. *Journal of Creative Behavior*, 36, 201–220.

(2003). The cost of the muse: Poets die young. *Death Studies*, 27, 813–822.

(2005a). The door that leads into madness: Eastern European poets and mental illness. *Creativity Research Journal*, 17, 99–103.

(2005b). Non-biased assessment: A supplemental approach. In *Children's handbook of multicultural school psychology*, edited by C. L. Frisby and C. R. Reynolds, 824–840. New York: John Wiley.

(2006). Self-reported differences in creativity by gender and ethnicity. *Journal of Applied Cognitive Psychology*, 20, 1065–1082.

(2010). Using creativity to reduce ethnic bias in college admissions. *Review of General Psychology*, 14, 189–203.

(2015). Why creativity isn't in IQ tests, why it matters, and why it won't change anytime soon . . . probably. *Journal of Intelligence*, 3, 59–72.

(2016). *Creativity 101*. 2nd ed. New York: Springer.

Kaufman, J. C., and Baer, J. (2002a). Could Steven Spielberg manage the Yankees? Creative thinking in different domains. *Korean Journal of Thinking and Problem Solving*, 12, 5–15.

(2002b). I bask in dreams of suicide: Mental illness and poetry. *Review of General Psychology*, 6, 271–286.

(2004a). Sure, I'm creative – but not in mathematics! Self-reported creativity in diverse domains. *Empirical Studies of the Arts*, 22, 143–155.

(2004b). The Amusement Park Theoretical (APT) model of creativity. *Korean Journal of Thinking and Problem Solving*, 14, 15–25.

(2005). The Amusement Park theory of creativity. In *Creativity across domains: Faces of the muse*, edited by J. C. Kaufman and J. Baer, 321–328. Mahwah, NJ: Lawrence Erlbaum.

(2006). Intelligent testing with Torrance. *Creativity Research Journal*, 18, 99–102.

Kaufman, J. C., Baer, J., and Gentile, C. A. (2004). Differences in gender and ethnicity as measured by ratings of three writing tasks. *Journal of Creative Behavior*, 38, 56–69.

Kaufman, J. C., and Beghetto, R. A. (2009). Beyond big and little: The four C model of creativity. *Review of General Psychology*, 13, 1–12.

(2013a). Do people recognize the four Cs? Examining layperson conceptions of creativity. *Psychology of Aesthetics, Creativity, and the Arts*, 7, 229–236.

(2013b). In praise of Clark Kent: Creative metacognition and the importance of teaching kids when (not) to be creative. *Roeper Review*, 35, 155–165.

Kaufman, J. C., Beghetto, R. A., Baer, J., and Ivcevic, Z. (2010). Creativity polymathy: What Benjamin Franklin can teach your kindergartener. *Learning and Individual Differences*, 20, 380–387.

Kaufman, J. C., Beghetto, R A., and Watson, C. (2016). Creative metacognition and self-ratings of creative performance: A 4-C perspective. *Learning and Individual Differences*, 51, 394–399.

Kaufman, J. C., Cole, J. C., and Baer, J. (2009). The construct of creativity: A structural model for self-reported creativity ratings. *Journal of Creative Behavior*, 43, 119–134.

Kaufman, J. C., Gentile, C. A., and Baer, J. (2005). Do gifted student writers and creative writing experts rate creativity the same way? *Gifted Child Quarterly*, 49, 260–265.

Kaufman, J. C., and Kaufman, A. B. (2004). Applying a creativity framework to animal cognition. *New Ideas in Psychology*, 22, 143–155.

Kaufman, J. C., Kaufman, S. B., and Lichtenberger, E. O. (2011). Finding creativity on intelligence tests via divergent production. *Canadian Journal of School Psychology*, 26, 83–106.

Kaufman, J. C., Niu, W., Sexton, J. D., and Cole, J. C. (2010). In the eye of the beholder: Differences across ethnicity and gender in evaluating creative work. *Journal of Applied Social Psychology*, 40, 496–511.

Kaufman, J. C., Plucker, J. A., and Russell, C. M. (2012). Identifying and assessing creativity as a component of giftedness. *Journal of Psychoeducational Assessment*, 30, 60–73.

Kaufman, J. C., Pumaccahua, T. T., and Holt, R. E. (2013). Personality and creativity in realistic, investigative, artistic, social, and enterprising college majors. *Personality and Individual Differences*, 54, 913–917.

Kaufman, J. C., Waterstreet, M. A., Ailabouni, H. S., Whitcomb, H. J., Roe, A. K., and Riggs, M. (2009). Personality and self-perceptions of creativity across domains. *Imagination, Cognition, and Personality*, 29, 193–209.

Luria, S. R., O'Brien, R. L., and Kaufman, J. C. (2016). Creativity in gifted identification: Increasing accuracy and diversity. *Annals of the New York Academy of Sciences*, 1377, 44–52.

Simonton, D. K. (1994). *Greatness: Who makes history and why*. New York: Guilford Press.

Sternberg, R. J. (2008). Applying psychological theories to educational practice. *American Educational Research Journal*, 45, 150–165.

(2010). *College admissions for the 21st century*. Cambridge, MA: Harvard University Press.

Sternberg, R. J., and Kaufman, J. C. (forthcoming). Societal forces that ERODE creativity. *Teacher's College Record*.

Sternberg, R. J., and Lubart, T. I. (1995). *Defying the crowd*. New York: Free Press.

CHAPTER 10

Creativity across the Seven Cs

Todd Lubart

During the last quarter of a century, I have been exploring creativity from an individual-differences perspective. The goal has been to grasp the essential nature of *Homo creativus*, which is a new term (from a dead language) that I use to describe the creative facet of the human spirit (Lubart et al., forthcoming). The term *Homo creativus* highlights the fact that humans are, by nature, producing constantly new ideas, actions, and behavioral traces. This novelty is more or less original, given the past productions of the individual (himself or herself), or his/her local social group, or professional field. The productions are also more or less valuable from the perspective, once again, of the individual, the local social context or the larger professional field. In terms of a working definition, creativity is defined as the ability to produce work that is original and valuable in its context. Creativity exists, however, at the interface between an individual (or small group) that produces work, which is more or less appreciated by the producer him/herself, and others in the proximal or distal social world. This approach is essentially relativistic, and interactionist.

The topic of creativity has been receiving increasing attention because it is viewed as a capacity that can contribute to personal development, daily problem solving, occupational success, and societal growth. In this context, creativity is often cited as a twenty-first-century skill, a key attribute for employability, an important ability for job success, and the source of future socially valuable solutions to numerous problems that face humanity. However, the first traces of human creativity can be found millions of years ago, when our ancestors, such as *Homo habilis*, invented the first tools by transforming natural materials such as wood, bone, and stone to facilitate hunting and other daily activities. This creative ability, which characterizes humans and contributes to survival, is present in various degrees for each individual. Examining the nature of these individual differences has led to several lines of research that will be presented briefly in this chapter.

The field of creativity research expanded greatly in the last decades. The four Ps with the creative person, process, product and press – has been, and still is, an organizing representation of the main topics in the field (Rhodes, 1961). Alternative systems have also been proposed. However, looking at the literature and contributions in which I have been involved, a seven-Cs perspective seems to be the most heuristically valuable (Lubart, 2017a). The "Seven Seas" refer historically to the seven main bodies of water on earth, with a metaphorical link between heavenly bodies and oceans on earth. To "sail the seven seas" involved making a complete trip around the earth, or more generally taking a comprehensive approach to a topic. Applied to the field of creativity, it is possible to describe the main lines of research in the field in terms of seven Cs: Creators, Creating, Collaborations, Contexts, Creations, Consumption, and Curricula. Consider each C with some illustrations of research.

Creators. This "C" refers to the people who create. Robert Sternberg and I developed a multivariate approach to creative potential in which we identified the cognitive, conative, emotional, and environmental components that contribute to creative potential (Sternberg and Lubart, 1991, 1995). These components combine in interactive ways to yield an individual's profile, which may be more or less compatible with the requirements for creative work in a domain or task (Lubart, 1999; Lubart, Mouchiroud, Tordjman, and Zenasni, 2015). In this perspective, some task and domain specificity in creative potential is expected, given each individual's personal set of abilities, traits, styles, and circumstances. Additionally, in this model, the wide range of creative output from very low, to moderate, to eminent cases can be understood and modeled through the multiple components and their interactive nature. Creative potential will be put into play when a person engages in a task, through the creative process, and then potential will be expressed in the production. It is possible to detect creative potential and develop creativity. This type of model allows, also, creative giftedness to be understood as a specific configuration of components that "fit" optimally with domain or task requirements leading to very high performance. In addition to the multivariate approach to creative ability, an investment theory was developed in which concepts from the financial domain were used to offer a new perspective on creativity (Sternberg and Lubart, 1995). For example, some people choose actively to invest their resources in a task with potential for original thinking. This investment may take the form of time, energy, or pecuniary resources being devoted to an idea or a project that is initially new, with little value but has growth potential. Strategies that people employ to choose which idea to pursue, the relative value of ideas, the rewards for investing in new ideas, and the opportunity costs of pursuing creative ideas versus more traditional, well-established ones that may offer a lower, but guaranteed result are some of the topics highlighted in the investment approach (Lubart, 1999).

This theoretical work focuses on creative potential and individual differences. Empirical studies were also conducted, such as Lubart and Sternberg (1995), in which adults completed several measures of cognitive and conative components that contribute to creative potential. Participants produced drawings, wrote stories, invented advertisement ideas for products, and offered solutions for societal-scientific problems. These productions were scored for creativity by qualified judges. Multiple regression was used to examine the extent to which individual differences in the cognitive and conative variables account for differences in creative performance. The role of both cognitive and conative variables was observed and there were some interactions between the predictors, with the specific regression models varying from one creative task domain to another. In later work, an expanded set of measures was conceived, with additional measures of cognitive abilities, personality-motivational, emotional and environmental factors, in order to form a tool called the creative profiler (Lubart, Zenasni, and Barbot, 2013). This profiler allows individuals to situate themselves with respect to a reference group who may be their peers, or a criterion-based group of people who have been creative in a certain task or domain.

In terms of children and adolescents, a different measurement approach was taken to assess creative potential. Instead of measuring directly the cognitive and conative components that contribute to creative potential, such as mental flexibility or openness, the alternative is to put individuals in a task situation in which they can provide a sample of their behavior, as if they were in a real task. Thus, the proposed tasks are a simulation of a real work situation, which would inherently be more complex. In this optic, my colleagues and I developed the battery entitled Evaluation of Potential Creativity (EPoC; Lubart, Besançon, and Barbot, 2011). In EPoC, individuals are presented with tasks to accomplish that engage their cognitive, conative, and affective resources in order to show the extent to which they can be creative. The tasks are organized by domain, to reflect the main domains of creative activity in scholastic and professional settings. These domains are: visual arts, verbal literary, social problem solving, scientific, mathematical, musical, and bodily movement. Within each domain, there are two types of tasks. These are divergent-exploratory and convergent-integrative ones, which reflect two modes of the creative process. As an example, in the visual arts domain, a divergent-exploratory task requires individuals to generate many, original drawings that use a shape that is provided. In a convergent-integrative task, individuals are provided with a set of visual stimuli, such as eight photos of objects, and they must make a drawing that includes at last four of the objects. In each measurement domain, there are divergent-exploratory and convergent-integrative tasks, which allow an individual's profile to be described (Barbot, Besançon, and Lubart, 2015, 2016). Using the norms, children and adolescents can also be situated with respect to others from their age group. The EPoC measures are available in several languages (including English, French, German, Arabic, Chinese, Turkish, Portuguese, Polish, and Slovenian) and norms are being developed in numerous countries.

Creating. The creative process is the sequence of thoughts, actions, and events that unfold over time and lead (in most cases) to a new production. Based on a review of the literature, a critical reading of work on the creative process (Lubart, 2000) led me to call into question the classic four-stage model, initially described by Wallas (1926). In addition, the creative process is by nature highly idiosyncratic, but the literature tends to look at the "general" process. These reflections led to theoretical and empirical contributions to process issues.

In terms of theoretical models, work on individual differences in creative potential resulted in a vision of the creative process as a dynamic interplay of two modes of thinking–divergent-exploratory and convergent-integrative modes. In divergent-exploratory thinking, the goal is a rich, expansive production marked by fluency and diversity, whereas in convergent-integrative thinking, the goal is one synthetic production that brings together several elements in a new way. This schematic view of the creative process is not radically different from many previous models and builds on numerous works. It has been a useful framework to think about specific cognitive, personality, emotional, and environmental components that can support each process mode. In addition, I worked on a specific model of creative associative thinking that focused on an individual's emotional experiences. This emotional-resonance model postulates that emotional traces in memory can serve as cues to connect concepts that are cognitively distant but emotionally similar (Lubart and Getz, 1997). As emotional experiences are complex and individualized, this is a potential source of idiosyncratic associations that can enter into the creative process.

In terms of empirical studies, I examined first the extent to which individual differences in the evaluation of ideas during the creative process, by the creators themselves, influences the creativity of the final production. Using both experimental and naturalistic, observational methods, evaluative thinking of work in progress was examined in students who wrote stories and made drawings. Participants evaluated their nascent productions relatively early in the process, relatively later in the process, or in a regular pattern over the process. In the case of short-story creation, early evaluation was related to more creative stories, as evaluated by external judges (Lubart, 2009). No particular pattern of evaluation was related to creativity in the drawing task.

In another, more recent set of studies, the question of tracing the natural creative process in several major domains was investigated (Lubart, forthcoming). This work concerned creators in visual arts, literature, design, music, and engineering domains. In a first set of studies, interviews with recognized creative people from each domain led to rich descriptions of their creative processes which were compared and contrasted (Botella et al., 2013; Glăveanu et al., 2013). Ultimately, a common set of terms was selected and used to construct a notebook-checklist method that allows people to trace their creative process activity over time and visualize the various chains of subprocesses that they follow as they create. The subprocesses include getting information on a topic, defining/redefining the problem, associating ideas, taking a break, and several others. Thus, it is possible to trace process activity, and to compare the traces of those who finally produce a highly creative work with those who produce a less creative work, in a given task. Several studies with advanced students in sculpture, scriptwriting, product and communication design, musical composition, and engineering were conducted (Botella and Lubart, 2016; Bourgeois-Bougrine et al., 2014; Botella, Zenasni, and Lubart, 2011).

When the process traces were compared, systematic differences were found between the more and less creative productions, although the exact nature of the different chains of process activity for the more and less creative students depends on the domain or task. As an example, in the artistic-sculpture task, when students came back from a break, some would start to associate freely or expand on their work in progress, whereas others would take stock of what they had done so far, evaluating their work and reconsidering task constraints or goals. The former tended to produce final sculptures judged as highly creative, whereas the latter tended to produce less original sculptures.

Collaborations. The term collaboration concerns all the social contacts that a creator has with others who participate directly in the creative work. For a creator who is part of a team, collaborations occur with team members. In some cases, a creator develops a special relationship with an external person who may serve as a first audience, a test ground, or someone in whom the creator can confide. Collaborations have been examined extensively in teams in the workplace but also through historical case studies. For example, Vincent Van Gogh, through his interactions and dense correspondence with his brother Theo, received valuable social and financial support. Van Gogh's particularly creative period in Arles was also, in part, a socially enriched phase of his life, thanks to Paul Gaugin's presence. In some previously described work about creative professionals' work process, it is interesting to note that contact with colleagues to get initial feedback on one's work is often viewed as an essential action. This was particularly clear in studies of scriptwriters (Glăveanu et al., 2013; Bourgeois-Bougrine et al., 2014). It may be interesting to add that the topic of collaborations is not necessarily limited to human-human interactions. In particular, a special issue on human-computer interactions led me to reflect on the ways that a computer could support or contribute collaboratively to creative work (Lubart, 2005). A computer with some artificial intelligence capacities can, for example, provide suggestions of sources to explore through keyword search that may be relevant to a task, or the computer may generate randomly new visual forms, new words, or word sequences that may then be selected and reworked by creators. The computer may therefore be considered as a collaborator (see also Burkhardt and Lubart, 2010). Of course, it is also possible to retrace these computational capacities to the source code that a human programmer created, and consider the programmer as a distant collaborator as well.

Contexts. The physical and social worlds provide the context in which creators create. Context has been a major topic of research, covering aspects such as family environment, professional environment, and societal or cultural environment. Some of my first work identified different influences that macro-level cultural variation can have on creativity (Lubart, 1990, 2010). For example, it is possible, to some extent, to identify and contrast "Western" and Eastern » views of creativity; the "Western" perspective is relatively individual-oriented and product-oriented, with a strong emphasis on radical-breakthrough ideas, whereas the "Eastern" perspective places special attention on the authenticity of the creative process, the reuse of existing cultural material in new ways, and the personal meaning attached to creative work. In terms of other cultural influences, there are variations in terms of activity domains that are considered most relevant to creativity (visual arts in some cultures are more emphasized than entrepreneurial creation, for example), or variations in social groups who are identified as those who create. Research on cultural dimensions, such as individualism-collectivism, power distance, and others have been a major source of findings, which have contributed greatly to understand the multilevel impact of culture on creativity (Lubart, Glăveanu, Storme,

Camrago and de Vries forthcoming; Taras, Kirkman, and Steel, 2010). There are additionally some cultural considerations that can be best examined at the organizational, or workplace level. These range from workplace climate to industry or professional domain "culture" (see Glăveanu and Lubart, 2014).

Approximately 99.9 percent of research about the impact of contextual factors has focused to date on real physical environments (such as the wall colors in offices) and the real social world (such as the diversity of team members), which we may call studies of context 1.0, or "reality" studies. For the past four years, my colleagues and I have been investigating the impact of virtual reality work environments on creativity. This research looks at creative thinking in multiuser virtual settings such as a virtual meeting room filled with participants who are represented by avatars. In this reality 2.0, participants try to generate creative ideas. The goal of this work is to examine whether certain environmental conditions impact creative performance in order, possibly, to implement the best features in a real 1.0 world. However, work and nonwork life activities may evolve toward virtualized settings, so reality 2.0 may become a real workspace in the future. In addition to reducing travel time and cost, virtual workspaces offer some features that are hard or impossible to create in standard physical conditions, such as the complete anonymity of each participant. Our team has designed procedures that allow virtual environments to be configured based on people's concepts of creative spaces (Guegan, Nelson, and Lubart, 2017). Also, we have results that show the positive impact of putting participants in creative-looking avatars, which boosts performance in idea generation tasks (Guegan, Buisine, Mantelet, Maranzana, and Segonds, 2016). This line of work opens new horizons within the context "C" of the seven Cs.

Creations. This term refers to the productions that result from creators engaging in the creative process. In the literature, numerous studies have examined the nature of work that leads it to be identified as "creative." In part, a production can be examined in terms of its formal characteristics, such as its statistical rarity compared with other similar works. This leads to studies that compare several ways to score the rarity of ideas, and extract meaningful indices such as mean originality (if a person produces several ideas) (see Mouchiroud and Lubart, 2001). Other work focuses on the implicit definitions that judges use when they evaluate productions for creativity. In this kind of study, interjudge agreement is always partially due to individual differences in the underlying criteria (novelty, value, aesthetic appeal, etc.), or to the relative weights attributed to each of the criteria, differences in the way each criterion is defined or implemented, or differences in background and expertise that each judge brings to the evaluation

(Storme and Lubart, 2012). Some work has examined the extent to which productions evaluated by judges and by formal methods of scoring tend to agree, or disagree. For example, in Lubart, Pacteau, Jaquet, and Caroff (2010), we examined this question using drawings from the TCT-DP test, and found relatively low correlations between these different scoring methods. In other work, Storme, Myszkowski, Celik, and Lubart (2014) examined the extent to which judges can be trained to score drawings and stories for creativity using a seven-point scale that was predefined for them. This work showed that high levels of interjudge agreement can be attained with relatively short training sequences. It was based on this type of work that we designed a judge-training system for the EPoC measures to help novice judges, such as teachers or psychologists with no particular prior experience scoring creativity, to understand quickly the judgment scale, acquire an idea of which kinds of productions get a each score (from 1 to 7), and reliably use the scale.

Consumption. This is the term used to conceptualize the adoption of novel productions by the public, in the "marketplace" of ideas or goods. Thus, this "C" concerns the receptive audience and its characteristics. In the literature, consumption of creative goods has been most studied in terms of adoption behaviors toward new products, such as buying novel technology items, literary works as opposed to classic works, listening to new music rather than well-established clips or groups, and being an early adopter of new services. However, consumption of creative "goods" can be conceived in a much broader way; for example, research on reactions to Charles Darwin's theory of evolution presented to the Royal Scientific Society showed that older, more established scientists were more critical of the new theory compared with younger scientists. Perhaps this difference may be attributed to vested interests that experts have in maintaining the status quo in their field.

A study that illustrates this "C" involving behavioral economics and economic psychology was conducted in our research group by Tavani, Caroff, Storme, and Collange (2016); adolescents were offered the opportunity to listen to music clips that were more or less "new" or "known." As listening time was limited, participants had to choose what they wanted to hear, and in some cases the "price" of each music clip was varied, within the listening session when participants had listening credits to use. The tendency to listen to original music was related to participants openness trait scores, but also to their own creativity as measured in creative production tasks. However, there were additional effects of "word-of-mouth" recommendations, and variation in price which allowed certain news clips to be tested for very few listening credits.

It is interesting to note that consumption can be, sometimes, itself a creative act because consumers bring something to the product, adapting it in some unexpected way and making it meaningful in their life. Thus, consumption of a novel production can be an act of co-creation. For example, Harley Davidson owners are known for their customizations of their motorcycles, which render their bikes unique and valuable. In addition, some of these ideas are later adopted for new models of Harleys. In work by Decotter, Burkhardt, Lubart, and Gonguet (2017), this kind of creative consumption was studied using a technological invention that was just entering the market at the time. A very small, transportable, "picoprojector," was presented to participants; it could be connected to a smartphone or computer, allowing videos to be projected onto any surface in a local way. Conditions in which consumers discovered this new invention, either in their home context or in a demonstration lab, either alone or in a group of other potential consumers, influenced the emergence of ideas that they had on how to use the new product.

Curricula. One of the major topics in the literature on creativity is how to teach and develop creativity. In children and adults, the question of the enhancement of creativity is important and has a potentially strong societal impact. In some work, the link between pedagogy and creative thinking was examined; Besançon and Lubart (2008) looked at children in France in traditional elementary schools and alternative schools. The alternative education focused on active learning, with both Montessori-inspired (private schools) or Freinet schools. Freinet was a French teacher who developed an active pedagogy in the public school system. Children from kindergarten to fifth grade participated in the study, with different children from each school grade tested in a cross-sectional design. All schools were matched on socioeconomic characteristics. Children completed a set of divergent-exploratory and convergent-integrative creative thinking tasks. In this study, it was hypothesized that students starting in kindergarten or first grade would all be similar in creative thinking but years of exposure to the pedagogical approach would have an effect. Cross-sectional data supported this concept because mean performance was very similar for younger elementary students, regardless of the pedagogical approach, but differences in performance on specific creative thinking tasks, notably divergent thinking tasks involving well-known objects, were found in the upper elementary grades in favor of children in alternative pedagogies.

In general, there are several avenues that can be pursued to favor the development of creative ability, both in children and adults (Besançon and Lubart, 2015; Besançon, Lubart, and Barbot, 2013). First, people may be offered opportunities to develop the "ingredients" of creativity, such as experiences that foster openness, situations that help develop risk taking, or exercises that require mental flexibility. Second, it is possible to provide role models through teachers' or team leaders' behaviors in which creative thinking is engaged, and this serves to inspire others to do the same. Third, it is possible to teach creative thinking techniques or methods, which people may use during their work. This last tradition has been widely used by consultants in business settings to foster creative thinking, and is the basis of methods such as creative problem solving (CPS; see Puccio, Firestien, Coyle, and Masucci, 2006). In order to foster individualized training, focusing on the most relevant attributes to be developed and the most useful creativity techniques to help a given person to be creative, we have used the creative profiler tool (Lubart, Zenasni, and Barbot, 2013). When an individual's profile of cognitive and conative components for creativity is measured and then compared to an ideal profile, certain components can be identified for further development, and certain creativity techniques that may be most relevant can be trained. The ideal profile is based on a task analysis and the use of reference groups of people who show high creative performance in a certain task or job (Caroff and Lubart, 2012). For example, being creative in a design task may require a high level of mental flexibility whereas being creative in a poetry task is particularly related to metaphorical thinking. These task characteristics can be used to identify key aspects in each individual's profile that may benefit from training.

Conclusion

Creativity is a vast topic. This chapter provides a synthetic view of work on creativity within a novel seven-C framework. In general, the work presented here draws on differential psychology, with a focus on intraindividual, interindividual, and naturally occurring group (cultural) differences. Illustrations of theoretical and empirical work on each C were drawn mainly from my own work, which was conducted collaboratively with numerous colleagues.

REFERENCES

Barbot, B., Besançon, M., and Lubart, T. (2015). Creative potential in educational settings: Its nature, measure, and nurture. *Education 3–13*, 43(4), 371–381.

(2016). The generality-specificity of creativity: Exploring the structure of creative potential with EPoC. *Learning and Individual Differences*, 52, 178–187.

Besançon, M., and Lubart, T. I. (2008). Differences in the development of creative competencies in children schooled in diverse learning environments. *Learning and Individual Differences*, 18, 381–389.

(2015). *La créativité de l'enfant (Children's creativity)*. Bruxelles: Mardaga.

Besançon, M., Lubart, T., and Barbot, B. (2013). Creative giftedness and educational opportunities. *Educational and Child Psychology*, 30(2), 79–88.

Botella, M., Glăveanu, V., Zenasni, F., Storme, M., Myszkowski, N., Wolff, M., and Lubart, T. (2013). How artists create: Creative process and multivariate factors. *Learning and Individual Differences*, 26, 161–170.

Botella, M., and Lubart, T. (2016). Creative processes: Art, design and science. In *Multidisciplinary contributions to the science of creative thinking*, edited by G. Corazza and S. Agnoli, 53–65. Singapore: Springer.

Botella, M., Zenasni, F., and Lubart, T. (2011). A dynamic and ecological approach to the artistic creative process of arts students: An empirical contribution. *Empirical Studies of the Arts*, 29(1), 17–38.

Bourgeois-Bougrine, S., Glăveanu, V., Botella, M., Guillou, K., De Biasi, P. M., and Lubart, T. (2014). The creativity maze: Exploring creativity in screenplay writing. *Psychology of Aesthetics, Creativity, and the Arts*, 8(4), 384–399.

Burkhardt, J.-M., and Lubart, T. (2010). Creativity in the age of emerging technology: Some issues and perspectives in 2010. *Creativity and Innovation Management*, 19(2), 160–166.

Caroff, X., and Lubart, T. I. (2012). Multidimensional approach to detecting creative potential in managers. *Creativity Research Journal*, 24(1), 13–20.

Decotter, D., Burkhardt, J.-M., Lubart, T., and Gonguet, A. (2017). The technology probe approach to support latent need analysis and creativity in design. Unpublished manuscript.

Glăveanu, V. P., and Lubart, T. (2014). Decentering the creative self: How others make creativity possible in creative professional fields. *Creativity and Innovation Management*, 23(1), 29–43.

Glăveanu, V., Lubart, T., Bonnardel, N., Botella, M., de Biaisi, P.-M., Desainte-Catherine, M., Georgsdottir, A., Guillou, K., Kurtag, G., Mouchiroud, C., Storme, M., Wojtczuk, A., and Zenasni, F. (2013). Creativity as action: Findings from five creative domains. *Frontiers in Psychology*, 4, Article 176.

Guegan, J., Buisine, S., Mantelet, F., Maranzana, N., and Segonds, F. (2016). Avatar-mediated creativity: When embodying inventors makes engineers more creative. *Computers in Human Behavior*, 61, 165–175.

Guegan, J., Nelson, J., and Lubart, T. (2017). The relationship between contextual cues in virtual environments and creative processes. *Cyberpsychology, Behavior, and Social Networking*, 20(3), 202–206.

Lubart, T. I. (1990). Creativity and cross-cultural variation. *International Journal of Psychology*, 25, 39–59.

(1999). Componential models of creativity. In *Encyclopedia of creativity*, edited by M. A. Runco and S. Pritzer, 295–300. New York: Academic Press.

(2000). Models of the creative process: Past, present and future. *Creativity Research Journal*, 13(3–4), 295–308.

(2005). How can computers be partners in the creative process? *International Journal of Human Computer Studies*, 63(4–5), 365–369.

(2009) Creative writing process. In *Psychology of creative writing*, edited by J. Kaufman and S. Kaufman, 149–165. Cambridge: Cambridge University Press.

(2010). Cross-cultural perspectives on creativity. In *The Cambridge handbook of creativity*, edited by J. C. Kaufman and R. J. Sternberg, 265–278. New York: Cambridge University Press.

(2017). The 7 C's of creativity. *Journal of Creative Behavior*. 51(4), 293–296.

(Ed.). (forthcoming). *The creative process across five domains*. New York: Palgrave Macmillan.

Lubart, T. I., Besançon, M., and Barbot, B. (2011). *EPoC: Evaluation of potential creativity*. Paris: Hogrefe.

Lubart, T., Botella, M., Caroff, X., Mouchiroud, C., Nelson, J., and Zenasni, F. (Eds.). (forthcoming). *Homo creativus*. Singapore: Springer.

Lubart, T. I., and Getz, I. (1997). Emotion, metaphor, and the creative process. *Creativity Research Journal*, 10(4), 285–301.

Lubart, T. I., Glaveanu, V., Storme, M., Camargo, A. and de Vries, H. (forthcoming). Creativity from a cultural perspective. In *The Cambridge handbook of creativity*, 2nd ed., edited by R. J. Sternberg and J. C. Kaufman. New York: Cambridge University Press.

Lubart, T., Mouchiroud, C., Tordjman, S., and Zenasni, F. (2015). *Psychologie de la créativité* [Psychology of creativity]. 2nd ed. Paris: Armand Colin.

Lubart, T. I., Pacteau, C., Jaquet, A. Y., and Caroff, X. (2010). Children's creative potential: An empirical study of measurement issues. *Learning and Individual Differences*, 20, 388–392.

Lubart, T. I., and Sternberg, R. J. (1995). An investment approach to creativity: Theory and data. In *The creative cognition approach*, edited by S. Smith, T. Ward, and R. Finke, 271–302. Cambridge, MA: MIT Press.

Lubart, T. I., Zenasni, F., and Barbot, B. (2013). Creative potential and its measurement. *International Journal of Talent Development and Creativity*, 1(2), 41–51.

Mouchiroud, C., and Lubart, T. I. (2001). Children's original thinking: An empirical examination of alternative measures. *Journal of Genetic Psychology*, 162(4), 382–401.

Puccio, G., Firestien, R. L., Coyle, C., and Masucci, C. (2006). A review of the effectiveness of CPS training: A focus on workplace issues. *Creativity and Innovation Management*, 15(1), 19–33.

Rhodes, M. (1961). An analysis of creativity. *The Phi Delta Kappan*, 42(7), 305–310.

Sternberg, R. J., and Lubart, T. I. (1991). An investment theory of creativity and its development. *Human Development*, 34, 1–31.

(1995). *Defying the crowd: Cultivating creativity in a culture of conformity*. New York: Free Press.

Storme, M., and Lubart, T. (2012). Conceptions of creativity and relations with judges' intelligence and personality. *Journal of Creative Behavior*, 46(2), 138–149.

Storme, M., Myszkowski, N., Celik, P., and Lubart, T. (2014). Learning to judge creativity: The underlying mechanisms in creativity training for non-expert judges. *Learning and Individual Differences*, 32, 19–25.

Taras, V., Kirkman, B. L., and Steel, P. (2010). Examining the impact of culture's consequences: A three-decade, multilevel, meta-analysis. *Journal of Applied Psychology*, 95(3), 405–439.

Tavani, J.-L., Caroff, X., Storme, M., and Collange, J. (2016). Familiarity and liking for music: The moderating effect of creative potential and what predict the market value. *Learning and Individual Differences*, 52, 197–203.

Wallas, G. (1926). *The art of thought*. New York: Harcourt, Brace, and Jovanovich.

CHAPTER II

Creative Thinking in the Real World
Processing in Context

*Michael D. Mumford, Robert Martin, Samantha Elliott,
and Tristan McIntosh*

Creativity has been defined in different ways by different scholars (Weisberg, 2015). Mumford and Gustafson (1988, 2007) have provided what has, perhaps, become one of the more widely accepted definitions of creativity. They hold that creativity involves the production of original, high-quality, and elegant solutions to a certain class of problems – novel, complex, and ill-defined, or poorly structured, problems (Mumford, Medeiros, and Partlow, 2012). The production of original, high-quality, and elegant solutions to complex, novel, ill-defined problems, is of some real practical interest. R&D departments exist to produce such problem solutions (Hemlin, 2009), creative problem solving is crucial for social innovation (Mumford, 2002), and it has been shown to be critical for economic growth above baseline (e.g., population, capital) expectations (Florida, 2002).

As an industrial and organizational psychologist interested in the assessment and development of high-level talent, much of my work has, over the last forty years, focused on creative problem solving. Broadly speaking, this work has sought to address two critical questions. One question was primarily substantive in nature – how do people go about solving the kinds of problems that call for creative thought? The other question was primarily pragmatic in nature – what attributes of firms encourage creative problem solving? In the present effort, we will examine the research my colleagues and I have conducted that we hope provides, at least, a partial answer to these two questions – one substantive and one practical.

Creative Problem Solving

Processes

Traditionally, people's ability to solve the kinds of problems that call for creative thought had been explained through a single ability – divergent thinking (Guilford, 1950; Merrifield, Guilford, Christensen, and Frick,

1962). Divergent thinking reflects the ability to generate multiple ideas to novel problems (e.g., what would happen if gravity was cut in half?). Although evidence is available for the validity of divergent thinking measures in accounting for creative problem solving (Vincent, Decker, and Mumford, 2002), one can argue divergent thinking per se cannot provide a complete understanding of creative problem solving. Remember a single, high-quality solution to a novel, complex, ill-defined problem may result in a noteworthy valuable, new product (Mumford and Mulhearn, 2015).

In my early work on eminent individuals (e.g., Nobel Prize winners), it had become apparent that creative achievement, an outcome of creative problem solving, only occurred after people had spent sufficient time in a field to acquire adequate expertise (Mumford, 1984). Expertise, however, provides only a necessary condition for creative problem solving. What is as critical, if not more critical, is how people work with this expertise to generate creative problem solutions. This observation is in no way unique. And, over the years, many models of the key mental operations – cognitive processes – involved in incidents of creative problem solving have been proposed (e.g., Dewey, 1910; Parnes and Noller, 1972; Sternberg, 1986; Wallas, 1926).

My colleagues and I (Mumford, Mobley, Reiter-Palmon, Uhlman, and Doares, 1991) reviewed the various models of creative problem-solving processes that had been proposed over the years. The model resulting from this review is presented in Figure 11.1. Basically, this model holds that eight key processing activities are involved in most incidents of creative problem solving: (1) problem definition, (2) information gathering, (3) concept selection, (4) conceptual combination, (5) idea generation, (6) idea evaluation, (7) implementation planning, and (8) solution monitoring. Effective execution of each of these processes was held to depend on problem-relevant knowledge and strategies for working with this knowledge during process execution. Moreover, these processes were held to operate in an interdependent, dynamic fashion. Thus, the products of problem definition determine the success of information gathering activities just as the products of conceptual combination determine the success of idea generation, with people cycling back to earlier processes, typically the preceding process, when process outputs were found to be inadequate.

We subsequently initiated a series of some twenty experimental studies intended to establish the validity of each of these processing activities. For example, Baughman and Mumford (1995) and Mobley, Doares, and Mumford (1992) have provided evidence for the impact of conceptual combination on creative problem solving. In these studies, participants

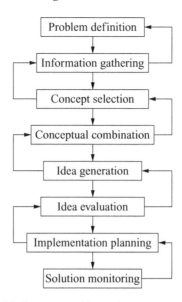

Figure 11.1 Model of creative problem-solving processes

were presented with three concepts defined by four exemplars (birds: owls, sparrows, robins, ostriches; or sporting equipment: bat, gloves, ball, oar). Participants were asked to combine these concepts to generate a new concept subsuming the presented exemplars, provide a label for this new concept, list additional exemplars of the new category, and write a story using this new category. Products were evaluated by judges for quality and originality. Instructional manipulations were used to influence how participants worked to combine categories. It was found that mapping of shared and nonshared features contributed to the production of more creative products.

In another study of information gathering, Mumford, Baughman, Supinski, and Maher (1996) asked participants to provide solutions to creative problems drawn from the public policy and business domains where judges appraised problem solutions for quality and originality. Prior to providing these problem solutions, participants were asked to work on a card reading task, where they were presented with various types of information–factual, diverse, irrelevant, inconsistent information, and time spent reading this information was recorded. It was found that solutions of the highest quality and originality were provided by those participants who spent more time reviewing key facts *and* anomalies – findings pointing to the importance of information gathering.

In still another study, Lonergan, Scott, and Mumford (2004) asked study participants to assume the role of a manager in a marketing firm. As a manager, they were to review the ideas provided by marketing teams and then prepare their own campaign. Judges appraised these campaigns for quality, originality, and elegance. Notably, the ideas presented to participants, drawn from an earlier study by Redmond, Mumford, and Teach (1993), were of varying quality and originality, and participants were asked to appraise the ideas presented with respect to different standards – operating efficiency or innovation standards. It was found that the most creative problem solutions (those of the highest quality, originality, and elegance) were obtained when they evaluated highly original ideas with respect to efficiency or high quality ideas with respect to innovation requirements. Thus, idea evaluation is not only a matter of appraising ideas, but appraising ideas in such a way as to improve them.

Other work by Licuanan, Dailey, and Mumford (2007); Mumford, Baughman, Supinski, and Maher (1996); Mumford, Supinski, Threlfall, and Baughman (1996); Osburn and Mumford (2006); Redmond, Mumford, and Teach (1993); and Reiter-Palmon, Mumford, and Threlfall (1998) has provided evidence for the operation of other processes–problem definition, concept selection, idea generation, and implementation planning, as distinct processes contributing to the promotion of high-quality and original solutions to various novel, complex, ill-defined problems drawn from various domains. Other work by Mumford, Supinski, Baughman, Costanza, and Threlfall (1997) has shown that effective execution of each of these processes makes a unique contribution to predicting the quality, originality, and elegance of creative problem solutions. Work by Vincent, Decker, and Mumford (2002) has shown effective process execution mediates between basic abilities (e.g., divergent thinking, intelligence) and performance on creative problem-solving tasks. Still, other work by Connelly et al. (2000), Mumford et al. (2005), and Zaccaro et al. (2015) has shown that effective execution of these processes is related to real-world performance on jobs calling for creative problem solving – not only producing positive relationships in the 0.40s but relationships that hold up over a twenty-year period.

All this evidence points to the validity of Mumford, Mobley, Reiter-Palmon, Uhlman, and Doares's (1991) model of the creative problem-solving process. Perhaps the most substantively important evidence for the validity of this model has been provided in a study by Friedrich and

Mumford (2009). Some 250 participants were asked to work on a marketing problem calling for creative thought where judges appraised problem solutions for quality, originality, and elegance. As participants worked through the problem solutions, "emails" presenting conflicting information with the general problem scenario were presented with the conflicting information being induced at different points with respect to execution of different processes (e.g., problem definition, information gathering). The conflicting information presented was intended to induce errors in process execution. In keeping with this process model, it was found that that disruption of earlier processes, for example problem definition, resulted in poorer performance in execution of subsequent processing activities. Thus, the flow-through features of the Mumford, Mobley, Reiter-Palmer, Uhlman, and Doares (1991) model seems to hold.

Knowledge

As noted earlier, Mumford, Mobley, Reiter-Palmon, Uhlman, and Doares's (1991) model of creative problem solving assumes processes are executed with respect to the knowledge acquired as a function of expertise – a deep understanding of the facts and concepts applying in a domain (Ericsson, 2004). In keeping with the proposition Vincent, Decker, and Mumford (2002), in a structural equations modeling effort, found that expertise, as evident in principle-based knowledge structures, had a strong positive impact on effective application of creative thinking processes. Along somewhat different lines, Antes and Mumford (2008) asked undergraduates to formulate plans for leading an experimental secondary school – plans appraised for quality, originality, and elegance. In this study, temporal orientation was manipulated through primes which encourage people to think about the past, the present, and the future. It was found that the most creative plans were obtained when people thought about the past, presumably because the past contains the specific knowledge needed for process execution.

Hunter, Bedell-Avers, Hunsicker, Mumford, and Ligon (2008) examined the kind of knowledge content used most effectively in process execution. We typically assume the three types of knowledge people work with in solving complex problems are conceptual (schematic), case-based (experiential), or associational (connectionist) knowledge (Mumford, Todd, Higgs, and McIntosh, 2016). Undergraduates were asked to solve a social innovation problem where problem solutions were appraised for quality, originality, and elegance. A training manipulation was used, or not used, to encourage application of conceptual, case-based, and/or associational knowledge in problem solving. They found not only that encouraging use of knowledge contributed to better creative problem solving, but that the use of conceptual and case-based knowledge resulted in production of the most creative solutions to social innovation problems. Thus, in creative problem-solving efforts, people combine concepts and experience to produce viable solutions.

It is not only the content of the knowledge which is critical for process execution. The way this knowledge is structured, or organized, is also important. Knowledge organization is typically held to be based on mental models of the performance domain at hand (Rouse and Morris, 1986). Mumford et al. (2012) asked undergraduates to solve a creative marketing problem and a social innovation problem. Prior to problem solving, however, participants were asked to complete a program where they were taught how to illustrate their mental models of various problems. Subsequently, attributes of their illustrations of their mental models were assessed on along with the quality, originality, and elegance of their problem solutions. It was found the most creative problem solutions were produced by those who used well-organized, conceptually based knowledge structures – albeit knowledge structures that were not necessarily highly novel or unusually complex. Thus, in creative problem solving, and process execution, the key issue is use of well-structured knowledge.

Strategies

The ways in which people work with this knowledge in process execution are also held to be critical for creative problem solving. A series of studies by Baughman and Mumford (1995); Caughron and Mumford (2008); Licuanan, Dailey, and Mumford (2007); Lonergan, Scott, and Mumford (2004); Mumford, Baughman, Maher, Costanza, and Supinski (1997); Mumford, Baughman, Supinski, and Maher (1996); Mumford, Baughman, Threlfall, Supinski, and Costanza (1996); Mumford, Marks, Connelly, Zaccaro, and Johnson (1998); and Osburn and Mumford (2006) have shown how the use of various strategies for working with knowledge contribute to more effective execution of certain, specific, creative problem-solving processes: creative people in (1) problem definition – define problems with respect to procedures and constraints rather than goals or facts (2) information gathering – seek key facts and anomalies with respect to these facts, (3) concept selection – seek adaptable, feasible, concepts of value over the course of problem solving, (4) conceptual combination – map shared and nonshared features of relevant concepts elaborating on emergent, new, conceptual features, (5) idea generation – new concepts are used to generate multiple workable ideas, (6) idea evaluation – ideas are appraised with respect to innovation potential and idea deficiencies are compensated for, (7) implementation planning – constraints are appraised, backup plans formulated, and emergent opportunities identified, and (8) monitoring – appraise critical problems and see problems as opportunities to reflect on.

Although these process-specific strategies all appear to contribute to creative problem solving, other strategies exist that may contribute to more effective execution of a number of processes. For example, multiple creative problem-solving processes, such as concept selection, conceptual combination, and idea evaluation, all might benefit from the analysis of key causes. Thus, Marcy and Mumford (2007, 2010) developed a self-paced instructional program where people were provided with viable approaches for causal analysis – for example, think about causes that have (1) large effects, (2) direct effects, (3) are controllable, or (4) affect multiple outcomes. They found that training people in these causal analysis strategies resulted not only in the production of high-quality, more original, and more elegant solutions to a series of social innovation problems; it also resulted in better performance on a simulation exercise calling for creative thought.

Another strategy likely to prove of value in executing a number of creative problem-solving processes is forecasting (Mumford, Steele, McIntosh, and Mulhearn, 2015), given the need for people to project the downstream implications of process outputs. In fact, studies by Byrne, Shipman, and Mumford (2010) and Shipman, Byrne, and Mumford (2010) have shown that forecasting also contributes to creative problem solving. They asked undergraduates to formulate advertising campaigns for a new product or formulate a plan for leading an experimental secondary school – products appraised by judges for quality, originality, and elegance. As participants worked on these plans, they were asked to forecast potential outcomes and various aspects of these forecasts were content analyzed. A subsequent factoring indicated the key dimensions of forecasting, forecasting extensiveness, and forecasting time frame emerged. More centrally, these two dimensions were positively related, in the $r = 0.25$–0.45 range, to the quality, originality, and elegance of participant's problem solutions.

Of course, other cross-process strategies, for example, self-reflection (Strange and Mumford, 2005) or judgment (Connelly et al., 2000), might also contribute to process execution. In this regard, however, it is important to recognize that the value of these cross-process, or process-specific, strategies will vary as a function of the type of knowledge people are working with in creative problem solving. Thus, Scott, Lonergan, and Mumford (2005) found that the strategies contributing to conceptual combination differed when people were working with conceptual, as opposed to case-based, knowledge. Similarly, Hester et al. (2012) found that the value of causal analysis for creative problem solving depended, in part, on the viability of people's mental models for understanding the problem at hand.

Creative Problem Solving in the Real World

The various streams of research discussed above have provided us with a stronger, a far stronger, basis for understanding creative problem solving. Creative problem solving is of interest, however, because it produces the basis for "real-world" innovation (Mumford and Hunter, 2005). What should be recognized here, however, is that the "real world" of firms, either for profit or not-for-profit firms, places a new set of demands on those doing the type of work which calls for creative problem solving. Although we have traditionally viewed these demands, firm-based demands, as factors inhibiting creative problem solving, recent research indicates that at least some of these demands may, in fact, contribute positively to creative problem solving.

Constraints

In the "real world," creative problem solving is subject to many potential constraints – client needs, resources, and technical support, to maintain a few. Traditionally, constraints have been held to inhibit creative thought (Osborn, 1953). More recent work, however, indicates that constraints may, in fact, encourage creative thought as people seek ways to manage, or work around these constraints (Haught, 2015; Stokes and Fisher, 2005). In fact, a recent study by Medeiros, Partlow, and Mumford (2014) provides some support for this proposition. Undergraduates were asked to develop advertising campaigns for a new product, a high-energy root beer, where judges appraised the resulting campaigns, the problem solutions, for quality, originality, and elegance. "Emails" from the participant's putative supervisor were used to induce constraints with respect to marketing firm fundamentals, marketing outcomes, environment, and objectives. They found that the most creative problem solutions emerged when some, but not an overwhelming number, of constraints were imposed on participants' creative problem-solving efforts.

Some support for the idea that in the "real world," creative problem-solving efforts must be appropriately constrained, has been provided in another study by Peterson et al. (2013). Here, participants were asked to formulate plans for leading an experimental secondary school, plans appraised for quality, originality, and elegance, after they had illustrated their mental model for understanding secondary school success. Prior to illustrating their mental model and formulating their plans, however, participants were asked to complete a set of self-paced instructional models where they were provided with strategies for managing constraints. It was found that providing people with more effective strategies for constraint management resulted in the production of more creative plans for leading this experimental secondary school.

Errors

The notion that "real-world" creative problem solving is subject to constraints implies that in the "real world," creative problem-solving efforts will be subject to error or failure. In fact, Blair and Mumford (2007) have shown that at least idea evaluation is subject to error due to people's tendency to discount risky, time consuming, and original ideas. Indeed, other, all other, creative problem-solving processes will be subject to error ranging from misspecification of the problem and discounting anomalies to failure to attend to critical contingencies in planning. Errors, however, may not always be detrimental, depending on how they are handled in execution of the creative problem-solving processes.

Some support for this observation has been provided in a study by Licuanan, Dailey, and Mumford (2007). They asked undergraduates to evaluate the originality of marketing campaigns, where the originality of the ideas provided by six different teams was varied. Manipulations were induced to encourage active analysis of the interactional processes occurring in these teams and the active analysis of the strengths and weaknesses of ideas provided – listing their strong and weak points. It was found that active analysis of team processes and explicit analysis of the strengths and weaknesses of ideas resulted in more accurate, less error prone, identification of original ideas.

In another study along those lines, Robledo et al. (2012) asked undergraduates to prepare plans for leading an experimental secondary school, where the resulting plans were appraised for quality, originality, and elegance. Prior to preparing these plans, however, participants were asked to complete a set of self-paced instructional modules where the participants were trained in strategies that might help them manage errors in creative problem solving: (1) think about emergent, downstream errors, (2) think about errors with respect to stakeholders, (3) think about errors that were controllable, and (4) think about errors which would be critical to attaining desired outcomes. Robledo et al. (2012) found that this error-management training resulted in the production of more creative solutions to a social innovation problem. Thus if people think about, and seek to manage potential errors, "real-world" creative problem solving may improve.

Criticism

People, of course, due to investment and framing (Hogarth, 1980), find it difficult to identify errors in their own work. Accordingly, in the real world, creative problem solutions are reviewed by others – others who seek to point out problems or deficiencies in the problem solution being proposed. Although for some time it has been argued that criticism may inhibit creative thinking (Grohman, Wodniecka, and Klusak, 2006), a more recent study by Gibson and Mumford (2013) suggests that at least certain types of criticism may prove of value in enhancing creative thought.

Gibson and Mumford (2013) asked 197 undergraduates to provide a written two-to-three page plan for marketing specialty clothing in the southern United States. Judges appraised the resulting marketing plans for quality, originality, and elegance. Prior to preparing these plans, however, participants reviewed descriptions of nine potential marketing ideas and an "e-mail" from their putative supervisor which requested an evaluation of these candidate ideas – ideas that must be considered by participants in preparing their campaigns. Written criticisms of these candidate ideas were appraised by judges with respect to (1) length, (2) number of critiques, (3) depth of critique, (4) usefulness of critiques, (5) range of critiques, (6) complexity of critiques, (7) isolation of critiques, (8) operational critiques, (9) risk appraisal in critiques, and (10) specificity of critiques. It was found that the highest quality, most original, and most elegant marketing plans were produced by people who provided deep, useful, and specific critiques of candidate ideas. Thus, the quality of others criticisms of ideas apparently contributes to creative problem solving, at least after criticisms are technical rather than personal.

Leadership

In firms, criticisms of creative problem solutions are sometimes provided by peers but are more often provided by those asked to lead the creative efforts.

It is common to assume that creative efforts, including "real-world" creative efforts, do not need leadership. Leaders, however, do many things critical to "real-world" creative problem-solving efforts. Yes, they provide criticisms but they also provide resources, they provide requisite professional contacts, they ensure team members have requisite expertise, they import locally needed expertise, and most centrally, they structure the nature of the work being done on people's creative problem-solving efforts (Mumford, Gibson, Giorgini, and Mecca, 2014). Thus, there is reason to suspect, suspicions that have, in fact, been supported in prior studies (e.g., Vessey, Barrett, Mumford, Johnson, and Litwiller, 2014), that leadership will influence people's creative problem solving.

Some rather compelling support for this proposition has been provided in a study by Marta, Leritz, and Mumford (2005). In this study, teams of three to seven individuals, fifty-five teams in all, were asked to formulate plans for turning around a failing automotive firm. Judges appraised the quality and originality of the plans produced by these teams. Prior to starting work on this task, the planning skills of all team members were assessed. After completing their turnaround plans, team members were asked to nominate the leader of their group. It was found that the teams producing the most creative turnaround plans were led by leaders who evidenced substantial planning skills. Moreover, the impact of these planning skills on team creativity was found to be moderated through more effective structuring of the team, and its tasks, by the leader. Thus, a key role played by leaders was the effective structuring, direction, of how team members worked through, and applied creative problem-solving processes, in formulating their turnaround plans.

Climate and Work

As noted above, however, leaders do many things aside from structuring the work of followers, or teams, as they work on creative problems. This observation is of some importance because these many varied activities of leaders define the environment, or climate, in which creative problem solving occurs. In fact, James, James, and Ashe (1990) have shown that leader behavior is the single most powerful determinant of climate perceptions. And prior work on the climate for creativity (e.g., Amabile, Conti, Coon, Lazenby, and Herron, 1996; Borrill, West, Shapiro, and Rees, 2000; Ekvall and Ryhammar, 1999) has shown that climate perceptions are powerful influences on creativity and innovation in "real-world" settings. Although we often assume that positive climate perceptions result in better team work (Taggar, 2001), positive perceptions of climate may also cause people to be willing to invest scarce cognitive resources into a demanding, a resource intensive, set of creative problem-solving processes.

Hunter, Bedell, and Mumford (2007) conducted a meta-analysis examining the magnitude of the effects of various climate studies on creativity as evident in "real-world" settings. Overall, climate perceptions were found to be strongly, positively, related (Cohen's $d = 0.75$) to creative problem solving at work. More centrally, in this work, the impact of specific dimensions of climate (e.g., positive peer group, autonomy, intellectual stimulation) as well as potential moderators of these relationships, such as the requirement for creativity on the job, team work requirements, and whether the job was, or was not, professional, were assessed. Of the various climate dimensions examined, the strongest effects of creative performance resulted from positive interpersonal exchange ($\Delta = 0.91$), intellectual stimulation ($\Delta = 0.88$) and challenge of the mission ($\Delta = 0.85$). Thus, an environment that encourages people to invest scarce resources in demanding creative problem-solving processes appears to contribute to "real-world" creative performance.

What should also be recognized here, however, is that the effects of climate perceptions were stronger when the job required creative work and the work was highly professionalized. These findings underscore an old adage – it is pointless to study creativity and creative problem solving, on jobs or tasks where it is not integral to performance. A broader implication of these findings, however, is that creative problem solving might not occur in the same way on all jobs, even in jobs where creativity is required.

Mumford, Antes, Caughron, Connelly, and Beeler (2010) conducted a study examining cross-field differences in the creative problem-solving processes required in different occupations. Here, 258 doctoral students, entry-level professionals, were asked to solve a series of field-relevant problems calling for creative thought where skill in executing the key creative problem-solving processes identified by Mumford, Mobley, Reiter-Palmon, Uhlman, and Doares (1991) were assessed. These doctoral students were working in the fields of health sciences, biological sciences, and the social sciences. The findings indicated that people working in different professional fields displayed different creative problem-solving skills – for example, health scientists were especially effective in problem definition and implementation planning, biological scientists were especially effective in information gathering, and social scientists were especially effective in conceptual combination and idea generation. Thus, different domains of work stress different creative problem-solving process, and may call for different strategies, as well as different forms of knowledge, as people attempt to solve the complex, novel, ill-defined problems that call for creative thought.

Conclusions

Before turning to the broader conclusions flowing from our work on creative problem solving, certain limitations in this research should be noted. To begin, although the available evidence does suggest we have isolated the key processes involved in most incidents of creative problem solving (Mumford, Medeiros, and Partlow, 2012), we have not conducted studies examining how each and every one of those problem-solving processes is applied in every domain of creative work. For example, no studies examining artists or engineers have been conducted at this juncture, although we know creative problem solving is important in these fields.

Along related lines, it should be recognized that we have not identified every strategy, process-specific strategies, that might contribute to effective execution of each of these processes. Although the process-specific strategies identified thus far, for example, gathering information bearing on key facts and anomalies, seem plausible (Mumford, Baughman, Supinski, and Maher, 1996), other strategies on other types of problems may also contribute to creative thought. Moreover, although evidence is available for the importance of forecasting and causal analysis (Byrne, Shipman, and Mumford, 2010; Marcy and Mumford, 2007), it is likely that a number of other cross-process strategies might also prove of some importance to creative problem solving.

It should also be recognized we have, for the most part, in these studies examined processes, strategies, and knowledge as unique, isolated, entities. Isolation, of course, is necessary in experimental studies where we seek to establish the existence and/or importance of any given phenomenon. By the same token, one must bear in mind the findings of Scott, Lonergan, and Mumford (2005), indicating that different strategies are needed for effective process execution when people are working with different types, case-based or conceptual, of knowledge. Potentially, other types of knowledge, for example spatial, or other types of mental models, might call for the use of different strategies or stress the use of certain processes in creative problem solving.

Even bearing these limitations in mind, we believe the work described in the present effort has real value. After years of speculating about the key processes involved in creative problem solving we now have a "pretty good" idea of what they are. Creative problem solving requires (1) problem definition, (2) information gathering, (3) concept selection, (4) conceptual combination, (5) idea generation, (6) idea evaluation, (7) implementation planning, and (8) solution monitoring. Thus, we have now moved past the point where we assume all creativity is simply a matter of generating lots of ideas or divergent thinking. Moreover, in this research we have begun to understand the strategies people should employ in executing these processes and the ways these strategies might be shaped by the types of knowledge people are working with in creative problem solving.

Creative problem-solving processes, however, are of practical interest because they provide the basis for the development and introduction of innovative new products. Put differently, creative problem solving is most often of value because it occurs in a "real-world" context where firms, or professions, seek innovative problem solutions. In fact, in our research, we have begun to examine how "real-world" phenomena act to influence effective execution of creative problem-solving processes. Constraints and criticism may help, not hinder, process execution. People in process execution should think about errors. Process execution should occur in a structured work environment where tasks are structured by leaders who encourage people to invest resources in process execution.

Although all these findings are noteworthy in their own right, they point to a need for further work. We need to know which processes, strategies, and knowledge structures contribute to creative thought on what jobs. And, we need to know how constraints, criticisms, error analysis, and leadership influence effective application of processing strategies, and knowledge, in creative problem solving. This is not a small venture but it may be a venture of great value. We know creative thinking skills can be developed (Scott, Leritz, and Mumford, 2004) and providing people with the knowledge and strategies for effective process execution apparently represents a viable approach for developing creative problem-solving skills (Hester et al., 2012; Marcy and Mumford, 2007). We hope the present effort provides an impetus for future work along those lines – efforts that may contribute much to our ability to develop creative potential and encourage its application to those "real-world" problems where innovation is critical.

REFERENCES

Amabile, T. M., Conti, R., Coon, H., Lazenby, J., and Herron, M. (1996). Assessing the work environment for creativity. *Academy of Management Journal*, 39, 1154–1184.

Antes, A. L., and Mumford, M. D. (2008). Temporal orientation and time pressure effects on creative thinking processes. Paper presented at the meetings of the Society for Industrial and Organizational Psychology, San Francisco, CA.

Baughman, W. A., and Mumford, M. D. (1995). Process-analytic models of creative capacities: Operations influencing the combination-and-reorganization process. *Creativity Research Journal*, 8, 37–62.

Blair, C. S., and Mumford, M. D. (2007). Errors in idea evaluation: Preference for the unoriginal? *Journal of Creative Behavior*, 41, 196–222.

Borrill, C., West, M. A., Shapiro, D., and Rees, A. (2000). Team working and effectiveness in health care. *British Journal of Health Care*, 6, 364–371.

Byrne, C. L., Shipman, A. S., and Mumford, M. D. (2010). The effects of forecasting on creative problem-solving: An experimental study. *Creativity Research Journal*, 22, 119–138.

Caughron, J. J., and Mumford, M. D. (2008). Project planning: The effects of using formal planning techniques on forecasting and plan development. *Creativity and Innovation Management*, 17, 1–12.

Connelly, M. S., Gilbert, J. A., Zaccaro, S. J., Threlfall, K. V., Marks, M. A., and Mumford, M. D. (2000). Exploring the relationship of leadership skills and knowledge to leader performance. *Leadership Quarterly*, 11, 65–86.

Dewey, J. (1910). *How we think*. Boston: Heath.

Ekvall, G., and Ryhammar, L. (1999). The creative climate: Its determinants and effects at a Swedish university. *Creativity Research Journal*, 12, 303–310.

Ericsson, K. A. (2004). Deliberate practice and the acquisition and maintenance of expert performance in medicine and related domains. *Academic Medicine*, 79, S70–S81.

Florida, R. (2002). *The rise of the creative class*. New York: Basic Books.

Friedrich, T. L., and Mumford, M. D. (2009). The effects of conflicting information on creative thought: A source of performance improvements or decrements? *Creativity Research Journal*, 21, 265–281.

Gibson, C., and Mumford, M. D. (2013). Evaluation, criticism, and creativity: Criticism content and effects on creative problem solving. *Psychology of Aesthetics, Creativity, and the Arts*, 7, 314–331.

Grohman, M., Wodniecka, Z., and Klusak, M. (2006). Divergent thinking and evaluation skills: Do they always go together? *Journal of Creative Behavior*, 40, 125–145.

Guilford, J. P. (1950). Creativity. *American Psychologist*, 5, 444–454.

Haught, C. (2015). The role of constraints in creative sentence production. *Creativity Research Journal*, 27, 160–166.

Hemlin, S. (2009). Creative knowledge environments: An interview study with group members and group leaders of university and industry R&D groups in biotechnology. *Creativity and Innovation Management*, 18, 278–285.

Hester, K. S., Robledo, I. C., Barrett, J. D., Peterson, D. R., Hougen, D. P., Day, E. A., and Mumford, M. D. (2012). Causal analysis to enhance creative problem-solving: Performance and effects on mental models. *Creativity Research Journal*, 24, 115–133.

162   MICHAEL D. MUMFORD ET AL.

Hogarth, R. M. (1980). *Judgment and choice: The psychology of decision.* New York: John Wiley.

Hunter, S. T., Bedell, K. E., and Mumford, M. D. (2007). Climate for creativity: A quantitative review. *Creativity Research Journal,* 19, 69–90.

Hunter, S. T., Bedell-Avers, K. E., Hunsicker, C. M., Mumford, M. D., and Ligon, G. S. (2008). Applying multiple knowledge structures in creative thought: Effects on idea generation and problem-solving. *Creativity Research Journal,* 20, 137–154.

James, L. R., James, L. A., and Ashe, D. K. (1990). The meaning of organizations: The role of cognition and values. In *Organizational climate and culture,* edited by B. Schneider, 40–84. San Francisco, CA: Jossey-Bass.

Licuanan, B. F., Dailey, L. R., and Mumford, M. D. (2007). Idea evaluation: Error in evaluating highly original ideas. *Journal of Creative Behavior,* 41, 1–27.

Lonergan, D. C., Scott, G. M., and Mumford, M. D. (2004). Evaluative aspects of creative thought: Effects of idea appraisal and revision standards. *Creativity Research Journal,* 16, 231–246.

Marcy, R. T., and Mumford, M. D. (2007). Social innovation: Enhancing creative performance through causal analysis. *Creativity Research Journal,* 19, 123–140.

(2010). Leader cognition: Improving leader performance through causal analysis. *Leadership Quarterly,* 21, 1–19.

Marta, S., Leritz, L. E., and Mumford, M. D. (2005). Leadership skills and the group performance: Situational demands, behavioral requirements, and planning. *Leadership Quarterly,* 16, 97–120.

Medeiros, K. E., Partlow, P. J., and Mumford, M. D. (2014). Not too much, not too little: The influence of constraints on creative problem solving. *Psychology of Aesthetics, Creativity, and the Arts,* 8, 198.

Merrifield, P. R., Guilford, J. P., Christensen, P. R., and Frick, J. W. (1962). Inter-relationships between certain abilities and certain traits of motivation and temperament. *Journal of General Psychology,* 65, 57–74.

Mobley, M. I., Doares, L. M., and Mumford, M. D. (1992). Process analytic models of creative capacities: Evidence for the combination and reorganization process. *Creativity Research Journal,* 5, 125–155.

Mumford, M. D. (1984). Age and outstanding occupational achievement: Lehman revisited. *Journal of Vocational Behavior,* 25, 225–244.

(2002). Social innovation: Ten cases from Benjamin Franklin. *Creativity Research Journal,* 14, 253–266.

Mumford, M. D., Antes, A. L., Caughron, J. J., Connelly, S., and Beeler, C. (2010). Cross-field differences in creative problem-solving skills: A comparison of health, biological, and social sciences. *Creativity Research Journal,* 22, 14–26.

Mumford, M. D., Baughman, W. A., Maher, M. A., Costanza, D. P., and Supinski, E. P. (1997). Process-based measures of creative problem-solving skills: IV. Category combination. *Creativity Research Journal,* 10, 59–71.

Mumford, M. D., Baughman, W. A., Supinski, E. P., and Maher, M. A. (1996). Process-based measures of creative problem-solving skills: II. Information encoding. *Creativity Research Journal,* 9, 77–88.

Mumford, M. D., Baughman, W. A., Threlfall, K. V., Supinski, E. P., and Costanza, D. P. (1996). Process-based measures of creative problem-solving skills: I. Problem construction. *Creativity Research Journal*, 9, 63–76.

Mumford, M. D., Connelly, M. S., Scott, G. M., Espejo, J., Sohl, L. M., Hunter, S. T., and Bedell, K. E. (2005). Career experiences and scientific performance: A study of social, physical, life, and health sciences. *Creativity Research Journal*, 17, 105–129.

Mumford, M. D., Gibson, C., Giorgini, V., and Mecca, J. (2014). Leading for creativity: People, products, and systems. In *The Oxford handbook of leadership and organizations*, 757–782. Oxford: Oxford University Press.

Mumford, M. D., and Gustafson, S. B. (1988). Creativity syndrome: Integration, application, and innovation. *Psychological Bulletin*, 103, 27–43.

  (2007). Creative thought: Cognition and problem solving in a dynamic system. *Creativity Research Handbook*, 2, 33–77.

Mumford, M. D., Hester, K. S., Robledo, I. C., Peterson, D. R., Day, E. A., Hougen, D. F., and Barrett, J. D. (2012). Mental models and creative problem-solving: The relationship of objective and subjective model attributes. *Creativity Research Journal*, 24, 311–330.

Mumford, M. D., and Hunter, S. T. (2005). Innovation in organizations: A multi-level perspective on creativity. In *Research in multi-level issues*, edited by F. Dansereau and F. J. Yammarino, 4:11–74. Oxford: Elsevier.

Mumford, M. D., Marks, M. A., Connelly, M. S., Zaccaro, S. J., and Johnson, J. F. (1998). Domain-based scoring in divergent-thinking tests: Validation evidence in an occupational sample. *Creativity Research Journal*, 11, 151–163.

Mumford, M. D., Medeiros, K. E., and Partlow, P. J. (2012). Creative thinking: Processes, strategies, and knowledge. *Journal of Creative Behavior*, 46, 30–47.

Mumford, M. D., Mobley, M. I., Reiter-Palmon, R., Uhlman, C. E., and Doares, L. M. (1991). Process analytic models of creative capacities. *Creativity Research Journal*, 4, 91–122.

Mumford, M. D., and Mulhearn, T. (2015). More than just a bright idea: The process for successful creative solutions. *Talent Quarterly*, 6, 44–50.

Mumford, M. D., Steele, L., McIntosh, T., and Mulhearn, T. (2015). Forecasting and leader performance: Objective cognition in a socio-organizational context. *Leadership Quarterly*, 26, 359–369.

Mumford, M. D., Supinski, E. P., Baughman, W. A., Costanza, D. P., and Threlfall, K. V. (1997). Process-based measures of creative problem-solving skills: V. Overall Prediction. *Creativity Research Journal*, 10, 77–85.

Mumford, M. D., Supinski, E. P., Threlfall, K. V., and Baughman, W. A. (1996). Process-based measures of creative problem-solving skills: III. Category selection. *Creativity Research Journal*, 9, 395–406.

Mumford, M. D., Todd, E. M., Higgs, C., and McIntosh, T. (2016). Cognitive skills and leadership performance: The nine critical skills. *Leadership Quarterly*, 28, 24–39.

Osborn, A. F. (1953). *Applied imagination, principles and procedures of creative problem-solving*. New York: Scribner.

Osburn, H. K., and Mumford, M. D. (2006). Creativity and planning: Training interventions to develop creative problem-solving skills. *Creativity Research Journal*, 18, 173–190.

Parnes, S. J., and Noller, R. B. (1972). Applied creativity: The creative studies project. *Journal of Creative Behavior*, 6, 164–186.

Peterson, D. R., Barrett, J. D., Hester, K. S., Robledo, I. C., Hougen, D. F., Day, E. A., and Mumford, M. D. (2013). Teaching people to manage constraints: Effects on creative problem-solving. *Creativity Research Journal*, 25, 335–347.

Redmond, M. R., Mumford, M. D., and Teach, R. J. (1993). Putting creativity to work: Effects of leader behavior on subordinate creativity. *Organizational Behavior and Human Decision Processes*, 55, 120–151.

Reiter-Palmon, R., Mumford, M. D., and Threlfall, K. V. (1998). Solving everyday problems creatively: The role of problem construction and personality type. *Creativity Research Journal*, 11, 187–197.

Robledo, I. C., Hester, K. S., Peterson, D. R., Barrett, J. D., Day, E. A., Hougen, D. P., and Mumford, M. D. (2012). Errors and understanding: The effects of error-management training on creative problem-solving. *Creativity Research Journal*, 24, 220–234.

Rouse, W. B., and Morris, N. M. (1986). On looking into the black box: Prospects and limits in the search for mental models. *Psychological Bulletin*, 100, 349.

Scott, G., Leritz, L. E., and Mumford, M. D. (2004). The effectiveness of creativity training: A quantitative review. *Creativity Research Journal*, 16, 361–388.

Scott, G. M., Lonergan, D. C., and Mumford, M. D. (2005). Conceptual combination: Alternative knowledge structures, alternative heuristics. *Creativity Research Journal*, 17, 79–98.

Shipman, A. S., Byrne, C. L., and Mumford, M. D. (2010). Leader vision formation and forecasting: The effects of forecasting extent, resources, and timeframe. *Leadership Quarterly*, 21, 439–456.

Sternberg, R. J. (1986). Toward a unified theory of human reasoning. *Intelligence*, 10, 281–314.

Stokes, P. D., and Fisher, D. (2005). Selection, constraints, and creativity case studies: Max Beckmann and Philip Guston. *Creativity Research Journal*, 17, 283–291.

Strange, J. M., and Mumford, M. D. (2005). The origins of vision: Effects of reflection, models, and analysis. *Leadership Quarterly*, 16, 121–148.

Taggar, S. (2001). Group composition, creative synergy, and group performance. *Journal of Creative Behavior*, 35, 261–286.

Vessey, W. B., Barrett, J. D., Mumford, M. D., Johnson, G., and Litwiller, B. (2014). Leadership of highly creative people in highly creative fields: A historiometric study of scientific leaders. *Leadership Quarterly*, 25, 672–691.

Vincent, A. S., Decker, B. P., and Mumford, M. D. (2002). Divergent thinking, intelligence, and expertise: A test of alternative models. *Creativity Research Journal*, 14, 163–178.

Wallas, G. (1926). *The art of thought*. New York: Harcourt.

Weisberg, R. W. (2015). Toward an integrated theory of insight in problem solving. *Thinking and Reasoning*, 21, 5–39.

Zaccaro, S. J., Connelly, S., Repchick, K. M., Daza, A. I., Young, M. C., Kilcullen, R. N., Gilrane, V. L., Robbins, J. M., and Bartholomew, L. N. (2015). The influence of higher order cognitive capacities on leader organizational continuance and retention: The mediating role of developmental experiences. *Leadership Quarterly*, 26, 342–358.

CHAPTER 12

It All Makes Sense Now That I Think about It
A Quarter-Century of Studying Creativity

Jonathan A. Plucker

The direction of my adventures with creativity was set fairly early in my career, back when I was a master's student at the University of Connecticut. As I neared the completion of my undergraduate degree in chemistry, an advisor noted that I had one course left to take that wouldn't be offered until the next year. I found myself with lots of time on my hands, and the professor leading my elective education seminar suggested I start my master's in educational psychology with a specialization in gifted education. It seemed like a better use of time than hanging out at the fraternity house all day,[1] and I began my studies. The program, under the direction of Sally Reis and Joe Renzulli, involved a great deal of talk and reading about creativity.

And, wow, did I hate creativity. It felt like a squishy, vague, not-serious-at-all waste of time, certainly not as serious and scientific as human intelligence, which fascinated me. But my fellow graduate students loved creativity, constantly talking about it, playing little creativity games, and just generally absorbing themselves in it. Creativity, creativity, creativity, all the time, usually (from my perspective) creativity just for the sake of creativity. Maybe it was my background as a science major – and an analytical one, at that – maybe it was an early indication of my aversion to going along with the crowd, or maybe it was simply me wanting to be a "serious" graduate student at the tender age of twenty-one. Regardless, creativity struck me as a silly distraction.

All of this was made worse by the fact that the major project for doctoral students in my program was a paper on intelligence and creativity. These papers routinely ran 100 pages or more, and there was an understanding that they should be as comprehensive as humanly possible. I hoped to get out of the paper given that I was a master's student, but Joe Renzulli disabused me of this notion very quickly.[2]

---

[1] It was.   [2] (Frustratedly): "Just write the paper, Jon."

I attacked the intelligence half of the paper with great enthusiasm, and much of that section served as the basis for our widely used and still functioning website on human intelligence theory (www.intelltheory.com). But the creativity portion still lay in front of me when I had to take a creativity course. To my surprise, I became intrigued by the topic – then mildly curious about current theory and research. About halfway through the semester, I had a moment of blinding clarity: This creativity stuff is important. It doesn't have to be playing silly games and making Rube Goldberg contraptions; it can be very serious, and very deliberate, and very – dare I say – utilitarian. A huge influence on my thinking that semester was Sternberg's (1988) *The Nature of Creativity*, which we used in class.[3] Those chapters, especially Csikszentmihalyi's (1988) description of his domain-field-individual model, changed the direction of my interests and, eventually, my career.

Here was a careful conceptual model of how humans produce ideas that are judged to be creative, and the model emphasized that creativity is a complex construct, cognitive yet social, objective yet subjective, but most importantly, a topic worthy of serious scientific study due to its importance to so many aspects of our lives. I began to attack the topic with gusto, eventually developing my own model of how ideas become "creative." My professors encouraged me to share my work with Bob Sternberg, Howard Gardner, and Mark Runco, which was very intimidating – who was I, as a master's student, to approach famous scholars whose work inspired me on a daily basis? To my surprise – and continued benefit – all three scholars made time for me, sending me comments about my work, providing advice on a range of intellectual and career-related topics, and generally encouraging me to pursue my interests in creativity. Gardner even shared my work with Csikszentmihalyi and reported back that he found the work to be "interesting." Never has one word lifted higher the spirits of a tired graduate student!

All of these interactions shaped how I approached the topic of creativity, and to this day I seek to answer the same basic questions that fascinated me more than twenty-five years ago in graduate school: What is the nature of creativity, and why is answering this question so difficult? And once we figure that out, how can we most effectively and efficiently foster creativity in others? I didn't realize it at the time, but I was essentially wondering if there is a science of creativity, the pursuit of which has occupied most of my time over the past twenty-five years.

---

[3] A signed copy of which has always resided on the bookshelf closest to my desk in all of my various offices over the years.

Defining Creativity

One day not long after arriving at Indiana University as an assistant professor, I guest lectured about creativity for a doctoral seminar. The professor in charge of the course, the late ecological psychologist Myrtle Scott, asked me to talk about creativity, and I shared some of my team's recent work. As we walked out after class, she thanked me and said, very matter-of-factly, "I'm just surprised your field hasn't figured out a common definition of creativity." I replied with my standard two-minute defense of the field, noting that a diversity of definitions was a good thing, having a plethora of definitions wasn't a big deal, etc. She listened politely, then said, "OK, sounds good. You still need a common definition."

I thought about this for a couple days, then I shared this experience with one of my students, Ron Beghetto, who strongly agreed that the field needed a better conceptual grasp of its terms.[4] He noted that other fields have wrestled with similar issues and benefited from the creation of common definitions. I also reflected on related experiences from my brief stint as an elementary school teacher. For example, I once mentioned to a colleague that one of our students had done creative work on a project. The teacher scoffed and replied, "I'm sure *someone* somewhere in the world has done that before." The flippant dismissal of the student's work seemed preposterous to me: Is the standard for creativity assessment really whether an act is truly and completely unique, judged against the entire history of human accomplishment? But such statements about creativity were not uncommon when I taught in that school, and they were quite frustrating. After considerable discussion, Ron and I decided to tackle this issue, and with the assistance of Gayle Dow, another of my students, we began studying the definitions – both explicit and implicit – used in creativity articles published in scholarly journals.

We found that fewer than 40 percent of the papers explicitly defined creativity, despite that being the focus of their paper. A similar percentage defined the term implicitly through the instrument selection or as being based on a specific theory or model that did define the term. More strikingly, nearly one in five did not define the term at all. Of the offered definitions, characteristics of originality and usefulness were most common. As a result of this investigation, we wrote an article for *Educational Psychologist*

---

[4] Throughout this chapter, I use the first person singular to describe actions that are more accurately described as team efforts. Even my sole-authored publications were influenced by discussions with several other people (e.g., my 1999 reanalysis of TTCT data was only possible because of extensive conversations with Paul Torrance about his data).

that shared the results, discussed the problems associated with this wide range of explicit and implicit conceptions, and proposed a definition:

> Creativity is the interaction among *aptitude, process, and environment* by which an individual or group produces a *perceptible product* that is both *novel and useful* as defined within a *social context*. (Plucker, Beghetto, and Dow, 2004, p. 90, italics original)

Including an emphasis on novelty and usefulness was obviously not original, but our recommendation that a creator's social context always be considered was unique at the time and reflected the growth of theories that emphasized the importance of context, such as Sternberg's (1985) work and sociocultural theories of learning (e.g., Packer and Goicoechea, 2000; Wertsch, del Río, and Alvarez, 1995). One aspect of the definition that raised eyebrows was our insistence that a creative product be perceptible. Weighing in so heavily on the need to focus on products that could be sensed in some way was not accidental. As educational psychologists, we wanted the definition to encourage educators to talk less about creative potential and focus more on providing opportunities for students to do actual creative work; less game playing, more time on real, creative products, such as one sees in the schoolwide enrichment model (Reis and Renzulli, 2003).

It is always fascinating to see how your work is received; in this case, the paper was rejected multiple times by different journals before being accepted;[5] the definition when published was rarely cited for several years, and one eminent scholar told us after a conference presentation that the work was "disappointing" and "boring." But a few years later, we heard the definition mentioned during some conference presentations, then it started to be cited – a lot. It is now our most highly cited work!

What made this particular contribution so appealing? We have lots of theories but no real answers. Our emphasis on the importance of social context addresses the eye-of-the-beholder issue that causes many educators to question their conceptions and beliefs about creativity. Giving context an elevated role in creativity also helps explain how creativity can be manifested across cultures (which we've explored via implicit theory studies, see Plucker, 2002; Plucker, Lim, and Lee, 2017; Lim and Plucker, 2001). And the pragmatism of our you-have-to-sense-it approach may appeal to educators and other people concerned primarily with practical creativity. In the end, the big take-aways for me are that people found the definition

---

[5] The editor of one highly prestigious journal liked it enough to encourage three revisions but not enough ever to accept it!

to be helpful, and you can never predict which of your creative products will take off (which is pretty much how I interpret chance configuration theory; see Simonton, 1988, 1989).

Subsequent attempts at definition are refinements of our criteria within specific contexts (e.g., Makel and Plucker, 2014; Runco and Jaeger, 2012; Simonton, 2012), which is exactly what we sought to emphasize in the definition. From our perspective, the paper served its purpose as it helped solidify the definitional issues of the field, and the paper's definition and emphasis on using it to address common myths and stereotypes about creativity became the foundation of my subsequent work with creativity.

Domain Generality versus Domain Specificity

Another area of interest related to conceptual issues, and perhaps my earliest work that made an impact on the field, dealt with whether creativity was essentially domain general or domain specific, in which I became identified as a strong proponent of the domain-general perspective. As sociocultural perspectives on learning and cognition became popular, the idea of domain-specific thinking and learning started to dominate educational psychology, and several researchers began to promote the idea that creativity was also domain specific and probably even task specific (e.g., Baer, 1991, 1993, 1996). The view that cognition was heavily context-embedded was becoming dominant in several subfields within psychology, sociology, and education, and a few scholars were pushing very hard to establish that creativity was also highly context-embedded.

Interestingly, I never said or wrote that creativity was domain, content, or task general; I just said that there was plenty of evidence that creativity was not *entirely* domain, content, or especially task specific. Since many creativity interventions and assessments were based on (or could be inferred to be based on) domain generality, their use was often being declared to be inappropriate and pointless. These conclusions were often paired with highly selective citations from the research literature. All of this felt like throwing out the baby with the bathwater, and it appeared to involve a misunderstanding of the strengths and limitations of the burgeoning sociocultural literature.

This was an important topic to me, as I was teaching in the educational psychology and cognitive science programs at Indiana University at the time, and my students and I were working through the explosion in sociocultural literature on a near constant basis. I was becoming worried that domain specificity was being oversold, and to see it begin to occur within one of my specialty areas was worrisome. Part of this is probably my aversion to groupthink – when I hear colleagues start to say things like, "There's no need to teach students about most of the older learning theories, because we all know that constructivism and other sociocultural perspectives are the only ones that matter now," I reflexively begin to question all the assumptions in that sentence. Do humans ever get to the point where researchers can truly say, "we all know . . . ?" I doubt it. And so began my quest to charge the windmills of domain and task specificity in creativity.

I began by partnering with John Baer (1998) in a debate on this issue in the *Creativity Research Journal* (Plucker, 1998). We outlined the case to be made for each position, with Baer summarizing the specificity perspective and me the generality case. This debate led to further discussion within the field, and I began a series of empirical studies and reviews of research conducted in other fields to investigate the issue further (e.g., Plucker, 1999b, 2005; Plucker and Zabelina, 2009). In particular, my approach was influenced by work on alternative assessment of student achievement, which was providing evidence that standardized assessments tend to produce data supporting unitary constructs, yet alternative assessments tend to produce data that looks multifaceted. I hypothesized a method effect, in which creativity data would follow a similar pattern, with alternative assessments suggesting domain specificity and more traditional assessments suggesting generality. That is basically what I found (Plucker, 2004), leading me to believe that our methods for studying specificity-generality are the most important factor in what we find, which in turn led me to think that perhaps the hybrid position really is the most accurate.

This debate has big implications for creativity in education. Many studies have shown that transfer of learning is a major problem for many people; learning scientists originally used this fact as a reason to argue for highly situation-specific forms of teaching and learning. But subsequent research provided evidence that transfer is especially tricky when learning occurs in highly contextualized settings. So although we do not want generalists who know all sorts of domain-general creative strategies but cannot apply them well to any particular domain or task, we also do not want functionally fixated creative specialists whose creativity is severely domain and task limited. Again, the hybrid position feels most appropriate, given our current theoretical and empirical understandings (Baer and Kaufman, 2005; Plucker and Beghetto, 2004).

This was among my most impactful early work, and I have no regrets in tackling it, but I also learned that one can get pigeon-holed pretty easily. For example, I began to receive invitations to write chapters and special issue articles as the "domain-general" representative, and most symposium invitations were in a similar vein. That was frustrating, not least because I didn't believe in the domain-general perspective!

The debate has lost a lot of its energy, in part because academia in general has tempered its fervor for the domain-specificity perspective. The hybrid position is largely taken for granted across a number of fields, including creativity. But like a game of whack-a-mole, extreme generality and specificity positions still pop up from time to time, and they need to be addressed vigorously whenever that happens.

Creativity Assessment

The conceptual work developed in parallel with my interest in the measurement of creativity. Joe Renzulli asked me to co-author a review of literature on creativity assessment for Sternberg's (1999) *Handbook of Creativity*, and given that it was my first major chapter, I threw myself into it, reading hundreds of studies on assessment issues.[6] The complexities of this aspect of the field fascinated me: The history is rich, the conventional wisdom of how the major assessments developed did not appear to be wholly accurate (satisfying my attraction to iconoclasm!), and a number of unique assessment strategies were being used.

This review informed the generality-specificity work, especially my belief that method effects are important to consider, and led to a number of subsequent studies that continue to this day on various measurement topics: examinations of the predictive validity of the Torrance Tests of Creative Thinking (Plucker, 1999a), development of new measures (e.g., the Runco Ideation Behavior Scales; Runco, Plucker, and Lim, 2001), and studies of how expertise is related to evaluation of the creativity of products (Plucker, Holden, and Neustadter, 2008; Plucker, Kaufman, Temple, and Qian, 2009), among other activities. This line of work also led to the book *Essentials of Creativity Assessment*, with James Kaufman and John Baer (Kaufman, Plucker, and Baer, 2008), in which we attempted to summarize the major developments in the field and provide concise advice to psychologists and educators on how to use the diverse assessments in the most useful ways. Of my sections in that book, the chapter on divergent thinking was probably the best piece I had written up to that time, and my background research for that chapter convinced me that DT assessments

---

[6] Coauthoring with one of my most highly regarded mentors for a book edited by another probably had something to do with my motivation, especially for my first chapter!

still had value to the field, although additional development was needed, especially in scoring (e.g., Plucker, Qian, and Schmalensee, 2014; Plucker, Qian, and Wang, 2011).

Although my assessment work has been more scattershot in its approach than other aspects of my creativity research, my hope is that organizing and cataloging the field's advances in this area (Plucker and Makel, 2010; Plucker and Renzulli, 1999; Plucker and Runco, 1998; Plucker, Makel, and Qian, forthcoming), with occasional studies meant to address holes in the research base, has given a structure to the efforts of others and helped move us forward.

Interventions

I have often told my students that in our role as educational psychologists, we have an obligation to think about practical application. We can still conduct basic research, of course, but our end goal should always be about making a difference in the lives of children. With this in mind, finding ways to foster creativity in K–12 settings has been a major focus throughout my career (e.g., Plucker, Guo, and Dilley, 2018; Plucker, McWilliams, and Alanazi, 2016). My initial motivation to do this work was more pragmatic, in that intervention efforts have largely been uncreative over the years, with few exceptions (Plucker and Beghetto, 2003). I was not convinced that all we were learning about creativity was making its way into programs that helped students become more creative.

Over the years, my intervention activity has fallen into two categories. The first, broader set of efforts is evaluating the effectiveness of various strategies for increasing creativity. For example, we have studied the relationship between drug use and creativity, generally finding little evidence that most drugs have an appreciable benefit (Plucker and Dana, 1998a, 1998b; Plucker, McNeely, and Morgan, 2009).[7] This is important for educators and parents because adolescents usually list "to be more creative" as one of their top excuses for experimenting with drugs. My colleagues and I have recently begun studying the role of modeling creative behavior (Yi, Plucker, and Guo, 2015), finding evidence that highly creative models influence verbal creativity but not necessarily artistic creativity. Modeling is interesting because schools have models built into every classroom in the

---

[7] This is a good example of how your research can and should surprise you occasionally. Robert Dana and I expected at least small creativity benefits from the use of alcohol, marijuana, LSD, psylocibin, etc., but there is little evidence to support positive benefits, and many studies suggest the opposite, including our own.

form of teachers and peers, suggesting that a careful modeling intervention could pay impressive dividends.

As a doctoral student at the University of Virginia, I was fortunate to serve as evaluator for a summer invention program at the School of Engineering and Applied Science under the direction of Mike Gorman. Evaluating and studying that program made a lasting impression on me, reinforcing the value of problem-based learning and real-life scenarios in creativity interventions (Gorman and Plucker, 2003; Gorman, Plucker, and Callahan, 1998; Plucker and Gorman, 1999) – also an emphasis in the schoolwide enrichment model (Reis and Renzulli, 2003).[8]

The second area of effort has been developing and implementing a model of creativity enhancement. This work was greatly facilitated by having the opportunity to teach in a presemester program at Indiana University for incoming freshmen. The goal of the program was to provide highly interactive courses to help students make the transition from high school to college, and the content was somewhat beside the point. As such, an experimental course on personal and group creativity didn't raise any eyebrows. The course was successful and eventually was taught during the regular academic year, where the model was expanded and evaluated. It also became the foundation of the minor in creativity, innovation, and entrepreneurship that I started at the University of Connecticut years later.

The focus of the model is on helping students understand the nature of creativity. In other words, the goal is to help them get to the point of thinking realistically about creativity that did not occur for me until graduate school.[9] We accomplish this by providing a series of problem-based learning activities in which they must use their creativity, individually and working with others, and then analyze their performance and reflect on what their actions can mean for creativity (Beghetto and Plucker, 2006, forthcoming). For example, precourse surveys indicate that around 75 percent of undergraduates enter the course believing that creativity is innate and cannot be taught, and roughly the same percentage report that they are not among the lucky few endowed with creativity. But by having them be creative then reflect on their actions, we find that their conceptions of creativity become much more complex and realistic (Plucker and Dow, 2010, 2017).

---

[8] I also learned that working with adolescents is, even on their best day, an exercise in herding cats, and that one needs to celebrate small victories, such as when they show up for class on time.

[9] Until writing this chapter, I didn't think about it this way. But as I thought about how to describe our courses, I realized some of my motivations here were deeply personal!

Our model for the course is fairly straightforward, focusing primarily on attitude change among students. We have come to believe that myths and stereotypes about creativity are the primary barriers to students developing their creativity, with learning specific cognitive techniques less useful for most people. We also help students explore the role of constraints in creativity, noting that constraints are not inherently good or bad, but rather the limits of one's reality that can often be modified or ignored. In many ways, our instructional model brings together most of my other work: The myths and stereotypes work is informed by the conceptual work (Plucker, Beghetto, and Dow, 2004), the attitude change piece is considered to be content general (Plucker and Dow, 2017), and we avoid teaching creativity techniques in a general way because we suspect this aspect of creativity is domain and perhaps even task specific (i.e., the hybrid model; Plucker and Beghetto, 2004). We use a battery of creativity assessments to (1) reinforce the multidimensional nature of creativity, (2) help students reflect on how they may be creative, and (3) obtain an understanding of the strengths and weaknesses of measurement in the social sciences. I also recently developed a text specifically to accompany courses taught using our model (Plucker, 2016a).

The intervention work is fulfilling in large part because it involves direct contact with students, allowing us to see firsthand the benefits of students learning to believe in their own creativity. Having the flexibility in a fairly low-stakes environment to try new things was invaluable, and I still apply that lesson today when managing my teams – people need space to experiment, which means being cool with the occasional failure. Some of my strategies in that creativity course failed spectacularly, but the context was such that my colleagues and I could sit down, discuss what went wrong, and try again the next class meeting. Compare that to the more common experience I have had in higher education, where I have occasionally needed formal approval to make small changes to my syllabus each semester.[10]

Articulation

At the beginning of this chapter, I noted the development of a new model of creativity as part of my big intelligence and creativity paper in graduate

---

[10] Seriously. One of my biggest frustrations is the steady increase in regulation of teaching at the college level. I understand wanting to create a minimum standard of quality for the classroom, but at many schools this intent has morphed into tight overregulation that squashes creativity in the classroom. If you're going to sign off on my reading list, you better know more about the topic than I do. And if that's the case, then why hire me in the first place?

school, but I did not divulge any details about it. Although I have worked on my model of creative articulation for over a quarter-century, I have only begun to publish on it (Plucker, 2016b); rather, it has lived on as a series of white papers that I share with colleagues and students on an infrequent basis, continually revising and developing the model based on everyone's feedback.

Our conceptual models of creativity have become more complex over the past few decades, in large part due to inclusion of the role of social contexts and audience factors in judgments of creativity. Creative articulation is a concept designed to help explain how creators select potential audiences for their creative work and use communication and persuasion to maximize the value of that work in the eyes of those audiences. I was trying to figure out if it were possible to design a model that explained how an individual or team influences how their work is judged to be creative by a domain or field (Csikszentmihalyi, 1988), or similarly, how that work moves from being considered little c creativity to Pro C creativity to Big C creativity (Kaufman and Beghetto, 2009). The goal was not to make the case that this sort of process was important, as others such as Stein (1974, 1975) and Sternberg and Lubart (1991, 1992) have done that already, but rather to help explore the mechanisms by which people can learn how to articulate their creativity more effectively. More to the point, the model's explanation has to guide K–12 educational interventions that would help students learn to be good creative articulators. Several scholars have touched on this basic idea, but no one to my knowledge has yet to elaborate on the mechanisms and environmental factors involved.

Although the full model cannot be described comprehensively in the available space, the basic framework is straightforward. The model has two tiers, and the components of the first tier are: communication, which involves putting the product in a form that is easily presented to and understood by the intended audience; audience selection, or deciding which group or groups constitute an audience which is likely to accept the product; selecting or creating the proper mood for the creative product; and alliance construction, which can be described as the process of finding advocates (e.g., peers, mentors, gatekeepers) who are in a position to help a product become accepted. The supportive factors that constitute the second tier include personality factors, physical factors, motivation, thinking skills, image, communication skills, and other processes and traits which influence articulation less directly than the general components of the first tier. Many of these skills and factors have been mentioned in the literature, independently of articulation, with respect to creativity, but part of what I am suggesting in the model is that perhaps some of these factors are more relevant for creative articulation than they are for creative processes.

Creative articulation can and should be taught in a variety of educational settings, otherwise students are only being taught part of the creative process. Most strategies for fostering articulation are straightforward and can be worked into many existing programs and units. In our creativity courses, for example, we ensure that every student presents their creative products to the class in an effort to learn how to best share one's work, respond to questions and concerns (or outright opposition!), and incorporate constructive criticism into revisions of the product. We also work with students on how to provide feedback that is constructive rather than just critical. Based on my personal observations, students (especially younger students) rarely present their work to their peers, let alone other groups outside the school walls, they do not have opportunities to persuade teachers that their work is indeed creative, and they do not learn how to provide constructive criticism. These are all easily fixable problems, and the articulation model provides a path forward for addressing them.

A lot of my career decisions and developments fit the model, which probably isn't a coincidence. For example, the model notes that some products take years to find the right environment, and our definition languished for a couple years before it captured people's attention. At the same time, we worked very hard to spread the word about the definition and its advantages over previous conceptions, trying multiple dissemination strategies and interacting with various gatekeepers and audiences (also part of the model). In the assessment work, I realized that our summative review chapters in major handbooks positioned us as gatekeepers, making it important to note the promising work of early career and out-of-field scholars, even if that work were in early stages of development. And articulation is a theme throughout our creativity courses and the intervention model on which they are based.

Is it weird to have the framework of one's career based on a largely unpublished idea from a quarter-century ago? Maybe, maybe not, but that is how it has worked out.[11] At this point, colleagues have recommended sharing the model in a series of articles, or maybe a book, or a combination of those formats with a healthy dose of social media mixed in. One nice thing about being later in one's career is that you can make such decisions based on what's best for scientific and educational advances, rather

---

[11] (Frustratedly): "Just write the paper, Jonathan."

than on what's best for getting tenure. In other words, you can think more directly about articulation.

Is There a Science of Creativity?

Returning to one of the foundational creativity questions with which I began my career, has the tremendous growth and development of our field brought us to the promised land of a science of creativity? My conclusion in a recent attempt to answer this question was a qualified yes (Plucker, 2017). The field has several well-regarded journals, lively conferences, a growing appreciation among academics, and a nascent sense among policymakers that creativity and innovation are important contributors to a wide range of valued outcomes. Much of this progress would have been hard to imagine twenty-five years ago. Should we be declaring victory? Part of me wants to celebrate, but part of me thinks there is much work to be done.

The pessimistic side of me is influenced by experience working in education policy, which is where much of my education-focused work has occurred in recent years. In interacting with policymakers, they do indeed appear to be grasping the importance of creativity, but their understanding of what we know about creativity is lacking. For example, I attended a conference about five years ago, during which the heads of important federal agencies spoke about twenty-first-century skills. I was excited at the beginning of each talk, as senior leaders from the National Institutes for Health, National Science Foundation, Institute for Education Sciences, and several major, private foundations all began their talks by stressing the importance of creativity – but toward the middle of each talk, each speaker pivoted abruptly to a harsh view of the field of creativity, concluding that it was conceptually weak, had poor assessments, and had no idea how to increase students' creativity. A well-known psychologist was sitting next to me in the back of the room,[12] and he whispered to me at one point, "This must be driving you crazy." It was, and it still does, as I continue to run into this attitude in Washington, DC, and state houses around the country. The good news is that people value my favorite construct; the bad news is that their knowledge of the field's accomplishments feels stuck in the mid-1970s.

This phenomenon is frustrating, but the field bears some responsibility for this state of affairs. Our work is rarely included in teacher preparation and business programs. When it is, personal experience leads me to believe

---

[12] Where academics are often placed at policy meetings!

that the instruction usually focuses on divergent thinking and the creativity game playing that drove me to distraction way back in graduate school. We need to push harder to get high-quality content in front of our future educators and business leaders. Consultants travel the globe preaching the values of brainstorming, a technique whose creative power has been vastly oversold. We need to be more forceful about providing research-supported workshops and trainings in these settings. Policymakers cannot be blamed for not having the time to research creativity interventions. We know so much, and our work is so important – we need to be much more proactive in how we disseminate our work.[13]

The benefits of pushing to apply as much of our work as possible are numerous. For example, I would argue that being able to scale an advanced battery of creativity measures/indicators, which would allow them to be used in state K–12 education accountability systems and districts assessment programs, is probably the "next step" for creativity assessment work. Several colleagues in the field agree with me, but everyone is reluctant to push in this direction, in large part because it is difficult work, it takes a tremendous amount of time (and probably funding), and inevitably leads to working with policymakers and test publishers. I understand why these barriers are daunting and not things everyone wants to or can tackle. But a thousand high-quality studies on scoring improvements for various creativity measures would be great; one statewide creativity assessment system would be game-changing and probably more impactful than those thousand studies.

It is an honor to be included in this volume, especially given that my enthusiasm for creativity only continues to grow. There are big questions still to be answered about creativity and how we can help people use it to improve their lives, and I am confident the field will look back in another twenty-five years and conclude that we were able to answer most of those questions. Then there will be more and better questions, which is the whole point!

REFERENCES

Baer, J. (1991). Generality of creativity across performance domains. *Creativity Research Journal*, 4, 23–39.
   (1993). *Creativity and divergent thinking: A task-specific approach.* Hillsdale, NJ: Lawrence Erlbaum.

---

[13] Again, articulation.

(1996). The effects of task-specific divergent-thinking training. *Journal of Creative Behavior*, 30, 183–187.

(1998). The case for domain specificity of creativity. *Creativity Research Journal*, 11, 173–177.

Baer, J., and Kaufman, J. C. (2005). Bridging generality and specificity: The Amusement Park Theoretical (APT) model of creativity. *Roeper Review*, 27, 158–163.

Beghetto, R. A., and Plucker, J. A. (2006). The relationship among schooling, learning, and creativity: "All roads lead to creativity" or "You can't get there from here"? In *Creativity and reason in cognitive development*, edited by J. C. Kaufman and J. Baer, 316–332. New York: Cambridge University Press.

(forthcoming). The relationship among schooling, learning, and creativity: "All roads lead to creativity" or "You can't get there from here"? In *Creativity and reason in cognitive development*, 2nd ed., edited by J. C. Kaufman and J. Baer. New York: Cambridge University Press.

Csikszentmihalyi, M. (1988). Society, culture, and person: A systems view of creativity. In *The nature of creativity: Contemporary psychological perspectives*, edited by R. J. Sternberg, 325–339. New York: Cambridge University Press.

Gorman, M. E., and Plucker, J. A. (2003). Teaching invention as critical creative processes: A course on technoscientific creativity. In *Critical creative processes*, edited by M. A. Runco, 275–302. Cresskill, NJ: Hampton Press.

Gorman, M. E., Plucker, J. A., and Callahan, C. M. (1998). Turning students into inventors: Active learning modules for secondary students. *The Phi Delta Kappan*, 79, 530–535.

Kaufman, J. C., and Beghetto, R. A. (2009). Beyond big and little: The four c model of creativity. *Review of General Psychology*, 13, 1–12.

Kaufman, J., Plucker, J. A., and Baer, J. (2008). *Essentials of creativity assessment*. New York: John Wiley.

Lim, W., and Plucker, J. A. (2001). Creativity through a lens of social responsibility: Implicit theories of creativity with Korean samples. *Journal of Creative Behavior*, 35, 115–130.

Makel, M. C., and Plucker, J. A. (2014). Creativity is more than novelty: Reconsidering replication as a creative act. *Psychology of Aesthetics, Creativity, and the Arts*, 8, 27–29.

Packer, M. J., and Goicoechea, J. (2000). Sociocultural and constructivist theories of learning: Ontology, not just epistemology. *Educational Psychologist*, 35, 227–241.

Plucker, J. A. (1998). Beware of simple conclusions: The case for content generality of creativity. *Creativity Research Journal*, 11, 179–182.

(1999a). Is the proof in the pudding? Reanalyses of Torrance's (1958 to present) longitudinal study data. *Creativity Research Journal*, 12, 103–114.

(1999b). Reanalyses of student responses to creativity checklists: Evidence of content generality. *Journal of Creative Behavior*, 33, 126–137.

(2002). What's in a name? Young adolescents' implicit conceptions of invention. *Science Education*, 86, 149–160.

(2004). Generalization of creativity across domains: Examination of the method effect hypothesis. *Journal of Creative Behavior*, 38, 1–12.

(2005). The (relatively) generalist view of creativity. In *Creativity across domains: Faces of the muse*, edited by J. C. Kaufman and J. Baer, 307–312. Mahwah, NJ: Lawrence Erlbaum Associates.

(2016a). *Creativity and innovation: Theory, research, and practice*. Waco, TX: Prufrock Press.

(2016b). Creative articulation. In *Creativity and innovation: Theory, research, and practice*, edited by J. A. Plucker, 151–163. Waco, TX: Prufrock Press.

(2017). Toward a science of creativity: Considerable progress but much work to be done. *Journal of Creative Behavior*, 51, 301–304.

Plucker, J. A., and Beghetto, R. (2003). Why not be creative when we enhance creativity? In *Rethinking gifted education*, edited by J. H. Borland, 215–226. New York: Teachers College Press.

(2004). Why creativity is domain general, why it looks domain specific, and why the distinction does not matter. In *Creativity: From potential to realization*, edited by R. J. Sternberg, E. L. Grigorenko, and J. L. Singer, 153–167. Washington, DC: American Psychological Association.

Plucker, J. A., Beghetto, R. A., and Dow, G. (2004). Why isn't creativity more important to educational psychologists? Potential, pitfalls, and future directions in creativity research. *Educational Psychologist*, 39, 83–96.

Plucker, J. A., and Dana, R. Q. (1998a). Alcohol, tobacco, and marijuana use: Relationships to undergraduate students' creative achievement. *Journal of College Student Development*, 39, 472–481.

(1998b). Creativity of undergraduates with and without family history of alcohol and other drug problems. *Addictive Behaviors*, 23, 711–714.

Plucker, J. A., and Dow, G. T. (2010). Attitude change as the precursor to creativity enhancement. In *Nurturing creativity in the classroom*, edited by R. Beghetto and J. Kaufman, 362–379. New York: Cambridge University Press.

(2017). Attitude change as the precursor to creativity enhancement. In *Nurturing creativity in the classroom*, 2nd ed., edited by R. A. Beghetto and J. C. Kaufman, 190–211. New York: Cambridge University Press.

Plucker, J. A., and Gorman, M. E. (1999). Invention is in the mind of the adolescent: Evaluation of a summer course one year later. *Creativity Research Journal*, 12, 141–150.

Plucker, J. A., Guo, J., and Dilley, A. (2018). Research-guided programs and strategies for nurturing creativity. In S. I. Pfeiffer, E. Shaunessy-Dedrick, and M. Foley-Nicpon (Eds.) *APA handbook of giftedness and talent* (pp. 387–397). Washington, DC: American Psychological Association.

Plucker, J. A., Holden, J., and Neustadter, D. (2008). The criterion problem and creativity in film: Psychometric characteristics of various measures. *Psychology of Aesthetics, Creativity, and the Arts*, 2, 190–196.

Plucker, J. A., Kaufman, J. C., Temple, J. S., and Qian, M. (2009). Do experts and novices evaluate movies the same way? *Psychology and Marketing*, 26, 470–478.

Plucker, J. A., Lim, W., and Lee, K. (2017). Viewing through one prism or two? Discriminant validity of implicit theories of intelligence and creativity. *Psychology of Aesthetics, Creativity, and the Arts*, 11, 392–402.

Plucker, J. A., and Makel, M. C. (2010). Assessment of creativity. In *The Cambridge handbook of creativity*, edited by R. J. Sternberg and J. C. Kaufman, 48–73. New York: Cambridge University Press.

Plucker, J. A., Makel, M. C., and Qian, M. (forthcoming). Assessment of creativity. In *The Cambridge handbook of creativity*, 2nd ed., edited by R. J. Sternberg and J. C. Kaufman. New York: Cambridge University Press.

Plucker, J. A., McNeely, A., and Morgan, C. (2009). Controlled substance-related beliefs and use: Relationships to undergraduates' creative personality traits. *Journal of Creative Behavior*, 43, 94–101.

Plucker, J. A., McWilliams, J., and Alanazi, R. (2016). Creativity, culture, and the digital revolution: Implications and considerations for education. In *Palgrave handbook of creativity and culture research*, edited by V. Glăveanu, 517–533. London: Palgrave Macmillan.

Plucker, J. A., Qian, M., and Schmalensee, S. L. (2014). Is what you see what you really get? Comparison of scoring techniques in the assessment of real-world divergent thinking. *Creativity Research Journal*, 26, 135–143.

Plucker, J. A., Qian, M., and Wang, S. (2011). Is originality in the eye of the beholder? Comparison of scoring techniques in the assessment of divergent thinking. *Journal of Creative Behavior*, 45, 1–22.

Plucker, J. A., and Renzulli, J. S. (1999). Psychometric approaches to the study of human creativity. In *Handbook of creativity*, edited by R. J. Sternberg, 35–60. New York: Cambridge University Press.

Plucker, J. A., and Runco, M. A. (1998). The death of creativity measurement has been greatly exaggerated: Current issues, recent advances, and future directions in creativity assessment. *Roeper Review*, 21, 36–39.

Plucker, J. A., and Zabelina, D. (2009). Creativity and interdisciplinarity: One creativity or many creativities? *ZDM: The International Journal on Mathematics Education*, 41, 5–12.

Reis, S. M., and Renzulli, J. S. (2003). Research related to the Schoolwide Enrichment Triad Model. *Gifted Education International*, 18(1), 15–39.

Runco, M. A., and Jaeger, G. J. (2012). The standard definition of creativity. *Creativity Research Journal*, 24, 92–96.

Runco, M. A., Plucker, J. A., and Lim, W. (2001). Development and psychometric integrity of a measure of ideational behavior. *Creativity Research Journal*, 13, 393–400.

Simonton, D. K. (1988). Creativity, leadership, and chance. In *The nature of creativity: Contemporary psychological perspectives*, edited by R. J. Sternberg, 386–426. New York: Cambridge University Press.

(1989). Chance-configuration theory of scientific creativity. In *The psychology of science: Contributions to metascience*, edited by B. Gholson, W. R. Shadish Jr., R. A. Neimeyer, and A. C. Houts, 170–213. New York: Cambridge University Press.

(2012). Taking the US Patent Office criteria seriously: A quantitative three-criterion creativity definition and its implications. *Creativity Research Journal*, 24, 97–106.

Stein, M. I. (1974). *Stimulating creativity: Vol. 1. Individual procedures.* New York: Academic Press.

(1975). *Stimulating creativity: Vol. 2. Group procedures.* New York: Academic Press.

Sternberg, R. J. (1985). *Beyond IQ: A triarchic theory of human intelligence.* New York: Cambridge University Press.

(Ed.). (1988). *The nature of creativity: Contemporary psychological perspectives.* New York: Cambridge University Press.

(Ed.). (1999). *Handbook of creativity.* New York: Cambridge University Press.

Sternberg, R. J., and Lubart, T. I. (1991). An investment theory of creativity and its development. *Human Development*, 34, 1–31.

(1992). Buy low and sell high: An investment approach to creativity. *Current Directions in Psychological Science*, 1, 1–5.

Wertsch, J. V., del Río, P., and Alvarez, A. (Eds.). (1995). *Sociocultural studies of mind.* New York: Cambridge University Press.

Yi, X., Plucker, J. A., and Guo, J. (2015). Modeling influences on divergent thinking and artistic creativity. *Thinking Skills and Creativity*, 16, 62–68.

CHAPTER 13

Creative Cognition at the Individual and Team Levels
What Happens before and after Idea Generation

Roni Reiter-Palmon

In the last few decades, interest in understanding creativity – the factors that facilitate or inhibit it – has grown tremendously. In part, this interest has stemmed from creativity being recognized as an important skill in the twenty-first century. A survey of more than 1,500 CEOs of companies from across the globe indicated that creativity is an important skill for managers that must deal with nonroutine problems and adapt to changing business environments (IBM, 2010). Similarly, according to the global digital citizen foundation (globaldigitalcitizen.org), educators indicate that creativity is an important twenty-first-century skill for students. Creativity has also been described as an end in itself (Cropley, 1990) and as a means to other ends, such as health and happiness (Richards, 2007). As such, the concept of creativity has been investigated in multiple subfields of psychology (Reiter-Palmon, Beghetto, and Kaufman, 2014).

As an industrial/organizational (I/O) psychologist, my interest has always been in studying creativity and its application to business and industry. The definition that guides research in the area of business, management, and I/O psychology has focused on the creative product. Specifically, creativity has been defined as a "novel product, idea, or problem solution that is of value to the individual and/or the larger social group" (Hennessey and Amabile, 2010, p. 572). Although the focus on the product can be found also in the study of creativity in general, it is the outcome that is important as businesses are not interested in creativity for the sake of creativity.

This focus on the product underlies our research. The factors that lead to creative products are complex and as such models that focus on explaining creativity include multiple factors at the individual and contextual level (Amabile, 1988; Hennessey and Amabile, 2010; Mumford and Gustafson, 1988; Woodman, Sawyer, and Griffin, 1993). Many of these models incorporate aspects of cognition and thought processes as important predictors or facilitators of creativity. There are a number of models that specifically focus on the cognitive processes associated with creativity (Finke, Ward, and Smith, 1992; Merrifield, Guilford, Christensen, and Frick, 1962; Mumford, Mobley, Uhlman, Reiter-Palmon, and Doares, 1991; Sternberg, 2012, forthcoming; Wallas, 1926).

Mumford et al. (1991) developed a cognitive process model of creativity based on the integration of various process models of creativity with models from the cognitive literature regarding problem solving. The Mumford et al. (1991) model includes eight processes: problem construction, information encoding, category search, specification of best fitting categories, category combination, idea evaluation, implementation, and monitoring.

Although idea generation is not directly specified, it is implied in the category combination process. The idea generation process of creative problem solving has received tremendous attention in the literature. Work on idea generation blossomed after Guilford's (1950) APA address, and a significant amount of research focused on divergent thinking as the outcome of interest, conflating idea generation with creativity (Hornberg and Reiter-Palmon, 2017; Kaufman, Plucker, and Baer, 2008). At the team level, brainstorming (Osborn, 1953) provides the equivalent of divergent thinking. As with individual-level research, much of the work on creativity in teams uses quantity of ideas generated as the main outcome, and refers to idea generation as creativity (Larey and Paulus, 1999; Mullen, Johnson, and Salas, 1991).

Although the quantity of ideas may be of importance in certain circumstances, organizations do not usually care about number of ideas. Rather, what is important is to have ideas or solutions that work, that solve a problem or need, and that are novel. Therefore, a better assessment is found through evaluating quality and originality of the solution. Not only is divergent thinking typically evaluated for fluency, which is a limited and inconsistent predictor of real-world creativity (Runco, Plucker, and Lim, 2000), but focusing primarily on divergent thinking provides scientific understanding regarding only one of the processes associated with creativity and creative problem solving. In order to gain a full understanding of creativity we must move beyond divergent thinking or idea generation, and understand what role do other processes such as problem identification and construction, idea evaluation and selection, and implementation planning, play in creativity. Unfortunately, these processes have not received as much attention in the literature (Mumford, Mobley, Reiter-Palmon, Uhlman, and Doares, 1991; Reiter-Palmon, Herman, and Yammarino, 2008).

Problem Construction

The increasing uncertainty facing organizations means that employees are confronted with more ill-defined and ambiguous problems than in the past. Ill-defined problems are characterized by multiple possible goals, multiple ways of solving the problem, and multiple possible and acceptable solutions. It is this ambiguity that allows for creative solutions to arise (Mumford, Mobley, Reiter-Palmon, Uhlman, and Doares, 1991; Schraw, Dunkle, and Bendixen, 1995). Given this ambiguity, the creative problem solver must first construct the problem to be solved. During the problem construction process, the problem solver engages in a number of activities: the problem solver must recognize that there is a problem to be solved, define the problem parameters of the problem, and construct the problem constructed (Reiter-Palmon and Robinson, 2009).

Although early theoretical approaches to creativity have included problem identification and construction (Wallas, 1926), empirical work was lacking. The seminal studies by Getzels and Csikszentmihalyi (1975, 1976) marked the beginning of empirical work on problem construction. However, even after the publication, research on problem construction lagged. Only in the 1990s have we seen a substantial increase in the empirical study of problem construction. A theoretical model of problem construction was then developed by Mumford, Reiter-Palmon, and Redmond (1994) (see Figure 13.1).

The cognitive process model suggested by Mumford, Reiter-Palmon, and Redmond (1994) indicates that problem construction starts with a signaling event, and situational cues that need to be perceived and attended to. Cues that are attended to tend to be salient because, for example, they are personally meaningful or incongruent (Mumford, Reiter-Palmon, and Redmond, 1994). The cues in turn trigger one or more problem representations, which are mental representations or schemas of past experience in problem-solving episodes (Holyoak, 1984). Problem representations contain information about the goals of the problem-solving effort, any constraints or restrictions, information needed and processes to be used (Gick and Holyoak, 1983).

The salience of the cue and the strength of the cue's association to past experiences are related to the strength of the activated problem representations. In addition, as problems increase in complexity, so do the cues and resulting problem representations associated with them. That is, a complex and ambiguous problem may result in a number of problem representations being activated. Depending on the number and complexity of

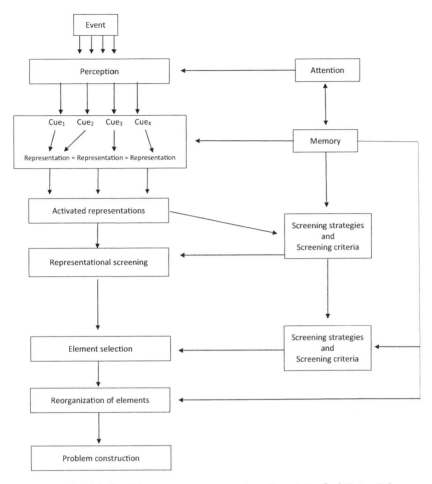

Figure 13.1 Model of problem construction operations. From Mumford, Reiter-Palmon, and Redmond (1994)

the problem representations that are activated, a screening strategy is used (Mumford, Reiter-Palmon, and Redmond, 1994). Routine problems that have been encountered before may result in one problem representation being strongly activated and adopted. However, novel problems are more likely to elicit multiple problem representations. Therefore, the problem representations need to be screened and limited to the ones that will be used further (Mumford, Reiter-Palmon, and Redmond, 1994). The screening strategy chosen could vary depending on the goals of the problem-solving effort and individual differences.

Once the screening strategy and criteria are defined and employed, the problem representations should be reduced to elements that will contribute to the constructed problem. However, if too many elements are retained, then an element selection strategy must be employed, which would reduce the number of elements included in the final problem representation. The element selection strategy might be based on goals or retained key knowledge, events or procedures central to or salient in one or more of the representations from which the elements were derived. Finally, these elements are reorganized into a coherent form. If no other changes occur, then the elements will contribute the resulting constructed problem.

This model has a number of implications that have been supported by research. First, problem construction provides the basis for the processes that follow by providing structure to ill-defined and ambiguous problems (Reiter-Palmon and Hullsiek, 2010). As such, effective and creative problem identification and construction result in increased creativity. In fact, early research has focused on the relationship between problem construction and creative outcomes. The seminal study by Getzels and Csikszentmihalyi (1975, 1976), using art students, found that behavioral measures of problem construction observed as the students created and painted a still life picture were related to originality and aesthetic evaluation of the painting. Even more impressive is that these problem construction measures predicated long-term success as an artist seven and eighteen years later. Rostan (1994) found that critically acclaimed artists and scientists devoted more time to problem construction as compared to professionally competent artists and scientists. Voss, Wolfe, Lawrence, and Engle (1991) compared experts in political science to novices solving a political science problem, and noted that experts devoted more time to defining and constructing the problem. Similar results were obtained by Sternberg (1981) with nonentrentched tasks.

Other work evaluated problem construction more generally, and found it related to predictors of creativity such as divergent thinking (Okuda, Runco, and Berger, 1991), participation in creative activities outside of school (Okuda, Runco, and Berger, 1991), and developing more creative solutions to a problem-solving exercise (Mumford, Supinski, Baughman, Costanza, and Threlfall, 1997; Reiter-Palmon, Mumford, O'Connor Boes, and Runco, 1997; Reiter-Palmon, Mumford, and Threlfall, 1998). In addition, a meta-analysis by Ma (2009) found that problem construction had the strongest effect on creativity compared with other cognitive processes. While research supported the finding that engagement in problem construction was related to creativity, one important aspect that has not been studied was the direct relationship between problem construction of the specific problem and the resulting solution. We therefore conducted a study to specifically evaluate this. We found that the quality and originality of the problem restatements were predictive of the quality and originality of the solutions generated for that specific problem, above and beyond problem construction ability and divergent thinking ability (Arreola and Reiter-Palmon, 2016).

Second, the model suggests that problem construction tends to be automatic. Problem construction can occur more automatically when the problem solver frames the problem in ways that fit with past experiences and existing problem representations (Bagozzi and Dholakia, 2005; Johnson, Daniels, and Huff, 2001; Mumford, Reiter-Palmon, and Redmond, 1994). However, when problem construction is more effortful or deliberate, the resulting solution tends to also be more creative. Past research supports the notion that active engagement in problem construction is related to improved creativity. Active engagement has typically been accomplished through instructions to engage in the process prior to solving the problem (Baer, 1988; Redmond, Mumford, and Teach, 1993; Vernon and Hocking, 2016). The importance of active engagement is further supported by research on the effects of training in problem identification and construction on creativity. A meta-analysis conducted by Scott, Leritz, and Mumford (2004) on creativity training and its relation to creativity outcomes, and found that a focus on problem construction was related to improved creative performance across multiple studies.

Third, the model suggests that attention, perceptions, and the specific cues that are attended to are particularly important in shaping how the problem is constructed and then solved. Specifically, I suggest that the presence of inconsistent cues would result in the elicitation of multiple and different problem representations. Elicitation of these multiple problem representations is likely to result in the creation of a new problem representation, which would then result in increased creativity. Theoretical models on post-Piagetian thought (Arlin, 1975). Indeed, research evaluating the effects of cues or paradox on creativity has found this to be the case. Specifically, Reiter-Palmon, Mumford, O'Connor Boes, and Runco (1997) found that creativity was enhanced when participants solved problems that included inconsistent cues compared with cues that were consistent with the rest of the problem.

Work on dialectical thinking and creativity provides additional support for the role of inconsistent cues or paradox. Dialectical thinking refers to the ability of a problem solver to approach or perceive a situation or problem from multiple, seemingly inconsistent perspectives. Paletz and Peng (2009) found that that undergraduates who scored higher on a dialectical thinking measure demonstrated more originality on a creativity task than students with lower scores. Similarly, Yang, Wan, and Chiou (2010) found that undergraduates whose beliefs were more dialectical scored higher across six measures of divergent thinking than those with more confirmatory or normative belief patterns.

Another way in which inconsistency and paradox were studied was though the manipulation of inconsistent goals. Paletz and Peng (2009) manipulated dialectical thinking by asking undergraduate students to write a story about when their lives were full of either contradiction and change or stability and consistency. They found that participants writing the dialectical story were more original on an unrelated creative problem-solving task. Miron-Spektor, Gino, and Argote (2011) used manipulations to prime participants to adopt paradoxical frames during creative problem solving. A series of four studies utilizing different tasks found that those participants primed with paradoxical frames performed more creatively. Finally, Reiter-Palmon and McFeely (2017) evaluated the degree of paradox in problem restatement generated and the relationship between paradox in problem construction and creativity. Degree of paradox in the problem restatements was positively related to both quality and originality of the solution generated.

Another implication of the model is the importance of both divergent and convergent processes in the problem construction process. The model indicates both divergent elements (problem representation elicitation) and convergent elements (selection of problem representations and elements). However, past research has focused almost exclusively on the divergent aspects of problem construction by asking participants to generate multiple restatements (Baer, 1988; Reiter-Palmon, Mumford, O'Connor Boes, and Runco, 1997). Wigert (2013) has evaluated the role of both divergent and convergent thinking in problem construction. Results from this study indicated that participants that were asked to diverge and then converge on problem restatements were more creative than participants that only engaged in divergent thinking during the problem construction phase.

Team Problem Construction

Empirical research evaluating problem construction in teams is limited. Reiter-Palmon, Herman, and Yammarino (2008) suggested that project teams, interdisciplinary teams, and other teams that include heterogeneous members are more likely to face differences during the problem construction stage. Research indicates that creative teams suffer when the problem frameworks vary across team members, and the goal states identified through problem construction cannot be reconciled in a single solution, providing support for this proposition (Cronin and Weingart, 2007; Goh, Goodman, and Weingart, 2013). Cronin and Weingart (2007) refer to these differences as *representational gap* or rGaps. Teams with larger rGaps tend to have difficulty during problem construction, leading to poor cognitive integration as a team and lower creativity (Weingart, Cronin, Houser, Cagan, and Vogel, 2005). However, other research has suggested that larger rGaps may increase team creativity when teams identify the discrepancies early and use them to communicate about alternative pathways to solving the problem (Weingart, Todorova, and Cronin, 2008).

A qualitative study by Leonardi (2011) found that people from different departments had differences in aspects of the problem representation. Specifically, differences were found in the goals identified, key problems, strategies to solve the problem, knowledge required, and criteria that a solution should meet, which negatively influenced the innovation process. In addition, people were largely unaware that other departments were constructing the problem differently. Leonardi further found that when leaders encouraged teams to discuss problem features they were able to develop a shared framework, a common problem representation that in turn guided the innovation process. Similarly, Gish and Clausen (2013) found that preexisting knowledge guided the way individuals within teams constructed the problem. This led to conflict and disagreements during idea generation because team members were unaware that they were constructing the problem differently and were unable to resolve team conflict. This conflict, in turn, resulted in lowered creativity. However, when additional information was introduced that facilitated divergence in problem construction to identify multiple problem definitions, diverse teams were more effective at generating an innovative solution.

Lastly, my own work has explored how we can manipulate problem construction in teams. We wanted to see if instructions to engage actively in problem construction would have an effect on creativity. Our first study (Reiter-Palmon et al., 2011) compared teams that were asked to generate problem restatements prior to solving the problem to teams that were only asked to solve the problem. Solutions were then rated for quality and originality. The results of the study provided a surprising outcome – teams asked to restate the problem performed worse than those that did not. Probing further, we found that when more restatements were generated, the solutions were more creative. That is, effort in the problem construction phase was related to creativity – teams that generated more restatement and therefore exerted more effort – developed more creative ideas. However, just asking the team to engage in problem construction may be detrimental to creativity.

To further investigate the effects of instructions to engage in problem construction, I have conducted a second study (Reiter-Palmon, 2017) in which different approaches to problem construction were evaluated. In addition to replicating the two previous conditions (problem construction in teams and no problem construction), two conditions were added. In the third condition, after generating restatements individually, participants were asked to solve the problem as a team – they may have discussed their restatement or they may have not. In the fourth conditions, participants were asked to also discuss the restatements as a team and list team restatements prior to solving the problem as a team. The first analysis evaluated whether there were any differences between the three problem construction conditions (team only, individual only, both individual and team) in terms of solution quality and originality, and no differences were found. Therefore, all analyses compared problem construction combined across the three groups to no problem construction. There were no differences in the quality of the solution generated between these two conditions; however, marginal differences were found for solution originality. Contrary to the previous study, teams that engaged in problem construction generated more original solutions compared with those that did not engage in problem construction.

Team processes were also evaluated for differences between these two groups. Results indicated that both outcomes and process satisfaction were higher when teams engaged in problem construction compared with teams that did not. In addition, task conflict, relationship conflict, and process conflict were lower for teams that engaged in problem construction (regardless of the form of problem construction) compared with teams that did not. These findings suggest that team problem construction can be beneficial for creativity potentially through its effects on originality. It is possible that the specific instructions for problem construction reduced some of the ambiguity associated with solving ill-defined problems, and therefore reduced conflict and increased satisfaction. The results of this study were more in line with studies evaluating problem construction at the individual level, in finding a positive effect on creativity, but in contrast to the first study, in which negative effects were found.

Problem Construction: Conclusions and Future Directions

Overall, the research discussed suggests that although we have some basic understanding of problem construction at the individual level, much more work needs to be done. Although we know that engaging in problem construction is beneficial for creativity for individuals, we are still not quite clear on what causes individuals to engage in problem construction and the best ways to elicit problem construction. Furthermore, the model proposed by Mumford, Reiter-Palmon, and Redmond (1994) has not been fully investigated. For example, we know that cues elicit representations, but we have limited information on which cues are attended to and how these cues elicit different representations. The research on paradox suggests that potentially paradoxical cues or ones that do not fit with other information in the problem may elicit multiple representations, which will in turn result in more creative solutions. However, there may be additional mechanisms that operate in terms of attention to cues and types of cues that are relevant that should be investigated. For example, whether individuals attend to specific cues or consider them to be irrelevant. It is also likely that experience and expertise may play a role in problem construction and attention to cues (Voss, Wolf, Lawrence, and Engle, 1991). Holyoak (1984) suggested that problem representations are based on past experiences. However, research directly connecting past experience with how problems are constructed is not available.

   In addition, our understanding of factors that influence the effectiveness of the problem construction process is still limited. We know that that effort during the problem construction and identification process matters, but motivational factors, such as creative self-efficacy, intrinsic motivation, or task interest, have not been fully studied with respect to problem construction. Similarly, the role of personality variables such as openness to experience or tolerance for ambiguity is not clear. It is possible that individuals who are open or tolerant will be more likely to exert more effort during the problem construction process, whereas those that are less open and less tolerant may be more likely to want to reach closure and construct the problem more rapidly. Other personality variables may also influence how individual construe ambiguous situations (Reiter-Palmon, Mumford, and Threlfall, 1998). For example, aggressive individuals may be more likely to view ambiguous situations in terms of harm or aggressiveness (Harris, Reiter-Palmon, and Kaufman, 2013; Harris, Reiter-Palmon, and Ligon, 2014).

At the team level, we have only started to gain an understanding of the role of problem construction. Reiter-Palmon, Herman, and Yammarino (2008) suggest that as a result of different past experiences, knowledge, and educational background, as well as personality and motivational factors, individual team members are likely to frame the problem differently. These differences are likely to be more pronounced in diverse teams. Furthermore, individuals in teams will be less likely to be aware that other individuals are framing the problem in a different way (Cronin and Weingart, 2007; Gish and Clausen, 2013), leading to disagreements about the best solution. Teams may address the presence of multiple perspectives and therefore multiple problem constructions in different ways, for example, ignoring the differences and focusing on similarities, selecting the majority view, or integrating the diverse problem constructions in a unique new way to view the problem. Future research should determine the factors that would lead to specific ways of addressing the diversity of problem constructions. Furthermore, future research should evaluate the relationship between these various approaches to solution creativity. In addition, individual differences in personality may also play a role. For example, more conscientious individuals may be more likely to try to make sure that different conceptualizations and constructions are discussed. Introverted individuals may be more reluctant to share their construction, especially if it is different from others. These speculations suggested that team composition in terms of individual differences, and not just experience and education may have a significant effect on team problem construction.

The studies on team creativity and problem construction have also suggested that how teams manage conflict is important, and also emphasizing the role of the leader for problem identification and construction and conflict management. Reiter-Palmon (2017) found that encouraging teams to actively engage in problem identification and construction was related to reduced perceptions of conflict and increased satisfaction, suggesting that this indeed may be one mechanism by which problem construction may operate in teams. However, more research is needed on the interaction between social processes such as leadership, conflict, or trust and the cognitive process of problem construction in teams.

Finally, the issue of measurement of problem construction still needs investigation. At the individual level, problem construction has been measured and evaluated using think-aloud protocols or observations (Getzels and Csikszentmihalyi, 1975, 1976), by asking participants to restate the problem in as many ways as they can (Baer, 1988; Reiter-Palmon, Mumford, and Threlfall, 1998), or by focusing on goals and constraints (Mumford,

Baughman, Threlfall, Supinski, and Costanza, 1996; Wigert, 2013). In all cases, the process of problem construction becomes conscious, and therefore, our ability to study how problem construction occurs more naturally is limited (Reiter-Palmon and Robinson, 2009). In addition, additional research is needed to determine if indeed these methods are equivalent, not only in terms of their effect on the creativity of the solution, but also in terms of the processes associated with problem construction and problem solving.

At the team level, observations of problem construction may be somewhat easier. That is, as teams discuss the problem, statements relating to how the problem should be defined and constructed may occur more naturally. However, it is also possible that teams will not engage in this process and proceed almost immediately to the solution (Gish and Clausen, 2013; Reiter-Palmon, Herman, and Yammarino, 2008), thus preventing the researchers from studying the problem construction process. In addition, research on how to instruct teams to engage in problem construction (individually or as a team) is only starting, and additional research on whether teams should focus on restatements, goals, constraints, or all of these are lacking.

Idea Evaluation and Selection

Idea evaluation and selection refer to the process of evaluating ideas with respect to specific standards or goals, and then the selection of an idea to implement. Mumford, Lonergan, and Scott (2002) proposed that idea evaluation and selection include three major activities: forecasting possible consequences and outcomes of selecting and implementing an idea; judging how well the characteristics of an idea fit with specific standards and criteria; and choosing, revising, or rejecting the idea as a solution. The idea evaluation and selection process is typically viewed as more convergent; however, it also includes divergent elements (Runco and Chand, 1995), such as the need to forecast, for example, which requires thinking about various options and their impact. Idea evaluation and selection are critical for creative problem solving; in organizational settings, many ideas are generated, but only a few of the ideas reach the implementation phase (Sharma, 1999). Furthermore, the quality and originality of the final idea selected for implementation will depend on the quality of the evaluation and selection process.

One important question is whether people are able to accurately evaluate ideas. Runco and his colleagues, in a series of studies on idea evaluation, have found that indeed individuals are able to accurately evaluate ideas for originality and novelty (Basadur, Runco, and Vega, 2000; Runco and Basadur, 1993; Runco and Chand, 1995; Runco and Smith, 1992; Runco and Vega, 1990). However, it has also been suggested that individuals are likely to be more accurate in their evaluation of ideas and choose a creative idea if they are creative themselves (Basadur, Runco, and Vega, 2000; Benedek et al., 2016; Berg, 2016; Blair and Mumford, 2007; Kaufman and Beghetto, 2013; Kaufman, Beghetto, and Watson, 2016). That is, creative individuals are more likely to recognize creativity. In addition, individuals are more likely to select creative ideas if they are instructed to choose creative ideas (Lonergan, Scott, and Mumford, 2004).

Another issue raised regarding evaluation is the optimal timing for evaluation. Early work suggested that engaging in evaluation during the generation phase could be detrimental, which is the foundation for the brainstorming rule of suspending evaluation (Osborn, 1953). Supporting this, research on artists suggests that the role of evaluation increases during the creative process (Botella, Zenasni, and Lubart, 2011; Fürst, Ghisletta, and Lubart, 2012). However, other work has suggested that early evaluation may actually increase creativity (Fürst, Ghisletta, and Lubart, 2017; Lubart, 2009). Domain may play a role in the effect of timing. Lubart (2001) found that early evaluation was beneficial for a creative writing task, but no differences between early and later evaluation were found for drawing. The specific domain likely is important not only on the effect of timing of the evaluation but also on the standards used for evaluation. Feist (1999) suggested that evaluation will depend on the domain, such that evaluation of art is more intuitive while evaluation of science is more analytical. In a study designed to assess these domain differences, Sullivan and Ford (2005) have found that the type of problem presented to participants (strategic choice versus advertising) resulted in different evaluations of choices. The strategic choice evaluations produced two specific factors of novelty and value, whereas a combined factor emerged for the advertising campaign.

Research also evaluated the relationship between quality, originality, and evaluation of creativity. Benedek and colleagues (2016) suggested that people tend to underestimate the creativity of ideas presented to them, and that those with higher intelligence and openness to experience (both predictors of creativity) tend to mitigate against this bias. Similarly, Diedrich, Benedek, Jauk, and Neubauer (2015) found that novelty was a stronger predictor of creativity relative to usefulness. The role of usefulness only emerged when ideas were highly novel. Rietzschel, Nijstad, and Stroebe

(2010) found that asking participants to exclude ideas that were not effective or to focus on including effective ideas did not influence idea selection. However, instructions to focus on choosing a creative idea resulted in the selection of more original ideas. Unfortunately, this also resulted in choosing ideas of lower quality at the same time. Finally, Blair and Mumford (2007) found that participants tended to reject highly original or risky ideas and were more likely to select ideas that were consistent with social norms, easy to understand, and likely to quickly lead to desirable outcomes, especially under high time pressure. Put together, these results indicate that when selecting ideas, individuals tend to prefer quality or usefulness unless specifically told to focus on creativity. However, the latter may result in selecting ideas that are not truly creative, in that individuals focus on originality at the expense of quality.

Given the results above, improving the accuracy of evaluations is an important topic for study. Licuanan, Dailey, and Mumford (2007) found that inducing people to actively analyze ideas was related to a more accurate evaluation of the creativity of those ideas. One way in which accuracy can be improved is through training individuals to understand the standards for creativity and how to go about such evaluations. Our work suggests that training improved evaluations of creativity of individuals but only when training included examples, practice, and detailed rubrics for quality and originality (McFeely, Reiter-Palmon, Ligon, and Schoenbeck, 2016).

Research sought to identify stable individual difference characteristics that can predict idea evaluation and selection. Silvia et al. (2008) found that openness to experience predicts evaluation accuracy. Promotion and prevention focus have been suggested as motivational variables that can influence creativity. Specifically, individuals with a promotion focus tend to have an approach motivation and is related to advancement and achievement, whereas individuals with a prevention focus work to prevent errors and focus on safety. Herman and Reiter-Palmon (2011) found that promotion regulatory focus was related to the accuracy of assessing originality, whereas prevention regulatory focus was related to the accuracy of assessing quality. Similarly, Zhou, Wang, Song, and Wu (2017) found that individuals with promotion regulatory focus were more likely to recognize creative ideas as such. Finally, expertise is an important factor. Experts show better interrater agreement on creative products than novices (Kaufman, Baer, Cropley, Reiter-Palmon, and Sinnett, 2013; Kaufman, Baer, Cole, and Sexton, 2008; Kaufman, Niu, Sexton, and Cole, 2010) and their creativity judgments are not related to novice judgments (Kaufman and Baer, 2012).

Team Idea Evaluation and Selection

Early work on team idea evaluation and selection has focused on comparing nominal groups with interactive groups (Faure, 2004; Girotra, Terwiesch, and Ulrich, 2010; Putman and Paulus, 2009; Rietzschel, Nijstad, and
Stroebe, 2006). Nominal groups are not really groups at all, but rather, a
collection of individuals. That is, individuals work on the same task, and
their responses are pooled for a comparison. For example, in a divergent
thinking task, we can use a group of three individuals working together
to generate ideas, or we can use three individuals, each working alone, and
add the responses across all three. These studies found that nominal groups
generated more ideas, and more original ideas, than interactive groups,
whereas interactive groups generated more feasible ideas. However, ideas
selected for final consideration were of equivalent quality, suggesting that
groups may not be better than individuals or the collection of individual
responses.

As a result of these findings, researchers have tried to understand the processes associated with idea evaluation and selection in teams. Kennel and
Reiter-Palmon (2012) examined team creative idea evaluation and selection
outcomes. Teams were presented with ten ideas that were previously rated
for quality and originality. Teams were asked to evaluate the quality and
originality of each of the ideas following a specific rubric prior to coming
to consensus in selecting the best solution to solve the problem. Teams that
more accurately evaluated the quality of the set of solutions chose ideas of
higher quality to solve the problem, whereas teams that more accurately
evaluated the originality of the set of solutions chose ideas of higher creativity (i.e., originality *and* quality). Consistent with the notion that evaluations guide the choice of solutions (Basadur, 1995; Faure, 2004), Kennel
and Reiter-Palmon's study suggested that better idea evaluation outcomes
related to better idea selection outcomes. However, overall, teams did not
always select the best ideas out of those presented. Only 55 percent of the
teams selected high-quality or creative ideas. The other teams chose ideas
that they evaluated as being good but were of low or moderate quality as
assessed by experts.

Harvey and Kou (2013) sought to identify the relationship between idea
generation and idea evaluation by using a qualitative approach and observing teams generate and evaluate ideas. They have found that idea evaluation did not always follow from idea generation, and that in some cases,
the two co-occurred. Harvey and Kou suggested that engagement in evaluation processes supports the development of a shared framework for the

problem at hand and directs collective attention to ideas to guide feedback and decisions of how well ideas address the problem. This finding is also in line with individual-level findings regarding the timing of evaluation, indicating that early evaluation while still generating may be beneficial.

Other research has sought to identify ways in which the process of idea evaluation and idea selection can be structured and therefore be made more effective. Reiter-Palmon, Kennel, de Vreede, and de Vreede (forthcoming) attempted to provide a structure for both the idea evaluation and idea selection phase. During idea evaluation, teams were either provided a rubric for quality and originality evaluation or were just provided definitions. During the selection phase, teams were either asked to select their best idea or to first select their top five ideas and then choose the best one. Using a rubric to evaluate solutions resulted in selecting a solution of higher originality. There was also an interaction between structure for evaluation and selection. When teams were provided with structure for both, more original ideas were selected. When teams were given structure for selection but not evaluation, the least original solutions were selected. However, these structure effects were not found for quality. Given the tendency to favor quality over originality in both evaluation and selection, the ability to improve the selection of high-originality solutions, without hurting quality, is important. In fact, in this study, over 75 percent of the teams selected ideas that were either high quality (but not original) or creative (high quality and high originality). This is compared to the findings by Kennel and Reiter-Palmon (2012), in which only 55 percent of the teams selected high-quality or creative ideas. This comparison suggests that providing more structure at both the evaluation and selection phases may indeed benefit teams allowing for the selection of better (and more creative) ideas. Furthermore, it is possible that the rubrics used and the narrowing of the pool of ideas, allowed teams to create a shared framework for discussing the merits of ideas.

Mumford, Feldman, Hein, and Nagao (2001) evaluated the role of shared frames and priming on evaluation and selection of creative ideas. They found that the factors that influenced individual and group creativity were different. Individuals benefited from priming and generated more alternatives compared to the no-priming condition. This in turn was related to selecting a more creative solution. For groups, although priming led to the development of more alternatives, it did not necessarily lead to the selection of a more creative solution. Instead, groups benefited from having all individuals exposed to the same training when no prime was available. Moreover, this group outperformed all individuals as well as all other groups in the study. Mumford, Feldman, Hein, and Nagao (2001) suggested that the reason groups perform better when fewer alternatives are available, was that time and coordination requirements are minimized. However, because fewer resources are used to review multiple alternatives, groups are able to fully elaborate and expand on the better, more optimal choices for the solution to be implemented. In addition, having a shared understanding or a shared mental model facilitates production and the selection of creative solutions in groups. These results further underscore the importance of having an appropriate and shared understanding of the problem, or a problem representation. In this context, a shared understanding of the problem representation also created a shared understanding of how to evaluate the solutions generated or standards, which in turn allowed the selection of the most creative solution.

Idea Evaluation and Selection: Conclusions and Future Directions

The research on idea evaluation and selection indicates that individuals can identify creative ideas, but typically only when those individuals are creative themselves. Furthermore, individuals tend to prefer usefulness and feasibility over originality or novelty, resulting in the selection of routine rather creative ideas. The research on the standards used to guide idea evaluation and ultimately selection indicates that we need to have a better understanding of how these standards are developed and adopted. It has been suggested that standards may be developed during the problem identification and construction processes, such as in the form of a goal (Reiter-Palmon et al., 2008); however, no research directly connects problem construction with idea evaluation and idea selection. Additionally, identifying how to support the evaluation and selection of creative ideas is critical, given the tendency of individuals to choose practical ideas. Furthermore, given the results that the push for selecting original ideas may increase originality but lower quality of the chosen solution, it is important to identify ways in which individuals can be led to choose truly creative ideas that are high in originality and quality.

Only limited research exists on the relationship between individual differences (expertise, personality, and motivation) in idea evaluation and selection. Additional research should investigate not only the role of the Big Five beyond openness to experience, but also additional variables such as creative self-efficacy, creative identity, and tolerance for ambiguity. For example, those individuals with high creative self-efficacy and creative identity may be more likely to select ideas that are creative, as these align with their conception of themselves. Similarly, individuals who are tolerant of ambiguous situations may be more likely to positively evaluate creative ideas as the ambiguity associated with these ideas is not as troubling or difficult for them. Finally, understanding contextual factors that may facilitate or hinder accurate evaluation and selection of creative ideas is needed. Understanding how leadership may facilitate team selection of creative ideas can be a fruitful avenue for research as well as practical implications for organizations. Ina addition, understanding how guidance and training can facilitate more accurate evelution as well as selection of creative ideas needs to continue.

Results at the team level mirror that of individuals, and in fact teams have not been found to perform better than individuals on idea evaluation and selection tasks (Faure, 2004; Rietzschel, Nijstad, and Stroebe, 2006). It is however, unclear whether teams use the same standards that individuals do, whether teams show the same preference for practical ideas, or may even show a greater preference due to groupthink (Janis, 1972). In addition, if individuals within a team have difference standards for evaluation, it is unclear how these discrepancies are settled. Additional research studying how teams develop standards for evaluation and how teams address different standards by different individuals is needed. Some team research has sought to identify the factors that influence more accurate evaluation and selection of ideas, such as training, team composition, and guidance or structure during the process. However, the number of studies is still limited and the results do not show a consistent pattern. Some consistency seems to be emerging that shared frames may provide support for accurate evaluation and selecting creative ideas. However, additional research is needed to identify how best to create these shared frames.

REFERENCES

Amabile, T. M. (1988). A model of creativity and innovation in organizations. *Research in Organizational Behavior*, 10(1), 123–167.

Arlin, P. K. (1975). Cognitive development in adulthood: A fifth stage? *Developmental Psychology*, 11, 602–606.

Arreola, N. J., and Reiter-Palmon, R. (2016). The effect of problem construction creativity on solution creativity across multiple everyday problems. *Psychology of Aesthetics, Creativity, and the Arts*, 10(3), 287–295.

Baer, J. M. (1988). Long-term effects of creativity training with middle school students. *Journal of Early Adolescence*, 8, 183–193.

Bagozzi, R. P., and Dholakia, U. M. (2005). Three roles of past experience in goal setting and goal striving. In *The routines of decision making*, edited by T. Betsch and S. Haberstroh, 21–38. Mahwah, NJ: Lawrence Erlbaum.

Basadur, M. (1995). Optimal ideation-evaluation ratios. *Creativity Research Journal*, 8, 63–75.

Basadur, M., Runco, M. A., and Vega, L. A. (2000). Understanding how creative thinking skills, attitudes and behaviors work together: A causal process model. *Journal of Creative Behavior*, 34(2), 77–100.

Benedek, M., Nordtvedt, N., Jauk, E., Koschmieder, C., Pretsch, J., Krammer, G., and Neubauer, A. C. (2016). Assessment of creativity evaluation skills: A psychometric investigation in prospective teachers. *Thinking Skills and Creativity*, 21, 75–84.

Berg, J. M. (2016). Balancing on the creative highwire: Forecasting the success of novel ideas in organizations. *Administrative Science Quarterly*, 61(3), 433–468.

Blair, C. S., and Mumford, M. D. (2007). Errors in idea evaluation: Preference for the unoriginal? *Journal of Creative Behavior*, 41(3), 197–222.

Botella, M., Zenasni, F., and Lubart, T. (2011). A dynamic and ecological approach to the artistic creative process of arts students: An empirical contribution. *Empirical Studies of the Arts*, 29(1), 7–38.

Crockett, L. W. (2016). The critical 21st century skills every student needs and why. http://globaldigitalcitizen.org/21st-century-skills-every-student-needs.

Cronin, M. A., and Weingart, L. R. (2007). Representational gaps, information processing, and conflict in functionally diverse teams. *Academy of Management Review*, 32(3), 761–773.

Cropley, A. J. (1990). Creativity and mental health in everyday life. *Creativity Research Journal*, 3(3), 167–178.

Diedrich, J., Benedek, M., Jauk, E., and Neubauer, A. C. (2015). Are creative ideas novel and useful? *Psychology of Aesthetics, Creativity, and the Arts*, 9(1), 35–40.

Dillon, J. T. (1982). Problem finding and solving. *Journal of Creative Behavior*, 16(2), 97–111.

Faure, C. (2004). Beyond brainstorming: Effects of different group procedures on selection of ideas and satisfaction with the process. *Journal of Creative Behavior*, 38(1), 13–34.

Feist, G. J. (1999). The influence of personality on artistic and scientific creativity. In *The handbook of creativity*, edited by R. J. Sternberg, 273–292. London: Cambridge University Press.

Finke, R. A., Ward, T. B., and Smith, S. M. (1992). *Creative cognition: Theory, research, and applications*. Cambridge, MA: MIT Press.

Fürst, G., Ghisletta, P., and Lubart, T. (2012). The creative process in visual art: A longitudinal multivariate study. *Creativity Research Journal*, 24(4), 283–295.

(2017). An experimental study of the creative process in writing. *Psychology of Aesthetics, Creativity, and the Arts*, 11(2), 202–215.

Getzels, J. W., and Csikszentmihalyi, M. (1975). From problem-solving to problem finding. In *Perspectives in creativity*, edited by I. A. Taylor and J. W. Getzels, 90–116. Chicago: Aldine.

(1976). The creative vision: A longitudinal study of problem finding in art. *Journal of Aesthetics and Art Criticism*, 36(1), 96–98.

Gick, M. L., and Holyoak, K. J. (1983). Schema induction and analogical transfer. *Cognitive Psychology*, 15(1), 1–38.

Girotra, K., Terwiesch, C., and Ulrich, K. T. (2010). Idea generation and the quality of the best idea. *Management Science*, 56(4), 591–605.

Gish, L., and Clausen, C. (2013). The framing of product ideas in the making: A case study of the development of an energy saving pump. *Technology Analysis and Strategic Management*, 25(9), 1085–1101.

Goh, K. T., Goodman, P. S., and Weingart, L. R. (2013). Team innovation processes: An examination of activity cycles in creative project teams. *Small Group Research*, 44(2), 159–194.

Guilford, J. P. (1950). Creativity. *American Psychologist*, 5(9), 444–454.

(1967). *The nature of human intelligence*. New York: McGraw-Hill.

Harris, D. J., Reiter-Palmon, R., and Kaufman, J. C. (2013). The effect of emotional intelligence and task type on malevolent creativity. *Psychology of Aesthetics, Creativity, and the Arts*, 7(3), 237–244.

Harris, D. J., Reiter-Palmon, R., and Ligon, G. S. (2014). Construction or demolition: Does problem construction influence the ethicality of creativity? In *The ethics of creativity*, edited by S. Moran, D. Cropley, and J. C. Kaufman, 170–186. London: Palgrave Macmillan.

Harvey, S., and Kou, C. Y. (2013). Collective engagement in creative tasks: The role of evaluation in the creative process in groups. *Administrative Science Quarterly*, 58(3), 346–386.

Hennessey, B. A., and Amabile, T. M. (2010). Creativity. *Annual Review of Psychology*, 61(1), 569–598.

Herman, A., and Reiter-Palmon, R. (2011). The effect of regulatory focus on idea generation and idea evaluation. *Psychology of Aesthetics, Creativity, and the Arts*, 5(1), 13.

Holyoak, K. J. (1984). Mental models in problem solving. In *Tutorials in learning and memory: Essays in honor of Gordon Bower*, edited by J. R. Anderson and S. M. Kosslyn, 193–218. San Francisco: W. H. Freeman.

Hornberg, J., and Reiter-Palmon, R. (2017). Personality and the Big Five personality traits: Is the relationship dependent on the creativity measure? In *The Cambridge handbook of creativity and personality research*, edited by G. J. Feist, R. Reiter-Palmon, and J. C. Kaufman, 275–294. Cambridge: Cambridge University Press.

Janis, I. L. (1972). *Victims of groupthink: A psychological study of foreign-policy decisions and fiascoes*. Oxford: Houghton Mifflin.

Johnson, P., Daniels, K., and Huff, A. (2001). Sense making, leadership, and mental models. In *The nature of organizational leadership: Understanding the performance imperatives confronting today's leaders*, edited by S. J. Zaccaro, and R. J. Klimoski, 79–103. USA: Pfeiffer.

Kaufman, J. C., and Baer, J. (2012). Beyond new and appropriate: Who decides what is creative? *Creativity Research Journal*, 24, 83–91.

Kaufman, J. C., Baer, J., Cropley, D. H., Reiter-Palmon, R., and Sinnett, S. (2013). Furious activity vs. understanding: How much expertise is needed to evaluate creative work? *Psychology of Aesthetics, Creativity, and the Arts*, 7(4), 332–340.

Kaufman, J. C., Baer, J., Cole, J. C., and Sexton, J. D. (2008). A comparison of expert and nonexpert raters using the consensual assessment technique. *Creativity Research Journal*, 20(2), 171–178.

Kaufman, J. C., and Beghetto, R. A. (2013). In praise of Clark Kent: Creative metacognition and the importance of teaching kids when (not) to be creative. *Roeper Review*, 35, 155–165.

Kaufman, J. C., Beghetto, R A., and Watson, C. (2016). Creative metacognition and self-ratings of creative performance: A 4-C perspective. *Learning and Individual Differences*, 51, 394–399.

Kaufman, J. C., Niu, W., Sexton, J. D., and Cole, J. C. (2010). In the eye of the beholder: Differences across ethnicity and gender in evaluating creative work. *Journal of Applied Social Psychology*, 40(2), 496–511.

Kaufman, J. C., Plucker, J. A., and Baer, J. (2008). *Essentials of creativity assessment.* Hoboken, NJ: John Wiley.

Kennel, V., and Reiter-Palmon, R. (2012). Teams and creativity: Accuracy in idea evaluation and selection. Paper presented at the 120th American Psychological Association Conference, Orlando, FL, August.

Larey, T. S., and Paulus, P. B. (1999). Group preference and convergent tendencies in small groups: A content analysis of group brainstorming performance. *Creativity Research Journal*, 12(3), 175–184.

Leonardi, P. M. (2011). Innovation blindness: Culture, frames, and cross-boundary problem construction in the development of new technology concepts. *Organization Science*, 22(2), 347–369.

Licuanan, B. F., Dailey, L. R., and Mumford, M. D. (2007). Idea evaluation: Error in evaluating highly original ideas. *Journal of Creative Behavior*, 41(1), 1–27.

Lonergan, D. C., Scott, G. M., and Mumford, M. D. (2004). Evaluative aspects of creative thought: Effects of appraisal and revision standards. *Creativity Research Journal*, 16(2–3), 231–246.

Lubart, T. I. (2001). Models of the creative process: Past, present and future. *Creativity Research Journal*, 13(3–4), 295–308.

(2009). In search of the writer's creative process. In *The psychology of creative writing*, edited by S. B. Kaufman and J. C. Kaufman, 149–165. London: Cambridge University Press.

Ma, H. H. (2009). The effect size of variables associated with creativity: A meta-analysis. *Creativity Research Journal*, 21(1), 30–42.

McFeely, S. M., Reiter-Palmon, R., Ligon, G., and Schoenbeck, M. (2016). Differential effects of creativity rater training on quality and originality. Poster presented at the 31st annual Society for Industrial/Organizational Psychology Meeting, Anaheim, CA, April.

Merrifield, P. R., Guilford, J. P., Christensen, P. R., and Frick, J. W. (1962). The role of intellectual factors in problem solving. *Psychological Monographs: General and Applied*, 76(10), 1–21.

Miron-Spektor, E., Gino, F., and Argote, L. (2011). Paradoxical frames and creative sparks: Enhancing individual creativity through conflict and integration. *Organizational Behavior and Human Decision Processes*, 116(2), 229–240.

Mullen, B., Johnson, C., and Salas, E. (1991). Productivity loss in brainstorming groups: A meta-analytic integration. *Basic and Applied Social Psychology*, 12(1), 3–23.

Mumford, M. D., Baughman, W. A., Threlfall, K. V., Supinski, E. P., and Costanza, D. P. (1996). Process-based measures of creative problem-solving skills: Problem construction. *Creativity Research Journal*, 9(1), 63–76.

Mumford, M. D., Feldman, J. M., Hein, M. B., and Nagao, D. J. (2001). Tradeoffs between ideas and structure: Individual versus group performance in creative problem solving. *Journal of Creative Behavior*, 35(1), 1–23.

Mumford, M. D., and Gustafson, S. B. (1988). Creativity syndrome: Integration, application, and innovation. *Psychological Bulletin*, 103(1), 27–43.

Mumford, M. D., Lonergan, D. C., and Scott, G. (2002). Evaluating creative ideas: Processes, standards, and context. *Inquiry: Critical Thinking across the Disciplines*, 22(1), 21–30.

Mumford, M. D., Marks, M. A., Connelly, M. S., Zaccaro, S. J., and Johnson, J. F. (1998). Domain-based scoring in divergent-thinking tests: Validation evidence in an occupational sample. *Creativity Research Journal*, 11(2), 151–163.

Mumford, M. D., Mobley, M. I., Reiter-Palmon, R., Uhlman, C. E., and Doares, L. M. (1991). Process analytic models of creative capacities. *Creativity Research Journal*, 4(2), 91–122.

Mumford, M. D., Reiter-Palmon, R., and Redmond, M. R. (1994). Problem construction and cognition: Applying problem representations in ill-defined domains. In *Problem Finding, Problem Solving, and Creativity*, edited by M. A. Runco. New York: Ablex.

Mumford, M. D., Supinski, E. P., Baughman, W. A., Costanza, D. P., and Threlfall, K. V. (1997). Process-based measures of creative problem-solving skills: V. overall prediction. *Creativity Research Journal*, 10(1), 73–85.

Okuda, S. M., Runco, M. A., and Berger, D. E. (1991). Creativity and the finding and solving of real-world problems. *Journal of Psychoeducational Assessment*, 9(1), 45–53.

Osborn, A. F. (1953). *Applied imagination, principles and procedures of creative thinking*. Oxford: Oxford University Press.

Paletz, S. B., and Peng, K. (2009). Problem finding and contradiction: Examining the relationship between naive dialectical thinking, ethnicity, and creativity. *Creativity Research Journal*, 21(2–3), 139–151.

Putman, V. L., and Paulus, P. B. (2009). Brainstorming, brainstorming rules and decision making. *Journal of Creative Behavior*, 43(1), 29–40.

Ray, D. K., and Romano, N. C. (2013). Creative problem solving in GSS groups: Do creative styles matter? *Group Decision and Negotiation*, 1(29).

Redmond, M. R., Mumford, M. D., and Teach, R. (1993). Putting creativity to work: Effects of leader behavior on subordinate creativity. *Organizational Behavior and Human Decision Processes*, 55(1), 120–151.

Reiter-Palmon, R. (2017). The effect of problem construction on team process and creativity. Paper presented at the 12th annual conference for INGroup, St. Louis, MO, July.

Reiter-Palmon, R., Beghetto, R., and Kaufman, J. C. (2014). Looking at creativity through the business-psychology-education (BPE) lens: The challenge and benefits of listening to each other. In *Creativity research: An interdisciplinary and multidisciplinary research handbook*, edited by E. Shiu, 9–30. New York: Routledge.

Reiter-Palmon, R., Herman, A. E., and Yammarino, F. (2008). Creativity and cognitive processes: A multi-level linkage between individual and team cognition. In *Multi-level issues in creativity and innovation*, edited by M. D. Mumford, S. T. Hunter, and K. E. Bedell-Avers, 7:203–267. Copenhagen: JAI Press.

Reiter-Palmon, R., and Hullsiek, B. (2010). The role of creativity in JDM. *Industrial and Organizational Psychology: Perspectives on Science and Practice*, 3(1), 431–433.

Reiter-Palmon, R., Kennel, V., de Vreede, T., and de Vreede, G. J. (forthcoming). Structuring team idea evaluation and selection of solution: Does it influence creativity? In *Palgrave handbook of social creativity research*, edited by I. Lebuda and V. Glăvenou. New York: Palgrave Press.

Reiter-Palmon, R., and McFeely, S. (2017). The effect of paradoxical and convergent thinking during problem construction on creative problem solving. Paper presented at the 125th annual convention of the American Psychological Association, Washington, DC.

Reiter-Palmon, R., Mumford, M. D., O'Connor Boes, J., and Runco, M. A. (1997). Problem construction and creativity: The role of ability, cue consistency, and active processing. *Creativity Research Journal*, 10(1), 9–23.

Reiter-Palmon, R., Mumford, M. D., and Threlfall, V. K. (1998). Solving everyday problems creatively: The role of problem construction and personality type. *Creativity Research Journal*, 11(3), 187–197.

Reiter-Palmon, R., and Robinson, E. J. (2009). Problem identification and construction: What do we know, what is the future? *Psychology of Aesthetics, Creativity, and the Arts*, 3(1), 43–47.

Reiter-Palmon, R., Wigert, B., Morral-Robinson, E., Hullsiek, B., Arreola, N., and Crough D. (2011). Team cognition and creativity: The case of problem construction. Poster presented at the 1st Israel Organizational Behavior Conference, Tel-Aviv, Israel, December.

Richards, R. (Ed.). (2007). *Everyday creativity and new views of human nature: Psychological, social, and spiritual perspectives*. Washington, DC: American Psychological Society.

Rietzschel, E. F., Nijstad, B. A., and Stroebe, W. (2006). Productivity is not enough: A comparison of interactive and nominal brainstorming groups on idea generation and selection. *Journal of Experimental Social Psychology*, 42(2), 244–251.

(2010). The selection of creative ideas after individual idea generation: Choosing between creativity and impact. *British Journal of Psychology*, 101(1), 47–68.

Rostan, S. M. (1994). Problem finding, problem solving, and cognitive controls: An empirical investigation of critically acclaimed productivity. *Creativity Research Journal*, 7(2), 97–110.

Runco, M. A. (1999). Tests of creativity. In *Encyclopedia of creativity*, edited by M. A. Runco and S. Pritzker, appendix, pp. 755–760. San Diego, CA: Academic Press.

Runco, M. A., and Basadur, M. (1993). Assessing ideational and evaluative skills and creative styles and attitudes. *Creativity and Innovation Management*, 2(3), 166–173.

Runco, M. A., and Chand, I. (1995). Cognition and creativity. *Educational Psychology Review*, 7(3), 243–267.

Runco, M. A., and Mraz, W. (1992). Scoring divergent thinking tests using total ideational output and a creativity index. *Educational and Psychological Measurement*, 52(1), 213–221.

Runco, M. A., Plucker, J. A., and Lim, W. (2000). Development and psychometric integrity of a measure of ideational behavior. *Creativity Research Journal*, 13, 391–398.

Runco, M. A., and Smith, W. R. (1992). Interpersonal and intrapersonal evaluations of creative ideas. *Personality and Individual Differences*, 13(3), 295–302.

Runco, M. A., and Vega, L. (1990). Evaluating the creativity of children's ideas. *Journal of Social Behavior and Personality*, 5(5), 439–452.

Schraw, G., Dunkle, M. E., and Bendixen, L. D. (1995). Cognitive processes in well-defined and ill-defined problem-solving. *Applied Cognitive Psychology*, 9(6), 523–538.

Scott, G., Leritz, L. E., and Mumford, M. D. (2004). The effectiveness of creativity training: A quantitative review. *Creativity Research Journal*, 16(4), 361–388.

Sharma, A. (1999). Central dilemmas of managing innovation in large firms. *California Management Review*, 41(3), 146–164.

Silvia, P. J., Martin, C., and Nusbaum, E. C. (2009). A snapshot of creativity: Evaluating a quick and simple method for assessing divergent thinking. *Thinking Skills and Creativity*, 4(2), 79–85.

Silvia, P. J., Winterstein, B. P., Willse, J. T., Barona, C. M., Cram, J. T., Hess, K. I., Martinez, J. L., and Richard, C. A. (2008). Assessing creativity with divergent thinking tasks: Exploring the reliability and validity of new subjective scoring methods. *Psychology of Aesthetics, Creativity, and the Arts*, 2, 68–85.

Sternberg, R. J. (1981). Intelligence and nonentrenchment. *Journal of Educational Psychology*, 73, 1–16.

(2012). The assessment of creativity: An investment-based approach. *Creativity Research Journal*, 24(1), 3–12.

(2018). A triangular theory of creativity. *Psychology of Aesthetics, Creativity, and the Arts*, 12, 50–67.

Sullivan, D. M., and Ford, C. M. (2005). The relationship between novelty and value in the assessment of organizational creativity. *Korean Journal of Thinking and Problem Solving*, 15, 117–131.

Tomasco, S. (2010). IBM 2010 global CEO study: Creativity selected as most crucial factor for future success. May. www.03.ibm.com/press/us/en/pressrelease/31670.wss.

Vernon, D., and Hocking, I. (2016). Beyond belief: Structured techniques prove more effective than a placebo intervention in a problem construction task. *Thinking Skills and Creativity*, 19, 153–159.

Voss, J. F., Wolfe, C. R., Lawrence, J. A., and Engle, R. A. (1991). From representation to decision: An analysis of problem solving in international relations. In *Complex problem solving: Principles and mechanisms*, edited by R. J. Sternberg and P. A. Frensch, 119–158. Mahwah, NJ: Lawrence Erlbaum Associates.

Wallas, G. (1926). *The art of thought*. London: Jonathan Cape.

Weingart, L. R., Cronin, M. A., Houser, C. J. S., Cagan, J., and Vogel, C. M. (2005). Functional diversity and conflict in cross-functional product development teams: Considering representational gaps and task characteristics. In *Understanding teams*, edited by L. L. Neider and C. A. Schriesheim, 89–110. Greenwich, CT: IAP.

Weingart, L. R., Todorova, G., and Cronin, M. A. (2008). Representational gaps, team integration and team creativity: The mediating roles of conflict and coordination. Paper presented at the meeting of Carnegie Melon University Research Showcase, Pittsburg, PA, March.

Wigert, B. G. (2013). The influence of divergent and convergent problem construction processes on creative problem solving. Doctoral dissertation retrieved from Proquest (3604561).

Woodman, R. W., Sawyer, J. E., and Griffin, R. W. (1993). Toward a theory of organizational creativity. *Academy of Management Review*, 18(2), 293–321.

Yang, C. C., Wan, C. S., and Chiou, W. B. (2010). Dialectical thinking and creativity among young adults: A postformal operations perspective. *Psychological Reports*, 106(1), 79–92.

Zhou, J., Wang, X. M., Song, L. J., and Wu, J. (2017). Is it new? Personal and contextual influences on perceptions of novelty and creativity. *Journal of Applied Psychology*, 102(2), 180–202.

CHAPTER 14

The Malleability of Creativity
A Career in Helping Students Discover and Nurture Their Creativity

Joseph S. Renzulli

> In children creativity is a universal. Among adults it is almost nonexistent. The great question is: What has happened to this enormous and universal human resource? This is the question of the age and the quest of our research.
> – Harold H. Anderson, *Creativity and Its Cultivation*

My early work in creativity focused on developing and researching student creativity training activities (Callahan and Renzulli, 1975; Renzulli, 1972a; Renzulli and Callahan, 1972) and providing guidance for teachers in both the use of these activities and the strategies for developing their own activities and infusing them into standard curricular areas. Following some general background thoughts about my pragmatic approach to teacher training, this chapter will describe the approach I have taken to developing creative activities and creativity in children, particularly, ways of influencing teacher behaviors to identify, promote, and develop creative teaching and the strategies for infusing creativity in educational experiences.

General Background

Thinking and writing about creativity immediately causes us to reflect upon our own experiences and wonder whether or not we think of ourselves as being creative people. Growing up in the 1940s and 1950s, the idea of "creativity" was ignored in the schools I attended. Most young children thought of their academic potential only in terms of how good they were in meeting traditional school requirements, such as paying attention in class, knowing a bunch of facts, and getting good grades on tests as well as the "conduct" or "behavior" ratings. In fact, the conduct grades were the first things my parents reviewed on my quarterly report card. I was never considered to be a top student in my small elementary school and constant reminders from my elementary school teachers about my smarter older brother caused a lot of self-doubt about my future. My teachers' report card comments referred to me as "mischievous," and an "instigator," which translated into being a person who was prone to getting himself and others into trouble. Too often I did things that earned me Ds and Fs in the conduct box on my report card. And yet, I always seemed to come up with good ideas about fixing things, developing endless money-making schemes, and making up stories that wiggled me out of the mischievous situations that caused my friends and me to be sent to the principal's office or, occasionally, even the police station.

Hundreds of books and tens of thousands of articles have been written about creativity over the years and I believe that it is one of the most important areas of inquiry in the social sciences. Indeed, the continuation of life on this planet is dependent upon the creative contributions of people who can address the unending challenges that face mankind. Although I have been involved in both research and learning theory development for over five decades (Renzulli, 2012, 2016), my greatest satisfaction has come from seeing the theories and ideas that I have developed translated into the practical applications that take place on a regular basis in schools and classrooms. The functions of thought, theory, and research certainly have important heuristic values, but my work has generally focused on a practical approach to problems and affairs that strike a balance between theory and research, on one hand, and the pragmatism that guides practical applications and actions in schools and classrooms, on the other. I also believe that opportunities to develop creativity in young people should be infused into regular curricular area and students' creative self-selected work rather than being taught as an isolated lesson. My first creativity program described below, for example, was specifically designed to be infused into traditional reading and language arts curriculum.

My professional journey in creativity began when I was a graduate student in School Psychology and one of my professors was asked by an editor to review a book manuscript that was being considered for publication. At the conclusion of our Thursday evening class, she called me aside and asked if I would read the manuscript and give her some "talking points," meaning that she would get the honorarium and I would do the work. "When do you need it?" I asked. "By Monday," she responded. There goes the weekend, I thought, but being the slow reader that I was and still am, and considering the brownie points that would at least be some recompense for pleasing this professor, I reluctantly dug into the review at about 10:00 PM that evening. The next thing I knew that the sun was coming up and I still hadn't put that manuscript down. The book turned out to be Getzels and Jackson's (1962) popular book entitled *Creativity and Intelligence:*

Explorations with Gifted Students. While the manuscript didn't give me any immediate revelations about the directions my future career might take, it did lead to an explosion of reflections of conscious and subconscious thoughts relating to my own capabilities and ideas.

A second major influence occurred when I was a middle school teacher in the late 1950s and ran across a mimeographed copy of the Minnesota Test of Creative Thinking, later to become the world-famous Torrance Tests of Creative Thinking. As I studied the items, I quickly came to two conclusions. First, I was doing absolutely nothing in my teaching that promoted the kinds of skills measured by these tests; and second, these skills were "teachable," and could be readily integrated into almost any of the memory-oriented content that was unfortunately what I thought at the time teaching was all about. And if these things could be taught, reasoned the entrepreneurial part of my brain, there was an opportunity to do some research and earn a buck at the same time. Thus, I embarked on a multi-year research project that resulted in a five book series on creativity entitled *New Directions in Creativity* (NDC), briefly explained below.

My more recent and I believe, more important work in my work on creativity, has related to creative productivity and my belief that children can produce highly creative work when given the opportunities described in our well-known schoolwide enrichment model (SEM; Renzulli and Reis, 1985). After the development of NDC and prior to the development of the SEM, I included Creativity as one of the clusters in my three-ring conception of giftedness (Renzulli, 1978, 2002, 2005), defining it as that cluster of traits that encompasses curiosity, originality, innovation, imagination, ingenuity, and a willingness to challenge convention and tradition. For example, there have been many gifted scientists throughout history, but the scientists whose work we revere, whose names have remained recognizable in scholarly communities and among the general public, are those scientists who used their creativity to envision, analyze, and ultimately help resolve scientific questions in new, original ways. Both the SEM and the three-ring conception of giftedness are described briefly below.

Sally Reis and I have spent the last three decades developing the SEM (Renzulli and Reis, 1985, 1997, 2014), a programming model that enables students to develop their creative productivity. The schoolwide enrichment model (SEM) is a programming model based on the vision that schools should be places for talent development. By providing a detailed plan for total school innovation and student creative productivity, schools that implement the SEM develop a unique program based on local resources, student populations, school leadership dynamics, and faculty strengths and creativity. The SEM was designed to develop creativity productivity in children, and includes three levels of enrichment: Type I (exposure), Type II (differentiated training in specific thinking and process skills), and Type III (investigations of self-selected topics) as well as opportunities for differentiated instruction and an assessment of students' interests, learning styles, and product styles. The SEM has been used across the world to increase achievement and create a setting in which academic excellence and innovation is expected and creativity is celebrated in all students. The development of creativity is accomplished when children find an area in which they desire and choose to develop their creativity, usually when an interest is activated. Our decades of experience with the SEM has demonstrated that when children experience and enjoy creative and productivity experiences, such as independent or small-group investigative projects, they will be more likely to seek additional creative and productive experiences later in life. These projects, called Type III Enrichment in the Enrichment Triad Model, cast the young learner as a young creative producer. And the SEM is integrated into my most recent theory of knowledge (Renzulli, 2016) underlying the SEM approach is designed to guide teachers in how students can use received and analyzed knowledge in applied ways to produce Type III outcomes that approximate the work of persons who use an investigative approach and creative mindset to become creative producers of, rather than, consumers of knowledge. These three initiatives are the cornerstone of my work in creativity over the decades, and each is more fully and briefly described below.

Earliest Work: New Directions in Creativity Program (NDC)

Since my graduate studies taught me that it is always necessary to have a theoretical rationale for research, I used Guilford's (1967) structure of intellect (SOI) model for the theoretical concept of my Creativity Program. Guilford defined the three dimensions by which the human mind processes information (Operations, Products, and Content). The five operations of mind are listed as Cognition, Memory, Convergent Production, Divergent Production, and Evaluation. Divergent Production, which served as a guide for the development of training activities in the NDC series, is described as the generation of information from given information to produce novel solutions to problems. Emphasis in divergent production is on the variety and quantity of output and it is the operation that most clearly involves fluency, flexibility, originality, and elaboration, the four factors most frequently found in definitions of creativity. By examining the specifications of each of the cells in the divergent production operation of the SOI, I had a template that differentiated activities according to Guilford's Content dimension of mind (Figural, Symbolic, Semantic, and Behavioral) and Product dimensions of mind (Units, Classes, Relations, Systems, Transformations, and Implications). Thus, for example, I could creative both semantic transformation activities as well as symbolic relations activities.

Whenever teachers ask me how I became interested in creativity and why I developed a creativity training program for children, I usually answer by referring to the quotation above. The quotation from Harold Anderson's book points out the great loss in human potential for creative development that takes place between childhood and adulthood. Although this loss takes its toll by limiting the number of people who make creative contributions to our society, a more serious and far-reaching consequence is that many adults never have the opportunity to experience the satisfaction and enjoyment that results from the act of creating. Somehow the joys associated with childhood fantasy and imaginary excursions into the world of the improbable seem to disappear as we engage in the business of growing up. Although growing up is indeed a serious business, I often wonder if the emphasis that our culture places on practical and utilitarian goals causes most people to arrive at adulthood without the full creative ability that they possessed as children.

Many writers have summarized problems that have made schools unfriendly places for creativity and have pointed out some of the ways that these problems can be overcome. One suggestion common to many writers is that classrooms need to be more engaging, creative, and interactive places, and that youngsters need to be given greater opportunities to imagine, create, and express themselves. The NDC program represents my earliest attempt to provide both teachers and students with a set of materials that will help them learn a variety of ways for expressing their creative potential. I have come to believe that creativity is a dynamic process that involves "a way of looking at things"; therefore, the activities included in this program are designed to broaden the way that youngsters look at their world. The program is not an end in itself, but rather a series of first steps that provide teachers and students with the basic skills involved in creative production.

Over the past fifty years, I have worked with thousands of teachers in courses and workshops dealing with creativity and creative productivity. These experiences have shown me that a minimum amount of instruction and a maximum amount of actual involvement with the NDC materials created the biggest changes in teachers' understanding and application of creativity training activities. The old saying "The best way to learn how to do it is to do it" is a guiding principle in my approach to teaching teachers the skills of creative production. Once these skills have been assimilated, they can be applied to all areas of the curriculum and to most of the learning experiences that take place in the classroom.

Purpose and Description of the NDC Program

The NDC includes five volumes: *Mark A, Mark B, Mark 1, Mark 2,* and *Mark 3* (Renzulli, 1972a, 1972b; Renzulli and Callahan, 1972; Renzulli, Renzulli, Ford, and Smith, 1976a, 1976b). The NDC program is designed to help teachers develop the creative thinking abilities of primary and middle-grade youngsters, and the premise of NDC is that almost all children have the potential to think creatively and that creative production can be improved by providing systematic learning experiences that foster the use of imagination.

The general purpose of NDC can best be explained by contrasting the creative or *divergent* production abilities with the *convergent* production abilities emphasized in most elementary school classrooms. In most traditional teaching-learning situations, an emphasis is placed on locating or converging upon correct answers. Teachers raise questions and present problems with a predetermined response in mind, and student performance is usually evaluated in terms of the correctness of a particular answer and the speed and accuracy with which youngsters respond to verbal or written exercises. Thus, the types of problems raised by the teacher or textbook and the system of rewards used to evaluate student progress cause most youngsters to develop a learning style that is oriented toward zeroing in on the "right" answer as quickly and as efficiently as possible. Although this ability has its place in the overall development of the learner, most teachers would agree that impressionable young minds also need opportunities to develop their rare and precious creative thinking abilities.

Divergent production is the kind of thinking that is characterized by breaking away from conventional restrictions on thinking and letting one's mind flow across a broad range of ideas and possible solutions to a problem. The real problems humanity confronts do not have the kinds of predetermined or "pat" answers that a great deal of instruction focuses on in the convergent-oriented classrooms. Yet we give our children too few opportunities to practice letting their minds range far and wide over a broad spectrum of solutions. The philosopher Alan Watts (1964) originally discussed these two kinds of thinking in terms of what he calls the "spotlight mind" and the "floodlight mind." The spotlight mind focuses on a clearly defined area and cannot see the many alternative possibilities or solutions to a problem that may exist outside that area. Floodlight thinking, on the other hand, reaches upward and outward without clearly defined borders or limitations. The floodlight thinker is free to let his or her imagination wander without the confinements or limitations that usually lead to conformity. Both types of thinking are valuable, and to pursue one at the expense of the other is clearly a disservice to the children for whose development we are responsible. NDC enabled students to have multiple an opportunities to break away from conventional restrictions on their thinking and generate responses that are relevant to particular kinds of problems and that fall within reasonable bounds.

Specific Abilities Developed by the NDC Program

The NDC was designed to develop each of the following creative thinking abilities:

1 Fluency. The ability to generate a ready flow of ideas, possibilities, consequences, and objects
2 Flexibility. The ability to use many different approaches or strategies in solving a problem; the willingness to change direction and modify given information
3 Originality. The ability to produce clever, unique, and unusual responses
4 Elaboration. The ability to expand, develop, particularize, and embellish one's ideas, stories, and illustrations

Each activity in the program promoted one or more of these four general abilities. The activities are also classified according to (1) the types of information involved in each exercise and (2) the ways that information is organized in each exercise (units, classes, relations, systems, transformations, implications, and elaborations). These two dimensions are described in detail in the teacher's manual that accompanies the program. The activity-by-activity lesson guides include the specific objectives for each activity and suggestions for follow-up activities designed to develop further the specific abilities toward which the respective exercises are directed. Although many of the objectives and suggestions for follow-up activity are directed toward the development of traditional skills in language arts, these skills are always "piggybacked" on the four major creative thinking skills. Extensive field testing on the NDC found that students are more motivated to pursue

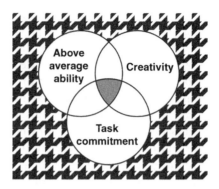

Figure 14.1 The three-ring conception of giftedness. The houndstooth background represents personality and environment, factors that give rise to the three clusters of traits

traditional language arts skills when such skills are based upon activities that make use of their own creative products.

In schools where these activities were field tested, participating teachers began to develop their own materials and activities for creativity training. In many cases, the teacher-made activities were highly original and skillfully integrated with various aspects of the regular curriculum. We also found that once teachers understood the general nature of the creative process, they were quickly able to apply the same basic strategies to other areas of the curriculum. Therefore, we encouraged teachers to view this creativity training program as a starting point that will eventually lead to the development of a "creativity orientation" on the part of teachers.

The Three-Ring Conception of Giftedness

My early work in Creativity led to much deeper reflection about its role in the development of potential, ultimately leading to my often cited three-ring conception of giftedness. This conception of creative-productive giftedness, accompanied by decades of research (Renzulli, 1978, 2005; see Figure 14.1), was purposefully designed for a programming model that develops both academic or high-achieving and creative-productive types of giftedness (Renzulli and Reis, 1997, 2014) as both of these types of giftedness are important and often interact, and both should be encouraged in special programs. This conception of giftedness identifies three interlocking clusters of abilities, as its name derives from the conceptual framework of the theory, three interacting clusters of traits: (1) *above average* but not necessarily superior ability as measured by cognitive ability and achievement tests, (2) *task commitment*, and (3) *creativity*. The conception emphasizes the relationship of these clusters in the development of what I prefer to call "gifted behaviors," which is the overlap between and among these clusters.

Perhaps the most salient aspect of my theory is that it is the *interaction* between and among these clusters of traits brought to bear upon a particular problem situation and/or performance area that creates the conditions for the creative-productive process to begin and flourish. Additionally, these clusters of traits emerge in certain people, at certain times, and under certain circumstances. The Enrichment Triad Model (Renzulli and Reis, 2014; Renzulli, 1977) is the compatible learning theory from which we promote educational circumstances that create the conditions for stimulating interaction between and among the three rings as described below.

Above average ability encompasses both general (e.g., verbal and numerical reasoning, spatial relations, memory) and specific (e.g., chemistry, ballet, musical composition, experimental design) performance areas and is the most constant of the rings. That is, any student's performance within the parameters of this ring is minimally variable, as it is linked most closely with traditional cognitive/intellectual traits. The reason that this ring makes reference to "above average ability" (as opposed to, for example, "the top 5 percent" or "exceptional ability") derives from research suggesting that, beyond a certain level of cognitive ability, real-world achievement is less dependent upon ever-increasing performance on skills assessment than upon other personal and dispositional factors (e.g., task commitment and creativity; Renzulli, 1978, 2005). The sole use of intelligence tests, aptitude, and/or achievement tests to identify candidates for "gifted programs" has been universally discussed and dismissed in the field.

Task commitment represents a nonintellective cluster of traits found consistently in creative-productive individuals (e.g., perseverance, determination, will power, positive energy). It may best be summarized as a focused or refined form of motivation – energy brought to bear on a particular problem or specific performance area. The significance of this cluster of traits in any definition of giftedness derives from myriad research studies, as well as autobiographical sketches of creative-productive individuals (Reis and Renzulli, 2003; Renzulli, 2002, 2012). Simply stated, one of the primary ingredients for success among persons who have made important contributions to their respective performance areas is their ability to immerse themselves fully in a problem or area for an extended period of time and to persevere even in the face of obstacles that may inhibit others.

Creativity encompasses curiosity, originality, innovation, imagination, ingenuity, and a willingness to challenge convention and tradition. For example, there have been many gifted scientists throughout history, but the scientists whose work we revere, whose names have remained recognizable in scholarly communities and among the general public, are those scientists who used their creativity to envision, analyze, and ultimately help resolve scientific questions in new, original ways.

A frequently raised question relates to whether creativity and task commitment must be present in order for a person to be considered "gifted." In the study of human abilities, traditionally measured achievement tends to remain constant over time (indeed, this is the reason for the high reliability of cognitive ability and achievement tests). Task commitment and creativity, on the other hand, are not always present or absent; rather, they emerge and are developed within certain contexts and circumstances that are the result of experiences and effective teaching to promote them. Creativity and task commitment, unlike traditionally measured academic achievement traits included in the above average ability circle, are developmental and therefore subject to the kinds of experiences provided for both young people and adults. They are the result of the opportunities, resources, and encouragement that are provided to spark a creative idea or develop the motivation that causes a person or group to want to follow through on the idea.

In many cases, creativity and task commitment "feed" upon one another. For example, a person notices a problem that needs to be solved (e.g., bullying in a school). She becomes interested and develops the task commitment to do something about it. She may then begin to explore various creative ways to start an awareness campaign, complete a questionnaire study about bullying, obtain a video to be shown to the students in their school, or prepare some posters or discussion groups that address this issue.

The reciprocal relationship between creativity and task commitment may also work in the opposite direction. A group of students may, for example, have a creative idea about starting an organization that helps senior citizens in their town. They must now develop their task commitment and executive function skills to actually get the job done. Task commitment requires the time, energy, and the organizational and management skills necessary for their creative idea to become a reality.

The three-ring conception of giftedness is based on an overlap and interaction between and among these three clusters of traits that create the conditions for developing and applying gifted behaviors. Giftedness is not viewed as an absolute or fixed state of being (i.e., "you have it or you don't have it"). Rather, it is viewed as a developmental set of behaviors that can be applied to creative endeavors and problem-solving situations. Varying kinds and degrees of gifted behaviors can be developed and displayed in certain people, at certain times, under certain circumstances, and within certain domains or contexts. In a certain sense, we might view the most important role of teachers is to provide young people with the opportunities, resources, and encouragement to generate creative ideas and the skills necessary to follow through on their ideas. In other words, in individuals with above average ability, our most important goal is to create the creativity and task commitment traits specified in the three-ring conception of giftedness and to bring the circles together to enable gifted behaviors to coalesce and be activated.

The Schoolwide Enrichment Model

My latest and I believe, my most important work in creativity, is our SEM, developed from over four decades of research and field testing (Gubbins, 1995; Reis and Renzulli, 2003; Renzulli and Reis, 1994). A guiding principle that summarizes this work is a belief that the creative and productive experiences of children who complete and enjoy highly engaging Type III experiences will lead them to further develop and seek additional creative and productive experiences later in life. That is, we believe that students who experience the joys and challenges and intensities of creative-productive work in elementary and secondary school, and indeed even in college, will be more likely to continue to pursue creative work in their vocation or avocation in their adult lives.

The SEM combines my previously developed Enrichment Triad Model (Renzulli, 1977) with a more flexible approach to identifying high-potential students, and it has been implemented in thousands of school districts worldwide. Extensive evaluations and research studies indicate the effectiveness of the model, resulting in independent researchers Van Tassel-Baska and Brown (2007) labeling it one of the mega-models in the field. This research suggests that the model is effective at serving high-ability students in a variety of educational settings and works well in schools that serve diverse ethnic and socioeconomic populations (Reis and Renzulli, 2003; Renzulli and Reis, 1994).

In the SEM, students receive several kinds of services. First, interest, learning styles, and product style assessments are conducted with talent pool students using the program Renzulli Learning. Each student creates a unique profile that identifies his or her unique strengths and talents, and

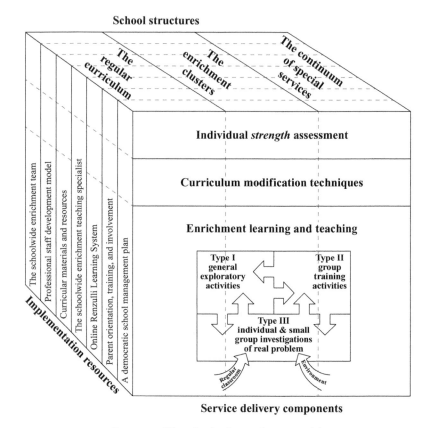

Figure 14.2 The schoolwide enrichment model

teachers can identify patterns of student's interests, creative products, and learning styles across the three classes. These methods are being used to both identify and create students' interests and to encourage students to develop and pursue these interests in various ways. Learning style preferences assessed include projects, independent study, teaching games, simulations, peer teaching, programmed instruction, lecture, drill and recitation, and discussion. Product style preferences include the kinds of products students like to do, such as those that are written, oral, hands-on, artistic, displays, dramatization, service, and multimedia.

The curriculum/instructional focus in the SEM for all learning activities is the Enrichment Triad Model (Renzulli, 1977), which was initially implemented in school districts as a gifted and talented program, and is often now integrated into whole school programming. Research on the use of the Enrichment Triad Model and its integration into the SEM has consistently shown the positive outcomes of the use of this approach with students, finding that the enriched and accelerated content can reverse underachievement and increase achievement (Reis and Renzulli, 2003). The Enrichment Triad Model is designed to encourage creative productivity on the part of students by exposing them to various topics, areas of interest, and fields of study, and to further train them to *apply* advanced content, process-training skills, and methodology training to self-selected areas of interest. Accordingly, three types of enrichment are included in the Enrichment Triad Model. In order for enrichment learning and teaching to be applied systematically to the learning process of all students, it must be organized in a way that makes sense to teachers and students, and the Enrichment Triad Model can be used for this purpose.

The Enrichment Triad Model is based on the ways in which people learn in a natural environment rather than the artificially structured environment that characterizes most classrooms. External stimulation, internal curiosity, necessity, or combinations of these three starting points cause people to develop an interest in a topic, problem, or area of study. Children are, by nature, curious and they enjoy the use of problem solving but in order for them to act upon a problem or interest with some degree of commitment and enthusiasm, the interest must be sincere and they must feel a personal reason for taking action. In the Enrichment Triad Model, the *interaction* among the following three types of enrichment is as important as any single type of enrichment (Type I, II, or III). The ultimate goal of the SEM is the development of creative and productive work and each year, we receive hundreds of examples of highly creative work from children in schools across the world that celebrates their creativity and task commitment applied to problems and areas of intense interest.

The Challenge of Change in the Real World of Schools

Bringing about change in education and especially infusing more creativity into both identification of talented students and the learning process has fascinated me since I entered academe more than fifty years ago. I have come to believe that practice in real-world settings should drive theory and research rather than the other way around and that you can "teach" theory and research appreciation more effectively by beginning with teaching the practical applications in schools that don't have the luxury of random assignment to experimental and control groups and the other features that define a respectable research design. There is an indefinable thing that I call "a teacher's way of knowing," and it is this that determines whether or not teachers will buy into the unending "innovations" that the academic community beams at them on a regular basis.

Unless teachers have practices that they both enjoy using and that produce positive results in their students they will not pay attention to and even revolt against the most elegant theories and sophisticated research findings. I believe that all theorists and researchers who want to have an impact on the change process in schools and classrooms should invest as much time on developing, refining, and implementing the practical applications of their theories and research as they do on theory and research development. And they should do this in the uncontrolled environments of real world of schools rather than in laboratories that are far removed from these real worlds of the teachers we expect to implement our recommendations.

REFERENCES

Callahan, C. M., and Renzulli, J. S. (1975). Developing creativity training activities. *Gifted Child Quarterly*, 19, 38–45.
Gretzels, J. W., and Jackson, P. W. (1962). *Creativity and intelligence*. New York: John Wiley.
Gubbins, E. J. (Ed.). (1995). *Research related to the enrichment triad model* (RM95212). Storrs: University of Connecticut, National Research Center of the Gifted and Talented. http://nrcgt.uconn.edu/wp-content/uploads/sites/953/2017/04/rm95212.pdf.
Guilford, J. P. (1967). *The nature of human intelligence*. New York: McGraw-Hill.
Reis, S. M., and Renzulli, J. S. (2003). Research related to the Schoolwide Enrichment Triad Model. *Gifted Education International*, 18(1), 15–40.
Renzulli, J. S. (1972a). *New directions in creativity*. Vol. 1. New York: Harper and Row.
———. (1972b). *New directions in creativity*. Vol. 2. New York: Harper and Row.
———. (1977). *The Enrichment Triad Model: A guide for developing defensible program for the gifted and talented*. Mansfield Center, CT: Creative Learning Press.
———. (1978). What makes giftedness? Re-examining a definition. *The Phi Delta Kappan*, 60, 180–184.
———. (2002). Expanding the conception of giftedness to include co-cognitive traits and to promote social capital. *The Phi Delta Kappan*, 84, 33–40, 57–58.
———. (2005). The three-ring conception of giftedness: A developmental model for promoting creative productivity. In *Conceptions of giftedness*, 2nd ed., edited by R. J. Sternberg and J. Davidson, 217–245. Boston: Cambridge University Press.

(2012). Reexamining the role of gifted education and talent development for the 21st century: A four-part theoretical approach. *Gifted Child Quarterly*, 56, 150–159.

(2016). The role of blended knowledge in the development of creative productive giftedness. *International Journal for Talent Development and Creativity*, 4(1), 13–24.

Renzulli, J. S., and Callahan, C. M. (1972). *New directions in creativity*. Vol. 3. New York: Harper and Row.

Renzulli, J. S., and Reis, S. M. (1985). *The schoolwide enrichment model: A how-to guide for educational excellence*. Mansfield Center, CT: Creative Learning Press.

(1994). Research related to the Schoolwide Enrichment Triad Model. *Gifted Child Quarterly*, 38, 7–20.

(1997). *The schoolwide enrichment model: A how-to guide for educational excellence*. 2nd ed. Mansfield, CT: Creative Learning Press.

(2014). *The schoolwide enrichment model: A how-to guide for educational excellence*. 3rd ed. Waco, TX: Prufrock Press.

Renzulli, J. S., Renzulli, M. J., Ford, B. G., and Smith L. H. (1976a). *New directions in creativity*. Vol. 4. New York: Harper and Row.

(1976b). *New directions in creativity*. New York: Harper and Row.

Van Tassel-Baska, J., and Brown, E. F. (2007). Toward best practice: An analysis of the efficacy of curriculum models in gifted education. *Gifted Child Quarterly*, 51, 342–358.

Watts, A. (1964). A psychedelic experience: Factor fantasy. In *LSD: The consciousness expanding drug*, edited by D. Soloman, 17–34. New York: G. Putnam.

CHAPTER 15

Everyday Creativity
Challenges for Self and World – Six Questions
Ruth Richards and Terri Goslin-Jones

Who is against creativity? It is fun and healthy, we want our own chance, and we want our kids to have it too. Plus accumulating evidence supports benefits for physical and psychological health, perhaps best known for arts-based therapies, for example, with depression, HIV, grief and loss, or trauma (Goslin-Jones and Herron, 2016a, 2016b; Richards, 2007a, 2010; Rogers, 2011; Zausner, 2007). Expressive writing about difficulties has even predicted relative elevations in immune function (Pennebaker, 1995).

Yet many questions remain, and six are below. These questions echo the interests of both authors – and share, temporally, the path of one of us (RR) with everyday creativity – from definition and assessment issues to questions of normalcy, health, and unhealth, to relational, social, and spiritual issues, nonlinear dynamics, and aesthetics. Dr. Richards comes with expertise in educational psychology, psychiatry, and everyday creativity, plus earlier math and physics; Dr. Goslin-Jones's background involves business, organizational coaching, consulting, psychology, and self-development processes using expressive arts. Both authors practice visual arts, have long-standing spiritual practices, and have come to share interests in expanded roles for creating as process and a way of life – with possible positive effects. This includes health, deeper inner knowing, and systems awareness as embedded and interconnected parts of a dynamic and nonlinear whole, with implications for our *worldview* and view of *self-in-world*. After some preliminaries, these six questions:

1   Is creativity beneficial for us, individually and together?
2   Linear or not? Is an interconnected view hurt by linear assumptions?
3   Normalcy and health – Is creative process destabilizing, hence resisted?
4   Mental Unhealth? – When is it actually a "Compensatory Advantage"?
5   Relational Creativity – Can we do more to honor our co-creating?
6   Can nuance herald creativity? Speculation on new directions.

Everyday creativity: Product definition. What is it, then, our "originality of everyday life"? After Barron (1969; see Richards, 2007a, 2010), we employ only two criteria: (1) *originality* and (2) *meaningfulness*. They encompass products not only in the arts and sciences, in traditionally creative areas, but in virtually any other area open to our freshness of vision. Abraham Maslow's (1968, 1971) *self-actualizing persons* too showed such outcomes in daily life. We omit criteria of social recognition, and also judgments of utility in a context. Some innovations may never be recognized; others may be recognized for the wrong reasons.

Everyday creativity is intended to apply broadly, whether painting a picture, landscaping the yard, writing a report, planning an ad campaign, or raising a child. As Barron (1969) said, originality is "almost habitual" with highly creative persons. Although one can talk about domain-specific talents, there is evidence for "core" creative factors across fields (Barron and Harrington, 1981; Plucker and Beghetto, 2004).

Dynamic and process focus. With process, *it is less what we do than how we do it.* One of us (RR), with Dennis Kinney and colleagues at Harvard Medical School, developed and validated the interview-based Lifetime Creativity Scales, to assess real-life originality at work and leisure (Kinney, Richards, and Southam, 2012; Richards, Kinney, Benet, and Merzel, 1988; Richards, Kinney, Lunde, and Benet, 1988). Though focused on *product*, creative *process* enters. Participants included a creative auto mechanic who designed his own tools, and extraordinary heroes who found ways to rescue innocent victims of persecution in wartime.

The other author (TGJ), a scholar-practitioner, has long emphasized creative process and mindfulness training toward personal growth and inner awareness, to enhance work/life integration, performance, and stronger relationships, and that author is now researching these. Use of multimodal expressive arts is not "art for art's sake," but a "means," offering powerful new ways of knowing (Leavy, 2015; Rogers, 1993, 2011).

Here, we turn the camera around from *product* – the usual focus – to explore how we too (the *creative person*) can be changed (Goslin-Jones, 2011; Moran, Cropley, and Kaufman, 2014; Richards, 2014). For instance, a thematic analysis of Richards's (2007a) edited *Everyday Creativity and New Views of Human Nature* yielded twelve process-related features: dynamic, conscious, healthy, nondefensive, open, integrating, observing actively, caring, collaborative, androgynous, developing, brave. Each is linked as well to a larger literature. Take androgyny, where high creativity muddies not only harmful gender stereotypes and group polarization but raises issues for ethnicity or SES too (Richards, 2007a).

"**Open systems**" **and self.** We all are changing even as we take a new breath. A key construct is "open systems" (Briggs and Peat, 1989). Albeit, from day to day, we remain recognizable, self-sustaining, *autopoetic* (Mitchell, 2009), manifesting a "self-maintaining process by which a system . . . functions as a whole to continually produce the components" (p. 298), we are also processes-in-motion, in metabolism with our environs.

Open systems concern both ongoing change, and integrity of certain life systems, at least during a finite life-span. Humans breathe, hear, communicate, live in a continual give-and-take exchange with each other and the world. You speak and my brain is changed! Memories, dendrites, neural networks, and beyond single being, a larger intersubjective context exists (Montuori, Combs, and Richards, 2004; Siegel, 2012). Yet we still hold our own unique center of consciousness, within multiple interconnections. We are more like YouTube than still photos.

Is Our Creativity Beneficial for Us, Individually and Together?

Surprisingly, many don't know the benefits of creativity. Areas of benefit range from art therapies to imagery-based interventions, even to vicarious creativity, to lifestyle and efforts to solve problems in the greater culture, with healing, connection, and greater life-meaning (Goslin-Jones and Herron, 2016b; Moran, Cropley, and Kaufman, 2014; Pilisuk and Parks, 1986; Ray and Anderson, 2000; Richards, 1997, 2010, 2014; Rogers, 1993, 2011). Whatever one's focus, we can access deeper inner awareness, ability to shift, adapt resiliently, know ourselves, reduce defensiveness, nurture the new. Once as children at play, our creating furthered emotional regulation, resilience, and adaptation; truly, play is a cornerstone of adult creativity (Runco and Pritzker, 2011; Russ, 2014).

Creativity can spur what Rhodes (1990), after Maslow, called movement from *deficiency creativity* to *being creativity*, in the arts and perhaps beyond. In writing about personal conflict (e.g., Pennebaker, 1995), we may become more apt to see universal themes and fundamental humanity (Moran, Cropley, and Kaufman, 2014; Richards, 1997, 2007b, 2014). Self-actualizing persons increasingly honor *being values*, such as truth and justice (Maslow, 1971).

Is there a "dark side"? There are "dark" paths and purposes as well, intentional and nonintentional (Cropley, Cropley, Kaufman, and Runco, 2010), be this in science, arts, or another domain. At times (for all of us), self-interest or shortsighted ignorance can dominate over spiritual, compassionate, or altruistic motives. World wisdom traditions have made contributions here (e.g., Thich Nhat Hanh, 1999). Yet is destructive creating on an equal footing with other sorts – or on the average, in the long run, will openness, nondefensiveness, and movement in values predict prosocial outcomes (Moran, Cropley, and Kaufman, 2014; Richards, 2014; Rogers, 2011)?

Expressive arts: Multimodal way of knowing self and world. Person-centered expressive arts, process-based, with a key reflective piece, can readily facilitate everyday creativity. Goals include personal and social well-being (Goslin-Jones, 2011). Founded by the late Natalie Rogers, PhD (1993, 2011), person-centered expressive arts use "art, movement, drawing, painting, sculpting, music, writing, sound, and improvisation in a safe and supportive setting, to develop authenticity, inner awareness, and spiritual growth" (p. 1). It incorporates, from Dr. Rogers's father, humanistic psychologist, Carl Rogers (1959), (1) empathy, (2) congruence, (3) unconditional positive regard, to enhance psychological safety.

Evolutionary issues. Surprising to many, a long misunderstood Charles Darwin (who once trained for the ministry), also celebrated higher human potential. Darwin expounded in his last writings – focused *within* the human species – on love, cooperation, and sympathy (meaning empathy); he rarely mentioned "survival of the fittest" (Loye, 2007; Richards, 2007a, 2014). We humans are, Darwin said, social beings, intended to honor our cooperative possibilities. Primate literature too supports such options (deWaal, 2013). Eastern Buddhist traditions (e.g., Loori, 2005; Trungpa, 2008) have their own writings/practices on creativity toward spiritual ends and a greater good.

Creativity plays a likely role in *Homo sapiens*'s past evolutionary paths and future emergent potential (Gabora and Kaufman, 2010; Loye, 2007; Morowitz, 2002). Whether inventing the wheel, or something more modest, both biological and cultural evolution can be affected. Witness our sparkling human variability, our "phenotypic plasticity," as per evolutionary biologist Dobzhansky (1962), or with DNA-environment interactions, our epigenetic potential as per Moore (2015). We can be flexible, adaptable, and escape from threatening situations – and not just live, but learn what we are living for.

In summary, we say *yes*: at best, our creativity is beneficial – and offers broader views of self and our co-creating in the world. Below, we ask if nonlinear modeling might change this.

Linear, or Not? Is an Interconnected View Hurt by Linear Assumptions?

Better late than never. Some see greater use of *nonlinear* models in psychology as long overdue, with their many delicate balances, and interactions between diverse factors (Carson, 2014; Runco and Pritzker, 2011; Russ, 2014). British mathematician Ian Stewart (2002) put it, "Today's science shows that nature is relentlessly nonlinear . . . If you draw a curve at random, you won't get a straight line" (p. 73). Or, "as the 18th century believed in a clockwork world, so did the mid-20th century in a linear one" (p. 73). Chaos theorists Guastello and Liebovitch (2009) add, "Psychology is not the first science to break out of the linear rut . . . physical science made the transition more than a half-century ago" (p. 1). Shakespeare, long ago, in *Julius Caesar*, addressed the nonlinearity of larger systems to which we are subject; even if we work steadily, fortunes may be based on the tides of life:

> There is a tide in the affairs of men;
> Which, taken at the flood, leads on to fortune;
> Omitted, all the voyage of their life;
> Is bound in shallows and in miseries.

Nonlinear, multivariate, complex. If you learned in Psychology 101 that $y = ax$ and twice the x leads to twice the y, well, it can work that way over a limited range. But often not. Consider severe stress and health (Field and Schuldberg, 2011), where modulators like social support can lower risk. Or those dangerous opioids: Too little, no pain response, too much, one can die.

Like it or not, *control* is *not* our middle name; changes (and sudden "bifurcations") often occur, for example, effect of summer rail closures in New York City. "Life," as the saying goes, "happens while we are making other plans." With our very real limitations, awe, wonder, and humility might serve us better – particularly with a violent age and threatened biosphere.

Two constructs from nonlinear dynamics. How often do people assume a linear reductionist model – where output is proportional to input, where confounding variables are, first, apparent, and then appear controllable? Where it seems we can build from the ground up, the "whole is equal to the sum of its parts." Where can we know, predict, and control? Some mistakenly think we are in charge, even above nature. This may be enacted – with industry and scientific know-how – while forgetting larger interconnected systems, including global climate change.

Two circumstances follow "metaphorically at minimum" (as a figure of speech, which will not *necessarily* apply literally): Butterfly Effect and Emergence. For more detail see resources including (Guastello, Koopmans, and Pincus, 2009; Mitchell, 2009; Richards, 2001; Schuldberg, 2007; Smith, 2007; Strogatz, 2015).

Butterfly Effect – and sudden insight? Many have heard of the Butterfly Effect, even a movie by this name. Metaphorically, with our butterfly, *at a key point*, a small puff of air in Paris leads to a storm system over the Northeastern United States. Here is "sensitivity to initial conditions." Yet don't blame it all on the Butterfly. Unstable global weather patterns can span the globe. The supercomputer has made analyses of these phenomena possible (Mandelbrot, 1983).

Criteria for chaos (see Smith, 2007) include multiple deeply interconnected, feedback-dependent, deterministic, and highly sensitive variables. *Chaos* does *not* mean all is random or anarchic; deeply ordered deterministic patterns and punctuations exist – as part of a hidden beautiful order. Such sudden changes are also seen in the stock market, viral Internet videos, earthquakes, and much more. Skarda and Freeman's (1987) findings, for instance, support resonant and sudden brain reorganization on encountering new smells.

People have long cited Butterfly Effect type phenomena as models for creative insight (Abraham, 1996; Briggs and Peat, 1989; Guastello, 1995; Richards, 1996; Zausner, 1996). A brainstorm, an avalanche of mind (Richards, 2010). The final datum arrives and, Aha!

It makes sense too, energetically. We are dissipative systems, situated "far from equilibrium"; we have real fuel in the creativity tank. Like being at the top of the hill, we've found a little basin to move about or settle in (in phase space), until something better sends us zipping over the side to alternative solutions (Abraham, 1996; Combs, 1996, 2002). Our creative system is designed for fast moves and new conclusions.

Then there is ongoing creativity – keeping the insights coming. With creative *person* variables or cognitive style, can we *statistically* raise the odds of more creativity in our partial black box of mind? Traits such as "openness to experience," or "preference for complexity," are predictive, or low latent inhibition combined with cognitive balancing factors (e.g., Carson, 2014; Kaufman, 2009; Richards, 2014). Using a popcorn analogy, Richards (2010) has suggested ways to help insights come faster, that is, statistically, to help the popcorn pop. Metaphorically turn up the heat! Yet we still don't know which kernel will pop and why.

Emergence: New patterns "out of nowhere." Much in life *emerges*, as per that saying, "The whole is greater than the sum of its parts!" We neither predict nor control it. A flock of birds suddenly emerges, flying in beautiful formation. How did they "know"? Take Internet growth, which has changed the world in twenty-plus years. Our immune systems (for which Prigogine got the Nobel Prize) are constantly organizing and reorganizing to keep us alive. Speculatively, we can go further, looking at whole societies (Sawyer, 2005), or a speculative leap to the Big Bang, and emergence of life itself (Morowitz, 2002).

Emergence does not need a clear overriding internal/external leading force (Mitchell, p. 13). It shows nonlinear connections among the parts, also with complex levels and hierarchies of internal organization (Holland, 2014, p. 5), and multiple influences, lower levels on the higher and vice versa. If relevant to creative process, however, can one untangle the threads? One author (RR) is doing interviews of experience of creative people to appreciate lived experiences at a conscious (or intuitive) level. The potential of neurophenomenology to relate first- and third-person data holds promise here. For example, consider sudden nonlinear findings such as the alpha "brain blink," then "gamma burst" (Kounios and Beeman, 2015) related to creative insight.

In summary, we say *yes*; nonlinearity is often important in creativity – and in all of life. The next question concerns the perceived "normalcy" of such creators, who threaten the status quo.

Normalcy and Health: Is Creative Process Destabilizing, Hence Resisted?

Social normalcy, or its normalcy statistically – what the typical person is often doing (including us!) – can at times be mindless and conformist. With our young people we might wish they would put down their cell phones and pay attention. Yet a more reflective creativity with challenge and change has its price, in schools, at home, in culture (Beghetto and Kaufman, 2010; Richards, 2007a). The creator is initially *destabilizing* things, pulling something apart to replace it (e.g., Flach, 1990). Add to this the stereotypes.

If we search on Google Images, the pictures of these creative upstarts (try "mad creator"!) are not flattering. So concerned with the latest insight, their hair is uncombed, and they are running into walls. Is this how nonconformity can appear in a more conformist setting?

For "normal college students," Schuldberg (1994) found some so-called pathologic traits, Eysenck showed elevated "psychoticism," Barron and others found abnormal MMPI pathology scores (except for high "ego strength," suggesting creators could go deep into nonconscious realms, while in touch with consensual reality – Runco and Richards, 1997; Richards, 2007a, 2014). Schuldberg (1994) wrote too about "giddiness and horror" (how useful for a playwright). Yet it can be *healthy* to go deep (Pennebaker, 1995). As Barron (1963) said, in a well-known quote, "The creative person is both more primitive and more cultivated, more destructive and more constructive, occasionally crazier and yet adamantly saner, than the average person" (p. 234).

"Creative normalcy." Focus not just on the mean, but also on the variation, as in the standard deviation. With creativity we hope for *variation*, the brilliant colors of our many ways of being; it's Dobzhansky's (1962) "phenotypic plasticity." We are talking too about self as "open system" in a culture that is either more receptive or not. Recent politics provide examples. Can we support healthy new norms as well as diverse behavioral "niches" (Richards, 1997) in evolving creative systems. Some wish to live closer to change than others, yet we can all benefit.

Creative norms can also better oppose the specter of conformity, even a pathologic "group think" self-organization. In psychology, this has included the Milgram Study, where shocks by participant-teachers punished test errors, and the Stanford Prison Experiment, intended as guard-prisoner "role-playing," yet ending early with some participants seeking therapy (Zimbardo, Johnson, and McCann, 2014). Researchers were shocked how readily participants conformed to social context; such studies can no longer be done.

Mindful awareness. This is not to demean our learned habits, which make parts of life simpler; we don't want to drive the car off the road. Yet to what extent can we inject mindful awareness, and interrupt, certain patterns? And then dare to be different. As above, we can assess and creatively reframe an ethically suspect situation and apply ethical reasoning (Sternberg, 2014). Hopefully, early experience or modeling has also helped build creative courage; the smallest departure can sometimes plant those early seeds (e.g., Richards, 1994/2017).

Mindfulness itself takes work and training, but what returns! Varied definitions exist, all involving conscious and broad nonjudgmental attentiveness, of evident value to creativity (Goslin-Jones and Herron, 2016a, 2016b; Kaufman and Gregoire, 2015; Langer, 2016). Mindfulness (Rahula, 1959; Siegel, 2007, 2012) is generally good for us physically and psychologically. Training can be done as sitting meditation or more actively. Used secularly in Mindfulness-Based Stress Reduction (MBSR) programs, now found around the world, such practice is helpful for stress, heart rate, blood pressure, relaxation, and more (Kabat-Zinn, 1994).

Yet – many of us hope that this secular use won't bypass higher values, intrinsic to this discipline (needn't imply "religion") as in many world wisdom traditions. On the Buddhist path, for instance, the Four Foundations of Mindfulness – mindful awareness of body, sensations or feelings, mind, and objects of mind (Thich Nhat Hanh, 1998; Rahula, 1959) are part of *right mindfulness* training on the eightfold path, which also includes *right action*.

Now, perhaps all we want is to stop being on automatic pilot. A good start.

Levels of accomplishment in mindfulness can ascend to include "bare attention" and nonconceptual knowing. How promising! – a path toward enlightenment itself (Rahula, 1959). Should a result be "insight into the nature of things, leading to the complete liberation of mind," (p. 68) it offers intrinsic wisdom and compassion, for which ethical living and universal caring are a natural. One can see greater interconnection and movement toward a greater good (Moran, Cropley, and Kaufman, 2014; Richards, 2014; Sternberg, 2014).

How easy, though, to never question a conformist self-centered social norm, especially for a teacher with thirty-plus students! Or to project a negative creative norm onto odd-appearing groups (people unlike us), especially those showing certain creativity-psychopathology paradoxes. In summary, *the social norms do not always favor creativity, nor does a healthy creative norm always win social favor.*

Mental Unhealth? Or Is It Actually a "Compensatory Advantage"?

There are serious mental illnesses, and treatment can make a huge difference for one's life – and creativity (Jamison, 2017; Runco and Richards, 1997). *Plus there are many roads to creativity – this being just one.* Yet what follows is about *health*, not illness, and potentially affects many patients and relatives.

Evidence has accumulated (Kaufman, 2014; Kinney and Richards, 2011, 2014; Kinney et al., 2000–2001; Richards, 2000–2001a, 2007a; Runco and Richards, 1997) that carrying *risk* (here, a personal or family history of bipolar and schizophrenia *spectrum* disorders) raises the odds of a "compensatory advantage" for real-life everyday creativity. Dennis Kinney and Ruth Richards and associates studied these spectrum disorders with the well-validated Lifetime Creativity Scales (Kinney, Richards, and Southam, 2012). Supportive studies exist; yet few on *everyday* creativity looked at patients and well-documented pedigrees of relatives. A relevant literature goes back to the early twentieth century (see Jamison, 2017; Richards, 1981; also Kaufman, 2014; Silvia and Kaufman, 2010).

A so-called creative or "compensatory advantage" follows an "inverted-U" relationship. It favors relatively *better functioning* individuals, or people at their better functioning times. This is consistent with factors favoring unusual mental content (e.g., low latent inhibition, as per Carson or Kaufman, previously) aligned with psychological controls. Definitely a nonlinear pattern, and not "the sicker the better."

Creativity peaks with relatively *milder* clinical situations, as in cyclothymia, for bipolar disorders, or for *subclinical* states of two-plus schizotypal signs, for schizophrenia. Results suggested "psychiatrically normal relatives" (or subclinically affected ones) could also carry the creative advantage, with a diathesis running in families that can emerge in various ways, including healthy ones. Evolutionary factors are possible (Kinney and Richards, 2011, 2014; Richards, Kinney, Benet, and Merzel, 1988a). We roughly compared such situations to sickle-cell anemia, where the full disease is devastating yet the trait has the advantage of resistance to malaria. Here, how do we help boost *this* compensatory advantage for creativity and coping?

Eminent and exceptional creators. These creators have their own research issues (Kinney and Richards, 2011, 2014; Richards, 2007a; Silvia and Kaufman, 2010), yet we note the sad finding (Jamison, 2017) that bipolar poet Robert Lowell couldn't control his mood elevations, such that brilliant writing episodes came to a halt. Ludwig (1995) showed artistic versus scientific creators had particular psychopathology. Yet pathology was not the rule in this subgroup either – who were disciplined creators with the strength to reach eminence.

Swain and Swain (2014), addressing "nonlinearity in creativity and mental illness," gave eminent exemplars, including Nikola Tesla and Srinivasa Ramanujan, suggesting a balance of qualities favoring coping and extraordinary creating, but added speculations about what might have transpired had things been worse. (Still, let us beware "pathologizing" the "abnormal" just because it is different.) Jamison (2017) cites research where, among manic-depressives without a strong prognosis, outcomes varied but some did much better than expected. This reminds us that many factors interact. Swain and Swain (2014) offer a resonant nonlinear speculation:

> The difference, it seems, between creativity and mental illness is very much one of how much control one has over the non-linear wanderings of the mind to places – either via a chaotic route drifting father and farther away, or a catastrophic route, making sudden transitions to new states. (p. 139)

Hence we have a complex nonlinear interacting dynamic, including unknown factors. We can try to help yet there are limitations to our own influence and control; all we can do is try.

In summary, *yes*, one finds important links between everyday creativity and health in some with personal/family history of major psychopathology. Yet complex systems help affect outcome. The next question reminds us that we are not "lone creators" but in relationship with others.

Relational Creativity: Can We Do More to Honor Our Co-Creating?

"Uh huh . . . uh huh . . . ," says an inattentive conversationalist to his partner at the breakfast table, reading a paper. This is *not* the creative case. Consider these two:

Interpersonal case. At best, a relationship is more than isolated billiard balls clicking on a table; here is a system, and a larger potential identity of the interrelationship. Shenk (2014) explores creator-pairs completing each other, as in The Beatles' McCartney and Lennon. Note Sawyer's (2010) discussion of both individual and group emergence. What is our unit of analysis? Buber (1970) spoke of emergence in relationship, in the "between space." Our very brain development (and more – some Romanian orphans who weren't held actually died; Eisler, 2007) depends on early contact and intersubjectivity (Siegel, 2007, 2012). Guisinger and Blatt (1994) showed the evolutionary roots of our relational as well as individual identity and purposes – albeit our separation-individuation has been prioritized in the West.

Back to everyday creativity, and the pair at the table, now deeply discussing their relationship. *Product* meets *process*, more than in an excellent theater performance, it is authentic, deeply felt, interactive, spontaneous, empathetic, meeting criteria of *originality* and *meaningfulness*. There is willingness to hear – even be deeply changed (Jordan, Kaplan, Miller, Stiver, and Surrey, 1991; Richards, 2007b).

One of us (TGJ) has led a Creative Living Coaching Process, with groups, and one-on-one; effects are found in areas including communication, creativity, decision-making, empathy, and well-being (Goslin-Jones, 2011; Goslin-Jones and Herron, 2016a, 2016b; Goslin-Jones and Richards, forthcoming). One participant found expressive arts helped her to "get into flow, lose my sense of time (and she) felt refreshed and energized . . . offering more creative options at work . . . (and could) communicate differently." Here arts can engage, finesse defenses, unfold new insight (Rogers, 2011), while also adding a conscious processing in discussion, with trusted others.

Case of relationship with an art object. Let us take a leap (taken further in Question 6), finding a oneness with the portrayed. Catalog notes for paintings by Wu Chen (1350 AD) announced (Pope, 1961, p. 152): "This album might be called 'twenty portraits of the artist as bamboo.'" Here artist merges with art, subject with object; in some sense, duality is bridged. There is a belongingness, an identity, a knowingness for each segment of the bamboo, the blowing of the wind, the ruffling of each leaf. We too are there. A dialogue has perhaps occurred on paper, each brushstroke changing the whole and informing the next step. The wind is still blowing through the artist's hair. From a manual on Chinese brush painting (in Richards, 2007b):

> Paint with love and kindness for the materials and the subject portrayed, becoming one with both.

The new sciences reveal profound connections, even across light years, as with quantum field theory (e.g., Hiley and Peat, 1987; Ricard and Thuan, 2001). At our level, Buddhist monk Matthieu Ricard (2003) wrote of sacred dance and our higher potential:

> From a spiritual point of view, true creativity means breaking out of the sheath of egocentricity and becoming a new person or more precisely, casting off the veils of ignorance to discover the ultimate nature of mind and phenomena. (p. 32)

In summary, *yes*, let us further address creativity in relationship with other beings and with the world around us. More connected than we imagined. Next, we turn to "nuance."

Can *Nuance* Herald Creativity? Speculations on New Directions

Little Albert Einstein was five years old; his compass needle, a gift from his father, always pointed north. For this little boy, there was a fascination, a vague yet totally real wonder, a feeling, an urge – that in some form lasted all of his life. A "germ," said Henry James, in turn, of an amorphous impression that unfolded into a story. One of us (RR) is studying these "seeds" of creativity (Richards, 2015). Briggs and Peat (1989), with LaViolette, have spoken of *nuance*.

Nuance – beyond words? Briggs and Peat, experts in literature and physics, respectively, approach *nuance* as that unspoken subtlety which can draw us in. *Nuance* involves "a shade of meaning, a complex of feeling, or subtlety of perception for which the mind has no words or mental categories," adding that "nuances exist in the fractal spaces between our categories of thought" (pp. 194–195). Briggs (1990) gave numerous artistic examples in a book. Peat, in a volume honoring the late David Bohm (Hiley and Peat, 1987), went further on this intense wondering and complex pull.

Chaotic attractors and fractals. As they suggested, do *"nuances exist in the fractal spaces between our categories of thought"*? Does nature's beauty hold a message for us – framed in those *self-similar* fractal forms (similar at larger and smaller scales; the visual forms have been called the "fingerprints of chaos"; Richards, 1999)? Examples are trees, clouds, mountains, rivers, or the branchings of our arteries and veins; other forms are based on (relatively simple) math formulas. Might they bring us to conscious awareness and appreciation (Richards, 2001)? Might this also occur at a level of ideation – where in our minds, we sense something – in this fractal structure of mind in phase space, a potential for change, elaboration, and creative insight? There is inadequate space to elaborate on this speculation, while clarifying nonlinear dynamical issues about attractors, or fractals forms related to their microstructure.

Yet converging evidence is supporting a fractal organization within mind and memory (Kitzbichler et al., 2009; also see Goertzel, 1995a, 1995b; Pincus, 2009; Skarda and Freeman, 1987). "Chaotic attractors" linked to mental operations are already part of a conversation with new speculation (Marks-Tarlow, forthcoming), for a transpersonal journal. Might fractal geometry, so applicable to the natural world (Mandelbrot, 1983), help unravel the nature of human creativity? Whether valid or not, it shows where wonder, science, nonlinearity, interconnection, and a new mathematics may open promising new doors.

"Intimation." Could aspects of *nuance* resonate with what Wallas (1926) has called "intimation," that fifth yet often omitted part of Wallas's (1926) heuristic for creative process (*preparation-incubation-intimation-illumination-verification*)? Does it occur when we suspect an insight but don't yet know what it is. Even as an early clue (Goslin-Jones and Richards, forthcoming)? Could *nuance* resonate with Sundararajan's (2015) subtle processes of "savoring" in Chinese literature and culture – far beyond the manifest – also an indication of high culture and refinement? By whatever name, are we, as creative and questing human beings, somehow enlisted by the "unknown"?

Dr. Barbara McClintock. This remarkable geneticist and scientist's honors ultimately included a Nobel Prize in science and genetics, and a MacArthur Award. Long fascinated by corn, she had her own ways of staining samples, preparing slides, making microscopic observations, and dynamically visualizing – even entering into the results. Decades before others, this brilliant scientist discovered crossing-over phenomena in meiosis and the basis for genetic transposition in corn (Keller, 1983).

Unfortunately, it was harder for others to understand Dr. McClintock's findings without sharing her ways of knowing. One can speculate as well about gender issues (Spender, 1982). Her findings at first dismissed, Dr. McClintock was ultimately and overwhelmingly celebrated. Yet it took others replicating her meiotic and transposition results, decades later, using more conventional means, for her work to be recognized.

A moment reminiscent of Wallas's (1926) "intimation," occurred when McClintock was a visiting dignitary at Stanford, helping a colleague with problems in the meiotic cycle of *Neurospora*. She was on a bench under stately eucalyptus trees, thinking but not getting anywhere. Suddenly she "jumped up . . . couldn't wait to get back to the laboratory . . . knew I was going to solve it" (p. 115). She then solved everything in five days.

McClintock's description of her process with microscopic slides is vivid. Where she had seen disorder before, now she picked out chromosomes easily. Plus she found that

> the more I worked with them the bigger and bigger (they) got, and when I was really working with them, I wasn't outside, I was down there. I was part of the system . . . I was even able to see the internal parts of the chromosome . . . as if I were right down there and these were my friends. (p. 117)

If this might resonate with purpose, one-pointed focus, and magnification of Csikszentmihalyi's (1990) *flow*, does it link any less with artist Wu Chen's contact with his bamboo? Seven days later, Dr. McClintock gave a seminar at Stanford on the meiotic cycle of Neurospora.

Her colleague Evelyn Witkin noted how Dr. McClintock's medium "more closely resembles that of the artist . . . consensual validation requires a degree of intersubjectivity, of shared vision as well as shared language" (p. 151). One may note here that recognized scientists, including Nobelists, are more apt to be polymaths with major artistic interests than other scientists (Root-Bernstein and Root-Bernstein, 2004).

Empathy, beauty, truth. Here, empathy occurred – with maize. The Root-Bernsteins (1999) chose empathy as one of the "13 thinking tools of the world's most creative people." Charles Darwin celebrated empathy as well, calling it "sympathy" (Loye, 2007; Richards, 2007a). Let us also ask what "beauty" may call us? Could it here involve more abstract contents of mind, a deep simplicity, or the esthetic appeal and "elegance" (Barron, 1969) found in scientific discovery? Let us include *truth*, along with beauty, also found among Maslow's (1971) *being values*, and seen too as part of the moral integrity of both artists and scientists (Richards, 2014). These are areas for the future – less curious if we stop chopping up domains such as arts and sciences, and putting them in silos, and then wondering why they are separate.

In summary, *yes*, nuance, *by this or another name*, could *herald potential for new insights*. Let us proceed here with our own wonder and awe; there is much more to be learned.

Last Words: A Bigger Picture

The six questions in brief involve creativity and (1) benefits, (2) nonlinearity, (3) "normalcy," (4) compensatory advantage, (5) relational creativity, (6) plumbing the unknown. Unfolding these helps informs the nature of creativity and who we are: our *worldview* and view of *self-in-world*.

Many of the healthy benefits of creativity are sadly not well known. Some delicate and nonlinear balances or steady states, not fully understood, may be one part of this. Use of new models could help, while lessening a linear preoccupation with prediction and control. Some representations become nonlinear, dynamic, open, emerging, interconnected, and multivariate; they ask us, as open systems, to value our larger context, allow outcomes we cannot imagine, and honor process at least as much as product. Here is a different view of *self-in-world*!

Some features now considered "normal" in popular culture may appear static, mindless, and conformist – while to that earlier cohort, the mindful, present, connected creator might seem odd indeed. Yet health lies in the dynamic and open direction, as do benefits of diversity. We can honor our many co-creations while drawing our own uniqueness into the larger picture.

Still, health gets turned upside down at times, for example, with personal/familial links between an everyday creative "compensatory advantage" and mental illness. Should we therefore want to be ill? Good heavens, *no!* Creating might even offer rich awareness, resilient coping, and treatment or primary prevention for those at risk – while benefiting society.

Hopefully future work can reveal more about seeming prosocial and ethical benefits in two directions: (1) *broader, systems thinking* and (2) *deeper inner self-knowledge*. Also it might help in finding the epigenetic and other conditions for more prosocial directions. It is not just our teenagers who can be deeply – and unconsciously – influenced by context. Let us find some new conscious paths.

Regarding *nuance* (or subtle cues in creativity, however named), we can stand more comfortably in wonder before what we don't know – which is just about everything. Humility and awe in turn open new doors. A process-based and open identity is also consistent with many world wisdom traditions. If of evolutionary significance, culturally, it may also bring greater well-being personally, as we become more tolerant (of self as well as other) and more interesting and experimental ourselves. This can also diminish stereotypes that limit creativity.

Greater openness – to each other and new insights – can also facilitate cultural creativity (including eminent creativity, sprung from a grassroots base), our caring for each other, and change in a crazy world. We can honor diverse connections, rather than unlikely images of pseudo-independence or reductionist science. We can move toward a worldview based in change, connection, and complex adaptive systems – and hopefully also a greater good.

REFERENCES

Abraham, F. D. (1996). The dynamics of creativity and the courage to be. In *Non-linear dynamics in human behavior*, edited by W. Sulis and A. Combs, 364–400. Singapore: World Scientific.

Barron, F. X. (1963). *Creativity and psychological health*. Princeton, NJ: Van Nostrand.

(1969). *Creative person and creative process*. New York: Holt, Rinehart, and Winston.

Barron, F. X., and Harrington, D. (1981). Creativity, intelligence, and personality. *Annual Review of Psychology*, 32, 439–476.

Beghetto, R. A., and Kaufman, J. C. (Eds.). (2010). *Nurturing creativity in the classroom*. New York: Cambridge University Press.

Briggs, J. (1990). *Fire in the crucible: Understanding the process of creative genius*. Los Angeles, CA: J. P. Tarcher.

Briggs, J., and Peat, F. D. (1989). *Turbulent mirror*. New York: Perennial/Harper and Row.

Buber, M. (1970). *I and thou*. New York: Touchstone.

Carson, S. (2014). The shared vulnerability model of creativity and psychopathology. In *Creativity and mental illness*, edited by J. Kaufman, 253–280. New York: Cambridge University Press.

Combs, A. (1995). Psychology, chaos, and the process nature of consciousness. In *Chaos theory in psychology*, edited by F. D. Abraham and A. R. Gilgen, 129–137. Westport, CT: Praeger.

(1996). Consciousness: Chaotic and strangely attractive. In *Nonlinear dynamics in human behavior*, edited by W. Sulis and A. Combs, 401–411. Singapore: World Scientific.

(2002). *Radiance of being*. 2nd ed. St. Paul, MN: Paragon House.

Cropley, D. H., Cropley, A. J., Kaufman, J. C., and Runco, M. A. (2010). *The dark side of creativity*. New York: Cambridge University Press.

Csikszentimihalyi, M. (1990). *Flow: The psychology of optimal experience*. New York: HarperPerennial.

DeWaal, F. (2013). *The bonobo and the atheist: In search of humanism among the primates*. New York: W. W. Norton.

Dobzhansky, T. (1962). *Mankind evolving: The evolution of the human species*. New Haven, CT: Yale University Press.

Dossey, L. (2002). How healing happens: Exploring the nonlocal gap. *Alternative Therapies*, 8, 12–15, 103–110.

Eisler, R. (2007). Our great creative challenge: Rethinking human nature – and recreating society. In *Everyday creativity and new views of human nature*, edited by R. Richards, 261–284. Washington, DC: American Psychological Association.

Field, R. J., and Schuldberg, D. (2011). Social-support moderated stress: A nonlinear dynamical model and the stress-buffering hypothesis. *Nonlinear Dynamics, Psychology, and the Life Sciences*, 15(1), 53–85.

Flach, F. (1990). Disorders of the pathways involved in the creative process. *Creativity Research Journal*, 3(2), 158–165.

Florida, R. (2007). *The flight of the creative class*. New York: HarperCollins.

Gabora, L., and Kaufman, S. B. (2010). Evolutionary approaches to creativity. In *The Cambridge handbook of creativity*, edited by J. C. Kaufman, and R. J. Sternberg, 279–300. New York: Cambridge University Press.

Goertzel, B. (1995a). Belief systems as attractors. In *Chaos theory in psychology and the life sciences*, edited by R. Robertson and A. Combs, 123–134. Mahwah, NJ: Erlbaum.

(1995b). A cognitive law of motion. In *Chaos theory in psychology and the life sciences*, edited by R. Robertson and A. Combs, 135–153. Mahwah, NJ: Erlbaum.

Goslin-Jones, T. (2011). Using expressive arts to transform the workplace. In *The creative connection for groups: Person-centered expressive arts for healing and social change*, edited by N. Rogers, 354–357. Palo Alto, CA: Science and Behavior Books.

Goslin-Jones, T., and Herron, S. (2016a). Cutting edge person-centered expressive arts. In *The person-centered counseling and psychotherapy handbook*, edited by C. Lago and D. Charr, 199–211. New York: Open University Press/McGraw-Hill Education.

———. (2016b). Person-centered expressive arts therapy: An experiential psychology of self-realization. In *Person centered and experiential therapies*, edited by P. Wilkins, 89–103. Thousand Oaks, CA: Sage.

Goslin-Jones, T., and Richards, R. (forthcoming). Mysteries of creative process: Explorations at work and in daily life. In *International handbook of creativity at work*, edited by L. Martin and N. Wilson. London: Palgrave Macmillan.

Guastello, S. J. (1995). *Chaos, catastrophe, and human affairs*. Mahwah, NJ: Erlbaum.

Guastello, S., Koopmans, M., and Pincus, D. (Eds.). (2009). *Chaos and complexity in psychology*. New York: Cambridge University Press.

Guastello, S. J., and Liebovitch, L. S. (2009). Introduction to nonlinear dynamics and complexity. In *Chaos and complexity in psychology*, edited by S. Guastello, M. Koopmans, and D. Pincus, 1–40. New York: Cambridge University Press.

Guisinger, S., and Blatt, S. J. (1994). Individuality and relatedness: Evolution of a fundamental dialectic. *American Psychologist*, 49(2), 104–111.

Hiley, B. J., and Peat, F. D. (Eds.). (1987). *Quantum implications: Essays in honour of David Bohm*. London: Routledge.

Holland, J. H. (2014). *Complexity: A very short introduction*. New York: Oxford University Press.

Jamison, K. R. (2017). *Robert Lowell: Setting the river on fire*. New York: Knopf.

Jordan, J., Kaplan, A., Miller, J. B., Stiver, I. P., and Surrey, J. L. (1991). *Women's growth in connection*. New York: Guilford Press.

Kabat-Zinn, J. (1994). *Wherever you go, there you are: Mindfulness meditation in everyday life*. New York: Hyperion.

Kaufman, J. C. (2014). *Creativity and mental illness*. New York: Cambridge University Press.

Kaufman, J. C., and Sternberg, R. J. (2010). *The Cambridge handbook of creativity*. New York: Cambridge University Press.

Kaufman, S. B. (2009). Faith in intuition is associated with decreased latent inhibition in a sample of high achieving adolescents. *Psychology of Aesthetics, Creativity, and the Arts*, 3(1), 28–34.

Kaufman, S. B., and Gregoire, C. (2015). *Wired to create*. New York: Perigee.

Keller, E. F. (1983). *Feeling for the organism: The life and work of Barbara McClintock*. New York: W. H. Freeman.

Kinney, D. K., and Richards, R. (2011). Bipolar mood disorders. In *Encyclopedia of creativity*, 2nd ed., 140–148. New York: Academic Press.

———. (2014). Creativity as "compensatory advantage": Bipolar and schizophrenic liability and the Inverted-U Hypothesis. In *Creativity and mental illness*, edited by J. Kaufman, 295–317. New York: Cambridge University Press.

Kinney, D. K., Richards, R., Lowing, P. A., LeBlanc, D., Zimbalist, M. E., and Harlan, P. (2000–2001). Creativity in offspring of schizophrenics and controls. *Creativity Research Journal*, 13(1), 17–26.

Kinney, D. K., Richards, R. L., and Southam, M. (2012). Everyday creativity, its assessment, and the Lifetime Creativity Scales. In *The creativity research handbook*, edited by M. A. Runco, 3:285–319. New York: Hampton Press.

Kitzbichler, M. G., Smith, M., Christensen, S. R., and Bullmore, E. (2009). Broadband criticality of human brain network synchronization. *PLoS Computational Biology*, 5(3), e1000314.

Kounios, J., and Beeman, M. (2015). *The Eureka factor*. New York: Random House.

Krippner, S. (1999). Altered and transitional states. In *Encyclopedia of creativity*, edited by M. A. Runco and S. Pritzker, 1:59–70. San Diego, CA: Academic Press.

Langer, E. (2016). *The power of mindful learning*. Boston: Da Capo.

Leavy, P. (2015). *Method meets art: Arts-based research practice*. 2nd ed. New York: Guilford Press.

Loori, J. D. (2005). *The Zen of creativity*. New York: Ballantine.

Loye, D. (2007). Telling the new story: Darwin, evolution, and creativity versus conformity in science. In *Everyday creativity and new views of human nature*, edited by R. Richards, 153–173. Washington, DC: American Psychological Association.

Ludwig, A. M. (1995). *The price of greatness*. New York: Guilford Press.

Mandelbrot, B. B. (1983). *The fractal geometry of nature*. New York: W. H. Freeman.

Marks-Tarlow, T. (forthcoming). A fractal epistemology for transpersonal psychology. *International Journal of Transpersonal Psychology*.

Maslow, A. (1968). *Creativity in self-actualizing people: Toward a psychology of being*. New York: Van Nostrand Reinhold.

——— (1971). *The further reaches of human nature*. New York: Penguin.

Miller, W. R. (1999). *Integrating spirituality into treatment*. Washington, DC: American Psychological Association.

Milne, J. (2006). *GO! The art of change*. Wellington, New Zealand: Steele Roberts.

Mitchell, M. (2009). *Complexity: A guided tour*. New York: Oxford University Press.

Montuori, A., Combs, A., and Richards, R. (2004). Creativity, consciousness, and the direction for human development. In *The great adventure: Toward a fully human theory of evolution*, edited by D. Loye, 197–236. Albany: SUNY Press.

Moore, D. S. (2015). *The developing genome: An introduction to behavioral genetics*. New York: Oxford University Press.

Moran, S., Cropley, D., and Kaufman, J. C. (2014). *Ethics of creativity*. London: Palgrave Macmillan.

Morowitz, H. J. (2002). *The emergence of everything: How the world became complex*. New York: Oxford University Press.

Pennebaker, J. (1995). *Emotion, disclosure, and health*. Washington, DC: American Psychological Association.

Pilisuk, M., and Parks, S. (1986). *The healing web*. Lebanon, NH: University Press of New England.

Pincus, D. (2009). Fractal brains: Fractal thoughts. www.psychologytodaycom/node/32616.

Plucker, J., and Beghetto, R. (2004). Why creativity is domain general, why it looks domain specific, and why the distinction does not matter. In *Creativity: From potential to realization*, edited by R. Sternberg, E. Grigorenko, and J. Singer, 153–167. Washington, DC: American Psychological Association.

Pope, J. (1961). *Chinese art treasures: Catalog for selected groups of objects exhibited in the U.S. by the Government of the Republic of China*. Lausanne, Switzerland: Skira.

Rahula, W. (1959). *What the Buddha taught*. New York: Grove Press.

Ray, P. H., and Anderson, S. R. (2000). *The cultural creatives: How 50 million people are changing the world*. New York: Three Rivers Press.

Rhodes, C. (1990). Growth from deficiency creativity to being creativity. *Creativity Research Journal*, 3, 287–299.

Ricard, M. (2003). *Monk dancers of Tibet*. Boston: Shambhala.

Ricard, M., and Thuan, T. X. (2001). *The quantum and the lotus: A journey to the frontiers where science and Buddhism meet*. New York: Crown.

Richards, R. (1996). Does the Lone Genius ride again? Chaos, creativity, and community. *Journal of Humanistic Psychology*, 36(2), 44–60.

———. (1981). Relationships between creativity and psychopathology: An evaluation and interpretation of the evidence. *Genetic Psychology Monographs*, 103, 261–324.

———. (1994/2017). *Everyday creativity: Coping and thriving in the 21st century*. Raleigh, NC: Lulu.

———. (1997). When illness yields creativity. In *Eminent creativity, everyday creativity, and health*, edited by M. Runco and R. Richards, 485–540. Stamford, CT: Ablex.

———. (1999). The subtle attraction: Beauty as a force in awareness, creativity, and survival. In *Affect, creative experience, and psychological adjustment*, edited by S. Russ, 195–219. Philadelphia: Brunner/Mazel.

———. (2000–2001a). Creativity and the schizophrenia spectrum? More and more interesting. *Creativity Research Journal*, 13(1), 111–131.

———. (2000–2001b). Millennium as opportunity: Chaos, creativity, and J. P. Guilford's structure-of-intellect model. *Creativity Research Journal*, 13(3–4), 249–265.

———. (2001). A new aesthetic for environmental awareness. *Journal of Humanistic Psychology*, 41(2), 59–95.

——— (Ed.). (2007a). *Everyday creativity and new views of human nature: Psychological, social, and spiritual perspectives*. Washington, DC: American Psychological Association.

———. (2007b). Relational creativity and healing potential: Power of Eastern thought in Western clinical settings. In *Cultural healing and belief systems*, edited by J. Pappas, B. Smythe, and A. Baydala, 286–308. Calgary, Alberta: Detselig.

(2010). Everyday creativity: Process and way of life – Four key issues. In *The Cambridge handbook of creativity*, edited by J. C. Kaufman and R. J. Sternberg, 189–215. New York: Cambridge University Press.

(2014). A creative alchemy. In *The ethics of creativity*, edited by S. Moran, D. Cropley, and J. Kaufman, 119–136. London: Palgrave Macmillan.

(2015). Subtleties of creative longing, perception, and power. Presented at the 123rd annual convention of the American Psychological Association, Toronto, ON, August.

Richards, R., Kinney, D. K., Benet, M., and Merzel, A. (1988). Assessing everyday creativity: Characteristics of the Lifetime Creativity Scales and validation with three large samples. *Journal of Personality and Social Psychology*, 54, 476–485.

Richards, R., Kinney, D. K., Lunde, I., and Benet, M. (1988). Creativity in manic-depressives, cyclothymes, their normal relatives, and control subjects. *Journal of Abnormal Psychology*, 97, 281–288.

Rogers, C. (1959). Toward a theory of creativity. In *Creativity and its cultivation*, edited by H. Anderson, 69–82. New York: Harper and Row.

Rogers, N. (1993). *The creative connection: Expressive arts as healing*. Palo Alto, CA: Science and Behavior Books.

(2011). *The creative connection for groups: Person-centered expressive arts for healing and social change*. Palo Alto, CA: Science and Behavior Books.

Root-Bernstein, R., and Root-Bernstein, M. (1999). *Sparks of genius: The thirteen thinking tools of the world's most creative people*. Boston: Houghton Mifflin.

(2004). Artistic scientists and scientific artists: The link between polymathy and creativity. In *Creativity: From potential to realization*, edited by R. J. Sternberg, E. L. Grigorenko, and J. L. Singer, 127–151. Washington, DC: American Psychological Association.

Runco, M., and Richards, R. (Eds.). (1997). *Eminent creativity, everyday creativity, and health*. Stamford, CT: Ablex/Greenwood.

(Eds.). (2011). *The encyclopedia of creativity*. 2nd ed. 2 vols. San Diego, CA: Academic Press.

Russ, S. W. (2014). *Pretend play in childhood*. Washington, DC: American Psychological Association.

Sawyer, R. K. (2005). *Social emergence: Societies as complex systems*. New York: Cambridge University Press.

(2010). Individual and group creativity. In *The Cambridge handbook of creativity*, edited by J. C. Kaufman and R. J. Sternberg, 366–380. New York: Cambridge University Press.

Schuldberg, D. (1994). Giddiness and horror. In *Creativity and affect*, edited by M. Shaw and M. Runco, 87–101. Norwood, NJ: Ablex.

(2007). Living well creatively: What's chaos got to do with it? In *Everyday creativity and new views of human nature*, edited by R. Richards, 55–73. Washington, DC: American Psychological Association.

Shenk, J. W. (2014). *Powers of two: Finding the essence of innovation in creative pairs*. Boston: Houghton Mifflin.

Siegel, D. J. (2007). *The mindful brain*. New York: W. W. Norton.

    (2012). *The developing mind: How relationships and the brain interact to shape who we are*. 2nd ed. New York: Guilford Press.

Silvia, P. J., and Kaufman, J. C. (2010). Creativity and mental illness. In *The Cambridge handbook of creativity*, edited by J. C. Kaufman and R. J. Sternberg, 381–394. New York: Cambridge University Press.

Skarda, C., and Freeman, W. (1987). How brains make chaos in order to make sense of the world. *Behavioral and Brain Sciences*, 10, 161–173.

Smith, L. (2007). *Chaos: A very short introduction*. New York: Oxford University Press.

Spender, D. (1982). *Women of ideas*. London: Pandora.

Sternberg, R. J. (2014). Creativity in ethical reasoning. In *The ethics of creativity*, edited by S. Moran, D. Cropley, and J. C. Kaufman, 62–74. London: Palgrave Macmillan.

Sternberg, R. J., Grigorenko, E. L., and Singer, J. L. (2014). *Creativity: From potential to realization*. Washington, DC: American Psychological Association.

Stewart, I. (2002). *Does God play dice? The new mathematics of chaos*. 2nd ed. Malden, MA: Blackwell.

Strogatz, S. H. (2003). *Sync: How order emerges from chaos in the universe, nature, and daily life*. New York: Hyperion.

    (2015). *Nonlinear dynamics and chaos*. Philadelphia: Westview Press.

Sundararajan, L. (2015). *Understanding emotion in Chinese culture*. New York: Springer.

Swain, J. E., and Swain, J. D. (2014). Nonlinearity in creativity and mental illness: The mixed blessings of chaos, catastrophe, and noise in brain and behavior. In *Creativity and mental illness*, edited by J. Kaufman, 133–144. New York: Cambridge University Press.

Thich Nhat Hanh. (1998). *The heart of the Buddha's teaching*. Berkeley, CA: Parallax Press.

Trungpa, C. (2008). *True perception: The path of dharma art*. Boston: Shambhala.

Wallas, G. (1926) *The art of thought*. New York: Harcourt Brace.

Zausner, T. (1996). The creative chaos. In *Nonlinear dynamics in human behavior*, edited by W. Sulis and A. Combs, 364–400. Singapore: World Scientific.

    (2007). *When walls become doorways: Creativity and the transforming illness*. New York: Harmony.

Zimbardo, P. G., Johnson, R. L., and McCann, V. (2014). *Psychology: Core concepts*. Boston: Pearson.

CHAPTER 16

Authentic Creativity
Mechanisms, Definitions, and Empirical Efforts

Mark A. Runco

This chapter summarizes approximately forty years of thinking about creativity. It explores a definition that follows directly from a theory of creativity. Empirical tests of that theory are summarized, as are the implications for how to best measure and develop creativity. Something must also be said about "how creativity matters to society." These are the topics covered herein, but when you study creativity you realize that it is a good thing to be rebellious once in a while, at least in ways that do no harm, so I will begin with the question of "how creativity matters" rather than end with it. This leads to an interesting path among the various topics covered in this chapter.

How Creativity Matters to Individuals and to Society

Creativity matters because it contributes to health, learning and growth, problem solving, evolution and advance, the quality of life, and several other important aspects of life. There is overlap among these varied benefits, and a good place to start with Bruner's (1962) claim that education must prepare today's students for a future that is not foreseeable. This idea may be a reflection of Zeitgeist, given that it seems to fit so well with what scientists in various other domains were saying at just about the same time (e.g., Wilson, 1975). Bruner and those others were clearly thinking a great deal about (1) the difference between cultural evolution and biological evolution, (2) the rapid rate and acceleration of the former, and (3) the impact of accelerating change on humans. While biological evolution tends to be quite slow, cultural evolution is essentially immediate: What is introduced in one generation, if it proves useful or engaging, remains a part of common knowledge from that point forward. The problem is that humans may adapt to one state of affairs only to have the state abruptly change. This is where creativity comes into play, and one reason that it matters: it allows humans to deal with rapid change. This is not to say that creativity

246

is just a kind of adaptability. Creativity is certainly not synonymous with adaptability. After all, sometimes adapting means to conform and fit in, and conformity is not a part of creativity.

That being said, creativity does require that people are both divergent (and rebellious) and conventional, and sometimes even conforming. This follows from the fact that humans are social animals, which means that although originality and creativity are useful, so too is conventionality sometimes useful. Thus a balance is best, and this gives us a start on the definition of creativity promised in the first paragraph of this chapter, as well as a start on the question of how to best develop creativity. Anyone intending to support creativity, including parents and teachers, should strive for optimal creativity which is both original but also effective. This is why my own suggestions for developing creativity emphasize *discretion*, so individuals will know when to be original, divergent, and rebellious, and when to act in a conventional fashion instead (Runco, 1996).

Something more must be said about "how creativity matters." The first point was that creativity matters because changes are coming at us faster and faster, and creativity allows us to create new understandings and thus adapt. From that perspective creative efforts are reactions to change. The flip side is also true: Creativity contributes to advance and evolution. Indeed, all systematic advance, both individual and societal, depends on creative efforts.[1] (We would really be shooting ourselves in the foot if we used creative actions to advance but then were unable to use creativity to adapt to the resulting changes!) Also relevant is that creativity supports both individual and societal health (Simonton, 1997). And for these reasons (i.e., adaptability and health), creativity is important for quality of life.

Sadly, the effect of creativity on our quality of life is frequently overlooked. Too often the social results of creativity are mentioned, but one of the most important benefits of creativity is quality of life. This should be emphasized because it is so far-reaching. Quality of life is something that touches every one of us (not just the gifted and talented, and certainly not just the geniuses), and it may do so every day. It is, in a sense, omnipresent. Later in this chapter I will need to discuss this position because it is not universally accepted. There are views that creativity is not universal and

---

[1] The various Ps of creativity and the hierarchical framework (Runco, 2007) both implied that it might be best to avoid the noun "creativity." There is so much ambiguity with that noun. Is it referring to creative personality, perhaps, or to creative places or products? It is probably best to use the adjective "creative" instead of the noun, for that requires specificity. Using the adjective will require precision and point directly to creative performance, *or* creative products, *or* creative achievement, *or* the creative process, and so on.

is, for example, just used by individuals who produce socially acceptable creative products (Kasof, 1995), a position with which I strongly disagree (Runco, 1995, 2017). Richards (2007), Cropley (1990), and a number of others working in this field agree and also write about *everyday creativity*, a wonderful concept that holds that creativity is related to quality of life and the experiences we have each and every day.

Creativity also matters because it is associated with learning. That means that all good education must target creativity, but of course learning is both formal and informal, which in turn underscores the view that creativity is useful everyday – or at least those days where learning is useful! The tie to learning follows from the definition of creativity as *the construction of original and effective interpretations of experience* (Runco, 1996, 2017). That is not a widely recognized definition and requires some explanation, which will be offered after one last idea about "how creativity matters" is presented. This may be the most obvious reason for creativity, and it is related to some of what was already said, but it must be stated that creativity matters because there are such serious problems facing humanity right now. Humanity has always been faced with problems, but now weapons can annihilate life on earth. Pollution has long been a health issue, but now it may destroy the ozone and all of earth will suffer, in a large number of ways. The enormity of various moral and political problems is also staggering. Many of the problems of today are such that creativity must be applied for our very survival, and for the survival of democracy and freedom. You might say, then, that creativity matters everyday, but it also matters in the grand scheme of things. Now we can focus on defining creativity and flesh out those ideas about originality, effectiveness, and the construction of meaning.

Defining Creativity

The brief discussion of how creativity benefits individuals and society required that several key parts of its definition be made explicit. Note, for example, the idea that creativity requires originality and effectiveness. This is the so-called Standard Definition (Runco and Jaeger, 2012), which is quite useful for various concerns, including scientific research. Bruner (1962) could again be cited here, for he referred to creativity as "effective surprise" (p. 3). Actually, as uncovered by Runco and Jaeger (2012), some sort of effectiveness has been included in definitions of creativity since before 1900! The earliest definitions did not use the term "creativity," however, but instead referred to inventiveness and the like. Stein (1953) may have been the first to be entirely clear about the Standard Definition.

The Standard Definition is useful but not comprehensive. There are all kinds of intriguing suggestions for improving it (Acar, Burnett, and Cabra, 2017; Corraza, 2016; Simonton, 2012; Weisberg, 2015). The one that may be the most compelling adds *authenticity* as a requirement. This would allow the definition of creativity to apply across cultures (Kharkhurin, 2012) and fit nicely with the *personal creativity* that is discussed throughout this chapter (and one emphasis of my own work for the past several decades). Authenticity also fits well with the humanistic perspective on creativity offered by Rogers (1959), Maslow (1968), and Richards (2007). Authenticity would help us to avoid questions such as "creative for whom," which often arise and can be directed to both originality and effectiveness.

In one sense the standard definition is limited in that it merely points to criteria that can be used to recognize creativity. It does not say anything about the underlying processes nor about the mechanism used when people are creative. That is probably the most important question facing research on creativity: what is the mechanism (Jay and Perkins, 1997; Runco, forthcoming). Without understanding the mechanism, efforts to define, encourage, support, and measure creativity are uncertain and may very well be inaccurate and ineffective.

This is one advantage of the definition of creativity as *the construction of original meaning*. That points to a process and to particular cognitive mechanisms. It can also be applied to all cultures, domains, and levels of creativity. This definition leads to a view of creativity as a kind of learning, as implied above. That is not to say that the construction of original interpretations covers all there is to creativity. Several times I have suggested that *intentions* and *discretion* be recognized as well (Runco, 1996). Recall here what I wrote earlier about discretion being necessary so individuals know when to be conventional and when to bend or break the rules. Intentions are involved very much like intrinsic motivation is involved (Amabile, 1990; Rubenson and Runco, 1992). As we shall see below, intentions also help to distinguish creative work that is serendipitous from that which is the direct result of an individual's persistence and effort. Serendipitous creativity is unintentional, a matter of luck as much as anything else.

The emphasis on such personal constructions applies broadly, but it may sound as if it is unrelated to definitions that point (only) to socially recognized creativity. Personal constructions are involved in all creativity, including socially recognized and high-level creative achievements in that everything starts with personal creativity. Sometimes the original idea or insight that results goes no further and is only useful to the individual, in which case it may improve his or her life, solve a personal problem, or boost his or her quality of life. Sometimes the original interpretation and construction of meaning is shared and value is attributed to it. We might use systems theory at this point, for the individual's creativity may, if shared, influence fields and eventually domains, and eventually influence novices just entering the field. But it all starts with personal creativity, and it is creativity because it is original and effective (and perhaps authentic).

The construction of meaning thus applies to both personal and social creativity, though it can be argued that really only the former is actually creativity. The latter requires several things that are not part of creation in a literal sense. Socially recognized creativity requires that a judgment is proffered, and that in turn begs the question, who it to judge? Different groups of judges often disagree (Runco and Smith, 1992), which is why attributions of creativity tend to change through history (Runco et al., 2010; Runco et al., 2016). Quite some time ago, Murray (1959) explored this problem and posed the question, "who is to judge the judges? And the judges of the judges?" Then there is the fact that socially recognized creativity is often conflated with fame, and fame can result from salience, reputation, or even luck or serendipity (Runco, 2014). The possible relevance of luck is why personal creativity usually includes intentions, along with the construction of meaning and discretion (Runco, 2003).

Creativity as the construction of original meaning parallels Piaget's (1976) thinking that "to understand is to invent." Piaget went into detail about the processes underlying such meaningful invention. His own work relied on empathic inference, which lacks rigor, but his theory does provide a framework and language to describe key processes. His work is also relevant in its rejection of products. Like socially recognized creativity, products can also be misleading and say nearly nothing about how creativity comes about. Research on products is useful in other ways (Amabile, 1982; Runco, 1989). One recent investigation looked to patents granted and offered some important ideas about liberal versus conservative styles of thought may be related to innovation and creativity (Runco, Acar, and Cayirdag, 2017). The data uncovered a negative relationship between highly conservative thinking and the likelihood of patents being granted. It also showed that ethic diversity was positively related to the likelihood of successful patents.

Not surprisingly, the concept of parsimony is useful when examining definitions of creativity. This is no surprise because creativity research has been becoming more and more scientific for decades, and parsimony is one of the tenets of science. Parsimony is at the heart of one approach, which (also unsurprisingly) is labeled, *parsimonious creativity* (Runco, Acar, and Cayirdag, 2017). That approach developed in reaction to the idea of a *creativity complex* and by employing a common tactic for creativity, namely *question assumptions*. The logic is as follows: First, all of the things included in sundry views of a *creativity complex* were identified. These included personality, attitude, motivation, values, settings, culture, and so on. In actuality, many of these are not always involved in creativity. They are sometimes involved, but not always. They therefore should not be included in a definition of creativity, or at least a parsimonious one. A parsimonious definition should recognize only requirements for creativity, and if something is required, it is always involved. Correlates and occasional influences should be recognized as such. They can be used in theory but should be recognized as mere influences. Second, many of the things studied in the creativity research are not causal factors. They are in fact results or effects. This is true of the attributions and judgments mentioned above, as well as the products already discussed. These are informative, but since they follow the creative act (or process), they should not be included in a theory that attempts to actually explain how creativity comes about. Again, they are results of the process and as such cannot influence the process. They are effects not causes, which is another way of saying that they are not vital. They may result from the creative process, but they may not, and in any case given that they follow the creation, they are not part of the causal mechanism.

What is left once the mere correlates and the results of the creative process are excluded? Not much, which is good for a parsimonious theory! One thing that is involved in all creativity, and is suggestive of process and thus mechanism, and can lead to original and effective things, is the construction of original meaning. If meaning is newly constructed, it is original, and if it is in fact "meaningful," it is effective. (If it was not effective it is likely that it is not meaningful.) The claim above that personal creativity precedes social creativity can be delineated a bit, with the construction of new meaning (by an individual) occurring first, and that meaning, in the form of an idea or insight, may subsequently be shared, judged, and recognized as creative. This too distinguishes the creativity from the possible reaction to it.

This line of thought is actually quite close to sytems system theories of creativity (Csikszentmihalyi, 1990). They describe creativity starting with an individual but eventually influencing fields and domains, and then cycling back on individuals. The difference between the parsimonious theory of creativity and systems theories is that the former views creativity as the result of individual mechanisms. The contributions of fields and domains are, in parsimonious theory, not required for creativity and in fact are reactions and attributions and as such more accurately described as part of the process of earning a reputation or, more simply, fame, which is not required for creativity. On the other hand, this line of thought is consistent with the view that creativity is often a kind of authentic self-expression and in part determines the quality of life. If someone actually constructs new meaning, it is new to that individual and not appropriated. Thus the authenticity. That may be why Maslow (1968) and Rogers (1959) eventually concluded that creativity is inextricable from self-actualization. They both depend on authenticity. Tan (2016) has recently related this kind of creativity to the thinking of Confucius, but the theory of personal creativity is quite broad and also applies to children's creativity, everyday creativity, and new meanings allowing humanity to cope with change.

Empirical Research and Advances in Measurement

My work on personal and parsimonious creativity has led me away from research relying on products and social recognition. In fact, I remain enormously interested in the idea of creative potential, in part because there are no doubt many people who are not creatively productive but have the capacity to be creatively productive. The concept of potential helps to describe those people. This in turn has led me to employ divergent thinking tests in much of my empirical research. These tests tell us quite a bit about ideation, and ideas can be original and effective and thereby satisfy the standard definition of creativity. Both individuals with mere potential and those creatively productive rely on ideas. In fact, note how well ideas can be integrated into the theory outlined above, with creativity starting with the personal construction of meaning (and often expressed or recognized as an idea) which is then shared and possibly socially recognized.

This is not to say that divergent thinking is synonymous with creativity. It merely assumes that divergent thinking is a useful indicator of the potential for creative problem solving. More than that, divergent thinking can help us to understand creative *problem finding* as well as *problem solving* (Okuda, Runco, and Berger, 1991; Runco, 1994). Research using divergent thinking tasks indicates that it, more than GPA or IQ, is predictive of many creative endeavors that occur in the natural environment (Runco, 1986; Runco, Millar, Acar, and Cramond, 2011; Wallach and Wing, 1969).

The usefulness of divergent thinking for empirical studies of creative potential is apparent in several recent investigations. Some of this research has examined how to best assess creative potentials. Results indicate that it is best to use several ideational indicators (originality, fluency, and flexibility) rather than fluency alone. Fluency is too often used alone, even though there is reliable and unique variance that is independent of fluency, and fluency is not as important as originality nor flexibility in theories of the creative process. This research also demonstrated how to use examinees' entire ideational output – what we called their *ideational pools* – for cost-efficient scoring (Runco and Mraz, 1992). The most recent research has utilized computer administration and computer scoring methods. Beketayev and Runco (2016), for example, confirmed that all ideational indicators can be calculated by computer. Simplifying some, programs can be written so the computer compiles ideas and determines how many ideas were given by each individual (for a fluency score) and how many were unusual or unique in the sample of examinees (for an originality score). In fact, that computer research with divergent thinking has introduce several new and meaningful ideational indicators, mostly based on semantic and associative networks. On new indicator represents semantic distance, which is the distance between the concepts used by a person's ideation. Some examinees produce ideas that covered large distances; interstices between any two of their ideas was sizable. Others take only small steps in their thinking, so each of their ideas is more closely related to the ideas that came before and those that came after. These new computer generated indices complement the traditional fluency, originality, and flexibility scores for divergent thinking tests.

The theory of divergent thinking has itself evolved. Acar and Runco (2014, 2015, 2017), for example, have reported tests of *literal divergent thinking* and *cognitive hyperspace*. The former was proposed after realizing that most examinations of divergent thinking have actually ignored divergence! The concept of divergence implies that things move apart and away from one another, but most tests of divergent thinking ignore this and just assume that original ideas are in fact divergent when they might have been found from remote association or another process that is linear and not literally divergent. The idea of literal divergent thinking requires an actual divergence of the thinking pathways.

The empirical work on literal divergent thinking, though in its early stages, suggests that ideas can be examined using a framework that credits ideas that are in fact literally divergent from one another. This line or work required an operationalization of *cognitive hyperspace* because one idea might diverge dramatically from the one that proceeded it, and as such it might go into a perpendicular direction. But if this kind of perpendicular thinking occurs more than twice, thinking has exhausted three dimensions and must go into cognitive hyperspace. Since thinking is not physical endeavor, there is no reason it cannot easily explore hyperspace. Acar and Runco reported tentative evidence for literal divergence and found it to correlate with independent criteria of creativity.

Speaking of criteria, another line of empirical research looks to actual creative activity and accomplishment rather than creative potential. An and Runco (2016), for example, found that it was possible to add a technological creativity scale to the *Creative Activity and Accomplishment Checklist* that has been used for many years (Holland, 1961; Hocevar, 1980). This check list is a self-report that asks respondents how many times that have been involved in various creative endeavors. It lists more than fifty such endeavors, from all of the recognized domains of creative performance, and has demonstrated its usefulness as a criterion of creativity many times over.

Even newer research is finding that creativity in the moral and political domains can be reliably assessed as well. Just as individuals can be asked how many times they have written software, designed a set for a play, composed a song, used mathematics to solve a problem in an original fashion (each examples from the CAAC), so too can they be asked how often they have organized a political activity, designed political flyers, or written political blogs, just to name three of the items from the political scale of the new CAAC.

Runco, Acar, and Cayirdag (2017) used the same *Creative Activity and Accomplishment Checklist* in their comparison of curricular (in school) and extracurricular (outside of school) creativity. This project replicated Holland's (1961) research from decades earlier, the key finding being that students display more creativity when they are outside of school compared to when they are in school. Runco et al. included several additional measures, and these suggested that students' creative attitudes and values, social preferences, and personality traits explained much of the discrepancy between curricular and extracurricular creativity. Quite a bit has been written about the problems schools have supporting students' creativity (Runco, 2016a, 2017).

One improvement in measurement was introduced by Runco, Acar, and Cayirdag (2017), namely the use of both quality of accomplishment and quantity of activity scales for each of the creative domains assessed (i.e., art, science, mathematics, writing, drama, politics, leadership, everyday creativity, technological creativity). The quality scales took the aforementioned idea of social recognition into account. The quantity scales were calculated as in Holland's work by simply counting the number of different creative activities in which an individual had been involved, but the quality scale was based on only socially recognized creative accomplishments. The pattern was very similar for both scales, with nearly all domains showing more creativity when the students were outside of school rather than in school, which is what Holland reported fifty years earlier, although there were two exceptions: everyday creativity and technological creativity. The first of these – everyday creativity – was a bit of a puzzle, though young students certainly can be creative in the way they dress and in other mundane ways, even at school – and perhaps they are motivated to do just that at school, around their peers. The second difference – in technological creativity – was easier to explain: it is likely that students have access to more apparatus and resources for technological creativity when they are in school rather than at home.

These results are relevant to the debate about exactly how the quantity of performance is related to its quality (Gruber, 1988; Runco, 1986; Simonton, 1988). They also suggest that students have untapped potential which they are displaying when they are outside of school but unable to use when they are in school. Data are currently being collected to compare the creativity of adults when they are at work with that displayed when they are not at work. The *Creative Activity and Accomplishment Checklist* is again being used in this research. It works well in just about every age group.

Education and Development

As is probably obvious at this point, many of my own suggestions about education and development point to intentions, discretion, and the construction of meaning (Runco, 2003, 2011, 2013). I have also offered three recommendations specifically for parents and teachers. These focus on *modeling*, presenting *opportunities* for creative self-expression, and appropriate *rewards*. The last of these must be appropriate in order to avoid the overjustification that can result when extrinsic reinforcement sometimes undermines the intrinsic motivation that can be so useful for creativity (Amabile, 1990). Feedback and rewards must be given carefully to avoid overjustification and to protect intrinsic motivation. Opportunities must of course be provided so children can practice creative self-expression and problem solving. It is likely that the technology for generalization and maintenance can be used as well so the creative skills children develop will be used in the natural environment (Runco, 1993, 2014). Modeling is straightforward – children learn through observation so parents and teachers should themselves be creative – but there is a second important benefit. That is, if parents and teachers do display creative behavior, there is an implicit message to go along with the manifest demonstration, namely that creativity is a valuable thing. Children will infer this much like they infer other values from the behavior of parents and teachers. If children do indeed internalize creativity as a valuable thing, they are likely to invest time and effort into being creative.

The theory of personal creativity mentioned earlier leads directly to suggestions for education and development. One implication is that discretion and decision-making must be targeted and supported. Given that discretion is under conscious control, it very well could be the most important part of creativity to support. There certainly is a large amount of evidence that decision-making plays one of, if not the, most important roles in creativity (Runco, Johnson, and Gaynor, 1999; Sternberg, 2000). Discretion can be supported by insuring that children have the opportunity to practice deciding when to be creative and when to act in a conventional fashion instead. The theory of personal creativity also implies that *ego strength* is important for children. After all, they will experience a large amount of peer pressure, which can lead them to conformity, but if they have ego strength, they can stand up to peer pressure and are more likely to think for themselves and make creative decisions.

Peer pressure may help explain the empirical result mentioned above where students are more creative outside of school rather than when in school. Very likely there are various reasons for this discrepancy, in addition to peer pressure. Not long ago I identified five challenges to educating for creativity. These may help to explain the discrepancy between curricular and extracurricular creativity. The first problem is that creativity is often misunderstood. Consider in this regard the distinction between little c creativity and Big C creativity (Merrotsy, 2013). This has intuitive appeal but is actually a false dichotomy, and as such potentially very misleading. If Big C and little c are viewed as truly distinct, educators may not realize that they are in fact connected such that a student might have little c creativity that can, with support, become Big C creativity, or at least manifest itself as creative productivity.

The second educational challenge identified earlier is similar but focuses on biases rather than misunderstandings. The *art bias*,is, unfortunately, alive and well. Apparently many educators (and non-educators) still assume that all creativity makes itself known in art, and only an art, when the truth of the matter is that creativity can take many different forms. These include the traditional domains studied in the research (e.g., science, mathematics, music, design) but also the everyday creativity, technological creativity, and political creativity mentioned earlier in this chapter.

Third problem for educators is a result of the fact that creativity requires originality, and by definition originality is not easy to predict. It is for this reason difficult to build originality into a curriculum. Most curricula are designed such that they target skills that have clear outcomes and definitions. Creativity is not like that. If something is original, it has not occurred before and is not easy to predict. For this reason educators are challenged by the need to design clear curricula but also the need to recognize and support (an unpredictable) originality.

The fourth challenge for educators who wish to support creativity is a reflection of the traditional structure of education. Think of a typical classroom: A white board, desks, and students. How many desks, how many students? Often there are twenty or more students for each teacher in a classroom. This kind of student:teacher ratio makes it very difficult to support the intrinsic motivation and autonomy that play a role in the creative process. Recall here the suggestion that parents and teachers should provide opportunities so their charges can practice creative thinking. It is difficult to provide such opportunities when intrinsic motivation and autonomy are required but the classroom contains twenty or more students. Consider also what was said earlier about personal creativity. The focus on personal creativity implies that students may need time to be alone and to think for themselves, at least early in the creative process. That is not easy to do in a classroom.

The fifth the last challenge arises because of administrative support for creativity – or lack thereof. Admittedly administrators in a situation where there are economic and political pressures, and these may lead to things like the aforementioned student:teacher ratios which make it difficult to support creativity. In addition, and for various reasons, administrators are often averse to risks, and the support for creativity is by its very nature risky. As noted above creativity depends on originality, and originality is unpredictable. This means that any investment in creativity is risky. You don't know what you're going to get! You very well could get something you don't expect. Teachers have this problem, but it also means that administrators, who make decisions about resources, must be risk tolerant and provide time and various other resources, even with unpredictable returns. That is especially difficult for many administrators these days, with a premium placed on accountability. Clearly accountability does not lend itself to risk tolerance.

Conclusions

This chapter started with comments on why creativity matters to individuals and society and then moved to issues surrounding definitions,

Creative potential   **Creative performance**

Person   **Products**
    Personality traits and characteristics   Ideas
Process   Poems, collages, designs, patents,
    Cognition   Inventions, and publications
Press   **Persuasion**
    Distal   Historical reputation
     •Evolution   Systems
     •Culture and zeitgeist   •Individual-field-domain
    Immediate environments   Social attributions
     •Places   **Interactions**
     •Settings   State x trait
                           Person x environment

Figure 16.1 Hierarchy of approaches to the study of creativity. Adapted from Runco (2007)

measurement, education, and development. The invitation for chapters to this volume asked authors to emphasize their own work, and for this reason this chapter gives special attention to the creative process, creative potential, parsimonious creativity, and personal creativity.

I have often wondered about these four emphases. They get me thinking about George Miller's (1956) oft-cited work on "the magic number seven, plus or minus two," which is a classic in cognitive psychology. I mention it because Miller opened his discussion by describing how the number seven seemed to follow him around. I have that kind of feeling but with the letter P! I may not be alone in this regard. Rhodes (1961) suggested that there were four strands in the creativity research, and each starts with a P: Creative Person, Creative Place, Creative Product, and Creative Process. Simonton (1995) also used a P when he added "Persuasion," the idea being that creative people and creative things change the way that others think. Later I added "Creative Potential" (and reorganized the entire framework into a hierarchy, which is presented in Figure 16.1) (Runco, 2007). Why so many Ps? Perhaps Arthur Miller (2009) was on to something when he described the obsessions of Wolfgang Pauli and Carl Jung, though they were hung up on the number 137 and not a letter of the alphabet.

The various Ps do make sense. Even in this chapter we saw that the *process* view correctly assumes that there is a need to identify underlying mechanisms that are required for creativity. Superficial descriptions of creativity are not enough. Theories of creativity must look for an explanatory mechanism – that is, a process. Similarly, *parsimony* has long been used in the sciences and, as I suggested above, it may help us move away from an ambiguous *creativity complex*, where causes and effects are all jumbled together in an uncertain way, to particulars specified by the logic of parsi-mony. For whatever the reason, Ps head many useful concepts in this field.

In fact, there is a bit more: The hierarchy presented in Figure 16.1 nicely distinguishes between creative potential and actual creative performance, but the older 4P could be used in a sort of chronology, starting with the creative *personality* that characterizes the individual who is likely to use a creative *process*, and if he or she is in a *place* that has appropriate supports and is free of inhibitions and barriers, the result may be a creative *product*. This chronology is consistent with one point made earlier in this chapter, namely that creative products are end results, and as such they may not tell us much, if anything, about the process that led up to them. At the very least inferences must be draw, moving backward from the product (result) to the (causal and explanatory) process which preceded the completion of the product.

There is one last point about the various P concepts, or at least the notion of creative potential. For years I argued that potential was the most impor-tant topic for anyone who wished to support or enhance creativity. Admit-tedly potential is latent (Lubart, Barbot, and Zenasni, 2013; Runco, 2016b) and thus a risky target – much riskier than creative products or any man-ifest display of creativity. Still, we are much more likely to get "more bang for our buck" if we invest in and study potential. The fulfillment of poten-tial can lead to enormous growth and increases in creative output. Perhaps it is not so difficult to argue for the focus on potential, given that there are numerous examples of how it is already used in the sciences (e.g., "firing potential" of neurons, "potential energy").

Now for the surprise ending. There is a problem with the concept of creative potential, at least the way I have used it for decades – as completely distinct from actual performance (see Figure 16.1). When defined in that fashion, potential may be viewed as only important because it can lead somewhere (i.e., to products or social recognized creativity). And that is incorrect, or at least misleading.

The easiest way to explain this new view – which rejects the assump-tion that creative potential is only important because it may eventually lead to actual creative performances – is to refer back to everyday creativ-ity, authenticity, and personal creativity. These are expressions of a creative capacity that may not be socially recognized, and they may not involve any productivity, but they are quite important – and quite common. Very likely each of us experiences them everyday. This is a nice point on which to end because we have now come the full circle. The new position, just described, where creativity is an ends in and of itself – even if it does not lead somewhere, such as a product or performance – is quite relevant to the first question addressed in this chapter of why creativity is important. Creativity is important because is it so often useful to each and every one of us. That is especially true of the personal creativity and capacity for authenticity which we all share.

REFERENCES

Acar, S., Burnett, C., and Cabra, J. F. (2017). Ingredients of creativity: Originality and more. *Creativity Research Journal*, 29, 133–144.

Acar, S., and Runco, M. A. (2014). Assessing associative distance among ideas elicited by tests of divergent thinking. *Creativity Research Journal*, 26, 229–238.

(2015). Thinking in multiple directions: Hyperspace categories in divergent thinking. *Psychology of Art, Creativity, and Aesthetics*, 9, 41–53.

(2017). Latency predicts category switch in divergent thinking. *Psychology of Aesthetics, Creativity, and the Arts*, 11, 43–51.

Amabile, T. M. (1982). Children's artistic creativity: Detrimental effects of competition in a field setting. *Personality and Social Psychology Bulletin*, 8, 573–578.

(1990). Within you, without you: The social psychology of creativity, and beyond. In *Theories of creativity*, edited by M. A. Runco and R. S. Albert, 61–91. Newbury Park, CA: Sage.

An, D., and Runco, M. A. (2016). General and domain-specific contributions to creative ideation and creative performance. *Europe's Journal of Psychology*, 12, 523–532.

Beketayev, K., and Runco, M. A. (2016). Scoring divergent thinking tests with a semantics-based algorithm. *Europe's Journal of Psychology*, 12(2), 210–220.

Bruner, J. (1962). The conditions of creativity. In *Contemporary approaches to creative thinking*, edited by H. E. Gruber, G. Terell, and M. Wertheimer, 1–30. New York: Atherton.

Csikszentmihalyi, M. (1990). The domain of creativity. In M. A. Runco and R. S. Albert (Eds.), *Theories of creativity* (pp. 190–212). London: Sage.

Corraza, G. (2016). Potential originality and effectiveness: The dynamic definition of creativity. *Creativity Research Journal*, 28, 258–267.

Cropley, A. J. (1990). Creativity and mental health in everyday life. *Creativity Research Journal*, 3, 167–178.

Gruber, H. E. (1988). The evolving systems approach to creative work. *Creativity Research Journal*, 1, 27–51.

Hocevar, D. (1980). Intelligence, divergent thinking, and creativity. *Intelligence*, 4, 25–40.

Holland, J. L. (1961). Creative and academic achievement among talented adolescents. *Journal of Educational Psychology*, 52, 136–147.

Jay, E., and Perkins, D. (1997). Creativity's compass: A review of problem finding. In M. A. Runco (Ed.), *Creativity research handbook*, vol. 1 (pp. 257–293). Cresskill, NJ: Hampton Press.

Kasof, J. (1995). Explaining creativity: The attributional perspective. *Creativity Research Journal*, 8, 311–366.

Kharkhurin, A. V. (2012). Creativity. 4in1: Four-criterion construct of creativity. *Creativity Research Journal*, 26(3), 338–352.

Lubart, T., Barbot, B., and Zenasni, F. (2013). Creative potential and its measurement. *International Journal for Talent Development and Creativity*, 1, 41–52.

Maslow, A. (1968). Creativity in self-actualizing people. In *Toward a psychology of being*, 135–145. New York: Van Nostrand Reinhold.

Merrotsy, P. (2013). A note on Big C creativity and little c creativity. *Creativity Research Journal*, 25, 474.

Miller, A. I. (2009). *137: Jung, Pauli, and the pursuit of a scientific obsession*. New York: W. W. Norton.

Miller, G. (1956). The magical number seven, plus or minus two: Some limits on our capacity for processing information. *Psychological Review*, 63, 81–97.

Murray, H. A. (1959). Vicissitudes of creativity. In *Creativity and its cultivation*, edited by H. H. Anderson, 203–221. New York: Harper.

Okuda, S. M., Runco, M. A., and Berger, D. E. (1991). Creativity and the finding and solving of real-world problems. *Journal of Psychoeducational Assessment*, 9, 45–53.

Piaget, J. (1976). *To understand is to invent*. New York: Penguin.

Rhodes, M. (1961). An analysis of creativity. *The Phi Delta Kappan*, 42, 305–310.

Richards, R. (2007). Everyday creativity: Our hidden potential. In *Everyday creativity and new views of human nature*, edited by R. Richards, 25–54. Washington, DC: American Psychological Association.

Rogers, C. R. (1959). Toward a theory of creativity. In *Creativity and its cultivation*, edited by H. H. Anderson, 69–82. New York: Harper and Row.

Rubenson, D. L., and Runco, M. A. (1992). The psychoeconomic approach to creativity. *New Ideas in Psychology*, 10, 131–147.

Runco, M. A. (1986). Divergent thinking and creative performance in gifted and nongifted children. *Educational and Psychological Measurement*, 46, 375–384.

(1989). The creativity of children's art. *Child Study Journal*, 19, 177–189.

(1993). Operant theories of insight, originality, and creativity. *American Behavioral Scientist*, 37, 59–74.

(1994). Conclusions concerning problem finding, problem solving, and creativity. In M. A. Runco (Ed.), *Problem finding, problem solving, and creativity* (pp. 272–290). Norwood, NJ: Ablex.

(1995). Insight for creativity, expression for impact. *Creativity Research Journal*, 8, 377–390.

(1996). Personal creativity: Definition and developmental issues. *New Directions for Child Development*, 72, 3–30.

(2003). Education for creative potential. *Scandinavian Journal of Education*, 47, 317–324.

(2007). A hierarchical framework for the study of creativity. *New Horizons in Education*, 55(3), 1–9.

(2010). Education based on a parsimonious theory of creativity. In *Nurturing creativity in the classroom*, edited by R. A. Beghetto and J. C. Kaufman, 235–251. New York: Cambridge University Press.

(2011). Personal creativity. In M. A. Runco and S. Pritzker (Eds.), *Encyclopedia of creativity* (2nd ed., pp. 220–223). San Diego, CA: Elsevier.

(2014). *Creativity: Theories and themes: Research, development, and practice.* Rev. ed. San Diego, CA: Academic Press.

(2016a). Creative interpretations of educational contradictions. In R. Beghetto and B. Sriraman (Eds.), *Creative contradictions in education: Cross disciplinary paradoxes and perspectives* (pp. 75–87). New York: Springer.

(2016b). Overview of developmental perspectives on creativity and the realization of potential. *New Directions for Child and Adolescent Development*, 151, 97–109.

(Ed.). (2017). *Major works on creativity and education.* London: Sage.

(forthcoming). Ideas for a creative 21st Century. In J. C. Penagos-Corzo (Ed.), *75 ideas in creativity & psychology for the XXI century.* Universidad de las Américas Puebla.

Runco, M. A., Acar, S., and Cayirdag, N. A. (2017). Closer look at the creativity gap and why students are less creative at school than outside of school. *Thinking Skills and Creativity*, 24, 242–249.

Runco, M. A., Acar, S., Kaufman, J. C., and Halladay, L. R. (2016). Changes in reputation and associations with fame and biographical data. *Journal of Genius and Eminence*, 1, 52–60.

Runco, M. A., Kaufman, J. C., Halladay, L. R., and Cole, J. C. (2010). Change in reputation as index of genius and eminence. *Historical Methods*, 43, 91–96.

Runco, M. A., and Jaeger, G. (2012). The standard definition of creativity. *Creativity Research Journal*, 24, 92–96.

Runco, M. A., Johnson, D., and Gaynor, J. R. (1999). The judgmental bases of creativity and implications for the study of gifted youth. In *Investigating creativity in youth: Research and methods*, edited by A. Fishkin, B. Cramond, and P. Olszewski-Kubilius, 113–141. Cresskill, NJ: Hampton Press.

Runco, M. A., and Kim, D. (forthcoming). The four Ps of creativity and recent updates. In E. G. Carayannis (Ed.), *Encyclopedia of creativity, invention, innovation and entrepreneurship*, 2nd ed. New York: Springer.

Runco, M. A., Millar, G., Acar, S., and Cramond, B. (2011). Torrance Tests of Creative Thinking as predictors of personal and public achievement: A 50 year follow-up. *Creativity Research Journal*, 22, 361–368.

Runco, M. A., and Mraz, W. (1992). Scoring divergent thinking tests using total ideational output and a creativity index. *Educational and Psychological Measurement*, 52, 213–221.

Runco, M. A., and Pina, J. (2013). Imagination and personal creativity. In *Oxford handbook of the development of imagination*, edited by M. Taylor, 379–386. New York: Oxford University Press.

Runco, M. A., and Smith, W. R. (1992). Interpersonal and intrapersonal evaluations of creative ideas. *Personality and Individual Differences*, 13, 295–302.

Runco, M. A., Turkman, B., Acar, S., and Nural, M. V. (2016). Idea density and the creativity of written works. *Journal of Genius and Eminence*, 2, 26–31.

Simonton, D. K. (1988). Quality and purpose, quantity and chance. *Creativity Research Journal*, 1, 68–74.

(1995). Exceptional personal influence: An integrative paradigm. *Creativity Research Journal*, 8, 371–376.

(1997). Political pathology and societal creativity. In *Eminent creativity, everyday creativity, and health*, edited by M. A. Runco and R. Richards, 359–377. Greenwich, CT: Ablex.

(2012). Taking the U.S. Patent Office criteria seriously: A quantitative three-criterion creativity definition and its implications. *Creativity Research Journal*, 24, 96–107.

Sternberg, R. J. (2000). Creativity is a decision. In *Teaching for intelligence*, edited by A. L. Costa, 2:85–106. Arlington Heights, IL: Skylight Training and Publishing.

Stein, M. I. (1953). Creativity and culture. *Journal of Psychology*, 36, 31–322.

Tan, C. (2016). Creativity and Confucius. *Journal of Genius and Eminence*, 1(1), 79–84.

Wallach, M. A., and Wing, C. W., Jr. (1969). The talent student: A validation of the creativity intelligence distinction. New York: Holt, Rinehart, and Winston.

Weisberg, R. (2015). On the usefulness of "value" in the definition of creativity. *Creativity Research Journal*, 27, 111–124.

Wilson, E. O. (1975). *On human nature*. Cambridge, MA: Harvard University Press.

CHAPTER 17

Pretend Play and Creativity
Two Templates for the Future

Sandra W. Russ

After forty-seven years of studying pretend play and creativity, I have come to the following conclusions:

- Pretend play can be used to assess a number of processes in children-especially creative processes.
- Emotion/affect in play is central to understanding creativity.
- Pretend play can be used as a vehicle to develop and enhance processes important in creativity and in other areas of adaptive functioning of children.

How did I come to these conclusions? My clinical experience pointed the way toward appreciating the power of pretend play in childhood. The theoretical and research literature was important in understanding what scholars and researchers have discovered, as were the descriptive accounts of highly creative individuals as they described their experiences. The research program that I and my students and colleagues have carried out has found some consistent results and raised questions for the future. My research program has developed two templates for future application-a play assessment template and a play intervention protocol template. Hopefully, these templates will be useful to future researchers and to individuals who work with children in a variety of settings.

Why did I study pretend play and creativity? I had been interested in creativity as an undergraduate at the University of Pittsburgh in the late 1960s. The creative process was exciting to read about, fit with the humanistic Zeitgeist of the times, and seemed to reflect optimal development of the individual (I was idealistic). My undergraduate research project and masters research was on the role of affect in the creative process. After I received my PhD in clinical psychology, I began to use play therapy in my work as a child therapist with children who were anxious and/or depressed. That's when the connection between play and creativity became apparent.

As these children became more open in their play with their ideas and emotions, they seemed to become more creative in their thinking in general. So I wondered if this connection was really occurring or was just in my imagination, and if it was a real connection, then what were the mechanisms that accounted for the association. Thus began a research journey.

Theoretical Link between Pretend Play and Creativity

Pretend play is symbolic behavior in which "one thing is playfully treated as if it were something else" (Fein, 1987, p. 282). Krasnor and Pepler (1980) conceptualized play as involving nonliterality, positive affect, intrinsic motivation, and flexibility. Creative products are those that are original, of good quality, and appropriate to the task (Sternberg, Kaufman, and Pretz, 2002). Creative processes are those abilities within the individual that have been found to be important in helping individuals develop creative products. Many of these creative processes occur in pretend play (Russ, 1993). There is a consensus in the field that creative products and creative processes are on a continuum. Therefore, creativity can be studied in all individuals and in children. Pretend play is a unique place in which to study creative processes. Pretend play can also be treated as a creative product.

Historically, pretend play has been a subject of much observation and theorizing. Anna Freud (1965) and Melanie Klein (1955) discussed the free association that occurred in play. All kinds of ideas, fantasy themes, and emotions are expressed in play in a free roaming manner. During normal development, children use play to modulate emotions and to deal with daily stresses and problems. Waelder (1933) described play as a leave of absence from reality. Illogical thinking occurs in play and children can repeat unpleasant emotional experiences until they are "digested" or become manageable. Similarly, Singer and Singer (1990) thought that cognition and affect interact in pretend play and that play helps children express and regulate emotions. Fein (1987) thought that affect in play is intertwined with fantasy and that play is a natural form of creativity in children. Fein emphasized that affect is important in pretend play and proposed an affect symbol system of mental representations of affect that gets activated in pretend play. As I read the literature, I noticed the consistency between Fein's theory of affect and creativity and psychoanalytic theory.

Psychoanalytic theory proposed that not being able to think about conflict-laden emotional content or content that is taboo will result in a general intellectual restriction. In other words, repression will interfere with the creative process (Freud, 1926). Kris (1952) built upon this concept and hypothesized that individuals who can easily access this affective and illogical content and integrate it into cognition will be more creative. This theory intrigued me because it fit with what I observed in my child clients. As they become comfortable with ideas, fantasy, and affective content through pretend play, they become more flexible and creative in their thinking. Could this link between openness to fantasy and affective content and creativity be demonstrated empirically?

In adults, there was a group of studies that found this association, usually in males but not females (Suler, 1980). What about in children? There was very little work with children. I did a series of studies using the Rorschach and found that children who expressed responses with affective content (scary monster; bears with blood) could generate more responses on a divergent thinking test (Russ, 1982, 1988). This was consistently true for boys, rarely for girls. Divergent thinking is the ability to generate a variety of ideas and solutions and is an important component of creative thinking (Runco, 1991).

The Rorschach studies answered the question of whether affect in ideation and fantasy is related to creativity (at least to divergent thinking) in children. There is a relationship for boys. But what about for girls? Perhaps the Rorschach was not as valid a measure of affect in fantasy for girls as for boys. It was time to move onto the area of pretend play and creativity.

Pretend Play Assessment Template

In order to study pretend play and creativity, it was necessary to have a measure of pretend play that captured the cognitive and affective processes that are important components of creativity. The first task was to identify which processes were most important for creativity. Research has found that the cognitive processes that are important in creative production include divergent thinking, broad associative ability, flexibility of thought, insight, and analogical thinking (Guilford, 1950; Runco, 2004). There had been much research on the cognitive aspects of creativity, but not as much on affective processes. One of my theoretical contributions was to synthesize different literatures to propose five affective processes important in creative production (Russ, 1993):

- openness to affect states – comfort with experiencing emotion
- openness to affect-laden thought-ideas, images, fantasies with affect themes
- joy and pleasure in challenge

Table 17.1 *Model of creativity and pretend play*

Creative processes in pretend play	Examples in play
Divergent thinking	Block transformations
Broad associations	Different story ideas and elements
	Wide fantasy and remote images
Cognitive flexibility/recombining ideas	Use toys in different ways
	Manipulating story elements
	Loosening of time and space
Insight and problem solving	Building novel objects
	Playing with mechanical objects
Perspective taking	Role-playing
	Pretending to be different characters
Narrative development	Story plots and sequences
Affect themes and symbols	Monsters; cops and robbers
	Yummy food
Emotional expression	Dolls fighting; dolls hugging
Joy in pretending	Pleasure and absorption in the play
Integration of affect/affect themes	Placing emotion in an appropriate narrative

- joy and pleasure in problem solving
- cognitive integration of the affect, for example, appropriate affect in a story narrative

This theoretical classification system was the conceptual basis of the measure I developed. Measures of pretend play had focused on cognitive components of play, but not on affective components. Rubin, Fein, and Vandenberg (1983) referred to this as the "cognification" of play and called for measures of affect in play. To meet this need, beginning in 1987, I developed the Affect in Play Scale (Russ, 1987). I wanted the scale to tap cognitive processes and affective processes, since both are important in creativity. I needed to identify what these different processes would look like in pretend play, so I developed a model of creative processes that occur in pretend play (see Table 17.1).

I developed the Affect in Play Scale (Russ, 1993) in order to fill the need for a comprehensive standardized measure that assesses both cognitive and affective processes and that could be used in many research programs. I followed the guidelines that Jerome Singer had outlined in 1973. Singer stressed the need to focus on specific variables, identify specific behavior samples, stay with observable behaviors, and train raters carefully. He emphasized systematic measurement of play samples. I also consulted with

Dr. Singer to make sure I had covered all relevant affect categories based on the emotion literature.

The Affect in Play Scale (APS; Russ, 1993, 2014) is a comprehensive measure of the processes important in creativity in the domain of play. It is a standardized five-minute play task developed to measure different processes in pretend play that are involved in creativity. The APS is now a well-validated measure of imagination and affect expression in pretend play. Children receive two puppets and three blocks and are given the following instructions:

> I'm here to learn about how children play. I have here two puppets and would like you to play with them any way you would like for five minutes. For example, you can have the puppets do something together. I also have some blocks that you can use. Be sure to have the puppets talk out loud. The video camera will be on so that I can remember what you say and do. I'll tell you when to stop. (Russ, 2014, p. 177)

The child is informed when there is one minute left. If the child stops playing during the five-minute period, the child receives the prompt, "There's still time left, keep playing." The task is discontinued if the child cannot play after a two-minute period.

In developing the play task, it was important to choose toys that children were comfortable with but that were unstructured enough to allow for individual differences to emerge. Puppets and blocks are appropriate and the instructions are unstructured, leaving lots of room for individual differences. In the pilot study, we determined that this task did allow for adequate individual differences in children six to ten years of age. The task is most appropriate for children in the first through third grades.

The child's play is scored from the videotape using a criterion-based rating scale. There are five main scores: (1) Organization, the quality of the plot and the complexity of the story, scored from 1 to 5; (2) Imagination, the novelty and uniqueness of the play and ability to pretend and transform the blocks, scored from 1 to 5; (3) Comfort, a global rating of the child's comfort engaging in play and their level of enjoyment, scored from 1 to 5; (4) Frequency of Affect, a total count of affect units expressed within the play narrative e.g., A child might have the puppets say "Yikes, a monster!" (fear) or "Whee! This slide is fun!" (happy), and (5) Variety of Affect, a total count of the number of affect categories out of eleven possible categories, expressed during the play. The frequency of affect units count both affect states and affect themes expressed in the narrative. There is also a rating of affect intensity, if relevant to a study. There are eleven categories of affect that can be subdivided into positive (happy; nurturing) or negative (aggression; sadness). Thus, based on the theoretical model, the APS assesses affect states; affect themes; joy, pleasure, and engagement in the task; and cognitive integration of the affect into an organized and imaginative narrative.

A detailed scoring manual for the APS has been developed (Russ, 1993, 2004, 2014). Past studies have reported the interrater reliability of the APS to be high, consistently in the 0.80s and 0.90s. Internal consistency for the frequency of affect scores on the APS using the Spearman-Brown split-half reliability is also high (0.85; Seja and Russ, 1999), when we compared the second and fourth minutes with the third and fifth minutes of the play samples.

The APS has a large body of validity studies demonstrating associations with theoretically relevant criteria in different research programs and countries (Russ, 2014). The APS as a measure of creative processes in play has been validated by relating it to other measures of creativity. In developing the construct validity studies, it was important to follow the principles set forth by Weiner (2004), including the need for a theoretical connection between the measure and the criterion, that the criterion be observable and that enough of the variance in the criterion should be accounted for by the construct that the test is measuring. We have now carried out a number of studies with the APS and creativity measures (for a review, see Russ, 2014). The first study was done by Russ and Grossman-McKee (1990) with forty-six first- and second-grade children. We found that frequency of affect and variety of affect categories in play related to divergent thinking with significant correlations of medium effect sizes ($r = 0.42$, $p < 0.001$; $r = 0.38$, $p < 0.001$, respectively). The cognitive scores of imagination and organization were also significantly associated with divergent thinking. Correlations were independent of verbal intelligence. This was an exciting finding. Both affect and imagination were related to divergent thinking, independent of intelligence, and the relationship was present for both boys and girls. This finding was the first validation of the APS but also supported the theory that affect in fantasy was associated with an important component of creativity – divergent thinking. Since this first study, we have replicated this finding in a number of studies with different child populations and examiners. The imagination and affect expression scores on the APS significantly relate to creativity measures in a number of studies (Russ, 2014). In addition, the APS has related to other measures of creativity such as creativity in stories and teacher ratings of make-believe (Kaugars and Russ, 2009). Interestingly, affect in play is associated with affect expression in memory descriptions (Russ and Schafer, 2006) and in stories (Hoffmann and Russ,

2012), suggesting a cross-situational ability of access to, and expression of affect-laden cognition. In addition, two longitudinal studies have found that the relationship between play and divergent thinking over a four-year period is stable (Russ, Robins, and Christiano, 1999; Wallace and Russ, 2015). Children who were better players in early grades were better divergent thinkers four years later, after verbal intelligence was controlled.

As we carried out this research, we started to look at differences between positive and negative affect in play. There were usually no gender differences in play ability except that boys had more negative affect in their play, driven by having more aggressive content in their play. In general, negative affect has been more strongly related to creativity in boys than in girls (Russ and Schafer, 2006).

One important question about the APS is whether the cognitive and affective scores form one factor or two – is there one general play ability or is affect a separate construct? In several factor analyses with small samples, we found two factors – one cognitive and one affective. The definitive study was done by Lis's research group at the University of Padua in Italy. They found, with a confirmatory factor analysis with a large sample of 519 children, two factors – one that is cognitive (organization, imagination, comfort) and one that is affective (frequency, variety of affect) (Chessa et al., 2011). They concluded that the two-factor model supported my theoretical model of play as consisting of two distinct cognitive and affective dimensions that influence each other reciprocally. The APS has also been related to other adaptive functions in children, such as coping ability (Christiano and Russ, 1996), emotional understanding (Hoffmann and Russ, 2012), and ego resilience (Yates and Marcelo, 2014).

The APS has proven to be a reliable and valid measure of play ability in children that is related to creativity measures. Does it make a good template that can be altered for different purposes? The answer is yes, in that slight modifications have proven to be useful in the following ways:

- APS-P–preschool version. For children four to five years old. Relates to divergent thinking and creative storytelling (Kaugars and Russ, 2009; Fehr and Russ, 2016). This version has more toys and more structured instructions for these young children. Basically, it has the same coding system.
- APS-BR and APS-P BR. Brief ratings of each version- rates play in vivo with no taping (Cordiano, Russ, and Short, 2008).
- APS-M. Adapted version of APS to rate other samples of play. We rated play samples from the Autism Diagnostic Observation Schedule

(ADOS) for atypical child populations (Zyga, Russ, Ievers-Landis, and Dimitropoulos, 2015). This adaptation enables the APS coding system to be used on other play samples.

- M-APS. Modified scoring of APS and APS-P Added more scores such as repetition of themes, number of different themes, number of block transformations for atypical child populations who need a more sensitive measure (Dimitropoulos, Zyga, and Russ, 2017). This modification has been validated for children as young as three.
- Dynamic Play Assessment Scale. Added assessment piece to child's behavior during instructions and play task for clinical populations (Hlavaty, Short, and Gross, 2017).

Future research should follow developmental trajectories of processes in play and their correlates. Marcelo and Yates (2017) are following a large sample of high-risk children who have received the APS-P several times. Their findings will be important to follow.

Ideally, the APS and APS-P could be used to identify creative potential in children. It could add to a battery of creativity measures that might increase predictive power of the assessment.

Play Intervention Protocol Template

If pretend play is associated with creativity, a key question is whether play can be used as a vehicle to increase imagination and creativity? Is there a causal link between play and creativity?

In general, the research is mixed about the effectiveness of play interventions on facilitating creativity. Dansky (1999) and Russ (2014) have concluded that there are well-done studies that have found effects. Lillard et al. (2013) concluded that there was no support for pretend play increasing creativity. She raised a number of important methodological problems that need to be addressed in future research.

In an early attempt in my research lab, a carefully controlled study by Russ and Kaugars (2000–2001) did not find an effect of play on divergent thinking. Eighty children were randomly assigned to one of four groups: a happy-puppet play group; an angry-puppet play group; a free-play group; and a control-puzzle group. Children were given different instructions about having the puppets play out a happy story, angry story, or neutral story. The Alternate Uses test (divergent thinking) was given immediately following the play, by the same examiner. There was no effect for any of the play conditions on divergent thinking. Why did we find no effects? The experimental affect manipulation did work for the angry group (on a mood check) but not for the happy group. So, the hypothesis remains untested for the positive-affect group. Perhaps a more appropriate outcome measure would have been a storytelling measure. This raises the methodological issue of choosing the outcome measure that makes the best conceptual sense in the study. Or perhaps one session was not sufficient for effects to emerge.

It is possible that a number of play intervention sessions are needed before effects are demonstrated. Christie (1994) has cautioned against brief one-trial studies in the play intervention area. It may take time for the development of processes in pretend play that would, in turn, facilitate creativity. There is evidence that when pretend play occurs in multiple sessions over time, increases in components of creativity occur. For example, Kasari, Freeman, and Paparella (2006), in a randomized controlled study with children with autism, found that a play intervention resulted in increased symbolic play. These studies were with young children from three to four years of age. This was a rigorous study that began the intervention at the child's current developmental level. The training involved modeling and prompting. Children received thirty hours of intervention weekly for six weeks on a daily basis. This was a rather intensive intervention but is necessary for children with autism. Children in the play group, compared with children in joint attention and control groups, had increased symbolic play that generalized to play with mothers.

I wanted to see if we could develop a multiple-session play intervention protocol that would affect creativity. The target of the intervention would be imagination, affect expression, and cognitive integration of the affect into the story narrative. Could we increase these processes in play which would, in turn, increase creativity? We have developed a play protocol that uses story stems and a variety of unstructured toys. Children are played with individually. In a pilot study by Russ, Moore, and Farber (2004), first- and second-grade children in an inner city school with a high degree of poverty received five individual twenty-minute play sessions following a standard play intervention protocol. Different examiners blind to the group assignment assessed baseline play and outcome play on the APS. There were two play groups (imagination and affect) and one control group (puzzles and coloring). The play groups had a variety of toys available and played with the adult facilitator. They were asked to play out specific story themes that focused on imagination (have a boy go to the moon) or affect (have a girl be happy at a birthday party). The adult played with the child and followed the child's lead in the story, but also praised, modeled, and asked questions.

We controlled for adult interaction in the control group as well (coloring sheets and puzzles).

The major result of this study was that the play interventions were effective in improving play skills on the APS. The affect play condition was most effective in that, after baseline play was controlled for, the affect play group had significantly higher play scores on all play processes. These children had more affect in their play (both positive affect and negative affect), a greater variety of affect content, and better imagination and organization of the story than did the control group. The imagination play group also had significantly more positive affect and variety of affect than the control group. Another major finding was that, on the outcome measure of divergent thinking, there were significant effects for group. Although the individual contrast comparisons did not reach significance, inspection of the profile plots indicated that the play groups (usually the affect play group) had higher scores on the divergent thinking test. However, one limitation of this study was that no baseline measure of divergent thinking was obtained.

In a follow-up study of these children four to eight months later by Moore and Russ (2008), the imagination group had improved play skills over time. The affect group did not maintain the play changes over this period. It may be that an increase in affect expression from a play intervention is temporary, whereas an increase in imagination and pretend in play could be longer lasting. In the follow-up study, there no longer was a significant group effect for divergent thinking. In fact, the control group now had higher scores. Perhaps booster sessions would have been useful in maintaining the initial group effects.

Because the affect intervention was more effective in the short term, and the imagination intervention had longer-term effects, in our current research we have combined the imagination and affect stories and prompts in each play intervention session.

The current play intervention protocol consists of the following:

- Toys. A group of toys that are relatively unstructured, such as plastic animals, small human figures, toy cars, blocks, Legos, etc.
- Story stems. Children are asked to make up a story about a boy going to the zoo; a girl living under water; a boy losing his dog and feeling sad; a girl going to a birthday party and feeling happy. We have a pool of about twelve story stems. Usually a twenty-minute session consists of four stories and then the child makes up his or her own story to end the session.

- Instructions. Make up a story and play it out. The adult plays with the child. For imagination stories, the child is told to use his or her imagination. For the affect stories, the child is told to express feelings. We mix imagination and affect stories into each session.
- Prompts. The play facilitator engages with the child; models pretend; labels feelings; models expressing feelings; summarizes the story; asks for different endings; observes with interest; follows the child's lead as much as possible.

In a group adaptation of the play intervention, Hoffmann and Russ (2016) found that small-group play sessions, when compared with a control group, did result in increased imagination and affective expression in play after six sessions. In addition, there was a transfer effect in that below-average players increased in imagination in play and also increased on a divergent thinking task. To date, in the Russ research program, we have been able to increase imagination and affective expression in pretend play with standardized play intervention sessions with elementary school children. There have been transfer effects to a divergent thinking measure in two studies. On the other hand, we did not find facilitation effects when a similar study was carried out with preschool children (Fehr and Russ, 2016). We think that preschool children need parental involvement in the home for the play intervention to have effects.

Another recent adaptation of this play intervention protocol has been to use a play intervention with a telehealth approach. Since research suggests that telehealth may serve as a feasible and effective means of remote delivery of psychological services, a major question is whether structured play tasks and interventions may be administered via videoconferencing methods, and whether children can be guided in pretend play by a partner over this remote platform. Can children engage in pretend ply in an authentic way through videoconferencing?

We examined the feasibility and acceptability of this direct telehealth play intervention with children ages six to twelve diagnosed with Prader-Willi Syndrome ($n = 8$). These children are developmentally delayed and rigid in their cognitions and behavior. We thought that a pretend play intervention would help increase their cognitive flexibility.

Children enrolled in this study underwent the following procedure: an in-person preintervention visit to measure baseline cognition, language, affect, behavior, and play ability; twelve remote play sessions over a six-week intervention period (two sessions per week); an in-person postintervention visit to measure change in baseline abilities. Participating families were given a standardized toy kit at the preintervention assessment, including blocks, a set of dolls, a toy car, toy animals, toy food and drink, and Legos. Both the play interventionist and the child had the same structured set of toys. Sessions averaged fifteen to twenty minutes in length, and the interventionist/play partner used story stems of varying complexity to directly engage the child toward each thematic goal (i.e., a happy story about going to the zoo, building up to a story that focuses on losing a toy, feeling sad, but learning to be okay with it). At the end of the twelve intervention sessions, participating children and their parents were seen for another in-person visit, to assess the same language, behavioral, affect, and play abilities measured at baseline. We then asked parents of the participating children to anonymously complete a modified version of the Behavioral Intervention Rating Scale (BIRS; Elliot and Treuting, 1991) to assess feasibility of this approach. Seven of the the eight participating families completed this survey, and overall results indicated that the children completed the program with minimal behavioral or technological difficulty (#sessions $M = 11.875/12$), and the BIRS results indicated good acceptability overall ($M = 5.54/6.00$) (Dimitropoulos, Zyga, and Russ, 2017). Most notably, results indicate that children with Prader-Willi Syndrome are able to play with a remote play partner over a video platform. Parents reported that children enjoyed the intervention and the interaction with the play partner.

One of the challenges in play intervention research is that the developmental process is slow and varied. It may be years before the advantages that engaging in pretend play provides are evident in a creative product. Nevertheless, it is important that we persist in trying to develop play protocols that gain empirical support and that are easy to use by parents and teachers.

We are encouraged by the promising results using this paly intervention and the fact that it is flexible in that it can be adapted for different purposes. To date, this play protocol has been adapted for the following:

- Small-group intervention. Four children in a group, with turn-taking in developing the story (Hoffmann and Russ, 2016)
- Telehealth intervention. Adding other elements in the play that target specific issues relevant to these children (Dimitropoulos, Zyga, and Russ, 2017)
- Parent coaching. For children with attention-deficit hyperactivity disorder to improve the parent–child relationship (Wallace, 2017)
- Reducing anxiety in pediatric populations. Major adaptation (Fehr, Russ, and Ivers-Landis, 2016)

A future goal is to disseminate this play intervention so that schools can use it to facilitate components of creativity in children. It is short, easy to do, and can be used with small groups. For younger preschoolers, a training program that involves parents is being developed and will be tested.

Why is this play facilitation research important? Because if we can provide children with good play skills, it will give them a tool that they can use on their own for a variety of developmental purposes.

My immediate to-do list is as follows:

1 Use the APS and APS-P to identify children with creative potential for schools and gifted and talented programs. It could be added to creativity batteries already in use.
2 Continue gaining empirical support for the play intervention protocol. It would be especially useful for children who need help in developing imagination, cognitive flexibility, and affect expression.
3 Develop parent-coaching protocols that enable parents to be good play partners.
4 Investigate gender differences in the role of positive and negative affect in creativity.

Words of Wisdom for Future Researchers

- Know the importance of graduate students in developing research programs. Graduate students have fresh ideas and often do not know what the obstacles are – so they just go ahead and do it. For example, Astrida Kaugars led the development of the preschool adaptation of the play scale (APS-P); Jessica Hoffmann developed the adaptation of the play intervention for small groups; Olena Zyga led the telehealth approach. I had my doubts about all of the above, but my students forged ahead. And they were right.
- Know all aspects of the variable you are studying. Barbara McClintock was a plant biologist who won the Nobel Prize for her discoveries about the corn plant. She talked about going deep into the topic. She described going "right down there with them (chromosomes) and everything got big. I even was able to see the internal parts of the chromosomes ... these were my friends" (Keller, 1983, p. 117). McClintock loved the corn plant.
- Follow the guidelines from the creativity research. Study what you love. And, for whatever unconscious and conscious reasons, I love play and creativity.

REFERENCES

Chessa, D., DiRiso, D., Delvecchio, E., Salcuni, S., and Lis, A. (2011). The Affect in Play Scale: Confirmatory factor analysis in elementary school children. *Psychological Reperts*, 109, 759–774.

Christiano, B., and Russ, S. (1996). Play as a predictor of coping and distress in children during an invasive dental procedure. *Journal of Clinical Child Psychology*, 25, 130–138.

Christie, J. (1994). Academic play. In *Play and intervention*, edited by J. Hellendoorn, R. Van der Kooij, and B. Sutton-Smith, 203–213. Albany: State University of New York Press.

Cordiano, T., Russ, S., and Short, E. (2008). Development and validation of Affect in Play Scale-Brief Rating Version (APS-BR). *Journal of Personality Assessment*, 90, 52–60.

Dansky, J. (1999). Play. In *Encyclopedia of creativity*, edited by M. Runco and S. Pritzker, 393–408. San Diego, CA: Academic Press.

Dimitropoulos, A., Zyga, O., and Russ, S. (2017) (forthcoming). Evaluating the feasibility of a play-based telehealth intervention program for children with Prader-Willi Syndrome. *Journal of Autism and Developmental Disorders*, 1–12.

Elliott, S. N., and Treuting, M. V. B. (1991). The Behavior Intervention Rating Scale: Development and validation of a pretend treatment acceptability and effectiveness measure. *Journal of School Psychology*, 29, 43–51.

Fehr, K., and Russ, S. (2016). Pretend play in preschool-age children: Association and brief intervention. *Psychology of Aesthetics, Creativity, and the Arts*, 10 296–308.

Fehr, K., Russ, S., and Ivers-Landis, C. (2016). Treatment of sleep problems in young children: A case series report of a cognitive-behavioral play intervention. *Clinical Practice in Pediatric Psychology*, 306–317.

Fein, G. (1987). Pretend play: Creativity and consciousness. In *Curiosity, imagination and play*, edited by P. Gorlitz and J. Wohlwill, 281–304. Hillsdale, NJ: Lawrence Erlbaum Associates.

Freud, A. (1965). *Normality and pathology in childhood: Assessment of development.* New York: International Universities Press.

Freud, S. (1926). Inhibition, symptoms, and anxiety. *Standard Edition*, 20, 87–172.

Guilford, J. P. (1950). Creativity. *American Psychologist*, 5, 444–454.

Hlavaty, L., Short, E., and Gross, S. (2017). The utility of play for understanding developmental differences in preschoolers diagnosed with ADHD, SLI, or ASD. Paper presented at SRCD, Austin, April.

Hoffmann, J., and Russ, S. (2012). Pretend play, creativity and emotion regulation in children. *Psychology of Aesthetics, Creativity, and the Arts*, 6, 175–184.

 (2016). Fostering pretend play skills and creativity in elementary school girls. *Psychology of Aesthetics, Creativity, and the Arts*, 10, 114–125.

Kasari, C., Freeman, S., and Paparella, T. (2006). Joint attention and symbolic play in young children with autism: A randomized controlled intervention study. *Journal of Child Psychology and Psychiatry*, 47, 611–620.

Kaugars, A. S., and Russ, S. W. (2009). Assessing preschool children's pretend play: Preliminary validation of the Affect in Play Scale – Preschool Version. *Early Education and Development*, 20, 733–755.

Klein, M. (1955). The psychoanalytic play technique. *American Journal of Orthopsychiatry*, 25, 223–237.

Krasnor, I., and Pepler, D. (1980). The study of children's play: Some suggested future directions. *Child Development*, 9, 85–94.

Kris, E. (1952). *Psychoanalytic explorations in art*. New York: International Universities Press.

Lillard, A., Lerner, M., Hopkins, E., Dore, R., Smith, E., and Palmquist, C. (2013). The impact of pretend play on children's development: A review of empirical evidence. *Psychological Bulletin*, 139, 1–34.

Marcelo, A., and Yates, T. (2017). The development of cognitive and affective play features in pretend play across childhood. Poster presented at SRCD, Austin, April.

Moore, M., and Russ, S. (2008). Follow-up of a pretend play intervention: Effects on play, creativity, and emotional processes in children. *Creativity Research Journal*, 20, 427–436.

Rubin, K., Fein, G., and Vandenberg, B. (1983). Play. In *Handbook of child psychology*, edited by P. Mussen, 4:693–774. New York: John Wiley.

Runco, M. (1991). *Divergent thinking*. Norwood, NJ: Ablex.

(2004). Everyone has creative potential. In *Creativity: From potential to realization*, edited by R. J. Sternberg, E. L. Grigorenko, and J. L. Singer, 21–30. Washington, DC: American Psychological Association.

Russ, S. (1982). Sex differences in primary process thinking and flexibility in problem solving in children. *Journal of Personality Assessment*, 46, 569–577.

(1987). Assessment of cognitive affective interaction in children: Creativity, fantasy, and play research. In *Advances in personality assessment*, edited by C. Spielberger and J. Butcher, 141–155. Hillsdale, NJ: Lawrence Erlbaum Associates.

(1988). Primary process thinking, divergent thinking and coping in children. *Journal of Personality Assessment*, 52, 539–548.

(1993). *Affect and creativity: The role of affect and play in the creative process*. Hillsdale, NJ: Lawrence Erlbaum Associates.

(2004). *Play in child development and psychotherapy: Toward empirically supported practice*. Mahwah, NJ: Lawrence Erlbaum Associates.

(2014). *Pretend play in childhood: Foundation of adult creativity*. Washington, DC: American Psychological Association.

Russ, S. W., and Grossman-McKee, A. (1990). Affective expression in children's fantasy play, primary process thinking on the Rorschach and divergent thinking. *Journal of Personality Assessment*, 54, 756–771.

Russ, S. W., Moore, M., and Farber, B. (2004). Effects of play training on play, creativity and emotional processes. Poster session presented at the annual meeting of the American Psychological Association, Honolulu, HI, July.

Russ, S. W., Robins, A., and Christiano, B. (1999). Pretend play: Longitudinal prediction of creativity and affect in fantasy in children. *Creativity Research Journal*, 12, 129–139.

Russ, S. W., and Schafer, E. (2006). Affect in fantasy play, emotion in memories and divergent thinking. *Creativity Research Journal*, 18, 347–354.

Russ, S., and Seja Kaugars, A. (2000–2001). Emotion in children's play and creative problem solving. *Creativity Research Journal*, 13, 211–219.

Seja, A., and Russ, S. W. (1999). Children's fantasy play and emotional understanding. *Journal of Clinical Child Psychology*, 28, 269–277.

Singer, D. G., and Singer, J. L. (1990). *The house of make-believe: Children's play and the developing imagination*. Cambridge, MA: Harvard University Press.

Sternberg, R. J., Kaufman, J. C., and Pretz, J. E. (2002). *The creativity conundrum*. New York: Psychology Press.

Suler, J. (1980). Primary process thinking and creativity. *Psychological Bulletin*, 88, 144–165.

Waelder, R. (1933). Psychoanalytic theory of play. *Psychoanalytic Quarterly*, 2, 208–224.

Wallace, C. (2017). Improving the parent–child relationship in ADHD: A pretend play intervention. Unpublished doctoral dissertation, Case Western Reserve University.

Wallace, C., and Russ, S. (2015). Pretend play, divergent thinking, and achievement in girls: A longitudinal study. *Psychology of Aesthetics, Creativity, and the Arts*, 9, 296–305.

Weiner, I. (2004). Rorschach assessment: Current status. In *Comprehensive handbook of personality assessment*, edited by M. Hilsenroth and D. Segal, 343–355. Hoboken, NJ: John Wiley.

Yates, T., and Marcelo, A. (2014). Through race-colored glasses: Preschoolers' pretend play and teachers' ratings of preschooler adjustment. *Early Childhood and Research Quarterly*, 29, 1–11.

Zyga, O., Russ, S., Ievers-Landis, C., and Dimitropoulos, A. (2015). Assessment of pretend play in Prader-Willi syndrome: A direct comparison to autism spectrum disorder. *Journal of Autism and Developmental Disorders*, 45, 975–987.

CHAPTER 18

An Interdisciplinary Study of Group Creativity

R. Keith Sawyer

I study creativity in individuals and in social groups. I received my undergraduate degree in computer science at MIT, where I focused on artificial intelligence, and I continued my studies with a PhD in psychology, focusing on a sociocultural approach that brought together psychology and anthropology. Although my two degrees are in different disciplines, my work in both was connected to the cognitive sciences, an interdisciplinary approach that studies both individual and group cognition (Gardner, 1993). In the process of conducting my empirical research studies of creative groups, I became convinced that a full explanation of creativity required a group level of analysis.

I define creativity as a sociohistorical process – one that involves acts by individuals, appropriately studied by psychology, and also involves social and cultural processes, appropriately studied by sociology, anthropology, and history. My empirical and theoretical work attempts to explore and explain how groups create, and the relationship between the creativity of a group, and the creativity of individual group members. I conduct ethnographic, observational studies of real-world creative groups, using the transcription methodologies of conversation analysis, and emergent coding methodologies associated with grounded theory. In this chapter, I describe my three largest ethnographic studies: conversation in children's pretend play (Sawyer, 1997); musical interaction in jazz (Sawyer, 2003a); and the improvised dialogues of Chicago improv theater groups (Sawyer, 2003b).

These empirical studies provide evidence that a purely psychological conception of creativity cannot fully explain group improvisational phenomena. To explain these empirical phenomena, I've developed a theory of *social emergence*. The theory of social emergence is grounded in sociological theory and the philosophy of science, and provides an explanation of the empirical observed relationships between individual creativity and group creativity (Sawyer, 2005). After I describe my empirical studies, I provide a brief description of this theoretical framework.

Intellectual History

I was introduced to creativity research in my first term of graduate school, fall 1990. I had just entered a doctoral program at the University of Chicago, in the Committee on Human Development, an interdisciplinary program that combined psychology and anthropology. My research goal was to study the social contexts of conversational interaction. I chose to attend the University of Chicago for graduate school because of the anthropology department's strengths in linguistic anthropology. I was particularly interested in studying with the legendary linguistic anthropologist, Dr. Michael Silverstein.

While registering for my first semester of classes in fall 1990, I noticed a class called "The Psychology of Creativity," taught by Dr. Mihaly Csikszentmihalyi. I recognized his name: he had been in the news quite a bit due to the phenomenal success of his recently published book, *Flow: The Psychology of Optimal Experience* (Csikszentmihalyi, 1990). But I didn't know that he also studied creativity. I had an opening in my schedule for an elective, and I registered for the course.

I was drawn to this course because of the important role of music in my life. I've been a pianist since a young age. Like many piano students, my training focused on the European classical music tradition. By the age of fifteen, I was playing and performing the "three Bs": Beethoven, Bach, and Brahms. I was able to sight read just about anything; with practice, I could perform very well while reading from a score. But I had never improvised. In fact, I didn't even know what improvisation was.

At the age of sixteen, my school's jazz band had an opening for a pianist, and I signed up. At the first rehearsal, I was surprised to find out that there was no written music! I didn't know that jazz pianists are expected to improvise their parts. I sat the piano, staring at the sheet music with a puzzled look. The band director noticed my dilemma; he came over to the piano and showed me a few basic chord voicings, just enough to get me started.

Over that school year, I taught myself how to improvise on piano by playing with other musicians. I discovered that jazz is an ensemble art form: you improvise with other musicians and almost never play alone. I enjoyed playing in a group because the improvisations of the other musicians gave me ideas for things I never would have created on my own. The performance emerged from all of our improvisational ideas: our individual creativity combined into group creativity.

In Dr. Csikszentmihalyi's class, I received a broad survey of the creativity research literature. I discovered that there had been almost no creativity research on jazz improvisation. For my course project, I decided to apply the methods and theories of creativity research to jazz creativity. I conducted an interview study with jazz musicians in the Chicago area, and this study was the basis for my first peer-reviewed journal article (Sawyer, 1992).

In my second year of graduate school, in a short hallway conversation between classes, another student found out that I was interested in improvisational creativity. She told me about improvisational theater – a style of theater that was improvised on stage. I had never heard of improv theater, and I didn't know that Chicago was the world headquarters of improvisational comedy. So I went to a few performances, and I was fascinated. A few weeks later, I noticed a handwritten piece of paper on a hallway door: it announced that a Chicago improv group was auditioning for a pianist. I decided to audition, and because I knew how to improvise, I was able to follow the improvised action on stage. I was selected at the audition; I then performed with the group for two years. This gave me a front-row seat to see how group improvisation worked.

Soon after our first performances, I realized that these staged improvisations could provide interesting data for interactional analysis – my original motivation for going to graduate school. I was already doing my dissertation on another topic, a study of dialogue in children's pretend play (Sawyer, 1997). But I didn't want to lose this unique opportunity to study improv theater up close. So I purchased a video camera and a tripod (this was pretty expensive for a graduate student in 1990), and I videotaped all of our performances. I planned to transcribe and analyze the data after I finished my dissertation.

Improv theater was an excellent site to study the social contexts of conversational interaction. My graduate school coursework trained me in the methodologies and theories of linguistic interaction, and the role of social and cultural context in linguistic interaction. I studied fields including conversation analysis (Psathas, 1995), ethnomethodology (Garfinkel, 1967), symbolic interaction (Blumer, 1969), Goffman's interaction ritual and frames (Goffman, 1967, 1974), and the creativity of ritual performance in performance genres in cultures around the world (Bauman and Sherzer,

1974). I used these traditions in my dissertation, to analyze children's play dialogues.

Because I was immersed in theater and children's play at the same time, I was able to see that improv and children's play shared several creative elements. The similarities were so profound, and so rich, that I used improvisation as a metaphor for children's play dialogues. My dissertation, and then my first book, elaborated the similarities between children's play and improvisation: I called it *Pretend Play as Improvisation* (Sawyer, 1997). After receiving my PhD in 1994, guided by a doctoral committee that included both Dr. Csikszentmihalyi and Dr. Silverstein, I then turned to the analysis of my improv theater videotapes, and I presented the findings in my book *Improvised Dialogues: Emergence and Creativity in Conversation* (Sawyer, 2003b).

The above intellectual history describes several unexpected developments. I entered graduate school to study the social context of conversation, not to study creativity; I didn't know it was possible to study creativity scientifically. After arriving at the University of Chicago, I noticed Dr. Csikszentmihalyi's fall 1990 course almost by accident, and I discovered the field of creativity research. (In yet another course, I studied children's discourse, and that gave me the idea for my dissertation research.) A year later, in a brief hallway conversation, I learned about Chicago improv theater. Months after that, I saw the handwritten notice that a group needed a pianist. I didn't start out to study creativity, and I didn't start out to study improvisation. You might say that my own career has been an improvisation, with its many twists and turns.

The Group Level of Analysis

In jazz and improv theater, each performer is creative. Psychologists would analyze their creativity using the methodologies and theoretical frameworks developed for studying individual personality and cognition. But individual psychology cannot provide a complete scientific explanation of group improvisation, because so much of the creativity is found in the conversational interactions between members of the group, and the links between these moment-to-moment exchanges. Each communication act looks backward, a response to the immediately previous action. Each act refers back to the entire past flow of the performance so far. Each act also looks forward, opening up creative possibilities for the other members of the group.

My research has found that improv groups display three characteristics that are difficult to analyze and explain using psychological methods and theories:

Unpredictability

In an effective improvisational performance, none of the performers knows what the next action will be. Each act must coherently follow from the prior flow of the performance, but that prior performance doesn't predict what this act will be. Actors are trained to improvise in this fashion, because they believe that the best performances emerge from the creativity of the group, not from any one actor. At any moment in the performance, the performer has available a broad range of possible action.

Ambiguity

In an effective improvisational performance, each person's actions are ambiguous, and this ambiguity opens up many possible paths forward. If an individual's creative act is too specific, then it overly narrows the range of options for the next performer. Improv theater actors have a pejorative term for such an action: They call it *driving* the scene. "Driving" means that a single person has taken an action that overly determines and predicts the subsequent flow of the scene. Such driving blocks the creativity of the group, and almost always results in a failed performance.

Retrospective interpretation

As a result of unpredictability and ambiguity, even a performer doesn't know what his own creative action means. Only when the interaction continues does the meaning of a single action become clear. Performers trust the collective creativity of the group to determine their own action's meaning. As a result, it's problematic to speak of the *creative intention* of the performer. Performers have to act without intention. Even a single performer's action cannot be explained using psychological analysis of individual creativity.

A Theoretical Framework: Social Emergence and Complex Systems

In my studies of jazz and theater, I have focused on the creativity of the group, rather than the creativity of the individuals in the group. Each single action is an individual creative act, no doubt. But the study of these individual moments would not provide an effective or complete explanation of the creativity of the group. Early in my career, I searched the literature for theoretical frameworks that I might use to explain group creativity. In my view, the existing theories were not adequate to explain group improvisation. So I began to develop a theoretical model of group dynamics, group symbolic interaction, and the unfolding flow of an encounter from moment to moment. I built on existing theories of culturally situated verbal performance, primarily in linguistic anthropology, and this theoretical account appears in my books *Improvised Dialogues* (Sawyer, 2003b) and *Social Emergence* (Sawyer, 2005).

These theoretical writings explore to how we might conceptualize group phenomena, and the relationship between group processes and individual-level phenomena. This relationship has been understudied in the social sciences, due to a disciplinary division of labor. Psychologists study individual thought and behavior; sociologists study groups and collectives. Psychologists tend to assume (even if implicitly and unstated) that social phenomena can be explained by analyzing the individual actions of the group's members, aggregated to the social level. This is a *reductionist* explanatory position. Inversely, sociologists tend to assume that the primary explanatory focus is social and collective, and they rarely include psychological states or behavior in their explanatory frameworks. This is a *holist* explanatory position.

In these two books (Sawyer, 2003b, 2005), I argue that neither position is adequate to explain group improvisational creativity. Jazz and theater performances cannot be reduced to explanations in terms of the creativity and creative actions of the individual performers. And yet, these performances cannot be fully explained at the group level, either. An adequate explanation of group improvisation must include accounts of both group and individual factors.

This theoretical stance, between reductionism and holism, is necessary to explain *emergent phenomena*. Emergence occurs when higher levels of analysis emerge from lower levels of analysis, and is typically found in complex systems. Simple systems are easy to explain with a reductionist strategy; for example, a crystal has many molecules, and from the systemic combinations of these molecules, a distinctive structure emerges. But every property of a crystal can be fully explained through reduction to properties of the individual molecules, and explanations of how those molecules interact.

At the other extreme, the interactions between a system's components can be so chaotic that no structures or patterns emerge. It's not possible to identify explanatory patterns at the collective level; at the same time, the reduction to an explanation at the component level is far too difficult to be accomplished. Chaotic systems are not amenable to scientific explanation.

To explain improvisational group creativity, I worked to develop theoretical frameworks that might account for the emergence of group creativity from individual creativity. I first began this work while analyzing my improvisational theater transcripts, and my first development of this theory appears in Sawyer (2003b). I engaged with a long tradition of exploring emergent phenomena in sociological theory and in the philosophy of the social sciences. This journey took longer than I originally expected. There had been substantial theoretical work on these topics in the past fifty years, but I also discovered important theoretical writings from the 1920s, and some prior to 1900. My theoretical research resulted in several contributions to sociological theory and to the philosophy of science – in a series of journal articles, and in my 2005 book *Social Emergence: Societies as Complex Systems*. My theoretical research convinced me that there existed social systems that could not be scientifically explained by reduction to the study of the people in these systems.

Drawing on this theoretical work, I argue that improvisational performances are complex systems, and that the relationship between individual and group levels of analysis is one of emergence. The performance emerges from the individual actions of the group members, successively contributed, over time. The emergent performance then constrains the possible creative actions of the performers: philosophers of science call this *downward causation*. In group improvisation, the dialectic of emergence and downward causation is so complex that the performance cannot be explained by reduction to individual performers and their actions.

Defining Creativity

Because improvising groups are emergent complex systems, their study has to be interdisciplinary, incorporating methods and theories from both psychology and sociology. My career has been interdisciplinary because my chosen topic of study requires it, not because of any a priori theoretical stance. Not all creative phenomena are socially emergent, and not all creativity research has to be interdisciplinary. Psychology will continue to be the proper disciplinary approach for creativity that can be analyzed solely at the individual level. For example, when a person combines two unrelated words to create a concept that is new to that person, this is an individual creative act that can be explained in terms of cognitive structures and processes, without reference to sociological mechanisms. Likewise, some creative phenomena can be best analyzed at the sociological level, without reference to psychology. For example, the development of scientific disciplines over decades and centuries is appropriately explained using theoretical frameworks of sociology and history, without the incorporation of psychological concepts or theories.

Having an interdisciplinary point of view, I see multilevel phenomena everywhere – including in most studies of creativity. I would argue that almost all creativity research incorporates both the individual and the group levels of analysis, as follows. Cognitive psychology studies *constructs* – hypothesized yet unobservable entities within individual minds, like memory, attention, and processing. Personality psychology also studies unobservable entities – personality traits or dispositions. Psychologists study these unobservable entities using the methodologies of individual psychology: defining a population, randomly sampling it, constructing control and experimental conditions, operationalizing a construct of interest so that it can be measured through observation, and statistically testing group differences in these measures.

This interdisciplinary approach has led me to the observation that the standard definition of a creative product, as being novel and useful or appropriate, is not a psychological definition. Likewise, a definition of creative people by reference to their created products, identified this way, is not a psychological definition, because it cannot be operationalized solely at the individual level of analysis. Novelty is defined by reference to the prior history of a discipline; appropriateness is defined by reference to a social and cultural process. These are both group-level phenomena. Because novelty and appropriateness are not properties at the individual level of analysis, what most creativity researchers study are the psychological correlates of social phenomena. Some creativity researchers acknowledge this more explicitly than others; for example, one of the best-known versions of the "novelty and appropriateness" definition of creativity is Csikszentmihalyi's (1988) *systems model*, which is explicitly sociocultural. In the systems model, creativity is conceived to be a property of a sociocultural system which includes the person, domain, and field.

Most studies of creativity have been studies of specific individuals who are identified as "creative" as a result of this sociohistorical process of acclaim, success, and acknowledgment. These studies are partly psychological, in that they are studies of internal constructs of these individuals. The constructs are correlates of the worldly success used for the identification criteria. But it is difficult to know to what extent these correlating individual properties represent "creativity," or some other traits or cognitions that are involved in societal success. Defining creative people as those who generate novel and appropriate products is an interdisciplinary and sociocultural definition. Our field has not fully acknowledged that its status vis-à-vis the discipline of psychology is complex and unresolved.

As Louis Sass (2000–2001) wrote in an issue of *Creativity Research Journal*,

> What merits the honorific term *creative* will vary according to the context of production and perspective, largely culturally determined, in which the product is seen, interpreted, and judged. (p. 57)

He continues:

> [Creativity research depends] on judgments of creativity...such judgments [are inseparable] from prevalent social values, attitudes, and conventions...Studies that use psychological tests of creativity must also rely on someone's judgment of what is a worthy, interesting, or creative response...What is being examined in such studies is not some timeless or intrinsic essence but, rather, an interaction between a given personality and the milieu in which the person finds him or herself. (p. 69)

Conclusion: Where Creativity Research Is and Where It Might Go in the Future

In my article for the *Journal of Creative Behavior*'s fiftieth anniversary (Sawyer, 2017), which I completed a few months ago, I described three historical shifts in creativity research that occurred between the field's origins in the 1950s through today:

- The first is a shift from Cold War concerns about conformity, socialism, and democracy, to a contemporary concern with economic success, entrepreneurship, and innovation.
- The second is a shift from the study of world-famous scientists and artists (I called this "elite creativity") to the study of the creative abilities that are possessed by everyone, and used every day.
- A third shift is away from the cultural and ethnic homogeneity of 1950s American society, to a more diverse and multicultural society today, and a more interconnected and global world.

All three of these shifts are driving a necessary transition in creativity research, from the psychological study of individuals, to the interdisciplinary study of creativity in groups, social networks, and cultural contexts:

- In a business context, successful creativity is based in teams and social networks; it requires a particular type of organizational culture; it requires well-structured incentives, and uniquely executed leadership. Business scholars have convincingly demonstrated that the lone genius entrepreneur is largely a myth, and that successful creativity requires groups who engage in a certain type of interaction. I reviewed this research in *Group Genius* (Sawyer, 2017).
- Everyday creativity is embedded in the moments of everyday life. Large portions of each day are spent in the presence of others: in hallway conversations, at lunch, or in business meetings. In our personal lives, we are often with friends and family.
- In the face of increasing social, cultural, and ethnic diversity, it is becoming increasingly clear that the standard definition of creativity, as socially and culturally determined, is problematic. As Sass (2000–2001) argues in the block quotation above: creativity is an "honorific term" that is "culturally determined" and defined by "prevalent social values" (pp. 57, 69).

I am excited by these developments. Creativity is more important to society than ever before. Our research is needed; we have a receptive audience. These sociohistorical developments make a focus on groups and societies ever more essential: creativity in business, creativity in everyday life, and creativity across cultural groups. In the second edition of *Explaining Creativity* (Sawyer, 2012), I argued that our field has advanced to an interdisciplinary stage, one that works to incorporate both individualist and sociocultural approaches to creativity.

The importance of collaborative creativity has accelerated in recent years, due to the growth of social media. Definitions of creativity have been *disintermediated*: No longer are creative products always selected by gatekeepers with disciplinary expertise; they are selected by distributed networks. Today, anyone can post creative products, and anyone can consume them: a video (YouTube), a photo (Instagram), a story (fan fiction websites), a new song (Sound Cloud). Anyone can pitch an idea for a new product, and accept donations to work on the project (Kickstarter).

I expect these historical trends to continue, and creativity will become increasingly distributed, networked, and collaborative. Creativity research should respond by drawing on multiple disciplines: using diverse methodologies to gather data at the individual and the group level of analysis, and developing explanatory frameworks that are both psychological and sociological. I hope that my studies of emergent creativity in complex systems might prove useful as the field responds to these developments.

REFERENCES

Bauman, R., and Sherzer, J. (Eds.). (1974). *Explorations in the ethnography of speaking*. New York: Cambridge University Press.
Blumer, H. (1969). *Symbolic interactionism: Perspective and method*. Englewood Cliffs, NJ: Prentice Hall.
Csikszentmihalyi, M. (1988). Society, culture, and person: A systems view of creativity. In *The nature of creativity*, edited by R. J. Sternberg, 325–339. New York: Cambridge University Press.
    (1990). *Flow: The psychology of optimal experience*. New York: HarperCollins.
Gardner, H. (1993). *The mind's new science: A history of the cognitive revolution*. New York: Basic Books.
Garfinkel, H. (1967). *Studies in ethnomethodology*. Englewood Cliffs, NJ: Prentice Hall.
Goffman, E. (1967). *Interaction ritual: Essays on face-to-face behavior*. New York: Pantheon Books.
    (1974). *Frame analysis: An essay on the organization of experience*. New York: Harper and Row.
Psathas, G. (1995). *Conversation analysis: The study of talk-in-interaction*. Thousand Oaks, CA: Sage.
Sass, L. A. (2000–2001). Schizophrenia, modernism, and the "creative imagination": On creativity and psychopathology. *Creativity Research Journal*, 13(1), 55–74.
Sawyer, R. K. (1992). Improvisational creativity: An analysis of jazz performance. *Creativity Research Journal*, 5(3), 253–263.
    (1997). *Pretend play as improvisation: Conversation in the preschool classroom*. Mahwah, NJ: Erlbaum.
    (2003a). *Group creativity: Music, theater, collaboration*. Mahwah, NJ: Erlbaum.
    (2003b). *Improvised dialogues: Emergence and creativity in conversation*. Westport, CT: Greenwood.
    (2005). *Social emergence: Societies as complex systems*. New York: Cambridge University Press.
    (2012). *Explaining creativity: The science of human innovation*. 2nd ed. New York: Oxford University Press.
    (2017a). Creativity research and cultural context: Past, present, and future. *Journal of Creative Behavior*, 51(4), 352–354.
    (2017b). *Group genius: The creative power of collaboration*. 2nd ed. New York: Basic Books.

CHAPTER 19

Creativity is Undefinable, Controllable, and Everywhere

Paul J. Silvia

I love William Zinsser's many books. He is best known for his classic *On Writing Well* (Zinsser, 2006), which has sold over a million copies and is a touchstone for modern nonfiction style. But like most eminent creators, his big hits overshadow a large body of more obscure works, from books on jazz to sports to travel (Zinsser, 1984, 1989, 1992). My favorite work in the Zinsser catalog might be *Writing to Learn* (Zinsser, 1988), a book that argues for nonfiction writing as a tool for generating and refining ideas. Instead of seeing writing as a mechanical process that wraps up the research process, writing can be the start of research. In writing we teach ourselves what we know and don't know, what we're committed to and what we're uncertain about.

My inner creativity researcher likes the idea of writing as an ideational tool, as a way for me to see what I think. So in that spirit, this chapter explores a few major themes in creativity research that motivate my research. I haven't made up my mind on these issues, but I hope that writing about them sparks some new ideas for both you and me on some hard problems in creativity research.

Creativity Is Undefinable

I think creativity researchers enjoy defining creativity and then arguing about it. Many creativity books, articles, and chapters start with a definition of creativity, which is odd when one realizes that few publications in cell biology start by defining *cell* or *biology*. Arguments about definitions of creativity break out occasionally online, and creativity scholars still publish papers that seek to shape, once and for all, what counts as creativity. Some call their definition "the standard definition" (Runco and Jaeger, 2012), perhaps to lend it some gravitas and scare off graduate students who might be tempted to innovate. The amount of time and energy creativity scholars put into defining creativity seems excessive. Social psychologists, for example, spend almost no time on defining complex, controversial concepts like *social, group, power,* and *interaction,* and they're doing okay.

These definitions usually claim that creative ideas meet two criteria: they are *novel* and *appropriate. Novel* is sometimes replaced by *new* or *original; appropriate* is sometimes replaced by *useful* or *effective.* An invention – perhaps an Apple iPeeler, for example – would be creative if it is both novel (a web-connected way to core and peel apples quickly while posting humble-bragging images of your denuded apple to social media) and appropriate (it functions as intended).

This novel-and-appropriate definition is in all the textbooks and first-paragraphs of articles, but the fact that creativity researchers still grouse about it shows that it has never really caught on. One suspects that its defenders who call it "*the* standard definition" are protesting too much. Many creativity theories reject appropriateness as a criterion (e.g., Weisberg, 2006), and it seems like the general public doesn't weigh it heavily when judging creativity (Diedrich, Benedek, Jauk, and Neubauer, 2015). And analytically, the definition fails because the concepts of *appropriate, useful,* and *effective* must be stretched beyond recognition – creativity researchers shift vagueness from *creative* to *appropriate.*

Consider a prototypical Western arts domain like poetry. What makes traditional poetry of the Robert Frost sort "appropriate" or "effective" or "useful"? Think of a few ways. Then consider other forms of poetry, like free or blank verse – do those ways still work? Some would. Now what about visual poetry (poetry without lines of text), asemic poetry (a poetry of nonmeaning that celebrates imaginary languages), algorithmic poetry (overdetermined poems generated by inputs to a created system), or concrete poetry (poems in which the words' visual form and layout participate in meaning)? Does the way that worked earlier work for all of these genres? Then what about found poems, which are texts not intended to be poems by their creators but are held up as such by the poets who find them?

It is hard to discern a sense of *effective* that these kinds of poetry share with each other, let alone a sense of *effective* that poetry shares with leadership, pastry decorating, and automotive engineering. My impression is that creativity researchers shift between different senses of *useful, appropriate,* and *effective* to fit the problem at hand. The sense of *useful* one sees for inventions is unlike the sense used for poetry, humor, pretend play, children's drawings, or imaginative daydreams. It is okay to shift between a word's many senses, but we should acknowledge that these standard definitions put *creativity* and *appropriate* on a semantic see-saw. We can have a consistent definition of creativity only if we have variable and vague implicit definitions of its constituent elements. To save the definition of *creativity*, we must sacrifice our definition of *appropriate* by allowing it to mean many, many things. But if we save our definition of *appropriate*, our tidy definition of creativity doesn't work anymore.

So the standard definition isn't a definition after all: it just hides the ambiguity of *creative* behind *effective* and *appropriate*. But let's dig into some more problems by returning to the easy, prototypical case of inventions: They are creative because they are novel while also functioning as intended and serving (or creating) a market need. And let's consider an easy case: Steve Jobs and Apple's iPod and iPhone. These were smashing market successes that were widely heralded as triumphs of consumer design, and Steve Jobs is now held up as a modern-day creative genius. By all accounts, the iPad and iPhone are surely "creative": novel and appropriate.

Even in this easy case, we can see a different criticism of the standard definition: who gets to define "appropriate" or "effective"? A capitalist would say "Hey, we all made a fortune and owned the tablet market – the iPad was effective." Design theorists in the cradle-to-cradle school of thought (McDonough and Braungart, 2002), on the other hand, would see these devices as inappropriate failures. Held together by glue and double-sided tape, your typical hard-to-fix, hard-to-recycle, short-life-cycle iPad represents all that is distasteful in unsustainable product design. Socialists and labor activists would point out that those iPads were made by thousands of poor developing-world laborers who worked in conditions so depressing that several flung themselves from the factory roof in despair (e.g., Foreman, 2010). One wonders if their families see the iPad as useful or effective or appropriate as a creative product. We needn't agree with the capitalists or design theorists or socialists to agree with the bigger point: *appropriate*, *useful*, and *effective* are not features of an idea but social claims about those objects, claims involving social, political, and economic power (cf. Glăveanu, 2010; Negus and Pickering, 2004).

Finally, who cares? Imagine that all the writers in this book got together in Davos, conferred over wine and shrimp, and issued a pretentious declaration that defined, once and for all, what creativity was. Would our creativity journals stop publishing research that slipped outside the definition, such as work on insight, animal behavior, pretend play, or mental imagery? Would we not let those researchers talk in creativity sessions at conferences? Would those research areas cease to interest "real creativity" researchers? Of course not.

So, to recap: the standard definition of creativity (1) is fraught and sensible only if we abuse the definitions of its constituent concepts,

(2) carries heavy ideological baggage regarding who gets to define what is new and appropriate, and (3) has zero implications for how we do and share our research. Yet despite not having a tidy definition, creativity research is flourishing. Perhaps you don't need a nailed-down, pithy definition of something to know a lot about it.

Creativity Is Controllable

Once we get over "defining" creativity, we can start to think about what creativity looks like and how it works. One of the most intriguing problems in the science of creativity, in my opinion, is whether creativity is controllable – and if it is, how do people control it? The romanticist tradition views creativity as a fickle and ineluctable force (Sawyer, 2006; Weisberg, 2006). Sometimes our inner creative spirit moves us; sometimes it doesn't. The romanticist view is widely held in Western culture, which views creativity as mysterious and geniuses as set apart (Glăveanu, 2010).

When I first started getting into the study of creative thought, around 2005 or so, I had the impression that the cognitive psychology of creativity was missing some obvious opportunities. The field's models of cognition were rooted in the cognitive psychology of the 1950s and were thus seriously dated. Even today, one still sees papers that view associative chains and spreading activation – one thought sparking the next and the next and the next – as the core mechanism behind creative thought. Associative models of creativity are romanticist models. Creativity goes where it goes: the mind hops and jumps and ambles toward good ideas at the frontier of the conceptual network. The process is bottom-up and undirected, and people have to patiently sit out all the bad early ideas until their mind wanders into those remote, hazy regions that contain the good ideas.

Spreading activation is a real thing, and this idea was fresh back when Mednick (1962), Guilford (1967), and Wallach and Kogan (1965) were breaking new ground, but cognitive psychology has evolved a few generations since then. In particular, creativity work struck me as having missed the executive revolution – the widespread interest in self-regulation and executive control that swept most area of psychology starting in the 1990s. Perhaps, I thought, the literatures on metacognition, cognitive control, inhibitory control, and strategy use have something to offer the study of creative thinking.

Another reason to think that creativity is controllable came from what my humanities pals call a *performative incongruity*. Divergent thinking research might claim that creative ideas flow from spontaneous, bottom-up associative processes, but divergent thinking researchers weren't training their students to come up with research ideas this way. Instead of encouraging them to follow random associative threads wherever they lead, we tell our students to read widely, reason through what they read, link their ideas to a field's abstract themes and enduring concerns, sift through their ideas to find the best ones, and then refine those ideas. In short, we train budding scientists as if people can learn to think creatively about scientific problems and thus exert control over the creative quality of their ideas. (Indeed, we were applying the wisdom of systems and sociocultural theories [Csikszentmihalyi, 1988; Sternberg and Lubart, 1996].)

It seemed intuitive to me, coming from a self-regulation background (Duval and Silvia, 2001), that people must use executive processes to come up with creative ideas. When trying to think of a cool new idea, you have to manage many ideas at once, inhibit all the old and irrelevant ideas that come to mind first, selectively retrieve the knowledge you need, identify and apply mental strategies, and keep your creative goal in mind. Associative processes are involved, without a doubt, but creative thought struck me as essentially directed and intentional much of the time.

We started our explorations into how well people can control creativity with the low-hanging fruit of individual differences in cognition. Many cognitive abilities reflect executive processes, such as fluid intelligence, broad retrieval ability, and working memory capacity. In our early work, we developed latent variable models of these cognitive abilities and examined how they predicted measures of creative thought. When people complete unusual uses tasks and are told to generate creative ideas, for example, variables like fluid intelligence (Nusbaum and Silvia, 2011) and retrieval ability (Benedek, Könen, and Neubauer, 2012; Silvia, Beaty, and Nusbaum, 2013) strongly predict the rated creativity of their ideas. The effect sizes range from medium to large, suggesting an important role for these cognitive abilities.

The links between executive abilities and the creativity of people's ideas on divergent thinking tasks have now been firmly established (Benedek, Franz, Heene, and Neubauer, 2012; Benedek, Jauk, Sommer, Arendasy, and Neubauer, 2014; Jauk, Benedek, Dunst, and Neubauer, 2013; Karwowski et al., 2016). But there's much more to creative thought than uses for bricks. Other research has explored how people generate creative metaphors. As we expected, the creativity of people's metaphors, assessed with both open-ended and constrained prompts, is strongly related to fluid intelligence (Beaty and Silvia, 2013; Primi, 2014; Silvia and Beaty, 2012). Humor, too, is strongly predicted by fluid intelligence. Smart people come up with much funnier jokes on an array of humor tasks (Christensen, Silvia, Nusbaum, and Beaty, forthcoming; Greengross and Miller, 2011; Howrigan and MacDonald, 2008).

Beyond the individual-differences approach, experimental studies have manipulated features of creativity tasks to illuminate the inner working of executive processes. For example, looking at why ideas tend to become more creative over the course of a task (Beaty and Silvia, 2012; Hass, 2017), studying how asking people to "be creative" works (Nusbaum, Silvia, and Beaty, 2014), provoking interference to see how people overcome it (Beaty, Christensen, Benedek, Silvia, and Schachter, 2017), and assessing people's natural strategies for tackling creativity tasks (Gilhooly, Fioratou, Anthony, and Wynn, 2007) have focused on the cognitive nuts-and-bolts of executive control, thus complementing the trait approach.

My goal in this line of research was to shift the conversation about creative thought toward executive mechanisms (Silvia, 2015). I don't dismiss, however, associative, implicit, and bottom-up approaches to creativity. To the contrary, the big question in modern research, as I see it, is understanding how executive and associative processes intersect. In our recent work, we have studied how large-scale brain networks associated with controlled (executive control network) and spontaneous (default mode network) forms of thought interact (Beaty, Benedek, Silvia, and Schacter, 2016; Beaty and Jung, forthcoming). When working on creative problems, these ordinarily antagonistic networks appear to cooperate (e.g., Beaty, 2015; Beaty, Benedek, Kaufman, and Silvia, 2015; Beaty, Silvia, and Benedek, 2017), which suggests that creative ideas somehow fuse executive and associative processes. Other approaches, such as think-aloud methods during realistic creative problems, suggest that creative ideas come about from a "meshed mode" of thought that combines both spontaneous and controlled modes of thinking (Pringle and Sowden, 2017). Other studies have examined the interactions between the structure of people's knowledge and their ability to executively retrieve and manage it (e.g., Benedek et al., 2017). I'm curious to see where this line of work goes.

Creativity Is Everywhere

Creativity research is a diverse field: you don't often find scholarly domains where neuroscientists, humanistic scholars, industrial-organizational psychologists, and educators all hang out and share ideas. The four-C model (Kaufman and Beghetto, 2009) – a way of thinking about creativity I find appealing – brings some structure to the gallimaufry of creativity research by structuring our research interests along an ordered continuum. At one end are *Big C* and *Pro C*, the domain-changing instances of creativity that archival and sociocultural scholars tend to emphasize. And at the other end are *little c* and *mini-c*, the humble creative activities, ideas, and insights that fill everyday life.

I like all the Cs, but I'm increasingly drawn to little c and mini-c, which are often called *everyday creativity* (Richards, 2010) or *ordinary creativity* (Bateson, 1999). When you look for it, creativity really is everywhere. But our traditional research methods – self-report scales, semistructured interviews, and cognitive tasks given in sterile research labs – are poorly suited to capture everyday creativity. Everyday creative acts and ideas are situated in people's idiosyncratic real-world environments. We thus need to get close to everyday creativity, to see what it looks like as it unfolds in its natural habitat.

Ecological studies of creativity strike me as a major emerging trend in creativity research (for details, see Cotter, Christensen, and Silvia, 2017). The technologies and statistical methods for ecological momentary assessment methods have matured to the point that it is much easier to assess creativity in people's everyday environments. Recently, studies using experience sampling and diary methods have explored some intriguing questions by sampling people's ordinary days. Some studies have looked at how often people work on creative goals and who is more likely to do so (Karwowski, Lebuda, Szumski, and Firkowska-Mankiewicz, 2017; Silvia et al., 2014). Others have explored the emotional correlates of working on creative goals in daily life (e.g., emotions, moods, and flow; Benedek, Jauk, Kerschenbauer, Anderwald, and Grond, 2017; Conner and Silvia, 2015; Fullagar and Kelloway, 2009) and suggested that spending time on creative hobbies boosts subjective well-being (Conner, DeYoung, and Silvia, 2018). Some studies take a more mini-c approach by exploring mind wandering, daydreaming, and mental imagery in everyday life. For example, people often report hearing music in their mind (Cotter and Silvia, 2017), and in many cases the musical imagery is something people are actively composing, improvising, or rehearsing for an upcoming performance (Beaty et al., 2013).

This is just a snapshot of the sorts of topics, from creative goals to mental imagery, that researchers have tackled using ecological assessment methods (Silvia, Cotter, and Christensen, 2017). So little is known about what creativity and the arts look like in everyday life that this area strikes me as an unusually fertile field for researchers interested in little c and mini-c creativity.

Conclusion: Teaching Yourself What You Know

Creativity is a sort of cognitive alchemy. We know things – experiences, ideas, images, words, concepts – and somehow from what is old and known comes something new. Zinsser's (1988) concept of writing to learn, of using writing to teach ourselves what we know, is about this alchemy. Writing is a way of stirring the cognitive cauldron. In this essay, I put a big paddle into my mental cauldron to see what I think about creativity, and I dare say a few new-to-me ideas came out (although I won't say which ones). From a writing to learn perspective, perhaps I knew these all along and just needed to sit patiently and learn these ideas from myself. Or perhaps I didn't know these new ideas before and created them anew while writing. And I hope that reading this chapter sparked a few new ideas of your own.

REFERENCES

Bateson, M. C. (1999). Ordinary creativity. In *Social creativity*, edited by A. Montuori and R. E. Purser, 1:153–171. Cresskill, NJ: Hampton.

Beaty, R. E. (2015). The neuroscience of musical improvisation. *Neuroscience and Biobehavioral Reviews*, 51, 108–117.

Beaty, R. E., Benedek, M., Kaufman, S. B., and Silvia, P. J. (2015). Default and executive network coupling supports creative idea production. *Scientific Reports*, 5, 10964.

Beaty, R. E., Benedek, M., Silvia, P. J., and Schacter, D. L. (2016). Creative cognition and brain network dynamics. *Trends in Cognitive Sciences*, 20, 87–95.

Beaty, R. E., Burgin, C. J., Nusbaum, E. C., Kwapil, T. R., Hodges, D. A., and Silvia, P. J. (2013). Music to the inner ears: Exploring individual differences in musical imagery. *Consciousness and Cognition*, 22, 1163–1173.

Beaty, R. E., Christensen, A. P., Benedek, M., Silvia, P. J., and Schachter, D. L. (2017). Creative constraints: Brain activity and network dynamics underlying semantic interference during idea production. *NeuroImage*, 148, 189–196.

Beaty, R. E., and Jung, R. E. (forthcoming). Interacting brain networks underlying creative cognition and artistic performance. In *The Oxford handbook of spontaneous thought: Mind-wandering, creativity, dreaming, and clinical disorders*, edited by K. Fox and K. Christoff. New York: Oxford University Press.

Beaty, R. E., and Silvia, P. J. (2012). Why do ideas get more creative across time? An executive interpretation of the serial order effect in divergent thinking tasks. *Psychology of Aesthetics, Creativity, and the Arts*, 6, 309–319.

  (2013). Metaphorically speaking: Cognitive abilities and the production of figurative language. *Memory and Cognition*, 41, 255–267.

Beaty, R. E., Silvia, P. J., and Benedek, M. (2017). Brain networks underlying figurative language production. *Brain and Cognition*, 111, 163–170.

Benedek, M., Franz, F., Heene, M., and Neubauer, A. C. (2012). Differential effects of cognitive inhibition and intelligence on creativity. *Personality and Individual Differences*, 53, 480–485.

Benedek, M., Jauk, E., Kerschenbauer, K., Anderwald, R., and Grond, L. (2017). Creating art: An experience sampling study in the domain of moving image art. *Psychology of Aesthetics, Creativity, and the Arts*, 11, 325–334.

Benedek, M., Jauk, E., Sommer, M., Arendasy, M., and Neubauer, A. C. (2014). Intelligence, creativity, and cognitive control: The common and differential involvement of executive functions in intelligence and creativity. *Intelligence*, 46, 73–83.

Benedek, M., Kenett, Y. N., Umdasch, K., Anaki, D., Faust, M., and Neubauer, A. C. (2017). How semantic memory structure and intelligence contribute to creative thought: A network science approach. *Thinking and Reasoning*, 23, 158–183.

Benedek, M., Könen, T., and Neubauer, A. C. (2012). Associative abilities underlying creativity. *Psychology of Aesthetics, Creativity, and the Arts*, 6, 273–281.

Christensen, A. P., Silvia, P. J., Nusbaum, E. C., and Beaty, R. E. (forthcoming). Clever people: Intelligence and humor production ability. *Psychology of Aesthetics, Creativity, and the Arts*.

Conner, T. S., DeYoung, C. G., and Silvia, P. J. (2018). Everyday creative activity as a path to flourishing. *Journal of Positive Psychology*, 13, 181–189.

Conner, T. S., and Silvia, P. J. (2015). Creative days: A daily diary study of emotion, personality, and everyday creativity. *Psychology of Aesthetics, Creativity, and the Arts*, 9(4), 463–470.

Cotter, K. N., Christensen, A. P., and Silvia, P. J. (2017). Creativity's role in everyday life. Unpublished manuscript.

Cotter, K. N., and Silvia, P. J. (2017). Measuring mental music: Comparing retrospective and experience sampling methods for assessing musical imagery. *Psychology of Aesthetics, Creativity, and the Arts*, 11, 335–343.

Csikszentmihalyi, M. (1988). Society, culture, and person: A systems view of creativity. In *The nature of creativity: Contemporary psychological perspectives*, edited by R. J. Sternberg, 325–339. New York: Cambridge University Press.

Diedrich, J., Benedek, M., Jauk, E., and Neubauer, A. C. (2015). Are creative ideas novel and useful? *Psychology of Aesthetics, Creativity, and the Arts*, 9, 35–40.

Duval, T. S., and Silvia, P. J. (2001). *Self-awareness and causal attribution: A dual systems theory*. Boston: Kluwer Academic.

Foreman, W. (2010). Tech: Apple supplier Foxconn suffers 10th death this year, asks workers to sign anti-suicide pledge. *The Huffington Post*, May 26. www.huffingtonpost.com/2010/05/25/foxconn-suffers-10th-deat_n_588524.html.

Fullagar, C. J., and Kelloway, E. K. (2009). "Flow" at work: An experience sampling approach. *Journal of Occupational and Organizational Psychology*, 82, 595–615.

Gilhooly, K. J., Fioratou, E. E., Anthony, S. H., and Wynn, V. V. (2007). Divergent thinking: Strategies and executive involvement in generating novel uses for familiar objects. *British Journal of Psychology*, 98, 611–625.

Glăveanu, V. P. (2010). Paradigms in the study of creativity: Introducing the perspective of cultural psychology. *New Ideas in Psychology*, 28, 79–93.

Greengross, G., and Miller, G. (2011). Humor ability reveals intelligence, predicts mating success, and is higher in males. *Intelligence*, 39, 188–192.

Guilford, J. P. (1967). *The nature of human intelligence.* New York: McGraw-Hill.

Hass, R. W. (2017). Tracking the dynamics of divergent thinking via semantic distance: Analytic methods and theoretical implications. *Memory and Cognition*, 45, 233–244.

Howrigan, D. P., and MacDonald, K. B. (2008). Humor as a mental fitness indicator. *Evolutionary Psychology*, 6, 652–666.

Jauk, E., Benedek, M., Dunst, B., and Neubauer, A. C. (2013). The relationship between intelligence and creativity: New support for the threshold hypothesis by means of empirical breakpoint detection. *Intelligence*, 41, 212–221.

Karwowski, M., Dul, J., Gralewski, J., Jauk, E., Jankowska, D. M., Gajda, A., Chruszczewski, M. H., and Benedek, M. (2016). Is creativity without intelligence possible? A necessary condition analysis. *Intelligence*, 57, 105–117.

Karwowski, M., Lebuda, I., Szumski, G., and Firkowska-Mankiewicz, A. (2017). From moment-to-moment to day-to-day: Experience sampling and diary investigations in adults' everyday creativity. *Psychology of Aesthetics, Creativity, and the Arts*, 11, 309–324.

Kaufman, J. C., and Beghetto, R. A. (2009). Beyond big and little: The Four C model of creativity. *Review of General Psychology*, 13, 1–12.

McDonough, W., and Braungart, M. (2002). *Cradle to cradle: Remaking the way we make things.* New York: North Point.

Mednick, S. A. (1962). The associative basis of the creative process. *Psychological Review*, 26, 220–232.

Negus, K., and Pickering, M. (2004). *Creativity, communication and cultural value.* London: Sage.

Nusbaum, E. C., and Silvia, P. J. (2011). Are intelligence and creativity really so different? Fluid intelligence, executive processes, and strategy use in divergent thinking. *Intelligence*, 39, 36–45.

Nusbaum, E. C., Silvia, P. J., and Beaty, R. E. (2014). Ready, set, create: What instructing people to "be creative" reveals about the meaning and mechanisms of divergent thinking. *Psychology of Aesthetics, Creativity, and the Arts*, 8, 423–432.

Primi, R. (2014). Divergent productions of metaphors: Combining many-facet Rasch measurement and cognitive psychology in the assessment of creativity. *Psychology of Aesthetics, Creativity, and the Arts*, 8, 461–474.

Pringle, A., and Sowden, P. T. (2017). Unearthing the creative thinking process: Fresh insights from a think-aloud study of garden design. *Psychology of Aesthetics, Creativity, and the Arts*, 11, 344–358.

Richards, R. (2010). Everyday creativity: Process and way of life – four key issues. In *The Cambridge handbook of creativity*, edited by J. C. Kaufman and R. J. Sternberg, 189–215. New York: Cambridge University Press.

Runco, M. A., and Jaeger, G. J. (2012). The standard definition of creativity. *Creativity Research Journal*, 24, 92–96.

Sawyer, R. K. (2006). *Explaining creativity: The science of human innovation*. New York: Oxford University Press.

Silvia, P. J. (2015). Intelligence and creativity are pretty similar after all. *Educational Psychology Review*, 27, 599–606.

Silvia, P. J., and Beaty, R. E. (2012). Making creative metaphors: The importance of fluid intelligence for creative thought. *Intelligence*, 40, 343–351.

Silvia, P. J., Beaty, R. E., and Nusbaum, E. C. (2013). Verbal fluency and creativity: General and specific contributions of broad retrieval ability (Gr) factors to divergent thinking. *Intelligence*, 41, 328–340.

Silvia, P. J., Beaty, R. E., Nusbaum, E. C., Eddington, K. M., Levin-Aspenson, H., and Kwapil, T. R. (2014). Everyday creativity in daily life: An experience-sampling study of "little c" creativity. *Psychology of Aesthetics, Creativity, and the Arts*, 8, 183–188.

Silvia, P. J., Cotter, K. N., and Christensen, A. P. (2017). The creative self in context: Experience sampling and the ecology of everyday creativity. In *The creative self: Effect of beliefs, self-efficacy, mindset, and identity*, edited by M. Karwowski and J. C. Kaufman, 275–288. Oxford: Elsevier.

Sternberg, R. J., and Lubart, T. I. (1996). An investment theory of creativity and its development. *Human Development*, 34, 1–31.

Wallach, M. A., and Kogan, N. (1965). *Modes of thinking in young children: A study of the creativity-intelligence distinction*. New York: Holt, Rinehart, and Winston.

Weisberg, R. W. (2006). *Creativity: Understanding innovation in problem solving, science, invention, and the arts*. Hoboken, NJ: John Wiley.

Zinsser, W. (1984). *Willie and Dwike: An American profile*. New York: Harper and Row.

(1988). *Writing to learn*. New York: Quill.

(1989). *Spring training: The unique American story of baseball's annual season of renewal*. New York: Harper and Row.

(1992). *American places: A writer's pilgrimage to 15 of this country's most visited and cherished sites*. New York: HarperCollins.

(2006). *On writing well*. 30th anniversary ed. New York: Harper Perennial.

CHAPTER 20

Genius, Creativity, and Leadership
A Half-Century Journey through Science, History, Mathematics, and Psychology

Dean Keith Simonton

As contemporary creativity researchers go, I'm definitely sui generis – a one-off or rara avis. You pick your favorite expression. If a multiple-choice test item asked you to identify the investigator who doesn't fit with the rest, the "odd-one-out," I would be it. Doesn't even matter who the other choices are. I'm almost certainly the biggest outlier with respect to the other chapter authors in this volume. This or that investigator will be distinguished by one thing or another, beyond any doubt, but I am likely to be set apart by any research criterion you can imagine. How so?

Let me start by naming some representative research "participants" (the quotes purposely indicating that absolutely *none* participated and almost all could *never* have done so). Yes, I can identify them by name! No confidentiality agreements violated whatsoever. And you probably have even heard of most of them before reading this paragraph. For starters, please ponder these: (1) Aristotle, Hypatia, Shen Kuo, Omar Khayyam, Isaac Newton, Charles Darwin, Marie Curie, Albert Einstein, and Srinivasa Ramanujan; (2) René Descartes, Francis Galton, William James, Ivan Pavlov, Alfred Binet, Anna Freud, and Eleanor Gibson; (3) Kong Fuzi, Socrates, Arete of Cyrene, Ibn Sina, Maimonides, Baruch Spinoza, and Jean-Paul Sartre; (4) Aeschylus, Virgil, Li Bai, Ferdowsi, Murasaki Shikibu, Dante Alighieri, Miguel de Cervantes, William Shakespeare, Phillis Wheatley, Fyodor Dostoevsky, and Rabindranath Tagore; (5) Phidias, Vitruvius, Zhao Mengfu, Michelangelo Buonarroti, Katsushika Hokusai, Vincent van Gogh, and Grandma Moses; (6) Ludwig van Beethoven, Giacomo Puccini, Bernard Herrmann, and Billie Holiday; (7) Archimedes, Cai Lun, James Watt, George Washington Carver, and Lillian Moller Gilbreth; and (8) Alfred Hitchcock, Akira Kurosawa, Oscar Micheaux, Orson Welles, Ingmar Bergman, and Lina Wertmüller. Don't recognize some? Just google their names: Wikipedia biographies guaranteed! Your favorite creator not named? Very likely "participated" nevertheless.

See the pattern in the above abbreviated list? Right! I have studied creators active in virtually every domain and in almost every major world civilization from antiquity to the present day. Yet I've also used your customary college undergraduates as participants (now sans quotes), namely, anonymous and ephemeral volunteers recruited from Occidental, Harvard, UC Davis, and Radboud University Nijmegen. Most remarkably, perhaps, the sizes of my research samples have ranged from $N = 1$ to $N = 15{,}518$. More concretely, the samples have extended from single-case studies of exemplary creators to the entire population of interest.

What about statistics? Although I've done standard laboratory experiments in which I applied analyses of variance to data from prototypical $2 \times 2 \times 2$ factorial designs – even getting three-way interaction effects! – that's a decided rarity in my career. I'm much more prone to utilize correlational statistics, thus doing my fair share of cluster and factor analyses (both exploratory and confirmatory), multiple regression and path analyses, latent variable and structural equation models, and a diversity of nonparametric stats. Yet I've also employed techniques that are very seldom if ever used by most creativity researchers, such as econometric dynamic time-series models, quasi-experimental cross-lagged correlation designs, and an artificial intelligence heuristic-search program for inferring causal relations in complex correlational data. Still, as if to forestall any misconceptions about my being a mere "quant man," I've also published empirical investigations that were purely qualitative, not a single statistic anywhere in sight.

In theory development, my breadth also stands out, and rigor too. I'm among a select few creativity researchers (if any) who has (1) solved differential equations to derive mathematical models and (2) generated and tested stochastic models of key phenomena. Better yet, these diverse theoretical approaches have become ever more tightly integrated over the course of my career – even if I'd be the first to admit that such integration still has a ways to go.

Finally, if the above facts do not suffice to make me stick out like a sore thumb relative to other creativity researchers, I have also conducted a considerable amount of research on leadership, including that displayed by military generals on the battlefield, European kings, queens, and sultans, US presidents, and even the First Ladies of those presidents. Accordingly, my research subjects have included Hannibal, Julius Caesar, Wu Zetian, Saladin, Mehmed the Conqueror, Martin Luther, Queen Elizabeth I, Toyotomi Hideyoshi, Catherine the Great, Alexander Hamilton, Napoleon Bonaparte, Abraham Lincoln, Andrew Carnegie, Emma

Goldman, Jomo Kenyatta, Indira Gandhi, Cesar Chavez, Che Guevara, Jacqueline Kennedy, and Martin Luther King, among *hundreds* of others. Even so, somehow this work on leadership still fits with my inquiries into creativity. Indeed, leaders and creators can rub shoulders in identical samples!

How did all these fluky oddities come about? No doubt much of who I am as a researcher dates back to my childhood. For example, early in elementary school I enjoyed poring over encyclopedia volumes, finding the numerous biographical entries especially fascinating. Yet to keep this autobiographical narrative within bounds, I will concentrate on three key phases in my unique intellectual journey as a creativity researcher: Oxy undergraduate, Harvard graduate student, and UC Davis professor – and then close with my current emeritus status.

Oxy Undergraduate

When I applied for admission to Occidental College more than fifty years ago, I was obliged to endure a face-to-face interview. Asked about my planned major, my immediate response was to say "History!" I saw from the interviewer's reaction that I had given the wrong answer. Given that my major sequence in high school was precisely identified as "Science – College Preparatory," she had reasonably supposed that I would pursue coursework in one of the sciences. So I quickly corrected myself, replacing history with chemistry (but without the exclamation mark). I was not about to risk admission to the college of my first choice.

Fortunately, a chemistry major at this liberal arts institution led to a Bachelor of Arts degree. One manifestation of its mandatory BA curriculum was a two-year team-taught course on the History of Civilization – meaning that I would be taking six-quarters of history anyway. Hence, for the first half of my undergraduate training I would necessarily combine science and mathematics courses with much broader exposure to the history of art, music, literature, philosophy, science, war, and politics from the ancient Sumerians (*The Epic of Gilgamesh*) to contemporary times (*The Autobiography of Malcolm X*). Yes, we studied primary sources. And we even read beyond Western civilization (e.g., *The Tale of Genji*). I always loved the class, even serving as a discussion group leader in my senior year!

A special feature of "Hist. Civ." was the persistent requirement to keep a regular journal recording our personal thoughts about our lectures, readings, and discussions. My natural inclination was to think about the course content in scientific and mathematical terms. For example, in contemplating all of the names, dates, and places, I observed the striking tendency to focus attention on the most eminent figures of history. Hence I speculated on how fame might be measured. Here's an actual journal entry that I jotted down in my very first quarter in October 1966:

> What is fame? Qualitatively it is name. But how can we measure it quantitatively? Basically, fame is directly proportional to the occurrence of name; that is, $F = n (N)$. To determine how famous a man is, all we have to do is count the number of times his name appears in writing and speech, or more pragmatically, in writing only. Then the person may be placed on a fame-scale and compared, quantitatively with others. (Simonton, 1990a, p. 96)

Please excuse any naiveté in this unedited remark as that of a beginning college student who may have been half asleep at the time he scribbled the entry! And, obviously, neither I nor my instructors had any idea that this operational definition of fame (aka achieved eminence) had already been devised many decades earlier. Nor could I imagine at the time that I would eventually develop this crude concept into a far more sophisticated multivariate measurement technique that provided dependent variables for numerous empirical studies published throughout my career (see Simonton, 1991c).

Nonetheless, the cross-talk between my chemistry major and my history class was not going anywhere fruitful – especially when I began applying the laws of thermodynamics! But then a remarkable event took place in my sophomore year: Having only a single slot in my crammed four-year course schedule to sneak in an elective, I selected introductory psychology. The experience was a revelation. I learned for the first time that a discipline existed that embraced the scientific study of phenomena closely related to my fascination with history. In particular, I discovered that some psychologists actually investigated such topics as genius, creativity, and leadership. Weren't the most acclaimed figures of history either geniuses, creators, or leaders – sometimes even all three at once? Like Benjamin Franklin, the very subject I had chosen for the required Oxy application essay on "who I most admire and why." I subsequently took an upper-division social psychology class, and soon found that I had fallen out of the rigid course sequence required to graduate on time. By the end of my junior year, I decided it was most opportune to change to a psychology major. About the same time, I was designated a "College Scholar," which gave me the freedom to create my own curriculum. I was thus enabled to canvass various theoretical and methodological options.

I ultimately conceived creativity and leadership as intimately connected. Both were principal forms of exceptional personal influence over numerous others – and the two main guises of genius besides. That is why I had no problem dedicating my honors thesis to a laboratory experiment on leadership in problem-solving groups. That is also why I chose to apply to a social psychology graduate program despite having a substantial interest in a subject (creativity) that was back then seldom if ever studied by social psychologists (quite unlike today). I was particularly attracted to the social psychology program at Harvard's Department of Social Relations which, at the time I applied, included sociology and cultural anthropology along with the less behavioristic subdisciplines of psychology – a truly interdisciplinary department that I assumed would allow me to freely explore my varied interests.

Harvard Graduate Student

My initial experience as a graduate student left much to be desired. The Social Relations department was in the midst of a nasty breakup. The sociologists and cultural anthropologists were leaving to form two more conventional departments, and concurrent negotiations were going on with the Department of Psychology for an equally traditional union of all psychologists. Worse still, I pretty much started out on the wrong foot with regard to my theoretical and methodological orientation. I brought from Oxy a thesis that was written "in partial fulfillment of the College Scholar Program" that I hoped would provide the basis for my doctoral dissertation. Although this theoretical integration did inspire my required "predissertation project," producing a preliminary laboratory experiment on intuitive versus analytical problem solving (Simonton, 1975b), I realized that it was not the direction that I wanted to pursue further. So I merely resigned myself to revising that thesis for eventual publication as a monograph (Simonton, 1980a).

Quite frankly, I didn't want to study college undergraduates. Instead, I sought to investigate the illustrious figures who highlight the history of world civilization. Trying to extrapolate from a student population to the creativity or leadership displayed by a Nicolaus Copernicus or a Genghis Khan just seemed like a prima facie ridiculous academic exercise. If I seek to understand history-making creators and leaders, why not study them directly rather than indirectly? But how? And as a scientist, not as a historian? That was the perplexing question.

The answer came quite by chance: Browsing in the Social Relations library, I spotted a recent publication entitled "Creativity: A

Cross-Historical Pilot Survey" (Naroll et al., 1971). The researchers were cultural anthropologists rather than psychologists, but that didn't matter one iota given my interdisciplinary orientation. More important was the fact that the authors attempted to investigate the contextual factors influencing the fluctuations in creative geniuses across the history of four civilizations (viz. Europe, the Middle East, India, and China). The dependent variable contained counts of the number of eminent creators listed in Kroeber's (1944) *Configurations of Culture Growth* (which was unknown to me at the time). The investigators found that a civilization's creativity was positively associated with the number of independent states it contains. The numerous city states of Classical Greece and Renaissance Italy constitute well-known examples.

The above investigation was no more than a "pilot survey" by the authors' own admission. Their methods were very makeshift and often inadequate. That said, the study at least made me realize that it was possible to scrutinize creativity of the highest order. After all, the sampled creators more or less defined the civilizations in which they were active. I just needed to immerse myself more thoroughly in the relevant methods. Besides learning cross-cultural techniques, I also mastered the econometric statistics that macroeconomists use to test their theoretical models. I would just substitute generational fluctuations in creative activity for quarterly fluctuations in economic prosperity. Suddenly I had a more promising basis for a doctoral dissertation.

Naturally, a dissertation based on such methods might not be well received by a department that was then converging on mainstream psychology. The only faculty member remaining in the merging departments who had any sympathy for cross-cultural and transhistorical data was David C. McClelland, the eminent personality psychologist who had used such data extensively in his monumental 1961 *The Achieving Society*. But McClelland was unavailable as a thesis supervisor, leaving me in a quandary.

Then luck struck again. In 1972, the same year that the Department of Psychology and Social Relations was officially formed, the new unit hired an assistant professor who had just earned his PhD under the famed social psychologist and methodologist Donald T. Campbell. That new hire was David Kenny, and he obviously needed his very first graduate student. With his encouragement and advice, I put together a "special topic paper" outlining the methods I hoped to use for my doctoral dissertation (Simonton, 1973). This document led directly to my thesis proposal, which eventually became fully actualized in my doctoral dissertation on *The Social Psychology of Creativity: An Archival Data Analysis* (Simonton, 1974). This dissertation was signed off in time for me to earn my PhD in early 1975 (with

McClelland among the signatories). My idiosyncratic research program had been successfully launched, and with the biggest possible splash: Generational time-series analyses predicted the fluctuations in more than 5,000 creative geniuses across more than 2,500 years of Western civilization. Creative florescence was a positive function of role-model availability, political fragmentation, and anti-imperial revolts, but a negative function of assassinations and coups d'etat (Simonton, 1975c).

Yet there remained a catch: I still had to get a job! And who was going to hire somebody with such unconventional research interests? Happily, the faculty at the University of Arkansas was willing to give me the urgently needed opportunity. With their full support, I published extensively, including publications in the top-tier *Journal of Personality and Social Psychology* and *Psychological Bulletin* (e.g., Simonton, 1976a, 1976b). In two years my CV accumulated a dozen new publications, making me sufficiently competitive to obtain a ladder-track position at the University of California, Davis.

University of California, Davis Professor

I wish I could say that life got easier from that point on, but that simply didn't happen. I still had to endure abundant skepticism from fellow psychologists. One episode stands out as especially disconcerting. Having submitted my eighth manuscript to the *Journal of Personality and Social Psychology* (the previous seven having already been accepted for publication but the current one on a totally different topic), the editor sent it out to two referees, both of whom recommended that the submission be accepted as is, without any revision whatsoever! Needless to say, that almost never happens to anybody. Indeed, it has never happened to me before or after that one instance. Even so, the editor could not help but rain on my parade by commenting in his acceptance letter that "it is possible that your well may be running dry; the present paper begins to show signs of strain" (Simonton, 2002, p. 247). No lie: that's a *literal* quote!

What a discouraging message for a young researcher who was just about to go up for tenure! Yet as anyone can verify via Google Scholar, my research program didn't dry up after 1979. Indeed, I did not attain my productive peak *until thirty years later*! For the year 2009 my CV lists twenty-nine publications, twenty-seven of them sole authored, mandating that the latter references undergo serial identification from 2009a to 2009aa! How often have other creativity researchers confronted this bibliographic peculiarity? My own second highest single-author seriation only goes to "u."

In any case, I advanced to tenure just fine, but only after the editor kindly abridged the decision letter so that it could be included in my promotion dossier. I merely needed a confirmation that the paper was actually in press (see Simonton, 1980b), not a prophecy that my creativity was already drying up at age thirty-one.

Associate Professor

In fact, once I became tenured in 1980, my creative well began to fill up and overflow. I was generating research ideas far faster than I could realize them. The reason for this surge was simple: I felt free to take even greater intellectual risks now that job security was no longer at stake. For instance, about this time I decided to expand my research into extraordinary leadership, with a special emphasis on presidential performance that lasted for more than three decades (Simonton, 2012b). I also became more willing to start my first book, one with the main title *Genius, Creativity, and Leadership* (Simonton, 1984a). Just ten years after my doctoral thesis I had accumulated enough research findings to help fill up a volume.

The book's subtitle, *Historiometric Inquiries*, was also noteworthy because it was the first time I so explicitly identified the core methodology of my research program. Although the term "historiometry" was invented more than a century ago (Woods, 1909, 1911), and pointedly used in one of the most impressive historiometric studies ever published (Cox, 1926), the usage had waned in the intervening years, largely to be replaced by the "archival data analysis" seen in my dissertation's subtitle. Yet because the old term features a far more specific meaning, I decided it needed a revival, a decision reinforced when I published the very first monograph exclusively devoted to the technique (Simonton, 1990b). All historiometric research is archival, but not all archival research is historiometric. Only historiometry specifically applies quantitative techniques to samples of historic figures, products, and events in order to test nomothetic hypotheses about superlative creativity or leadership.

By fully explicating my research program, that 1984 book certainly aided my advancement to the next rank in the professorial series.

Full Professor

Earlier I noted how tenure allowed me to take greater risks in my research program. Both the substantive issues and the methods used to address those issues considerably diversified. That diversification became more pronounced when I was promoted to full professor in 1985. Particularly important was my decision to expand my theoretical efforts regarding both creativity and leadership.

The theoretical work on creativity proved to be the most productive (cf. Antonakis, House, and Simonton, 2017; Simonton, 1984b, 1985, 1986). A quarter-century earlier, the doctoral mentor of my doctoral mentor had published his classic paper on "Blind Variation and Selective Retention in Creative Thought as in other Knowledge Processes" (Campbell, 1960). I integrated "BVSR" with sundry combinatorial processes and procedures to generate a series of mathematical models, Monte Carlo simulations, and research syntheses (e.g., Simonton, 1997a, 2003, 2010, 2011). It may not be too immodest to claim that the resulting conceptual system represents the most precise and comprehensive theory of exceptional creativity currently available. Notably, the theory not only successfully predicts the productive careers of thousands of eminent creators (Simonton, 1991a, 1991b, 1992, 2007a), but it even continues that success with respect to individual creative geniuses like Galileo Galilei, Thomas Edison, and Pablo Picasso (Damian and Simonton, 2011; Simonton, 2007b, 2012a, 2015). The theory sees both the forest and the trees – and even the leaves!

To be sure, not every creativity researcher would concur with the foregoing claim. Part of the problem is that I have been developing BVSR combinatorial theory since 1985. It has therefore gone through many transformations, and some early versions contained serious errors. Ironically, the most important mistakes came when I departed too far from Campbell's (1960) original formulation (viz. calling BVSR "Darwinian," equating "blind" with "random," and altering the unit of selection from "thought trials" to creative products). Yet these blunders have been rectified in the most recent versions.

Another problem with wide acceptance of BVSR combinatorial theory concerns a far more pernicious issue: Neither Campbell (1960) nor any other researcher had ever worked out a scientifically valid definition of creativity. Despite the commendable efforts in devising a profusion of rival creativity tests, researchers never really defined the actual subject matter of their measures. Instead, the research literature was riddled with inadequate, even contradictory definitions. Investigators reached no consensus regarding the specific criteria, the number of criteria, how the criteria were scaled and integrated, and even who actually assessed those criteria. As a result, the creativity literature is often a massive mess.

Consequently, in the past half-dozen years I have spent considerable effort working out a logically cogent definition of creativity (Simonton,

2016b, 2016c). Because the definition is more mathematical than the norm, I'll just describe it here in a more simplified and qualitative manner. First, an idea's creativity requires the joint convergence of three quantitative criteria (all assessed on a 0–1 scale): originality (low probability), utility (or usefulness, appropriateness, value, meaningfulness, etc.), and surprise (the proportional increment added to any prior knowledge about the utility). Second, because the integration of the three criteria is multiplicative rather than additive, each of these requirements is necessary but not sufficient; something that's unoriginal, useless, or obvious cannot be creative no matter what (to wit, zero times any number is zero). Third, each of the three criteria must be assessed at two main levels, the personal (or psychological) and the consensual (or social). The former merely incorporates the creator's final judgment at the time of completing a creative product, whereas the latter can assume multiple forms. For example, the consensual creativity of a film's plot can be evaluated by critics, consumers, or industry professionals, none of whom may agree in their evaluations (Simonton, 2009). Consensual creativity can also change over time – including the posthumous evaluation of the work of a "neglected genius." Emily Dickinson's poems come immediately to mind.

This definition of creativity has many critical implications, yet among the most telling is that BVSR combinatorial processes and procedures are unequivocally required for anyone to conceive a personally creative idea. In brief, BVSR follows inexorably from the only definition of creativity that can claim any logical coherence and completeness (Simonton, 2013). That necessity ensues directly from the axiom that the "blind" in BVSR essentially concerns the degree of prior ignorance regarding the final utility value. Conversely, any process or procedure that is perfectly "sighted," such as domain-specific algorithms, cannot possibly produce anything creative. It is no accident that the US Patent Office imposes an isomorphic three-part definition to evaluate patent applications at the consensual level: novel, useful, and nonobvious.

Thirty years after my dissertation was signed off, I received my last promotion – to distinguished professor of psychology.

Distinguished Professor Emeritus

After four decades of fulltime academic engagement, I finally decided to retire from my UC Davis professorship. Such retirement often encourages some retrospection about the cumulative accomplishments of any professorial career. That retrospective survey will necessarily examine research as well as teaching and service. And with respect to my own research, I would like to close with the following reflections.

In the process of diversifying my research, I have somehow managed to span a tremendous diversity of empirical and theoretical factors, variables, concepts, or phenomena – maybe a greater diversity than any other creativity researcher. To illustrate, here's an incomplete list of instances very roughly organized into eight categories.

1. Dependent variables: achieved eminence; cultural creativity; compositional productivity; scientific journal citations; quantity versus quality; recording and performance frequencies; movie awards, critical acclaim, and box office; philosophical beliefs; leader evaluation; military victory and battle casualties; presidential greatness and chief executive veto behavior.

2. Individual differences: intelligence (both psychometric and historiometric); versatility; expertise; personality (including the "Big Five"); psychopathology; physical health; power, achievement, and affiliation motivations; belief structure (breadth, consistency, and extremism); theoretical and methodological orientation; research program depth; creative potential; aesthetic preference; dogmatism; morality; leadership style, including charisma.

3. Cognitive processes: intuition and analysis; divergent and convergent thought; remote association; foresight and hindsight; dispositional versus situational attributions; ideation and elaboration; trial-and-error or generate-and-test problem solving; simultaneous versus sequential selection; combinatorial mechanisms; BVSR free will.

4. Product attributes: aesthetic significance, listener accessibility, melodic and metric originality; linguistic complexity (i.e., type–token ratio, adjective–verb quotient, and hapax legomena); thematic content, issue richness; quotability; incongruous juxtapositions; primary and secondary process imagery; sexual and violent content; literary, cinematic, musical, or operatic genre; the grade and simultaneity of multiple discoveries and inventions.

5. Developmental factors: emergenic inheritance; epigenetic growth; talent or giftedness; birth order, sibling gender configuration, family size; socioeconomic background; parental loss and other diversifying experiences; biographical typicality; creative precocity; formal education and deliberate practice; omnivorous reading; adulthood external stressors; social reinforcements; cumulative advantage; career

landmarks; chronological versus career age; creative longevity; life-span; swan songs; mode of death.

6. Professional networks: paragons, role models, and mentors; predecessors and successors; collaborators and associates; competitors or rivals; correspondents; friends, parents, siblings, children; pupils or disciples; imitators or admirers.

7. Demographic variables: gender; cohort; marital status; nationality; ethnicity; occupation; geographic, cultural, and professional marginality.

8. Political circumstances: revolutions and revolts; civil disturbances; imperialistic and defensive wars; assassination or anarchy; political fragmentation; persecution or oppression; vice-presidential succession; administration scandals; electoral mandates.

9. Social context: political ideologies; philosophical Zeitgeist; Comtean hierarchy; psychological ortgeist; religious milieu; cultural configurations; multiculturalism and ideological diversity; aesthetic styles or fashions; exponential growth; dialectical change; cultural diffusion; home field advantage.

Even more amazingly, the units of analysis used to study these diverse phenomena have spanned: (1) intraindividual melodies, sonnets, short stories, artistic sketches, patents, discoveries, symphonies, operas, films, and battles; (2) individuals like inventors, scientists, psychologists, novelists, poets, painters, composers, calligraphers, sword makers, polymaths, mystics, entrepreneurs, revolutionaries, assassins, monarchs, college undergraduates, and mid-level leaders in multinational private-sector companies; and (3) larger extraindividual aggregates such as years, congresses, reigns, and generations as well as disciplines, cultures, nations, and civilizations. Once more, I surely must seem a bona fide odd ball among creativity researchers. How many other investigators feel comfortable probing the aesthetic impact of sonnet couplets in one moment and then, in the next, scrutinizing scientific Golden Ages in whole sociocultural systems?

Despite the fact that this chapter's narrative has emphasized the progressive diversification of my research program, I must also stress the conspicuous continuities in my inquiries. For example, the highly distinctive generational time-series analyses that I introduced for Western civilization in my doctoral dissertation were later applied to Chinese, Japanese, and Islamic civilizations. These successive replications and extensions thus spread over more than four decades (e.g., Simonton, 1976c, 1988, 1997b, 2017). One-shot inquiries are extremely rare in my publication list. In truth, I've carried out several career-long lines of inquiry. If carefully disconnected, each separate inquiry might normally support a single creative career.

Among those multiple lines of continuing inquiry hides a more poignant example: From the very onset of my career I have been conducting investigations into the relation between age and creativity. The very first manuscript I had accepted for publication was on that particular topic (viz. Simonton, 1975a), and I have continued to publish on the subject ever since (e.g., Simonton, 2016a). Thus, nobody knows better than I do that I may be well past my creative prime. It's possible that the *Handbook of Genius* that I edited in 2014 embodies the culmination of my academic career. Even though I still have some big projects on my to-do (or bucket) list, who can guarantee that I will produce something that will surpass anything I have already accomplished? Certainly not me.

All I can confidently affirm is that I have made utterly unique contributions to scientific knowledge about those creators (and leaders) who have left the biggest imprint on world history. Anyone who wants the answers to the questions that I started asking some fifty years ago should really begin with my published theories, methods, and findings. If those contributions become the basis for their own advances to our understanding of these phenomena, then so much the better! I will not even mind having my work become outdated provided that future creativity researchers are standing on my shoulders rather than starting all over again from sea level. There must remain so very much to see well beyond the horizon.

REFERENCES

Antonakis, J., House, R. J., and Simonton, D. K. (2017). Can super smart leaders suffer too much from a good thing? The curvilinear effect of intelligence on perceived leadership behavior. *Journal of Applied Psychology*, March 30. doi:10.1037/apl0000221.

Campbell, D. T. (1960). Blind variation and selective retention in creative thought as in other knowledge processes. *Psychological Review*, 67, 380–400.

Cox, C. (1926). *The early mental traits of three hundred geniuses.* Stanford, CA: Stanford University Press.

Damian, R. I., and Simonton, D. K. (2011). From past to future art: The creative impact of Picasso's 1935 *Minotauromachy* on his 1937 *Guernica. Psychology of Aesthetics, Creativity, and the Arts*, 5, 360–369.

Kroeber, A. L. (1944). *Configurations of culture growth.* Berkeley: University of California Press.

McClelland, D. C. (1961). *The achieving society.* New York: Van Nostrand.

Naroll, R., Benjamin, E. C., Fohl, F. K., Fried, M. J., Hildreth, R. E., and Schaefer, J. M. (1971). Creativity: A cross-historical pilot survey. *Journal of Cross-Cultural Psychology*, 2, 181–188.

Simonton, D. K. (1973). Time-series and longitudinal analyses of archival data: A suggestion for the social psychology of innovation. Unpublished special topic paper, Harvard University.

——— (1974). The social psychology of creativity: An archival data analysis. Unpublished doctoral dissertation, Harvard University.

——— (1975a). Age and literary creativity: A cross-cultural and transhistorical survey. *Journal of Cross-Cultural Psychology*, 6, 259–277.

——— (1975b). Creativity, task complexity, and intuitive versus analytical problem solving. *Psychological Reports*, 37, 351–354.

——— (1975c). Sociocultural context of individual creativity: A transhistorical time-series analysis. *Journal of Personality and Social Psychology*, 32, 1119–1133.

——— (1976a). Biographical determinants of achieved eminence: A multivariate approach to the Cox data. *Journal of Personality and Social Psychology*, 33, 218–226.

——— (1976b). Philosophical eminence, beliefs, and Zeitgeist: An individual-generational analysis. *Journal of Personality and Social Psychology*, 34, 630–640.

——— (1976c). The sociopolitical context of philosophical beliefs: A transhistorical causal analysis. *Social Forces*, 54, 513–523.

——— (1980a). Intuition and analysis: A predictive and explanatory model. *Genetic Psychology Monographs*, 102, 3–60.

——— (1980b). Thematic fame, melodic originality, and musical Zeitgeist: A biographical and transhistorical content analysis. *Journal of Personality and Social Psychology*, 38, 972–983.

——— (1984a). *Genius, creativity, and leadership: Historiometric inquiries*. Cambridge, MA: Harvard University Press.

——— (1984b). Leaders as eponyms: Individual and situational determinants of monarchal eminence. *Journal of Personality*, 52, 1–21.

——— (1985). Intelligence and personal influence in groups: Four nonlinear models. *Psychological Review*, 92, 532–547.

——— (1986). Dispositional attributions of (presidential) leadership: An experimental simulation of historiometric results. *Journal of Experimental Social Psychology*, 22, 389–418.

——— (1988). Galtonian genius, Kroeberian configurations, and emulation: A generational time-series analysis of Chinese civilization. *Journal of Personality and Social Psychology*, 55, 230–238.

——— (1990a). History, chemistry, psychology, and genius: An intellectual autobiography of historiometry. In *Theories of creativity*, edited by M. Runco and R. Albert, 92–115. Newbury Park, CA: Sage.

——— (1990b). *Psychology, science, and history: An introduction to historiometry*. New Haven, CT: Yale University Press.

(1991a). Career landmarks in science: Individual differences and interdisciplinary contrasts. *Developmental Psychology*, 27, 119–130.

(1991b). Emergence and realization of genius: The lives and works of 120 classical composers. *Journal of Personality and Social Psychology*, 61, 829–840.

(1991c). Latent-variable models of posthumous reputation: A quest for Galton's G. *Journal of Personality and Social Psychology*, 60, 607–619.

(1992). Leaders of American psychology, 1879–1967: Career development, creative output, and professional achievement. *Journal of Personality and Social Psychology*, 62, 5–17.

(1997a). Creative productivity: A predictive and explanatory model of career trajectories and landmarks. *Psychological Review*, 104, 66–89.

(1997b). Foreign influence and national achievement: The impact of open milieus on Japanese civilization. *Journal of Personality and Social Psychology*, 72, 86–94.

(2002). It's absolutely impossible? A longitudinal study of one psychologist's response to conventional naysayers. In *Psychologists defying the crowd: Stories of those who battled the establishment and won*, edited by R. J. Sternberg, 238–254. Washington, DC: American Psychological Association.

(2003). Scientific creativity as constrained stochastic behavior: The integration of product, process, and person perspectives. *Psychological Bulletin*, 129, 475–494.

(2007a). Cinema composers: Career trajectories for creative productivity in film music. *Psychology of Aesthetics, Creativity, and the Arts*, 1, 160–169.

(2007b). The creative process in Picasso's *Guernica* sketches: Monotonic improvements or nonmonotonic variants? *Creativity Research Journal*, 19, 329–344.

(2009). Cinematic success, aesthetics, and economics: An exploratory recursive model. *Psychology of Creativity, Aesthetics, and the Arts*, 3, 128–138.

(2010). Creativity as blind-variation and selective-retention: Combinatorial models of exceptional creativity. *Physics of Life Reviews*, 7, 156–179.

(2011). Creativity and discovery as blind variation: Campbell's (1960) BVSR model after the half-century mark. *Review of General Psychology*, 15, 158–174.

(2012a). Foresight, insight, oversight, and hindsight in scientific discovery: How sighted were Galileo's telescopic sightings? *Psychology of Aesthetics, Creativity, and the Arts*, 6, 243–254.

(2012b). Presidential leadership: Performance criteria and their predictors. In *The Oxford handbook of leadership*, edited by M. G. Rumsey, 327–342. New York: Oxford University Press.

(2013). Creative thought as blind variation and selective retention: Why sightedness is inversely related to creativity. *Journal of Theoretical and Philosophical Psychology*, 33, 253–266.

(Ed.). (2014). *The Wiley handbook of genius*. Oxford: John Wiley.

(2015). Thomas Alva Edison's creative career: The multilayered trajectory of trials, errors, failures, and triumphs. *Psychology of Aesthetics, Creativity, and the Arts*, 9, 2–14.

(2016a). Are pure mathematicians the lyric poets of the sciences? In *I, mathematician II: Further introspections on the mathematical life*, edited by P. Casazza, S. G. Krantz, and R. D. Ruden, 165–174. Bedford, MA: Consortium for Mathematics and Its Applications.

(2016b). Creativity, automaticity, irrationality, fortuity, fantasy, and other contingencies: An eightfold response typology. *Review of General Psychology*, 20, 194–204.

(2016c). Defining creativity: Don't we also need to define what is not creative? *Journal of Creative Behavior*. Early view. doi:10.1002/jocb.137.

(2017). Intellectual genius in the Islamic Golden Age: Cross-civilization replications, extensions, and modifications. *Psychology of Aesthetics, Creativity, and the Arts*. Advance online publication. April 6. doi:10.1037/aca0000110.

Woods, F. A. (1909). A new name for a new science. *Science*, 30, 703–704.

(1911). Historiometry as an exact science. *Science*, 33, 568–574.

CHAPTER 21

The Triangle of Creativity

Robert J. Sternberg

I study what I stink at (Sternberg, 2014b). I first became interested in creativity at the end of my first year of graduate school at Stanford, which was back in 1973. I had had a successful first-year project on free recall, but the project was so successful, there seemed to be nowhere to go with it (Sternberg and Bower, 1974). I was never to repeat that kind of success in my career! I was not sure of what I wanted to do next. My undergraduate advisor, Endel Tulving, was visiting at the Center for Advanced Study in the Behavioral Sciences in Stanford, California, and invited me to visit him there. I did. His colleagues there asked me what I planned to do next. I said I did not know. I could see the pity in their faces – here was a guy who had one good idea his first year of graduate school and then proceeded to flame out right away. I wondered why I was so desperate for a creative idea. And I hoped, sometime during my career, to find out. Fortunately, all was not lost: I did get an idea later that summer, which led to my dissertation and much of my career (Sternberg, 1977). I did learn one thing that summer, for sure: Creativity is in large part a decision and an attitude toward life (Sternberg, 2002a). If I wanted to have a creative idea, I had to be open to it and willing to fight for it. And fight for it I did – creative ideas don't generally meet with a reaction of quick acceptance and gratitude!

As with intelligence (Sternberg, 1985b, 1986), there are various metaphors for understanding creativity. The metaphor here is one of defiance against authorities – the crowd, oneself, and the Zeitgeist, as explained below.

The Triangular Theory of Creativity

Creativity is, in large part, an attitude toward life. The attitude is one of defiance of – active assertion against – conventional views in favor of a new view. This chapter presents a new theory of creativity, the triangular

Table 21.1 *Three types of defiance in the triangular theory of creativity*

Type of defiance	Definition
Defying the crowd	Defying the beliefs, values, practices of one's field
Defying oneself	Defying (and moving beyond) one's own earlier values, practices, beliefs
Defying the Zeitgeist	Defying the often unconsciously accepted presuppositions and paradigms in a field

theory (Sternberg, forthcoming). The proposed triangular theory of creativity is an expansion of an investment theory of creativity (Sternberg and Lubart, 1991, 1992, 1994, 1995, 1996), according to which creativity can be understood in terms of defiance of "the crowd," or of conventional and widely shared beliefs. Structurally, although not at all with respect to content, the theory is isomorphic to my triangular theories of love (Sternberg, 1987, 1998, 2007) and hate (Sternberg, 2003a). Those triangular theories also create a typology based upon all possible combinations of the vertices of the triangles. (For a review of other theories of creativity, see Kozbelt, Beghetto, and Runco, 2010.)

The triangular theory expands upon the investment theory of creativity as well as on the three-facet model of creativity (Sternberg, 1988c; see, for related work, Amabile, 1996; Reiter-Palmon, 2014), according to which creativity can be understood in terms of intelligence, cognitive style (Sternberg, 1984, 1985b, 1988b; Zhang and Sternberg, 1998), and personality/motivation (see also Dai and Sternberg, 2004; Hennessey, 2010). The triangular theory (Sternberg, forthcoming) holds that creativity can be understood not just in terms of defying the crowd – that is, other people with more conventional conscious beliefs – but also, in terms of defying oneself and one's own beliefs as well as defying the usually unrecognized and presupposed the Zeitgeist – the unconscious field-based presuppositions upon which one's own and others' beliefs are embedded (see Csikszentmihalyi, 2013, 2014, who has ideas akin to these). The theory applies to all kinds of insightful thinking (Sternberg and Davidson, 1982, 1983). Csikszentmihalyi distinguished between the domain – the actual body of research in an area – and the field – the social organization of the domain – and that distinction is useful here.

Table 21.1 defines the three types of defiance that contribute to the theory.

Kinds of Defiance in Creativity

There are three kinds of defiance in the triangular theory – of the crowd, of the self, and of the Zeitgeist. Crowds and the Zeitgeist can be of different scopes. The crowd may be one's professional colleagues (e.g., if one is a scientist, lawyer, or medical doctor) or one's constituents (if one is a politician or civil-service worker). Or it may be both groups. Similarly, a Zeitgeist can exist in a professional field or in a society at large. Who or what one is defying depends on the kind of work one does and the audience to which one addresses one's work.

Defying the crowd. Creative people tend to defy the crowd – from the high levels of creativity shown by the great minds in history, such as Galileo Galilei, Albert Einstein, Franz Kafka, Louis Pasteur, Marie Curie, Toni Morrison, and Pablo Picasso – to the more mundane levels of creativity many of us show in our everyday life. It is hard to defy the crowd because others do not like their ideas being challenged, and often act in ways to suppress such challenges, as some scholars, such as Galileo and Copernicus, found out the hard way. Even today, however, things have not changed. Ideas that challenge the existing order often are very hard to get accepted (Hunter, Bedell, and Mumford, 2007; Kaufman and Gregoire, 2015; Mumford, 2002; Mumford, Medeiros, and Parlow, 2012; see essays in Sternberg, 2003b; Sternberg, Fiske, and Foss, 2016).

Defying the crowd is difficult because creative people, perhaps even more than some uncreative ones, want to be appreciated for their work. Part of what motivates them is the renown that may result from their creative ideas. But people, including creative ones, often become uncomfortable, irritated, or downright angry when their ideas are challenged. In the long term, creative people know that ideas that defy the crowd are the ones that change a field. But they also know that, in the short term, it is easier to get articles accepted, grant proposals funded, exhibition halls to show one's work, and concert-goers to listen to one's concerts if one, metaphorically or literally, plays to the crowd (see Sternberg, 2003b). As a result, often what pays off most in the long term with regard to creative performance – defying the crowd – pays off least in the short term.

Difficult as defying the crowd is, it actually may be easier than the other two kinds of defiance that can be crucial to creativity.

Defying oneself. An even greater challenge, at times, is defying oneself and one's own set of beliefs. It is a greater challenge, in part, because one does not easily recognize it as a challenge. Defying oneself is challenging because virtually everyone tends to become entrenched and tends to accept her own entrenchment, usually viewing others rather than themselves as problematical for creativity. In other words, one can be one's own worst enemy in generating creative ideas.

Simonton (2004, 2010) has suggested that, even among highly eminent individuals, the best way to maintain one's creativity is to start working in a new area. But most scholars do not do so and, moreover, even finding a new area can be a daunting creative challenge. In other words, scholars become less creative in part because they are unable to combat their own entrenchment – being used to, and comfortable, seeing things in a certain way.

Sometimes, creative individuals seek to work in an entirely new domain. The advantage is that they essentially reset their creativity: They start over. But when creative individuals try to be creative in an entirely new way, for example, in a new domain, they have to be careful, no matter how famous they are, to acquire a strong knowledge base in that field. People who defy themselves in moving into a new field can make seminal contributions, as in the case of Nobel Prize winners Herbert Simon or Daniel Kahneman, or can make serious mistakes, as in the case of two other Nobel Prize winners, William Shockley in his unscientific views on race and eugenics (see Shurkin, 2006) or Linus Pauling in his views of Vitamin C as something of a miracle drug for heart disease (Fonorow, 2008).

Research has shown the susceptibility of experts to entrenchment effects (e.g., Adelson, 1984; Frensch and Sternberg, 1989). Peter Frensch and I (Frensch and Sternberg, 1989) showed that when expert and novice bridge players played against a computer, novices were more susceptible to declines in performance from changes in the game if the changes were surface-structural; in contrast, experts were more susceptible if the changes were deep-structural – that is, fundamental changes in the nature of the game. One interpretation is that the experts had encoded thousands of patterns of play, based on their past experience (Chase and Simon, 1973); the novices had encoded few or none. It thus was far more costly for the experts than for the novices to endure a major change in the rules of the game. Simonton's (1999) model suggests that as one advances in one's career, it becomes harder to depart from past patterns. We tend to view others as the greatest obstacles to our creativity. But often, we are our own greatest obstacle. We may have the disposition to create – the attitude that we are willing to blaze our own path (Grant, 2016; Schank and Childers, 1988; Sternberg and Lubart, 1995), but we keep blazing the same path again and again.

In sum, when it comes to creativity, we often are our own worst enemy (Dweck, 2007). To be creative not just once, but repeatedly throughout a career, one needs to defy not just the crowd, but also oneself and one's own earlier ideas.

Defying the Zeitgeist. Gardner (2011) pointed out that creative contributions that truly defy convention are most likely to happen relatively early in a career, with what constitutes "early" differing somewhat from one field to another. Later contributions tend to be more of a synthetic nature. Why might that be?

The greatest threat to creativity, for most of us, is not the set of beliefs we or others (the crowd) are aware of having but rather the set of presuppositions we often do not even consciously know we have. They are the common-cultural presuppositions on which our field and often our world is built – the so-called Zeitgeist. Even those with a creative, defiant attitude cannot easily defy beliefs they do not consciously know they, or others have. The same assumptions that people hold about groups apply to scientific ideas (see Sawyer, 2008), as Thomas Kuhn (1970) pointed out in his work on the structure of scientific revolutions. For the most part, we buy into paradigms embedded in the Zeitgeist without even consciously realizing that these paradigms are the result of untested and often untestable assumptions.

As Kuhn (1970) recognized, revolutionary, Zeitgeist-defying creativity inconsistent with current paradigms in research is fundamentally different from normal creativity within a paradigm because it challenges the often unconscious assumptions we hold about what science (or art or literature or whatever) is and can be. Zeitgeist-defying creativity pits one up against a whole cultural way of thinking, whether it is a geographic culture, a scientific culture, an artistic culture, or whatever (see Glăveanu, 2015; Lubart, 1999, 2010; Niu and Sternberg, 2002, 2003; Sternberg, 2004). In Zeitgeist-defying creativity, the scientist or artist or writer questions the very presuppositions about what is acceptable for the discipline.

According to a propulsion model of creative contributions, there are several different forms of Zeitgeist-defying contributions (Sternberg, 1999a, 1999b; Sternberg, Kaufman, and Pretz, 2001, 2002). Redirection occurs when a field is moving in one direction and a researcher then moves it in a totally different direction. For example, parallel models of cognition, especially as realized in computer programs, constituted a redirection from serial models – they were based on a totally different set of assumptions (Rumelhart and McClelland, 1994). A reinitiation is a do-over: It occurs when someone starts a field anew, as Noam Chomsky (1957) did with his book, *Syntactic Structures*. A synthesis integrates Zeitgeists from different fields – it represents the integration of ideas from two entirely different disciplines. It is what made Herbert Simon so famous with his merging of economic, business, and psychological thinking (see also Gilson and Madjar, 2011).

One might argue that defying the crowd and defying the Zeitgeist are two regions on a continuum – that they differ quantitatively rather than qualitatively. But this seems not to be the case. Darwin's theory of evolution was qualitatively different from the various theories that existed before of how God created different creatures on different days of the week. Einstein's theory of relativity was qualitatively different from Newtonian theory, in that it recognized that Newtonian theory was merely a special case of a much more general set of phenomena that Newton could not even have envisioned. The Cubism of Picasso was qualitatively different from art that came before it, and atonal music such as that of Schoenberg is qualitatively different from the tonal music that preceded it. In contrast, most painters and musicians work within already established traditions rather than creating new ones.

Relations among the Three Types of Defiance

The three types of defiance are not entirely independent, as is also the case for the three elements of the triarchic theory of successful intelligence (Sternberg, 1981, 1988a, 1988d; Sternberg and Grigorenko, 2004), of the triangular theory of love (1987), and indeed of all major theories of intelligence (see Kim, Cramond, and VanTassel-Baska, 2010) except for Gardner's (1983). In the case of the elements of the triangular theory of creativity, both the self and others are embedded in a society that has various aspects to its Zeitgeist. One often does not realize how the Zeitgeist – and how other people – affect the way one thinks. And even when one defies the Zeitgeist and others, one inevitably relies on their past work, even if it is to tear it down.

All that said, the correlation between the three types of defiance will depend on one's environment. For example, one can defy the crowd but work within the existing Zeitgeist by proposing a new theory – such as a new information-processing theory – within existing ways of seeing things. Similarly, one can defy oneself by admitting that earlier work one did was incomplete or wrong without defying the crowd or the Zeitgeist. And one can defy the existing Zeitgeist but actually getting praise from one's

Table 21.2 *Types of creativity*

Kind of defiance	Type of creativity		
	Crowd	Individual	Zeitgeist
Lack of creativity	–	–	–
Sparse creativity	x	–	–
Minor creativity	–	x	–
Isolated creativity	–	–	x
Major creativity	x	x	–
Sparse major creativity	x	–	x
Quiet creativity	–	x	x
Consummate creativity	x	x	x

colleagues rather than opposition, as in the case of the Google X lab (a Skunk Works laboratory) and of Xerox PARC before it.

Combinations of Creative-Defiant Thinking

The three kinds of creativity all involve similar cognitive processes (see Finke, Ward, and Smith, 1996; Sternberg and Lubart, 1995; Ward and Kolomyts, 2010), although processes used with different ends. That is, they will be correlated. People who are defiant of one of the categories (crowd, individual, paradigm) may well tend, on average, to be defiant of others. At the same time, the theory suggests that there nevertheless will be wide individual differences in the extent to which their defiance crosses the categories. The extent of correlation across categories is an empirical question for the future, however.

Whereas the investment theory of creativity recognized one kind of creativity (defiance of the crowd), the triangular theory recognizes multiple kinds of creativity (cf. Sternberg, 2005a), in particular, three kinds of creativity, yielding seven different manifestations of creativity (plus lack of creativity, with null values on all three kinds of creativity). These kinds of creativity are based on all possible combinations of defiance of the crowd, the individual (oneself), and the Zeitgeist. The different kinds of creative-defiant thinking combine to yield different manifestations of creative thought. (Note that I refer to the three vertices of the triangle as "kinds" of creativity, and the seven combinations to which they give rise as "manifestations" of creativity.) Consider now the various manifestations, as shown in Table 21.2.

The typical individual, for better or worse, but probably for worse, never develops much or any of a creative attitude. Rather, he learns to conform to the expectations of society. In terms of my theory of successful intelligence (Sternberg, 2005b), such a person emphasizes analytical or possibly practical skills (Sternberg, 1997a; Sternberg and Hedlund, 2002; Sternberg and Smith, 1985) at the expense of creative ones. Analytical skills are important for success on jobs and in life. But they are not the skills that lead people to change the world. That said, not everyone has to be a world-changer.

Sparse Creativity (Defiance of the Crowd Only)

Sparse creativity can be seen in a person who is willing to defy the crowd but not himself and not the Zeitgeist. She is likely to generate one or a small number of creative ideas that defy the crowd, but after that, production diminishes rapidly. The sparsely creative person, because she is unwilling to defy herself – to go beyond her previous ideas – ends up producing variants of earlier work and then, when those variants flame out, so does her creativity. It is largely because of sparse creative scholars that colleges and universities wait six or seven years to award tenure (Sternberg, 2016). The institutions fear that the first major idea may be the last one.

Minor Creativity (Defiance of Oneself Only)

Minor creativity is by far the kind we most frequently encounter. It is close to what Kaufman (2016; Kaufman and Beghetto, 2009) refers to as "mini-c" creativity, the kind involved in learning. It also covers what Kaufman and Beghetto refer to as "little c" creativity, or the kind of creativity involved in small creative accomplishments. In the triangular view, these two kinds of creativity may differ from each other quantitatively, but they do not differ qualitatively. Minor creativity is what an individual displays in his daily life as he goes beyond what he has done before. He sees how to accomplish a task, such as fixing a leaking sink, in a new way. Or he sees a new way to save money on his purchases. Or he thinks of a new way to make his children happy. The individual keeps going beyond where he has been before, but does not do so at a level that defies the crowd or the Zeitgeist.

Isolated Creativity (Defiance of the Zeitgeist Only)

There are instances of individuals who defy the Zeitgeist but not the crowd or herself as an individual. This would be an individual who creates a shift in Zeitgeist without any opposition from the crowd (or from herself). That is, she has a world-changing idea and everyone immediately congratulates her and showers recognition and gratitude on her. All are grateful to have been shown how foolish they have been in what they did before and are immediately prepared to change their ways. Such an instantiation is relatively rare. There are certainly products that gain quick acceptance (e.g., hit movies such as the Star Wars or the Indiana Jones franchise), but usually the people behind these products (including George Lucas) had many challenges before they achieved success (Grant, 2010, 2016).

It might seem as though one could not defy the Zeitgeist without defying the crowd. But a defier of the Zeitgeist basically does not disagree with the answers of the crowd but rather with the questions the crowd asks. When someone defies the Zeitgeist, he basically labels the questions that the crowd is asking as irrelevant and suggests instead a different set of questions to ask. He may even agree with the crowd's answers to *their* questions. He just does not think those are the right questions to ask.

Defiers of the Zeitgeist may be isolated but not frustrated. In rare cases, they work in environments that actually encourage defiance of the Zeitgeist, such as the former XeroxParc, Google X (both mentioned earlier), or the various Skunk Works that companies set up to isolate creative thinkers from the pressures toward conformity that exist in most organizations. Such environments are relatively rare but certainly not unheard of.

Major Creativity (Defiance of the Crowd and of Oneself Only)

Major creativity is the kind one sees among skilled practitioners in a variety of professions. It comes closest to what Kaufman and Beghetto (2009) refer to as Pro c. Major creativity comprises willingness to defy the crowd and to defy oneself. It is not paradigm-changing, but rather tends to be a small to moderate step forward for a field, what Sternberg (1999b) refers to in the propulsion model as a forward propulsion. Major creativity is what enables fields to progress – to move forward within a paradigm. For example, Baddeley and Hitch (1974) published a seminal paper on working memory; thousands of forward incrementations then followed. The same happened for Festinger and Carlsmith's (1959) classic research on cognitive dissonance. Thousands of studies ensued. Major creativity in extending a paradigm is the bread and butter of creative endeavor – it is what keeps a field moving forward.

It might seem, at least at first, that forward propulsion, because it builds on rather than rejecting current ideas, is not in any sense defiant. On the contrary, it is defiant, although in a minimal way. In particular, the scientist who engages in forward propulsion rejects, within a given paradigm, the current state of knowledge and argues that it is possible to move on from that state of knowledge. It is defiance, although of a mild kind.

Major Sparse Creativity (Defiance of the Crowd and of the Zeitgeist Only)

Major sparse creativity occurs when an individual has one truly great idea that defies both the crowd and the Zeitgeist of the day.

J. D. Salinger flamed out early, from a certain point of view, but one of the works he produced when he was young, *Catcher in the Rye*, was read, at least for many years, by high school students throughout much of the United States. It was a radically new kind of novel, at least in some respects, and was banned in many schools. Reverend Thomas Bayes has become known for his revolutionary Bayes's theorem, which has transformed the way in which many statisticians (and psychologists!) view significance testing; the theorem was his only major contribution to statistics.

Quiet Creativity (Defiance of Oneself and the Zeitgeist Only)

Quiet creativity occurs when an individual makes major contributions to a field but basically works for himself or for an organization that keeps its creative work under wraps. The individual either has little or no interest in publicizing his work or he is unable to. Sometimes, the work is discovered only by happenstance. Or it may never be discovered at all, in which case whether it is actually "creative" becomes roughly comparable to the question of whether a tree that no one hears fall in a forest actually makes a noise.

People who work for defense agencies – the Central Intelligence Agency, the Defense Intelligence Agency, and so forth – may do highly creative work in the intelligence sector, but be unable to publicize the work. Similarly, hackers do highly creative work but often keep it a secret from the public. Indeed, the whole idea, for a hacker, often is to keep her work, or at least her identity, a secret. He or she may seek fame, but only under an assumed name so that no one can identify who actually did the work. The government was recently able to open the iPhone of the late terrorist primarily responsible for the San Bernardino massacre. Originally, neither the government nor Apple thought that the government would be able to open the iPhone without secret codes (themselves quietly creative) from Apple. But a hacker enabled the government to open the phone, in a major example of quiet creativity. The success was widely reported, but not how or by whom the phone was opened.

Consummate Creativity (Defiance of the Crowd, Oneself, and the Zeitgeist)

Consummate creativity involves all three components of the triangular theory – defiance of crowd, self, and Zeitgeist. It is what Kaufman (2016) and others refer to as Big C creativity. The great discoveries in science, for example, usually represent an evolution in thinking of their discoverers that culminate in revolutionary ideas – Darwin's theory of evolution, Einstein's theory of relativity, Pasteur's discovery of the principles of vaccination. It is what many scientists strive for but few achieve. Monet's Impressionism or Picasso's and Braque's cubism would be examples of consummate creativity in art, Chaucer's *Canterbury Tales* in literature, or Beethoven's Ninth Symphony in music.

Properties of Triangles of Creativity

Triangles of creativity have three important immediate properties – size, shape, and modifiability.

Size. The size (area) of the triangle is determined by the magnitude of the creative contribution, as judged by peers. Larger triangles correspond to creative contributions having larger impact. Size can increase because of high levels of all three kinds of defiance, or because of high levels of just one or two kinds.

Shape. The shape of the triangle is determined by the nature of the contribution – the extent to which it emphasizes the different components of the theory. A given contribution, for example, may represent a major advance for the individual, but a smaller advance for a field, and only a tiny advance in terms of moving the Zeitgeist. Or a contribution might represent a major shift in terms of defying the crowd, a major advance for an individual, but not much of a change in Zeitgeist. Different contributions make changes of different kinds in different amounts.

Modifiability. Creativity is defined in terms of an attitude toward life and work, not in terms of a fixed set of attributes determined at conception or birth. Although genetic factors no doubt play a role, in that underlying attributes such as openness to experience show some heritability (Jang, Livesley, and Vernon, 1996), genes interact with environment such that people can modify their attitudes toward producing creative work – or practically anything else (Gottesman, 2016). Moreover, as discussed below, abilities play a role as well.

Someone who starts off afraid to defy the crowd may change as a result of particular experiences. Indeed, many revolutionary thinkers started out as ordinary thinkers but became revolutionary in part as a result of circumstances. People like Benjamin Franklin, John Hancock, and Thomas Jefferson, for example, were not raised to become revolutionaries but became revolutionaries in part as a result of the times and circumstances in which they lived.

Gardner's (2011) and Simonton's (1997) models of development of creative careers both suggest that creative innovation may decrease over time. But whether it does decrease depends on a number of factors, including the individual's own self-efficacy for producing creative work and the amount of decline in the individual's fluid-thinking abilities.

In sum, creators can vary both in magnitude and in the kind of creative contribution they make with respect to defiance of the crowd, individual, and Zeitgeist. They also can change the magnitude and balance of their triangles of creativity as the circumstances of their lives change and as their motivations for being creative change.

Is There a Best Kind of Creativity?

It would seem, at first glance, that some manifestations of creativity are better than others – for example, consummate creativity would seem in some sense better than individual creativity. But what kind of creativity is "best" really depends on goals, much as does what kind of intelligence is needed to achieve specific goals (Sternberg, 1997b). What is "best" depends on the goals one is trying to reach. Unfortunately, though, smart and creative people are just as susceptible to foolish goals as are people with less intellectual endowment (Sternberg, 2002b). So the goals need not only to be reachable, but ones that contribute to one's own good, the good of others, and the good of society as a whole (Sternberg, 2003c, 2003d, 2010a, 2010b, 2013, 2014a).

Is There a Worst Kind of Creativity?

Unfortunately, there are a lot of awful examples of creativity in the world today. The rise of creative demagogues in the world, including in the United States, is an extremely ominous development. Most of the people alive today were not alive for World War II, and so there is a risk of repeating the same foolishness that led to that war, except with the possibility of far worse outcomes. Unfortunately, neither creativity nor intelligence provides any protection whatever against the rise of dema-gogues – narcissistic, sociopathic, Machiavellian individuals with extremely inflated views of themselves who are able to convince other people to fol-low their irresponsible and potentially deadly leadership (Sternberg, 2002, 2010b). The question, therefore, is whether creativity will be a force for good or for evil as we advance into the twenty-first century. At this point in time, it is unclear how things will go. It would be a shame if humans' creativity, which is capable of bringing so much good to the world, proved to be the source of the demise of the world as we know it. Such a fear may sound apocalyptic. It is, but so is the possible future that awaits us unless we temper creativity with common sense and wisdom (Sternberg, 2003d).

REFERENCES

Adelson, B. (1984). When novices surpass experts: The difficulty of a task may increase with expertise. *Journal of Experimental Psychology: Learning, Memory, and Cognition*, 10(3), 483–495.

Amabile, T. (1996). *Creativity in context: Update to "The social psychology of creativity."* Boulder, CO: Westview Press.

Baddeley, A. D., and Hitch, G. (1974). Working memory. In *The psychology of learning and motivation: Advances in research and theory*, edited by G. H. Bower, 8:47–89. New York: Academic Press.

Chase, W. G., and Simon, H. A. (1973). The mind's eye in chess. In *Visual informa-tion processing*, edited by W. G. Chase, 215–281. New York: Academic Press.

Chomsky, N. (1957). *Syntactic structures*. The Hague: Mouton.

Csikszentmihalyi, M. (2013). *Creativity: The psychology of discovery and invention*. New York: Harper Perennial.

(2014). *The systems model of creativity: The collected works of Mihaly Csikszentmi-halyi*. Dordrecht, Netherlands: Springer.

Dai, D. Y., and Sternberg, R. J. (Eds.). (2004). *Motivation, emotion, and cognition: Integrative perspectives on intellectual functioning and development*. Mahwah, NJ: Lawrence Erlbaum Associates.

Dweck, C. (2007). *Mindset: The new psychology of success*. New York: Ballantine.

Festinger, L., and Carlsmith, J. M. (1959). Cognitive consequences of forced com-pliance. *Journal of Abnormal and Social Psychology*, 58(2), 203.

Finke, R. A., Ward, T. B., and Smith, S. M. (1996). *Creative cognition: Theory, research, and applications*. Cambridge, MA: Bradford Books.

Fonorow, O. (2008). *Practicing medicine without a license? The story of the Linus Pauling therapy for heart disease*. Privately published.

Frensch, P. A., and Sternberg, R. J. (1989). Expertise and intelligent thinking: When is it worse to know better? In *Advances in the psychology of human intel-ligence*, edited by R. J. Sternberg, 5:157–188. Hillsdale, NJ: Lawrence Erlbaum Associates.

Gardner, H. (1983). *Frames of mind: The theory of multiple intelligences.* New York: Basic Books.

(2011). *Creating minds.* New York: Basic Books.

Gilson, L. L., and Madjar, N. (2011). Radical and incremental creativity: Antecedents and processes. *Psychology of Aesthetics, Creativity, and the Arts,* 5, 21–28.

Glăveanu, V. (2015). Culture and psychology: The first two decades and beyond. *Culture and Psychology,* 21, 429–438.

Gottesman, I. I. (2016). The view from the center of the triangle: Psychology, psychiatry, and genetics. In *Scientists making a difference: One hundred eminent behavioral and brain scientists talk about their most important contributions,* edited by R. J. Sternberg, S. F. Fiske, and D. J. Foss, 77–81. New York: Cambridge University Press.

Grant, A. (2010). Top 10 people who became famous after death. www.toptenz.net/top-10-people-who-became-famous-after-death.php.

(2016). *Originals: How non-conformists move the world.* New York: Viking.

Hennessey, B. A. (2010). The creativity-motivation connection. In *The Cambridge handbook of creativity,* edited by J. C. Kaufman and R. J. Sternberg, 342–365. New York: Cambridge University Press.

Hunter, S. T., Bedell, K. E., and Mumford, M. D. (2007). Climate for creativity: A quantitative review. *Creativity Research Journal,* 5, 69–90.

Jang, K. L., Livesley, W. J., and Vernon, P. A. (1996). Heritability of the Big Five personality dimensions and their facets: A twin study. *Journal of Personality,* 164, 577–591.

Kaufman, J. C. (2016). *Creativity 101.* 2nd ed. New York: Springer.

Kaufman, J. C., and Beghetto, R. A. (2009). Beyond big and little: The four C model of creativity. *Review of General Psychology,* 13, 1–12.

Kaufman, S. B., and Gregoire, C. (2015). *Wired to create: Unraveling the mysteries of the creative mind.* New York: TarcherPerigree.

Kaufman, J. C., and Sternberg, R. J. (Eds.). (2010). *The Cambridge handbook of creativity.* New York: Cambridge University Press.

Kim, K. H., Cramond, B., and VanTassel-Baska, J. (2010). The relationship between creativity and intelligence. In *The Cambridge handbook of creativity,* edited by J. C. Kaufman and R. J. Sternberg, 395–412. New York: Cambridge University Press.

Kozbelt, A., Beghetto, R. A., and Runco, M. A. (2010). Theories of creativity. In *The Cambridge handbook of creativity,* edited by J. C. Kaufman and R. J. Sternberg, 20–47. New York: Cambridge University Press.

Kuhn, T. S. (1970). *The structure of scientific revolutions.* 2nd ed. Chicago: University of Chicago Press.

Lubart, T. (1999). Creativity across cultures. In *Handbook of creativity,* edited by R. J. Sternberg, 339–350. New York: Cambridge University Press.

(2010). Cross-cultural perspectives on creativity. In *The Cambridge handbook of creativity,* edited by R. J. Sternberg, 265–278. New York: Cambridge University Press.

Mumford, M. D. (2002). Social innovation: Ten cases from Benjamin Franklin. *Creativity Research Journal*, 14, 253–266.

Mumford, M. D., Medeiros, K. E., and Parlow, P. J. (2012). Creative thinking: Processes, knowledge, and strategies. *Journal of Creative Behavior*, 46, 30–47.

Niu, W., and Sternberg, R. J. (2002). Contemporary studies on the concept of creativity: The East and the West. *Journal of Creative Behavior*, 36, 269–288.

  (2003). Societal and school influences on student creativity: The case of China. *Psychology in the Schools*, 40(1), 103–114.

Reiter-Palmon, R. (2014). Can we really have an integrative theory of creativity? The case of creative cognition. *Creativity: Theories, Research, Applications*, 1, 256–260.

Rumelhart, D. E., McClelland, J. L., and PDP Research Group (1994). *Parallel distributed processing: Foundations*. Vol. 1. Cambridge, MA: Bradford.

Sawyer, K. (2008). *Group genius: The creative power of collaboration*. New York: Basic Books.

Schank, R. C., and Childers, P. (1988). *The creative attitude: Learning to ask and answer the right questions*. New York: Macmillan.

Shurkin, J. (2006). *Broken genius: The rise and fall of William Shockley, creator of the Electronic Age*. New York: Palgrave Macmillan.

Simonton, D. K. (1997). Creative productivity: A predictive and explanatory model of career trajectories and landmarks. *Psychological Review*, 104, 66–89.

  (1999). Talent and its development: An emergenic and epigenetic model. *Psychological Review*, 106, 435–457.

  (2004). *Creativity in science: Chance, logic, genius, and Zeitgeist*. New York: Cambridge University Press.

  (2010). Creativity in highly eminent individuals. In *The Cambridge handbook of creativity*, edited by J. C. Kaufman and R. J. Sternberg, 174–188. New York: Cambridge University Press.

Sternberg, R. J. (1977). *Intelligence, information processing, and analogical reasoning: The componential analysis of human abilities*. Hillsdale, NJ: Lawrence Erlbaum Associates.

  (1981). A componential theory of intellectual giftedness. *Gifted Child Quarterly*, 25, 86–93.

  (1984). What should intelligence tests test? Implications of a triarchic theory of intelligence for intelligence testing. *Educational Researcher*, 13, 5–15.

  (1985a). Human intelligence: The model is the message. *Science*, 230, 1111–1118.

  (1985b). Teaching critical thinking, Part 1: Are we making critical mistakes? *Phi Delta Kappan*, 67, 194–198.

  (1986). Inside intelligence. *American Scientist*, 74, 137–143.

  (1987). Liking versus loving: A comparative evaluation of theories. *Psychological Bulletin*, 102, 331–345.

  (Ed.). (1988a). *Advances in the psychology of human intelligence*. Vol. 4. Hillsdale, NJ: Lawrence Erlbaum Associates.

  (1988b). Mental self-government: A theory of intellectual styles and their development. *Human Development*, 31(4), 197–224.

(1988c). A three-facet model of creativity. In *The nature of creativity*, edited by R. J. Sternberg, 125–147. New York: Cambridge University Press.

(1988d). *The triarchic mind*. New York: Viking.

(1997a). Managerial intelligence: Why IQ isn't enough. *Journal of Management*, 23(3), 463–475.

(1997b). Successful intelligence: A broader view of who is smart in school and in life. *International Schools Journal*, 17, 19–31.

(1998). *Cupid's arrow: The course of love through time*. New York: Cambridge University Press.

(Ed.). (1999a). *Handbook of creativity*. New York: Cambridge University Press.

(1999b). A propulsion model of types of creative contributions. *Review of General Psychology*, 3, 83–100.

(2002a). Creativity as a decision. *American Psychologist*, 57(5), 376.

(Ed.). (2002b). *Why smart people can be so stupid*. New Haven, CT: Yale University Press.

(2003a). A duplex theory of hate: Development and application to terrorism, massacres, and genocide. *Review of General Psychology*, 7(3), 299–328.

(Ed.). (2003b). *Psychologists defying the crowd: Stories of those who battled the establishment and won*. Washington, DC: American Psychological Association.

(2003c). WICS: A model for leadership in organizations. *Academy of Management Learning and Education*, 2, 386–401.

(2003d). *Wisdom, intelligence, and creativity synthesized*. New York: Cambridge University Press.

(2004). Culture and intelligence. *American Psychologist*, 59(5), 325–338.

(2005a). Creativity or creativities? *International Journal of Human Computer Studies*, 63, 370–382.

(2005b). The theory of successful intelligence. *Interamerican Journal of Psychology*, 39(2), 189–202.

(2007). Triangular theory of love. In *Encyclopedia of social psychology*, edited by R. Baumeister and K. Vohs, 2:997–998. Los Angeles, CA: Sage.

(2010a). *College admissions for the 21st century*. Cambridge, MA: Harvard University Press.

(2010b). The dark side of creativity and how to combat it. In *The dark side of creativity*, edited by D. H. Cropley, A. J. Cropley, J. C. Kaufman, and M. A. Runco, 316–328. New York: Cambridge University Press.

(2013). Personal wisdom in the balance. In *The scientific study of personal wisdom: From contemplative traditions to neuroscience*, edited by M. Ferrari and N. Weststrate, 53–74. New York: Springer.

(2014a). Creativity in ethical reasoning. In *The ethics of creativity*, edited by S. Moran, D. Cropley, and J. Kaufman, 62–74. New York: Palgrave Macmillan.

(2014b). I study what I stink at: Lessons learned from a career in psychology. *Annual Review of Psychology*, 65, 1–16.

(2016). *What universities can be*. Ithaca, NY: Cornell University Press.

(2018). A triangular theory of creativity. *Psychology of Aesthetics, Creativity, and the Arts*, 12, 50–67.

Sternberg, R. J., and Bower, G. H. (1974). Transfer in part–whole and whole–part free recall: A comparative evaluation of theories. *Journal of Verbal Learning and Verbal Behavior*, 13, 1–26.

Sternberg, R. J., and Davidson, J. E. (1982). The mind of the puzzler. *Psychology Today*, 16, 37–44.

(1983). Insight in the gifted. *Educational Psychologist*, 18, 51–57.

Sternberg, R. J., Fiske, S. T., and Foss, D. J. (Eds.). (2016). *Scientists making a difference: One hundred eminent behavioral and brain scientists talk about their most important contributions.* New York: Cambridge University Press.

Sternberg, R. J., and Grigorenko, E. L. (2004). Successful intelligence in the classroom. *Theory into Practice*, 43, 274–280.

Sternberg, R. J., and Hedlund, J. (2002). Practical intelligence, g, and work psychology. *Human Performance*, 15(1/2), 143–160.

Sternberg, R. J., Kaufman, J. C., and Pretz, J. E. (2001). The propulsion model of creative contributions applied to the arts and letters. *Journal of Creative Behavior*, 35(2), 75–101.

(2002). *The creativity conundrum: A propulsion model of kinds of creative contributions.* New York: Psychology Press.

Sternberg, R. J., and Lubart, T. I. (1991). An investment theory of creativity and its development. *Human Development*, 34(1), 1–31.

(1992). Buy low and sell high: An investment approach to creativity. *Current Directions in Psychological Science*, 1(1), 1–5.

(1994). An investment perspective on creative insight. In *The nature of insight*, edited by R. J. Sternberg and J. E. Davidson, 534–558. Cambridge, MA: MIT Press.

(1995). *Defying the crowd: Cultivating creativity in a culture of conformity.* New York: Free Press.

(1996). Investing in creativity. *American Psychologist*, 51(7), 677–688.

Sternberg, R. J., and Smith, C. (1985). Social intelligence and decoding skills in nonverbal communication. *Social Cognition*, 2, 168–192.

Ward, T. B., and Kolomyts, Y. (2010). Cognition and creativity. In *The Cambridge handbook of creativity*, edited by J. C. Kaufman and R. J. Sternberg, 93–112. New York: Cambridge University Press.

Zhang, L. F., and Sternberg, R. J. (1998). Thinking styles, abilities, and academic achievement among Hong Kong University students. *Hong Kong Educational Research Association Educational Research Journal*, 13, 41–62.

CHAPTER 22

Creativity as a Continuum

Thomas B. Ward

My focus on creativity has been mostly, though not exclusively academic. I do use photography and music as modes of expression, but I have not thought of myself as an especially creative person. In fact, one of my earliest creativity-related memories is of a bad feeling I had about a grade school painting I crafted. I had adorned it with a long blue squiggle (river), uniform brown lumps (mountains), and what looked like outsized broccoli crowns perched atop limbless telephone poles (trees). It didn't look that way for lack of trying; I wanted to make a realistic-looking scene. But I was disappointed, and as much as a young child can be convinced about such things, I was convinced that I was not destined to be an artist. I didn't take this seeming failure as an indicator of my being uncreative in general, just a bad artist. So, in retrospect, I must have held a domain-specific folk-psychological belief about creativity. It is perhaps surprising then that my first formal foray into systematic research and theorizing about creativity would be more consistent with a domain-general point of view, maintaining that a relatively small set of cognitive processes underlie most forms of creativity.

An Unanticipated Finding

My formal research on creativity emerged from a traditional cognitive-psychological focus on concepts and categories, a serendipitous turning point based on the results of a classroom exercise, and a happy confluence of collaborators at Texas A&M University. Graduate training at the University of Wisconsin had turned me into a hard-core experimental psychologist with an early focus on how children and adults form simple classifications of stimuli on the basis of dimensions such as the size, brightness, hue, and saturation of geometric forms (Ward, 1980, 1983; Ward, Foley, and Cole, 1986; Ward and Vela, 1986). Later, that work extended to consider how intentional versus incidental learning affected the structure of people's concepts (Ward and Scott, 1987; Ward and Becker, 1992) and to children's heavy reliance on shape in extending labels for objects (Becker and Ward, 1991; Ward, Becker, Hass, and Vela, 1991).

In the late 1980s and early 1990s I was also teaching Cognitive Psychology at Texas A&M, and wanted to develop in-class activities to make the constructs more real, including one to help students think about the nature of categories and concepts. For that one I had the students imagine a novel species of animals from a distant planet, draw two instances of it, and then draw another animal from a different species. They kept shape constant within species and varied it across species, which helped me explain Rosch's ideas about the basic level of categorization to them, since members of those types of categories tend to share the same shape (Rosch, Mervis, Gray, Johnson, and Boyes Braem, 1976). But beyond that result, the overall similarity of their imagined animals to animals on earth was striking; nearly all of them were bilaterally symmetric and had eyes and legs. It's not so much that that result was especially surprising, it's just that I had not considered that type of outcome one way or the other. Seeing it made me curious, and I realized that a systematically developed creative generation paradigm might yield interesting findings about category structure.

There were two sides to the same coin. One was that category structure could be studied using generative paradigms and not just the traditional receptive, learning, and classification paradigms that had been used up to that point. The other was that creativity might be studied by looking for largely implicit, systematic effects of people's existing concepts on what they produced when asked to generate novel ideas. So began a series of studies on conceptual expansion and "what's old about new ideas" (Ward, 1994, 1995).

Creative Cognition

Right around the time of the serendipitous finding from the class exercise, my colleague Steve Smith was beginning his studies on how mechanical engineers' designs for new devices were constrained by the properties of design examples they viewed before doing their task (Jansson and Smith, 1991). Whereas I was seeing the structuring effects of long-term, highly accessible category knowledge, he was seeing the effects of recently activated, exposure-based knowledge. Also, in that same time frame, Jyotsna Vaid and Ron Finke joined us on the faculty at Texas A&M, which resulted in a critical mass. Collaboratively, we produced four books and many joint papers as well as a spate of separate papers and chapters, focused on what we came to refer to as *creative cognition* (Finke, Ward, and Smith, 1992).

The choice of the term "creative cognition" reflected the fact that we came from cognitive-experimental psychology traditions rather than from programs directly concerned with creativity. We were deeply committed to understanding the cognition that underlies creativity. Without denying the importance of personality, motivation, environmental, and other factors (e.g., Amabile, 1983a, 1983b; Csikszentmihalyi, 1999; Lubart and Sternberg, 1995; Sternberg and Lubart, 1995), creative cognition concentrates on the mental operations that lead to the production of creative ideas. It characterizes the creative process as the application of basic cognitive processes to existing knowledge structures, which can lead to novel and useful outcomes. Understanding when and how those processes lead to creative as opposed to uncreative outcomes became an important mission.

Creative cognition received a major boost in 1995. Through the generous support of APA's scientific conferences program and matching funds from Texas A&M, Steve, Jyotsna, and I were able to hold a conference that was a showcase for research on the cognitive processes we saw as most promising to yield progress in understanding creativity (Ward, Smith, and Vaid, 1997). This included presentations from individuals we thought of as "hard-core" cognitive psychologists on multiple aspects of conceptual combination, conceptual expansion, metaphor, and analogy, among other phenomena. We also heard from individuals with deep roots in the creativity field, including David Perkins and Dean Keith Simonton. In their own way, they each challenged us to think more deeply about creative cognition (Perkins, 1997; Simonton, 1997).

Dean Simonton, in particular, raised the question of whether or not the same types of processes observed in laboratory studies could apply to real-world instances of high-level creativity. Reflecting his own strong concern with eminent creativity (Simonton, 1994), he rightly pointed to the vast range of creative accomplishment going from the mundane, everyday variety to the extraordinary and noted that understanding creativity required a focus on both ends of the continuum. Echoing that concern, an important ingredient in a complete creative cognition approach is *convergence*, considering both historical accounts of high-level creativity, and laboratory studies that attempt to operationalize the likely processes identified in those accounts (Ward and Kolomyts, 2010). In a later section of this chapter I return to the points Dean raised and discuss *creativity as a continuum*.

Structured Imagination and the Path of Least Resistance

For my own approach to understanding the process-creativity link, I developed a creative generation paradigm much like the classroom exercise described above (Ward, 1994). The initial goal was to go beyond the obvious point that people use their existing knowledge when they develop new ideas, to a more refined account of how and why known properties of particular concepts manifest themselves in newly formed ideas. In study 1, I simply asked college students to imagine animals that might exist on a planet somewhere in the galaxy that was very different from earth. I asked them to draw and describe the creature. As I had been observing in my classroom exercises, the vast majority of the imagined animals had standard appendages, such as legs and standard sense organs, such as eyes. The importance of that observation is that those are among the most commonly listed characteristic properties of animals in classic studies of category attributes (Ashcraft, 1978; Hampton, 1979; Rosch, Mervis, Gray, Johnson, and Boyes Braem, 1976; Tversky and Hemenway, 1984), revealing a direct relationship between the structure of people's animal concepts and the form of their new ideas. This occurred despite the fact that there are no necessary constraints that require animals to possess those properties on a planet described as being very different from earth.

Participants in Study 1 also generated a second member of the same species and a member of a different species. As I had found in the class exercise, the members of the same species tended to maintain the same basic shape as the first member, but differ in properties such as size and gender. Members of the different species differed from the first animal in shape. The result is consistent with the idea that participants' creations were influenced by a shape bias (Landau, Smith, and Jones, 1988) and basic-level category distinctions (Rosch, Mervis, Gray, Johnson, and Boyes Braem, 1976). That is, even young children have a tendency to extend novel labels they learn for an object to other objects of the same shape (Landau, Smith, and Jones, 1988). Participants in Ward (1994) were showing a *generative* version of a shape bias, using category membership to guide projections about shape rather than shape to guide categorization. In addition, the attributes people think of as characteristic of animals are not just disembodied abstractions with no relationship to one another. Rather, they are coherent collections organized into particular shapes (Tversky and Hemenway, 1984). Similarly, the evidence is clear that members of basic-level categories share the same identifiable shape (Rosch, Mervis, Gray, Johnson, and Boyes Braem, 1976). Thus, multiple aspects of conceptual structure, well established in the literature on noncreative tasks, were being shown to have reliable effects in determining the specific form of newly generated ideas.

Additional studies in Ward (1994) revealed the influence of other known properties of conceptual structure, such as the fact that attributes of natural categories tend to co-occur rather than being randomly distributed (Mervis and Rosch, 1981; Rosch, Mervis, Gray, Johnson, and Boyes Braem, 1976). When participants were told that the only known property of the creature was that it had feathers, they were more likely to produce imaginary animals that flew and had wings. In contrast, furry creatures were imagined to have four legs and be terrestrial. The effect was partly due to people retrieving birds versus mammals as starting points for their novel creations, but an additional study also revealed the influence of general world knowledge. When the planet was described as largely molten, with only a few islands of solid rock, participants tended to develop flying creatures, whereas for a fiercely windy planet, flying animals were rarely produced. In addition to showing the influence of specific instances of animals, and characteristic attributes and attribute co-occurrences, then, the study fit well with the assumption that categories are embedded in larger theoretical structures that provide coherence and context for understanding concepts (e.g., Murphy and Medin, 1985).

The results of Ward (1994) led me to the view that what's old about new ideas is as important as what's new about them for understanding creativity (Ward, 1995). They also led me to coin the term *structured imagination*. Far from being flighty and unpredictable, imagination tends to be governed in predictable ways by well-known properties of people's existing conceptual structures.

The why and how of structured imagination is described in the *path-of-least-resistance model*. When given a task of imagination, about two-thirds of participants report that they use specific known-category instances as their starting points, such as dogs for generating imaginary animals, apples for imaginary fruit, and football for sports (Ward, 2008; Ward, Patterson, Sifonis, Dodds, and Saunders, 2002). This is likely due to the power of the basic level (Rosch, Mervis, Gray, Johnson, and Boyes Braem, 1976) that guides our conceptual lives in general. On seeing a four-legged, furry creature, barking and playing fetch, for example, we could think of it as an animal, mammal, life-form, or something even more abstract, but our first tendency is to categorize it at the more specific basic level: a dog. It is an especially accessible level of abstraction. Similarly, it is the easiest path to follow in retrieving knowledge to help us in creative tasks. The properties of whatever is retrieved as the starting point are then projected onto the new idea being produced. As a result, otherwise novel creations possess a lot of the characteristic properties of existing entities.

Across several years, in collaboration with some exceptional graduate students and other talented collaborators, I have fleshed out more of the details of structured imagination, and other research teams have as well. It occurs across multiple conceptual domains, including animals, tools, fruit, sports, faces, and even religious figures (Bredart, Ward, and Marczewski, 1998; De Cruz, 2013; Ward, 2008; Ward, Patterson, Sifonis, Dodds, and Saunders, 2002). It also operates across cultures (Niu and Sternberg, 2001; Yi, Hu, Scheithauer, and Niu, 2013), as well as other modes of production, such as having participants use the software program Spore to perform the creature generation task (Cockbain, Vertolli, and Davies, 2013). It is also readily observable in virtual environments where real-world constraints need not apply but nevertheless influence what people create and what they do in those environments (Ward, 2015; Ward and Sonneborn, 2009).

Structured imagination is responsive to task instructions, in that people can be encouraged to retrieve and use more abstract information (e.g., that animals need some way to sense environmental conditions) (Ward, Patterson, and Sifonis, 2004). In addition, the specific, basic-level exemplars retrieved can be primed with prior pleasantness rating tasks in which participants judge particular category instances, but are not told of any connection between that task and the creative generation one (Ward and Wickes, 2009). But in spite of some malleability, certain concept attributes appear to be nearly immutable. For example, when asked to generate creatures wildly different from earth animals, even while they introduce some novel properties, most people still develop symmetric ones that have eyes and legs (Ward and Sifonis, 1997).

One consistent observation across these and other studies is that the participants who report retrieving specific category instances develop products rated as less original than those who report other approaches, such as accessing higher level information about the characteristic properties of life-forms in general. This finding makes sense, in that retrieved knowledge, whether at a specific or abstract level, is used in generating new ideas, thereby shaping their form, but the more specific information is more constraining. For example, if a novel creature is patterned after a retrieved cat, it will be more likely to possess two eyes symmetrically located in a head than if the creature results from retrieving the more abstract idea that life-forms tend to have some type of sense organs. The latter is less constraining and could be materialized in a multitude of ways, such as "gravitomagnetic" sensors that integrate information from gravitational pull and north-south orientation to guide the creature. Such an organism would certainly receive higher novelty ratings from coders, even though both it and a two-eyed creature would originate from retrieved knowledge. These findings are one example of how variations of the same processes, in this case knowledge retrieval, result in more versus less original outcomes.

Although intuition and data were consistent with the idea that retrieval of knowledge at more abstract levels can lead to products that are more original, there was a nagging sense that abstraction could also have a down side. Specifically, the more abstract the information, the more distant it is from any specific concrete realizations or successful implementation. This could compromise the practicality or workability of the idea. One study gave clear evidence to support this idea.

Ward (2008) had participants devise new sports. As in previous studies, some participants reported retrieving and using specific known-category instances (e.g., basketball and soccer), and others retrieved more abstract information (i.e., the properties of sports in general). Consistent with previous studies, retrieving more abstract knowledge led to sports that were rated as more original, but also as less playable. Specific information seems to provide a useful guiding force to tie novel ideas to coherent, concrete reality. Thus, modes of retrieval differentially affect the two key ingredients of creative products, their novelty and their usefulness.

My favorite example of the limits of abstraction is a device patented in 1965. It makes use of one of the most abstract ideas possible, centrifugal force. For what? To aid childbirth! Yes, to aid childbirth. The woman about to deliver rests on an inclined plane on a rotating platform. The rotation aids in bringing the baby down into the birth canal via centrifugal force from the rotation. For skeptics, I provide here the US Patent Office patent number 3,216,423. I don't have the engineering or medical expertise to evaluate the workability of the idea. I only have my own experience at the birth of my first child. There was much screaming (from her Mom) during a valiant but vain attempt at natural childbirth. I suspect that centrifugal force would have increased both its quantity and volume!

Laboratory studies of the type describe in this section do raise some concerns about their applicability to real-world creativity. One is that they rely almost exclusively on college students as participants. Additionally, the tasks can be somewhat contrived, there is generally a limited amount of time to perform them, and the participants are not chosen because of possessing any particular creative skill. In contrast, higher level real-world creativity can involve more complex problems, with an extended period of effort performed by professionals with a high level of motivation to succeed in their domains, operating at what Kaufman and Beghetto (2009) describe as the Pro C level of creativity. With those types of concerns in mind, Ward (1994) examined creatures envisioned by professional science-fiction writers for the same types of properties as those included by college students in laboratory studies. Specifically, he examined paintings shown in the book, *Barlowe's Guide to Extraterrestrials* (Barlowe and Summers, 1979). Barlowe, a painter, had chosen to depict creatures from the science-fiction literature that he found to be "challenging to the imagination." Coding revealed that roughly three-fourths of them possessed the eyes, legs, and symmetry that so dominated the college students creatures. Thus, structured imagination is not limited to college students performing contrived tasks with limited time.

There are also countless instances that reveal the role of specific existing knowledge in the development of real-world creative products. One example is the earliest railway passenger cars of the 1830s, whose most obvious observable feature was their striking similarity to stagecoaches, including the fact that conductors sat on benchlike attachments at the front of the vehicle (see White, 1978). It is clear that stagecoaches served as models, both mental and physical, for the new type of railway car, much as dogs serve as models for college students' imagined novel creatures. Thus, imagination, structured by retrieval of specific known instances does apply to real-world situations. In fact, the railway passenger case is an instance of the convergence principle in creative cognition.

It is also clear that reliance on specific known instances can aid invention and other technological advancements. Among the many examples is the fact that Eli Whitney's cotton gin was a modification of an earlier device that had been in use for centuries in India (Basala, 1988), and Edison's lightbulb was a variant on previous inventions that ran current through a filament in a vacuum encased in glass (Friedel, Israel, and Finn, 1987). Both inventions had striking consequences, culturally and economically, but they were relatively modest mental increments to what had come before. The amount of the modification and the magnitude of its effect are not correlated. Similarly, Weisberg (2006) has clearly identified the role of exposure to and use of other people's ideas in the development of well-known creators' real-world accomplishments. Returning, then, to Dean Simonton's challenge, when viewed as incremental change culminating in major breakthroughs, it is clear that the same basic processes can underlie small and big forms of creativity.

The Conformity Effect and the Upside and Downside of Examples

My focus on the influence of highly accessible long-term knowledge dovetailed with Steve Smith's concern with the impact of recently activated knowledge, and our collaboration led to important discoveries about how presented examples can help and hurt creativity. With an engineering colleague, David Jansson, Steve had examined what they called "design fixation" (Jansson and Smith, 1991). Across four separate experiments, they demonstrated that examples can hurt rather than help. To reach that conclusion, they asked design engineering students and practicing engineers to generate ideas for practical products, such as spill-proof coffee cups and car-mounted bicycle racks. Before the engineers began their work, Jansson and Smith showed half of them examples of designs that had flaws built into them, such as straws and mouthpieces that would leak if the cup tipped over, and a rack arrangement that would complicate mounting one of the bikes. Even though the flaws were evident and sometimes even directly pointed out, the students and engineers nevertheless included them in their own designs. They also generated a more narrow range of ideas than people who saw no examples prior to doing the task, tending instead to produce designs of the same basic type as the examples. The activated knowledge from recent examples clearly had a negative effect.

With graduate student Jay Schumacher, Steve and I extended the Jansson and Smith findings to a large group of college students who we asked to come up with ideas for new toys and imaginary animals (Smith, Ward, and Schumacher, 1993). Like the engineers, they copied properties of the examples, even when we asked them to make their ideas be different from the examples, and even when the examples were described as ones that we had found to restrict people's creativity. Study 2 in that paper also showed that the effects of examples persist for at least twenty minutes. When the toy and animal examples were all shown at the beginning of the task and participants generate items for the categories sequentially, they showed conformity effects for both the category they worked on first, and the one they worked on second, which happened after twenty-three minutes had elapsed since viewing the examples.

The phenomenon of copying the properties of presented examples came to be called the *conformity effect*, and several subsequent studies replicated it and extended it to other domains, such as generating novel words with and without exposure to examples (Landau and Lehr, 2004; Landau and Leynes, 2004; Marsh, Ward, and Landau, 1999). Other studies advanced understanding of the sources of the effect by noting situations that would increase or decrease it. Marsh, Landau, and Hicks (1996), for example, showed that the conformity effect could be increased by increasing the number of examples presented and by imposing a one-day delay between exposure and generation. The effect of the number of examples could indicate that participants form a kind of category or schema from them, much as people form and use schemas of analogical problem solutions from exposure to multiple instances of the same type (Gick and Holyoak, 1983). The effect of increased conformity with a one-day delay may implicate a failure of source monitoring. Features from the examples may come to mind and be incorporated into the participants' products without them explicitly recalling the source of that information being the examples they saw the day before. Without that correct source attribution, they do not have a reason to avoid using those properties in their creations.

But noting that people inadvertently conform their ideas to examples is not the same as saying examples reduce creativity. Can examples sometimes help? Can conformity be creative? The answer is Yes. For one thing, in the Marsh, Landau and Hicks (1996) study, whereas conformity to examples increased in going from one to nine examples, inclusion of uncommon properties did not concomitantly decrease. To the extent that including uncommon features can be taken as an indicator or creativity, then, increased conformity is not linked to decreased creativity. In addition, when examples are specifically selected because they had previously been rated as very creative, participants who view those examples develop more creative artistic products (both extraterrestrials and collages) than participants who view no examples (Yi, Plucker, and Guo, 2015).

It is also clear that examples can be used to increase the unusualness of people's creations, if the examples include unusual properties. Under the guise of having participants help in the development of a computer program that would generate novel nonwords, for example, Landau and Lehr (2004) had participants make up new words for members of familiar categories, such as insects and sports. Some participants were shown examples that were legal in English orthography (e.g., treb) and others were shown illegal examples made up of the same letters (e.g., btre). As in other conformity effect studies, participants were instructed "not to use any aspect of the preceding examples." Compared to participants in a control condition who saw no examples, both examples groups were more likely to incorporate properties of the examples, such as the four-letter word length, into their own creations, but those who saw illegal examples were also more likely to create illegal and unpronounceable words. They were conforming, but conforming to the more unusual aspects of the examples.

The Landau and Lehr study is also a good example of how the conformity effect is largely inadvertent. In a second study, all participants saw illegal examples, but the properties of the examples were made salient to some by having them assess each one in terms of its length and pronounceability. The manipulation did not reduce their tendency to copy those properties even though, as in the first study they were instructed not to copy any aspect of the examples. The finding makes it difficult to maintain the position that participants incorporate properties of examples because they do not know (consciously) what those properties are, and so cannot consciously avoid them. Multiple studies with various phrasing of instructions to not copy examples have been tried and for the most part the instructions are ineffective. On the other hand, Chrysikou and Weisberg (2005) replicated the main Jansson and Smith findings but found conformity to examples was reduced by very explicit identification of what properties of the examples should be avoided along with close, one-on-one interaction with the experimenter rather than more loosely structure group testing.

More recently, the power of examples to increase creativity was shown in a study by Okada and Ishibashi (2016). They examined the idea that examples that violate people's basic assumptions or frameworks can result in constraint relaxation and thereby increase creativity. They capitalized on a cultural constraint in Japan that favors realistic drawings over less realistic ones. Their assumption was that the participants in their study would come into the situation adhering to that constraint and that exposure to and interaction with examples that violate the constraint would lead to relaxing it and, as a result more creative drawings. The study took place over three days. On the first day, participants were shown objects found in nature, such as oranges, and asked to make original, creative drawings of them using provided pens and paper. On day two, participants in a copy condition were shown two drawings specifically created by artists for the study in an abstract style, and they were asked to copy them. The use of the abstract style in the examples was intended to provoke a relaxation of the "realistic" constraint in the participants' views about art. Participants in a control condition were not shown those examples, but were instead instructed to make two new original drawings that were different from the ones they made the day before. On the third day, all participants were again given natural objects and asked to make original, creative drawings. The drawings were rated by experts for creativity, technique, and aesthetics. There were no rated differences between the groups on day one drawings, but the copy group's drawings on day three were rated as more creative.

There were no appreciable changes or differences between the groups in rated technique or aesthetic quality.

Three additional findings are of importance. One is that having participants in another condition copy *realistic* drawings on day two did not increase their day three creativity. Presumably, copying realistic drawings did not challenge their default assumptions about the way drawing "should" be done. The second interesting finding is that intense consideration of the abstract examples was as effective as having participants copy them. That is, when participants took as much time inspecting the drawings and considering things such as the artist's intent, their creativity scores went up as much as those who actually physically copied the drawings. One final subtlety in the study was that participants in a reproduction condition also copied the examples on day two but on day three were instructed to produce drawings *in the style of the examples*. Ratings of similarity revealed that their day three drawings were more similar to the examples than those of people in the copy condition, indicating that the latter were not just copying the style but rather developing their own version of it. Thus, examples that challenge people's frameworks can result in constraint relaxation and increased creativity.

Creativity as a Continuum

I want to return to the idea of creativity as a continuum. Dean Simonton emphasized the idea that there are gaps or discontinuities in the range going from everyday creativity to extraordinary creativity (Simonton, 1997), for example from a student's dabblings into creative writing in a college course to the exquisite works of Shakespeare. I cannot help but think of traditional distinctions between little c and Big C creativity, with one enormous discontinuity, and the more refined approach of Kaufman and Beghetto (2009) in their four-C model, with several smaller gaps between mini-c, little C, Pro C, and Big C creativity.

My view is that the qualitative gaps, great or small, are more about factors other than the cognitive processes involved. As I noted earlier, from a process point of view, even major accomplishments in invention appear to result from an incremental process of retrieving, modifying and building on previous ideas rather than one involving huge leaps sparked by some type of extraordinary mental process. But from an impact point of view, relatively small modifications on earlier ideas occasionally have enormous observable impacts on our lives. Similarly, the four-C distinctions seem to be about external factors, such as the requirement of an observable product that a qualified audience would judge to be creative, and how the "just right" balance of accurate praise and constructive criticism, dubbed the Goldilocks principle, can move people from one mode to another, rather than about the processes that generate novelty being qualitatively different in each type.

Both Simonton's suggestions and the four-C model are extremely valuable. By identifying specific qualitatively distinct levels of creative accomplishment, we now have a framework for asking what is different across levels of creativity. I suppose we could add other levels and reduce the size of the gaps even more, but my guess is that one commonality across the levels will always be the operation of the same basic set of cognitive processes, hence the notion of *creativity as a continuum*.

REFERENCES

Amabile, T. M. (1983a). *The social psychology of creativity*. New York: Springer.

(1983b). Social psychology of creativity: A componential conceptualization. *Journal of Personality and Social Psychology*, 45, 357–377.

Ashcraft, M. H. (1978). Property norms for typical and atypical items from 17 categories: A description and discussion. *Memory and Cognition*, 6(3), 227–232.

Barlowe, W. D., and Summers, I. (1979). *Barlowe's guide to extraterrestrials*. New York: Workman.

Basala, G. (1988). *The evolution of technology*. London: Cambridge University Press.

Becker, A. H., and Ward, T. B. (1991). Children's use of shape in extending novel labels to animate objects: Identity versus postural change. *Cognitive Development*, 6, 3–16.

Bredart, S., Ward, T. B., and Marczewski, P. (1998). Structured imagination of novel creatures' faces. *American Journal of Psychology*, 111, 607–725.

Chan, J., and Schunn, C. (2015). The impact of analogies on creative concept generation: Lessons from an in vivo study in engineering design. *Cognitive Science*, 39(1), 126–155.

Christensen, B. T., and Schunn, C. D. (2007). The relationship of analogical distance to analogical function and pre-inventive structure: The case of engineering design. *Memory and Cognition*, 35, 29–38.

Chrysikou, E. G., and Weisberg, R. W. (2005). Following the wrong footsteps: Fixation effects of pictorial examples in a design problem-solving task. *Journal of Experimental Psychology: Learning, Memory, and Cognition*, 31(5), 1134–1148.

Cockbain, J., Vertolli, M. O., and Davies, J. (2014). Creative imagination is stable across technological media: The spore creature creator versus pencil and paper. *Journal of Creative Behavior*, 48(1), 13–24.

Csikszentmihalyi, M. (1999). Implications of a systems perspective for the study of creativity. In *Handbook of creativity*, edited by R. J. Sternberg, 313–335. Cambridge: Cambridge University Press.

Dahl, D. W., and Moreau, P. (2002). The influence and value of analogical thinking during new product ideation. *Journal of Marketing Research*, 39(1), 47–60.

De Cruz, H. (2013). Religious concepts as structured imagination. *International Journal for the Psychology of Religion*, 23(1), 63–74.

Dunbar, K. (1997). How scientists think: On-line creativity and conceptual change in science. In *Creative thought: An investigation of conceptual structures and processes*, edited by T. B. Ward, S. M. Smith, and J. Vaid, 461–494. Washington, DC: American Psychological Association.

Finke, R. A., Ward, T. B., and Smith, S. M. (1992). *Creative cognition: Theory, research, and applications*. Cambridge, MA: MIT Press.

Friedel, R. D., Israel, P., and Finn, B. S. (1987). *Edison's electric light: Biography of an invention*. New Brunswick, NJ: Rutgers University Press.

Gentner, D., Brem, S., Ferguson, R., Wolff, P., Markman, A. B., and Forbus, K. (1997). In *Creative thought: An investigation of conceptual structures and processes*, edited by T. B. Ward, S. M. Smith, and J. Vaid, 403–460. Washington, DC: American Psychological Association.

Hampton, J. A. (1979). Polymorphous concepts in semantic memory. *Journal of Verbal Learning and Verbal Behavior*, 18(4), 441–461.

Jansson, D. G., and Smith, S. M. (1991). Design fixation. *Design Studies*, 12, 3–11.

Kaufman, J. C., and Beghetto, R. A. (2009). Beyond big and little: The four C model of creativity. *Review of General Psychology*, 13, 1–12.

Landau, J. D., and Lehr, D. P. (2004). Conformity to experimenter-provided examples: Will people use an unusual feature? *Journal of Creative Behavior*, 38, 180–191.

Landau, J. D., and Leynes, P. A. (2004). Manipulations that disrupt the generative stage decrease conformity to examples: Evidence from two paradigms. *Memory*, 12, 90–103.

Landau, B., Smith, L. B., and Jones, S. S. (1988). The importance of shape in early lexical learning. *Cognitive Development*, 3(3), 299–321.

Lubart, T. I., and Sternberg, R. J. (1995). An investment approach to creativity. In *The creative cognition approach*, edited by S. M. Smith, T. B. Ward, and R. A. Finke, 269–302. Cambridge, MA: MIT Press.

Marsh, R. L., Landau, J. D., and Hicks, J. L. (1996). How examples may (and may not) constrain creativity. *Memory and Cognition*, 24, 669–680.

Marsh, R. L., Ward, T. B., and Landau, J. D. (1999). The inadvertent use of prior knowledge in a generative cognitive task. *Memory and Cognition*, 27, 94–105.

Mervis, C. B., and Rosch, E. (1981). Categorization of natural objects. *Annual Review of Psychology*, 32, 89–115.

Murphy, G. L., and Medin, D. L. (1985). The role of theories in conceptual coherence. *Psychological Review*, 92(3), 289–316.

Niu, W., and Sternberg R. J. (2001). Cultural influences on artistic creativity and its evaluation. *International Journal of Psychology*, 36, 225–241.

Okada, T., and Ishibashi, K. (2016). Imitation, inspiration, and creation: Cognitive process of creative drawing by copying others' artworks. *Cognitive Science*. doi:10.1111/cogs.12442.

Perkins, D. N. (1997). Creativity's camel: The role of analogy in invention. In *Creative thought: An investigation of conceptual structures and processes*, edited by T. B. Ward, S. M. Smith, and J. Vaid, 523–538. Washington, DC: American Psychological Association.

Rosch, E., Mervis, C. B., Gray, W. D., Johnson, D. M., and Boyes-Braem, P. (1976). Basic objects in natural categories. *Cognitive Psychology*, 8, 382–439.

Simonton, D. K. (1994). *Greatness: Who makes history and why*. New York: Guilford Press.

——— (1997). Creativity in personality, developmental, and social psychology: Any links with cognitive psychology? In *Creative thought: An investigation of conceptual structures and processes*, edited by T. B. Ward, S. M. Smith, and J. Vaid, 309–324. Washington, DC: American Psychological Association.

Smith, S. M., Ward, T. B., and Schumacher, J. S. (1993). Constraining effects of examples in a creative generation task. *Memory and Cognition*, 21, 837–845.

Sternberg, R. J., and Lubart, T. (1995). *Defying the crowd*. New York: Free Press.

Tversky, B., and Hemenway, K. (1984). Objects, parts, and categories. *Journal of Experimental Psychology: General*, 113(2), 169–193.

Ward, T. B. (1980). Separable and integral responding by children and adults to the dimensions of length and density. *Child Development*, 51, 676–684.

——— (1983). Response tempo and separable-integral responding: Evidence for an integral-to-separable processing sequence in visual perception. *Journal of Experimental Psychology: Human Perception and Performance*, 9, 103–112.

——— (1994). Structured imagination: The role of conceptual structure in exemplar generation. *Cognitive Psychology*, 27, 1–40.

——— (1995). What's old about new ideas? In *The creative cognition approach*, edited by S. M. Smith, T. B. Ward, and R. A. Finke, 157–178. Cambridge, MA: MIT Press.

——— (1998). Analogical distance and purpose in creative thought: Mental leaps versus mental hops. In *Advances in analogy research: Integration of theory and data from the cognitive, computational, and neural sciences*, edited by K. Holyoak, D. Gentner, and B. Kokinov, 221–230. Sofia: New Bulgarian University.

——— (2008). The role of domain knowledge in creative generation. *Learning and Individual Differences*, 18, 363–366.

——— (2015). Content, collaboration and creativity in virtual worlds. In *Video games and creativity*, edited by G. Green and J. Kaufman, 119–136. New York: Academic Press.

Ward, T. B., and Becker, A. H. (1992). Learning categories with and without trying: Does it make a difference? In *Percepts, concepts and categories: The representation and processing of information*, edited by B. M. Burns, 451–491. Amsterdam: Elsevier Science.

Ward, T. B., Becker, A. H., Hass, S. D., and Vela, E. (1991). Attribute availability and the shape bias in children's category generalization. *Cognitive Development*, 6, 143–167.

Ward, T. B., Foley, C. M., and Cole, J. (1986). Classifying multidimensional stimuli: Stimulus, task, and observer factors. *Journal of Experimental Psychology: Human Perception and Performance*, 12, 211–225.

Ward, T. B., and Kolomyts, Y. (2010). Creativity and cognition. In *The Cambridge handbook of creativity*, edited by J. Kaufman and R. J. Sternberg, 93–112. Cambridge: Cambridge University Press.

Ward, T. B., Patterson, M. J., and Sifonis, C. (2004). The role of specificity and abstraction in creative idea generation. *Creativity Research Journal*, 16, 1–9.

Ward, T. B., Patterson, M. J., Sifonis, C. M., Dodds, R. A., and Saunders, K. N. (2002). The role of graded category structure in imaginative thought. *Memory and Cognition*, 30, 199–216.

Ward, T. B., and Scott, J. G. (1987). Analytic and holistic modes of learning family-resemblance concepts. *Memory and Cognition*, 15, 42–54.

Ward, T. B., and Sifonis, S. M. (1997). Task demands and generative thinking: What changes and what remains the same? *Journal of Creative Behavior*, 31, 245–259.

Ward, T. B., Smith, S. M., and Vaid, J. (Eds.). (1997). *Creative thought: An investigation of cognitive structures and processes*. Washington, DC: American Psychological Association Books.

Ward, T. B., and Sonneborn, M. S. (2009). Creative expression in virtual environments: Imitation, imagination and individualized collaboration. *Psychology of Aesthetics, Creativity and the Arts*, 3, 211–221.

Ward, T. B., and Vela, E. (1986). Classifying color materials: Children are less holistic than adults. *Journal of Experimental Child Psychology*, 42, 273–302.

Ward, T. B., and Wickes, K. N. S. (2009). Stable and dynamic properties of graded category structure in Imaginative thought. *Creativity Research Journal*, 21, 15–23.

Weisberg, R. W. (2006). *Creativity: Understanding innovation in problem solving, science, invention, and the arts*. Hoboken, NJ: John Wiley.

White, J. H. (1978). *The American railroad passenger car*. Baltimore: Johns Hopkins University Press.

Yi, X., Hu, W., Scheithauer, H., and Niu, W. (2013). Cultural and bilingual influences on artistic creativity performances: Comparison of German and Chinese students. *Creativity Research Journal*, 25(1), 97–108.

Yi, X., Plucker, J. A., and Guo, J. (2015). Modeling influences on divergent thinking and artistic creativity. *Thinking Skills and Creativity*, 16, 62–68.

CHAPTER 23

Reflections on a Personal Journey Studying the Psychology of Creativity

Robert W. Weisberg*

Since I began my research career, in the mid-1960s, there have been enormous changes in the study of creativity and related topics. In examining those changes, I will concentrate on two interconnected areas in my research: experimental studies of the role of leaps of insight in problem solving; and analysis of the thought processes underlying real-world creative advances. I define creative advances differently than most researchers, who use the "standard definition" (Runco and Jaeger, 2012), according to which a creative advance is something that is novel and of value. However, including value in the definition is problematic (Weisberg, 2015a), so I define a creative advance as something that is novel and produced intentionally. If you intentionally produce something novel, it is creative, even if no one values it. It might be possible that even the creator might not value it. For example, an artist might try a new technique that she is not sure will work and, as she carries it out, she sees that it does not in fact work out well. Therefore, even the creator turns out not to value the new work. That work would still be creative however, so long as it was novel.

The direction of my career was not the result of a plan. First, I was offered a summer research assistantship before I started graduate school, and the professor was studying problem solving, which I had not been exposed to as an undergraduate. Thus, my initial exposure to the field was by chance. Studying problem solving naturally led to an interest in creative thinking more broadly, but at that time that area struck me as fraught with mystery. Ghiselin, in 1952, had published a collection of anecdotes from eminent creators, reporting how they brought new works into existence, and those reports indicated that the process involved were nothing like those I

* Thanks are due to Robert Sternberg and James Kaufman for comments on an earlier version of this chapter.

was comfortable thinking about. As one example, the poet Samuel Taylor Coleridge described his poem "Kubla Khan" as coming to him complete, in an opium-induced dream. He just had to write it down. Similarly, Mozart described melodies coming to him unbidden, and again, his task was simply to write them down. It seemed that creativity was all unconscious and without effort. I did not know how to deal with such phenomena. However, in 1981 Perkins published a book that for me was eye-opening. He raised questions about some of those reports. For example, it turned out that Coleridge wrote more than one draft of "Kubla Khan," indicating that, contrary to his report, the poem had not come to him complete (Schneider, 1953). Stimulated by Perkins, I did a little research on my own and found that Mozart's report also was probably not true (Weisberg, 1986). Thus, it seemed that the creative process might be less mysterious than people had assumed that it was.

The goal that has motivated my research is the desire to understand creative thinking without resorting to explanations that rely on processes that to me were mysterious. The most prominent of those processes is the notion that "leaps of insight" underlie creative advances.

Insight versus Analytic Thinking in Problem Solving

Analytic Thinking versus the Insight Sequence

There seem to be two modes of solving problems, and, more generally, in producing creative advances (e.g., Ohlsson, 2011; Weisberg, 2015b, forthcoming). One mode, called *analytic thinking* by modern psychologists, involves application of one's knowledge to a problem, and step-by-step working out of the solution. In contrast, *insight* involves a subjective experience very different than solution through analysis. In solving a problem through what has been called the "insight sequence" (Ohlsson, 1992), the individual tries to apply knowledge to the problem, but that results in failure and an impasse. To achieve insight, find a new direction from which to approach the problem. In response to an impasse, one may be able to break away from the past, and achieve a *restructuring* of the problem: a new way of analyzing the problem. A solution may then suddenly appear, in an Aha! or Eureka! experience. An insightful solution can bring with it a feeling of certainty concerning its correctness, even though the person has not worked it out in a step-by-step manner. That result has been taken as evidence for the role of unconscious processes in insight. A solution can suddenly appear in consciousness, complete and with a feeling of certainty, because it had all been worked out, outside of conscious awareness.

Those differences in subjective experiences have led researchers to postulate differences in underlying cognitive processes underlying analysis versus insight (Ohlsson, 2011). We have already seen that modern researchers take the occurrence of insight as evidence for the occurrence of unconscious thinking, while analytic thinking is conscious. In the original gestalt analysis of problem solving, analytic thinking was dismissed as "reproductive thinking," that is, one reproduced something old, with no real advance in thinking. Gestalt theory emphasized the importance of "productive thinking" in insight, which involved rejecting the past and dealing with the situation on its own terms. Once one has broken the "fixation" on the past, solution to the problem should come quickly and easily. The gestalt view is strongly supported by many modern researchers (e.g., Kounios and Beeman, 2015; Öllinger, Jones, and Knoblich, 2014; Perkins, 2000), a number of whom explicitly reject analytic thinking as being relevant to creativity, distinguishing between analytic and "creative" (i.e., insightful) thinking (e.g, Ohlsson, 2011; Wiley and Jarosz, 2012).

In explaining how an impasse might lead to restructuring of a problem, the Gestalt psychologists pointed to the reversible cube and other perceptual situations, wherein one's experience of the world suddenly and spontaneously changed, without the individual having control over what happened (see Figure 23.1). When viewing the reversible cube in Figure 23.1, it suddenly changes orientation, going from facing in one direction to facing in another (A ⇔ B). Restructuring of perceptual experience was seen as analogous to restructuring of a problem. If one reached an impasse while working on a problem, the situation might undergo spontaneous restructuring, the way the reversible cube does, and the individual would then experience the problem from a new perspective (Ohlsson, 2011, Chapter 4).

Fixation and Interference with Insight

The Gestalt psychologists discussed several "insight" problems, in which solution was assumed to be blocked because of a too-strong reliance – that is, "fixation" – on unwarranted assumptions (see Figure 23.2). Consider the gestalt analysis of the Nine-Dot problem, which requires that the person connect nine dots with four connected straight lines. Scheerer (1963), in a *Scientific American* article summarizing the gestalt view (see also Maier, 1930), claimed that the Nine-Dot problem was a simple problem, made difficult by the person's fixation on an incorrect assumption: driven by

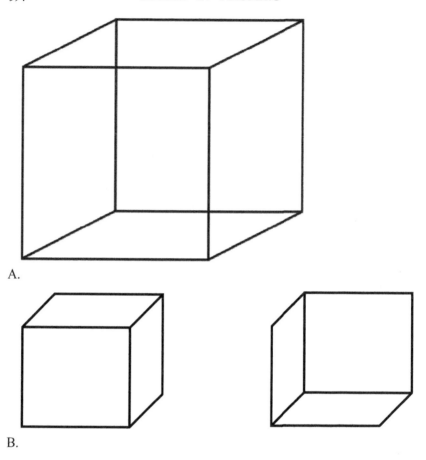

A.

B.

Figure 23.1 Reversible cube. The figure spontaneously reverses its orientation in depth as you watch, going back and forth from A to B. Those reversals are outside your control

perceptual factors, people assumed that the lines had to be drawn within the square shape of the dots. If that fixation could be overcome, the solution would follow easily. Scheerer presented no data to support his analysis. Nonetheless, the gestalt interpretation was adopted by other researchers. As one prominent example, Newell and Simon (1972, pp. 90–91), who carried out groundbreaking research formulating the information-processing theory of problem solving, specifically discussed the nine-dot problem. They noted that it was a difficult problem, because people represented the shape of the dots as a square, and that determined how they approached it.

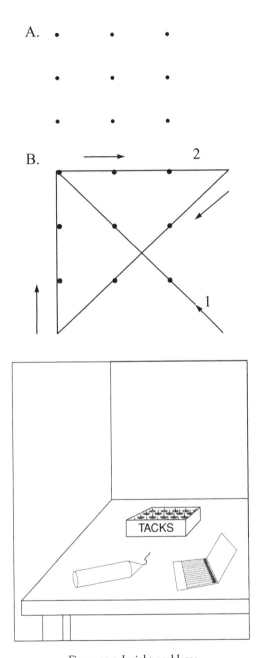

Figure 23.2 Insight problems

Similarly, Rumelhart (1977), another information-processing theorist, said the following about the nine-dot problem, among others:

> All of these problems have something in common. They are all very easy problems that are made very difficult by one thing only – our prior expectations about the allowable solutions to these problems . . . [With the nine-dot problem] the problem comes from the fact that the configuration forms a natural square and we tend to impose the constraint that our lines may not go outside the square. (p. 262)

Those researchers also presented no data supporting their assertions about the Nine-Dot problem. It thus seemed that the gestalt view had assumed the dominant position in discussions of problem solving, but without evidence.

Questions about the Gestalt View

I was struck by those interpretations of the Nine-Dot problem, because I had available informal evidence that contradicted them. I had presented the Nine-Dot problem as an exercise in numerous class discussions of problem solving. My students had a very hard time solving it, even when instructed to draw their lines outside of the square. That instruction, in the gestalt view, should have eliminated the fixation and made the problem easy. Thus, I began to believe that fixation was *not* the main cause of difficulty in the Nine-Dot problem. I therefore designed an experimental study, with Joe Alba's assistance, to test the gestalt analysis of the Nine-Dot problem (Weisberg and Alba, 1981, exp. 1). A control group was given the problem as presented in Figure 23.2A. To test the gestalt notion of fixation, an "outside hint" group was told that the only way to solve the problem was to draw lines outside the shape of the square. As in my class demonstrations, no one in the control condition solved the problem, indicating that it was very difficult. Contrary to gestalt theory, the outside hint did not make the problem easy: only 20 percent solved it. Everyone given the hint drew lines outside the square, indicating that the "fixation" had been broken, but most still did not solve the problem. Furthermore, those who solved after the hint needed more than five additional attempts to do so, further evidence that the hint did not provide immediate insight into the solution.

We also tested two other conditions: one group was given the outside hint plus line 1 from the solution (see Figure 23.2B), and the other received the outside hint plus lines 1+2. Those conditions produced significant levels of solution: 60 percent in the hint plus line 1 condition, and 100 percent in the hint plus lines 1+2 condition. Those results indicated that the difficulty with the Nine-Dot problem was that people did not know how to go about solving it, not that they were fixated on an incorrect assumption concerning the solution. It must be kept in mind that people given the "go outside" hint did indeed draw lines outside the square. The problem was not that they were *fixated*, which is defined in my dictionary as an obsessive or excessive interest or felling about someone or something. Rather, the difficulty was that they had no knowledge to fall back on concerning what to do when they went outside the square. Evidence to support that interpretation came from another study (Weisberg and Alba, 1981, exp. 2), in which we gave practice solving two problems where one had to draw lines outside the configuration of dots (see Figure 23.3A). A control condition was given practice that did not require them to think about going beyond the configuration (Figure 23.3B). The group given practice drawing lines outside the configuration solved the Nine-Dot problem significantly more frequently than the control group did. That result indicated that one needs to learn a lot before one can solve the Nine-Dot problem. Therefore, even after the hint to go outside the square, the problem remains very difficult (see also Kershaw and Ohlsson, 2004; Lung and Dominowski, 1985; Öllinger, Jones, and Knoblich, 2014).

Weisberg and Alba (1981) further suggested that the terms *insight* and *fixation* were not useful in describing the behavior of people attempting to solve the Nine-Dot problem, and perhaps should be abandoned. The reasoning behind that suggestion was as follows. Let us say I ask you to solve a problem in quantum mechanics, and you know nothing about that domain. If you cannot solve the problem, no one would be surprised, and we would not invoke "fixation" in explaining why you could not do so. The difference between a problem in quantum mechanics and the Nine-Dot problem is that, once you are shown the Nine-Dot solution, it seems so simple that you cannot understand why you did not solve it. When the researcher tells you about fixation, that seems a reasonable explanation. However, the solution to the Nine-Dot problem only *appears* simple: it is in actuality very complicated, involving a lot of knowledge, as evidenced by the mediocre performance of people given extensive hints or other information about the solution. Once one accepts that premise, then we do not have to bring forth fixation as an explanation of failures to solve the problem.

A. Nine-Dot problem: "outside" practice

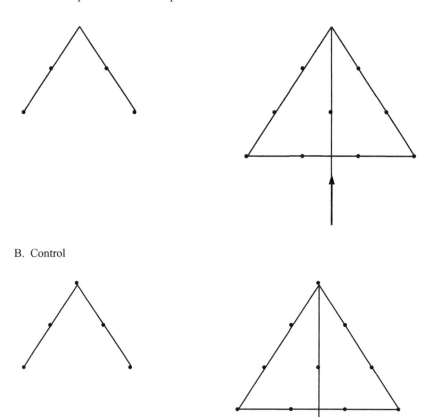

B. Control

Figure 23.3 Nine-Dot problem: (A) "outside" practice; (B) control

The Neo-Gestalt Response

In response to the proposal by Weisberg and Alba (1981; see also Perkins, 1981), modern supporters of the gestalt view – *neo*-gestalt researchers – carried out studies to demonstrate that the notions of insight and fixation were useful in describing people's behavior in solving problems, and in describing creative thinking more generally. Ohlsson (2011), for example, argued that insight was critical to our survival as a species. The world is constantly changing, so our knowledge quickly becomes outdated and irrelevant to the present (see also Perkins, 2000; Kounios and Beeman, 2015). Ohlsson (e.g., 1992, 2011) revised and elaborated gestalt theory; he and his colleagues then carried out studies presenting evidence they interpreted as supporting the gestalt view (e.g., Knoblich, Ohlsson, Haider, and Rhenius, 1999; Knoblich, Ohlsson, and Raney, 2001).

Other researchers presented additional evidence, which can only be very briefly sampled, in support of the sharp distinction between insight and analysis. Wiley and Jarosz (2012) and Fleck (2008) demonstrated that insight problems were solved with a lesser involvement of working memory than were analytic problems. Because working memory plays a critical role in executive functioning, that result was taken as evidence for a lack of conscious planning in insight. It was also reported that reasoning processes as exemplified by fluid intelligence – a critical component of analytic thinking – did not play an important role in solving problems through insight (for a review, see Chuderski, 2014). Here too, the conclusion was that analytic processes were not important in insight. Finally, Kounios and Beeman (2015) presented evidence supporting the conclusion that there were different patterns of brain activity underlying insightful versus analytic solutions to problems (for a critique, see Weisberg, 2013).

Insight versus Analysis?

However, other evidence has been presented that again raises questions about a sharp distinction between problem solving based on insight versus analysis. Fleck and Weisberg (2004, 2013) examined people's performance on a set of insight problems, such as those shown in Figure 23.2, and found a range of solution methods. Fewer than 10 percent of the "insightful" solutions came about through the insight sequence. That is, people solved the problems through restructuring, but did not go through the full insight sequence, which was postulated as being *necessary* for restructuring (Ohlsson, 2011, Chapter 4; Öllinger, Jones, and Knoblich, 2014). As one example, some people restructured a problem, but without first reaching impasse. The restructuring was based on a logical analysis of the information in the problem. Here, insight, in the sense of a solution based on restructuring of the problem, came about as the result of analysis. Other people solved problems through restructuring, based on new information that became available as they worked on the problem, again, not as a response to impasse, which never occurred. A problem situation changes as the solution process unfolds, providing new information to the individual. That new information can result in a new solution type coming to mind, without the person's having reached impasse. Thus, people can solve "insight" problems in a variety of ways (see also Weisberg, 2015b, forthcoming). The fact that the classic insight sequence occurs in a very small minority of the cases raises the question of whether we should be singling out that phenomenon for special attention.

Other evidence also supported this view. It has been shown that, contrary to earlier reports, working memory plays a significant role in problem solution through insight (e.g., Chein and Weisberg, 2014). Also, several large-scale investigations by Chuderski (e.g., 2014) demonstrated close links between insightful problem solving and performance on reasoning and other executive function tasks, which supports the idea that similar thought processes underlie analytic and insightful thinking.

Toward a Unified Theory of Problem Solving

Although there seem to be differences in the subjective states accompanying problem solving though insight versus analysis (e.g., Metcalfe and Wiebe, 1987), the underlying processes may have much in common (Weisberg, 2015b, forthcoming). Making a distinction between "creative" solutions, based on the insight sequence, versus those based on analysis (e.g., Ash, Cushen, and Wiley, 2009; Ohlsson, 2011; Perkins, 2000) overlooks the fact that analytic processes can produce "creative" solutions to problems, including "insightful" solutions based on restructuring. Rather than a dichotomy between insight versus analysis, it might be more useful to try to specify the processes leading to what are called insightful versus analytic solutions to problems.

One attempt at such a specification was provided by Fleck and Weisberg (e.g., 2013; see also Weisberg, 2015b, forthcoming). They presented a model of how people go about solving problems, a modified version of which is shown in Figure 23.4. All problem-solving activities arise from the match that a problem situation makes with a person's knowledge. Stage 1 centers on that process and its possible outcomes. If there is specific knowledge available (Stage 1A), the person will attempt to solve the problem by transferring an old method (Stage 1B). If that transferable method works, then the problem is solved, without impasse or restructuring (Stage 1C). If transfer fails, but new information arises out of that failure (Stage 1D), then the person searches memory again, with the possibility that a new method will come to mind (recycling through Stage 1A). Restructuring of

STAGE 1 – MATCHING PROBLEM WITH KNOWLEDGE

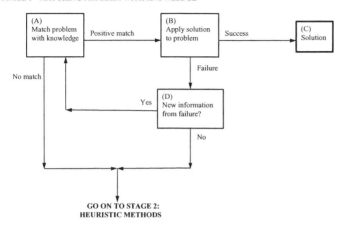

GO ON TO STAGE 2:
HEURISTIC METHODS

STAGE 2 - APPLYING HEURISTICS TO PROBLEM

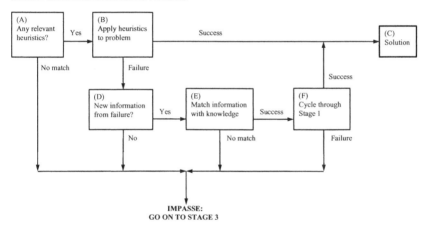

IMPASSE:
GO ON TO STAGE 3

STAGE 3 – RESTRUCTURING HEURISTICS IN RESPONSE TO IMPASSE

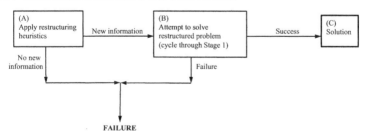

FAILURE

Figure 23.4 Outline of a model of problem solving

the problem may occur as the result of this recycling – the new information may bring to mind a new way of analyzing the problem, and bring solution – but there is no impasse.

If no match occurs at Stage 1A, or if no new information arises out of the failed solution in Stage 1D, then the person goes to Stage 2, and tries to apply heuristic methods – rules of thumb – to the problem. Heuristic methods, which are very general in their application, include logical analysis of the information in the problem, application of arithmetic, and working backward from the goal. If one of those methods matches the problem (Stage 2A), the person tries to carry it out (Stage 2B). If that attempt is successful, then the problem is solved (Stage 2C). If a heuristic method fails at Stage 2B, but new information arises out of that failure (Stage 2D), there is another search of memory (Stage 2E), which, if successful, can result in a new solution method being retrieved, which can produce restructuring and a new solution type (Stage 2F). If there is no solution and no new information (Stages 2D and E), then the person is at an impasse and goes on to Stage 3. At Stage 3A, the person may apply another set of heuristics to the situation, which Ohlsson (1992) called "switch when stuck" (that is, switch your way of analyzing the problem when you are stuck). Kaplan and Simon (1990) discussed a similar set of heuristics called "Try a Switch" (i.e., switch to something new). Those "restructuring heuristics," if successful (Stage 3B), can result in new information arising from the problem situation, which can in turn result in a solution (Stage 3C).

Application of the Framework

The way the framework in Figure 23.4 plays out can be made clear by considering two problems. The Water Lilies problem (Fleck and Weisberg, 2013), asks the person to determine the day when the lake is half full of lilies. This problem type is not familiar to most people (that is, they do not recognize that the language designates a geometric progression), so there is no match at Stage 1A. People then go to Stage 2, and apply a heuristic, their knowledge of arithmetic, to the problem (Stages 2A and 2B). To find when the lake is half covered: they divide the total time in half, producing thirty days as the answer. They are told that they are incorrect, which surprises them, so they try another heuristic: looking carefully at the problem information, to see where they went wrong. Some people then realize that the problem is not a simple arithmetic problem, and they reason out the solution. Insight in the Water Lilies problem is thus achieved through heuristic – that is, analytic – methods.

The Candle Problem (Fleck and Weisberg, 2004; see Figure 23.2B), in which people are asked to attach a candle to the wall so that they can read by its light, is more complicated. Most people have some knowledge that they can apply to the problem: they know how to use tacks and/or they know how to use melted wax as glue (Stage 1A). They therefore try to tack the candle to the wall, or "glue it" with melted wax (Stage 1B). Those solutions may fail, because it turns out that the tacks are too small to penetrate the candle; and the wax glue is not strong enough to hold it up (Stage 1D). That new information leads some people to consider using a shelf to hold up the candle (recycling through Stage 1A with that new information), and they turn to the tack box. Those people restructure the problem, but never reach impasse. Other people, however, solve the Candle Problem through the insight sequence. They try to tack the candle to the wall or to glue it, and then give up (Stage). They then go to Stage 2, but no relevant heuristics are found (Stage 2A). That leads to Stage 3A. Some people then examine the problem carefully, to determine if there is anything else they can use in a solution. They consider what they could do with the box, and they use it to solve the problem.

It should be noted, however, that the "box" solution is not the only way to solve the Candle Problem. A significant number of people solve the problem without using the tack box as a candle holder or shelf, because they are able to devise innovative ways of attaching the candle to the wall using the tacks and/or candle wax glue (Fleck and Weisberg, 2004; Weisberg and Suls, 1973). The "box" solution is sometimes described as *the* solution to the problem, but that is incorrect: there are many possible solutions. Also, sometimes we have asked people to actually attach a candle to the wall (Fleck and Weisberg, 2004) and other times we have presented a picture with objects and asked them to describe what they would do (Weisberg and Suls, 1973). The results in both conditions are the same, indicating that people think about the problem in the same way when they are actually manipulating objects versus when they are only thinking about what they might do.

Analysis and Insight: Summary

The outline in Figure 23.4 proposes that analytic thinking underlies all solutions to "insight" problems. The match between the problem and one's knowledge can result in retrieval of an old solution that can be transferred, or it can result in the application of heuristic methods to the problem. Stages 1 and 2 can result in solution, or, in case of failure, new information can become available, which can produce a restructuring of the problem (Stages 1D and 2D). Finally, the person may reach impasse (Stage 3). In response, there are several heuristic methods that have been suggested by researchers (Kaplan and Simon, 1990; Ohlsson, 1992). The insight sequence is based on the application at Stage 3 of heuristic methods of a high level of generality, which can change the person's overall orientation to the problem. In this view there is no basic difference between the insight sequence and other methods of solving problems: insight also depends on a set of heuristic methods, comparable to but more general than those that come into play earlier in the process. Insight – restructuring of a problem – is one outcome of analytic thought.

This conclusion represents an evolution in my thinking. Fleck and Weisberg (2004) assumed that the processes involved in resolving an impasse were different than those involving the earlier stages. That is, we assumed that the model was a *hybrid*, incorporating two different sorts of processes, with places for analytic thinking and also for the Gestalt psychologists' "spontaneous" restructuring. However, on further consideration, I have concluded that one can deal with all the solutions with analytic processes, if one includes heuristic methods within that category (Kaplan and Simon, 1990; Ohlsson, 1992). Thus, I am now of the opinion that it is not necessary to go beyond analytic processes in understanding "insightful" problem solving, i.e., problem solving based on the insight sequence.

The distinction between insight and analytic thinking has also been raised in discussions of creative thinking more broadly. Here, too, I was interested in the possibility of explaining creative thinking using cognitive mechanisms that were not different than those typically discussed by cognitive psychologists, for example, the retrieval of information from memory and logical reasoning. In other words, I was hoping that one could understand creative thinking through mechanisms of analytic thinking.

Analytic Thinking as the Basis for Creativity: Historical Case Studies

Neo-Gestalt researchers have argued for the importance of insight in creative thinking beyond the laboratory (e.g., Kounios and Beeman, 2015; Ohlsson, 2011; Perkins, 2000). Support for that argument involves presentation of real-world creative advances that purportedly arose through a leap of insight. The thinker went beyond the past and restructured a

Figure 23.5 Leonardo's aerial screw

problematic situation, making a connection where before none had existed. Here are two examples of creative advances presented as being the result of leaps of insight. For each of them, I have demonstrated that, contrary to the claims of the neo-gestalt researchers, there was in each case information available to the individual that could serve as the basis for a process of analytic thinking, linking the problem situation and the solution (Weisberg, 2015b, forthcoming).

Leonardo's Aerial Screw

Perkins (2000) discussed Leonardo's design of the "aerial screw," a flying machine, as an example of a leap of insight. The aerial screw (see Figure 23.5) is based on what seems to be a totally unprecedented idea: humans could fly – that is, rise in the air – if they could quickly turn a large-enough "screw" (the sail on the machine). As one drives a screw into a wooden ceiling, the aerial screw can be driven into the air. Perkins (2000) emphasized Leonardo's linking two unconnected ideas:

> Leonardo's insight made a connection between two very different things. He saw a relationship between screws and the challenge of flight. A propeller amounts to an air screw, holding on to air much as a wood screw holds on to wood, albeit less firmly. (p. 3)

Leonardo's discovery: Air is compressible

⇓

Leonardo's knowledge: Wood is compressible and a screw can be pulled through wood Birds soar in screw-shaped spiral paths through the air

⇓

A screw can be pulled through air
**(hypothesis/inference/
based on analogy)**

⇓

Aerial screw
Outcome (conclusion)

Figure 23.6 Possible conceptual links leading to Leonardo's invention of the aerial screw through analytic thinking

In Perkins's analysis, Leonardo's aerial screw was based on a "leap" Leonardo made, connecting "two very different things": a wood screw and the sail on his flying machine. Perkins emphasized how unrelated those two concepts were.

However, the wood screw and the sail were not so different in Leonardo's data base; there were in fact several connections in Leonardo's expertise between screws and flight (Laurenza, 2006, p. 47). In his scientific studies, Leonardo had analyzed the characteristics of air, and found that air was compressible, like wood. That was one link that could have led Leonardo to the possibility that a screw-shaped device, if rotated quickly, could bore through the air and lift itself in flight (see Figure 23.6). Leonardo had a long-standing interest in human flight, so the compressibility of air and wood might have been particularly noteworthy to him. Furthermore, in his notebooks describing birds' soaring flight paths, Leonardo described the flight paths as sometimes being spiral, "in the manner of a screw" (Richter, 1952, p. 97), which might have provided another link between wood screws and the aerial screw. Thus, Leonardo's making a connection between screws and flight was not a far-reaching leap connecting "two very different things." It was an extension of his expertise.

Arnold Wilkins and the Invention of Radar

Ohlsson (2011) discussed Wilkins's invention of radar in 1935 as an example of an almost incomprehensible leap of insight. Wilkins, a British physicist who specialized in radio transmission, worked at a government laboratory. His superior asked him to calculate whether concentrated radio waves could raise the temperature of eight pints of water from 98° Fahrenheit to 105°, at a distance of five kilometers and a height of one kilometer. There was fear in Great Britain concerning what looked like an inevitable war with Germany, and the purpose of the question was to determine whether radio waves could serve as a "death ray," to heat the blood of incoming enemy pilots, disabling or killing them. Wilkins concluded that the task could not be carried out with the available technology. His superior asked him if there was any way the laboratory might contribute to a war effort. Wilkins, "in a momentous act of inspiration" (Ohlsson, 2011, p. 53), conceived of using radio waves to specify the locations of incoming enemy planes, that could assist in intercepting and destroying them. In a leap of insight, Wilkins had conceived *radar*.

Here, too, the description ("a momentous act of inspiration") implies that there was no basis for the idea that Wilkins conceived. However, if we look at Wilkins's data base, we see that this situation also involved more than a leap of inspiration from nothing to a completely new idea (Weisberg, 2015b; see Figure 23.7). Wilkins was familiar with a recent governmental report addressing the problem of airplanes interfering with radio waves, *which is the basic idea on which radar is built* (Buderi, 1996, p. 55). There was thus a link in Wilkins's experience between the problem and his invention. His superior's request might have retrieved the information that aircraft interfered with radio waves (the request contained both "radio waves" and "aircraft"). Wilkins might then have inferred that such interference could provide information about an aircraft's location, which ultimately led to radar. Wilkins's advance involved a sequence of steps, building on his expertise, rather than a "momentous act of inspiration," independent of everything he knew.

I have elsewhere (Weisberg, 2006, Chapters 1 and 5; 2013) demonstrated that analytic thinking underlies numerous examples of seminal creative advances, including the discovery of the double helix by Watson and Crick; Picasso's creation of *Guernica*, his great antiwar painting; Frank Lloyd

Problem set to Wilkins:
Use radio waves in combating aircraft

Wilkins's knowledge: Aircraft interfere with radio waves

⇓

Interference provides information
about location of aircraft
(inference)

⇓

Direct waves at aircraft
(hypothesis/inference)

⇓

Determine location of aircraft
(outcome/conclusion)
⇓

Figure 23.7 Possible conceptual links leading to Wilkins's invention of radar through analytic thinking

Wright's creation of Fallingwater, the iconic house over the waterfall; and the Wright brothers' invention of the airplane. There is thus much evidence, beyond the case studies discussed here, for the role of analytic processes in creative advances of the highest order.

Experience and Creativity

I think that it is fair to say that the neo-gestalt researchers reject the direct role of experience in creative thinking. As one example, already briefly discussed, Ohlsson (1992, 2011) has argued that the ability to *suppress* one's knowledge and restructure problem situations underlies our survival (Ohlsson, 2011, p. 21). According to Ohlsson (2011, Chapter 1), the world is always changing rapidly and unpredictably; therefore, we cannot use what we know to predict what will happen. Thus, analytic thinking, which uses the past to deal with the new, is incapable of dealing with most situations that we face, especially the most important ones, those demand that we think in new ways. Ohlsson has proposed that the mechanisms of *deep learning* have evolved to deal with such situations. Deep learning allows us to

> abandon, override, reject, retract or suppress knowledge that we had previously accepted as valid in order to track a *constantly shifting and fundamentally unpredictable environment* and thereby indirectly create mental space for alternative or even contradictory concepts, beliefs, ideas and strategies. (p. 21, emphasis added)

Ohlsson here makes clear the distinction between situations in which we can apply our knowledge and those in which we must actively reject it.

Other researchers ascribe to variants of this perspective. Perkins also emphasized the difficulties arising when one tries to apply one's knowledge to the world. In his view, many problem situations in the world do not yield to analytic thinking. In Perkins's terms, the world is an "unreasonable" place, that is, a place where "reasonable" thought processes – those that compose analytic thinking – are doomed to fail. Success occurs only when one abandons analytic thinking and thinks "unreasonably," that is, by making connections between ideas that had not been connected. As a mechanism to make those connections, Perkins (2000) discussed *breakthrough thinking*, a concept very similar to Ohlsson's (2011) deep learning.

Wiley and her colleagues (e.g., Ash, Cushen, and Wiley, 2009; Wiley and Jarosz, 2012) have proposed a similar view, making a distinction between analysis and insight – restructuring in response to impasse – and equating insight with creativity. The critical shortcoming with analytic thinking is that there are problem situations in which it is not useful. "In these cases, prior experience elicits a problem representation that inappropriately constrains the search space or inappropriately combines problem elements" (Ash, Cushen, and Wiley, 2009, p. 7). The thinker must reject that problem representation, which is brought about through processes different than those involved in analytic thinking. "[R]estructuring is a mechanism that cannot be accommodated by classic heuristic-search accounts of problem solving, and requires an additional theoretical framework" (Ash, Cushen, and Wiley, 2009, p. 8).

Kounios and Beeman (e.g., 2015) have also emphasized the close relationship between creative thinking, restructuring, and insight. They defined creative thinking as

> the ability to reinterpret something by breaking it down into its elements and recombining those elements in a surprising way to achieve some

> goal . . . The less obvious the recombination, the more creative it is . . . When
> this kind of creative recombination takes place in an instant, it's an insight.
> (pp. 9–10)

This last statement makes clear the neo-gestalt take on the role of knowledge in creative thinking: knowledge provides the basic elements of
thought, but those elements must be combined in new – unobvious – ways
to produce new ideas.

My perspective, in contrast, is based on the assumption that one can
apply one's ideas relatively directly to new situations, using the structures
one already possesses, with minor "tweaking," to make them fit, rather
than dismantling them and building something new, from the foundation
up. The degree of precision of the match between the situation and one's
knowledge determines that processes that are activated. Thus, in my view,
"insight," defined as the restructuring of a problem in response to impasse,
is simply one example of the application of knowledge – general heuristics –
to a problem situation. Contrary to the claim by Ash, Cushen, and Wiley
(2009), restructuring does not require an additional theoretical framework,
beyond heuristic-search accounts of problem solving and creative thinking
(Weisberg, 2006).

Sternberg and Davidson (1982; Davidson, 1995) have proposed an analysis of insight which falls between the neo-gestalt view and the analytic
view presented in Figure 23.7. Sternberg and Davison argued that insight,
defined as the sudden realization of the solution to a problem, involves
three processes, that are used when the person faces a problem for which
he or she does not available a solution method. *Selective encoding* occurs
when a person suddenly becomes aware of a previously ignored aspect of a
situation. *Selective combination* occurs when the person puts information
together in a way that had previously not been obvious. *Selective comparison*
comes about when one discovers a relationship between new information
and already-known information.

As an example of how those processes are assumed to work, Darwin's
development of the theory of evolution is assumed to result from his selective combination of the facts that he had available, which resulted suddenly
in the development of the theory of *natural selection*, a coherent explanation of how species evolved. The commonality in the three processes is the
critical role of "selection and relevance" (Davidson, 1995, p. 129). In selective encoding, the person who exhibits insight is able in some way to select
the relevant information from the problem. In selective combination, he or
she sees how to combine available information in a relevant way, choosing

one out of many possible combinations. In selective comparison, the individual is able to select a relevant way of relating new and old information, out of many possible relations that might be drawn upon.

Sternberg and Davidson's analysis is similar to the one proposed here in the sense that more than a single process is assumed to underlie insight, although the specific processes are not the same as those proposed here. Also, Sternberg and Davidson's definition of insight is different than the gestalt definition, which involves restructuring of a problem. That difference makes it difficult make direct comparisons across theoretical views.

Analytic Thinking and Creativity: Conclusions

My research over the years has taken a consistent path. I have tried to analyze situations involving creative thinking, in the laboratory and in the real world, using the mechanisms of analytic thinking, which I have sometimes called "ordinary thinking" (Weisberg, 2006). In other words, I have tried to develop an analysis of creative thinking that assumes nothing beyond the mechanisms of thought discussed by cognitive psychologists analyzing such processes as retrieval of information from memory, and reasoning by deduction, induction, and analogy. This perspective leads to the intriguing possibility that creative advances come about through the thought processes that we all employ every moment of every day. That leads to the further conclusion that all people possess the capacity to think creatively. There is no difference in between the thought processes underlying the most radical creative advances and those underlying our ordinary interactions with the world. As far as thinking capacities are concerned, it is incorrect to say that some people are "more creative" than others. We can all think creatively to the same degree. The fact that some of us produce creative breakthroughs, while others do not, is due, not to differences in thinking, but to differences in what one could call motivation. If one has interest in some field that entails creativity, and a desire to make a contribution to that field, anyone can do so, assuming that they have the capacity to learn the field. Most people are not creative because they do not think they have the capacity to be creative, and so do not attempt to engage in creative activities.

In addition, the perspective proposed here implies that teaching people to think creatively is unnecessary, in the sense that we all possess the capacity to do so. What education should emphasize is the fact that anyone can produce new ideas and products, if they give themselves the chance to do so.

REFERENCES

Ash, I. K., Cushen, P. J., and Wiley, J. (2009). Obstacles in investigating the role of restructuring in insightful problem solving. *Journal of Problem Solving*, 2, 6–41.

Buderi, R. (1996). *The invention that changed the world*. New York: Simon and Schuster.

Chein, J. M., and Weisberg, R. W. (2014). Working memory and insight in verbal problems: Analysis of compound remote associates. *Memory and Cognition*, 42, 67–83.

Chuderski, A. (2014). How well can storage capacity, executive control, and fluid reasoning explain insight problem solving. *Intelligence*, 46, 258–270.

Davidson, J. E. (1995). The suddenness of insight. In *The nature of insight*, edited by R. J. Sternberg and J. E. Davidson, 125–156. Cambridge, MA: MIT Press.

Fleck, J. I. (2008). Working memory demands in insight versus analytic problem solving. *European Journal of Cognitive Psychology*, 20, 139–176.

Fleck, J. I., and Weisberg, R. W. (2004). The use of verbal protocols as data: An analysis of insight in the candle problem. *Memory and Cognition*, 32, 990–1006.

(2013). Insight versus analysis: Evidence for diverse methods in problem solving. *Journal of Cognitive Psychology*, 25, 436–463.

Kaplan, C. A., and Simon, H. A. (1990). In search of insight. *Cognitive Psychology*, 22, 374–419.

Kershaw, T. C., and Ohlsson, S. (2004). Multiple causes of difficulty in insight: The case of the nine-dot problem. *Journal of Experimental Psychology: Learning, Memory, and Cognition*, 30, 3–13.

Knoblich, G., Ohlsson, S., Haider, H., and Rhenius, D. (1999). Constraint relaxation and chunk decomposition in insight problem solving. *Journal of Experimental Psychology: Learning, Memory, and Cognition*, 25, 1534–1555.

Knoblich, G., Ohlsson, S., and Raney, G. E. (2001). An eye movement study of insight problem solving. *Memory and Cognition*, 29, 1000–1009.

Kounios, J., and Beeman, M. (2015). *The eureka factor: Aha moments, creative insight, and the brain*. New York: Random House.

Laurenza, D. (2006). Written text for Leonardo's machines: Da Vinci's inventions revealed. In *Leonardo's machines: Da Vinci's inventions revealed*, edited by M. Taddei and E. Zanon. Cincinnati, OH: David and Charles.

Lung, C., and Dominowski, R. L. (1985). Effects of strategy instructions and practice on nine-dot problem solving. *Journal of Experimental Psychology: Learning, Memory, and Cognition*, 11, 804–811.

Maier, N. R. F. (1930). Reasoning in humans: I. On direction. *Journal of Comparative Psychology*, 10, 115–143.

Metcalfe, J., and Wiebe, D. (1987). Intuition in insight and noninsight problem solving. *Memory and Cognition*, 15, 238–246.

Newell, A., and Simon, H. (1972). *Human problem solving*. New York: Prentice Hall.

Ohlsson, S. (1992). Information-processing explanations of insight and related phenomena. In *Advances in the psychology of thinking*, edited by M. T. Keane, and K. J. Gilhooly, 1:1–44. New York: Harvester Wheatsheaf.

——— (2011). *Deep learning: How the mind overrides experience.* Cambridge: Cambridge University Press.

Öllinger, M., Jones, G., and Knoblich, G. (2014). The dynamics of search, impasse, and representational change provide a coherent explanation of difficulty in the nine-dot problem. *Psychological Research*, 78, 266–275.

Perkins, D. N. (1981). *The mind's best work.* Cambridge, MA: Harvard University Press.

——— (2000). *The Eureka effect: The art and logic of breakthrough thinking.* New York: W. W. Norton.

Richter, I. (Ed.). (1952). *The notebooks of Leonardo da Vinci.* Oxford: Oxford University Press.

Rumelhart, D. (1977). *Introduction to human information processing.* New York: John Wiley.

Runco, M. A., and Jaeger, G. J. (2012). The standard definition of creativity. *Creativity Research Journal*, 21, 92–96.

Scheerer, M. (1963). Problem solving. *Scientific American*, 208(4), 118–128.

Schneider, E. (1953). *Coleridge, opium, and Kubla Khan.* Chicago: University of Chicago Press.

Sternberg, R. J., and Davidson, J. E. (1982). The mind of the puzzler. *Psychology Today*, 16, 37–44.

Weisberg, R. W. (1986). *Creativity: Genius and other myths.* New York: Freeman.

——— (2006). *Creativity: Understanding innovation in problem solving, science, invention, and the arts.* Hoboken, NJ: John Wiley.

——— (2013). On the "demystification" of insight: A critique of neuroimaging studies of insight. *Creativity Research Journal*, 25, 1–14.

——— (2015a). On the usefulness of *value* in the definition of creativity. *Creativity Research Journal*, 27(2), 111–124.

——— (2015b). Toward an integrated theory of insight in problem solving. *Thinking and Reasoning*, 21, 5–39.

——— (forthcoming). Problem solving. In *International handbook of thinking and reasoning*, edited by L. Ball and M. Thompson. New York: Psychology Press.

Weisberg, R. W., and Alba, J. W. (1981). An examination of the alleged role of "fixation" in the solution of several "insight" problems. *Journal of Experimental Psychology: General*, 110, 169–192.

Weisberg, R. W., and Suls, J. M. (1973). An information-processing model of Duncker's candle problem. *Cognitive Psychology*, 4, 255–276.

Wiley, J., and Jarosz, A. F. (2012). Working memory capacity, attentional focus, and problem solving. *Current Directions in Psychological Science*, 21(4), 258–262.

The Big Questions in the Field of Creativity
Now and Tomorrow

Robert J. Sternberg and James C. Kaufman

We hope you have enjoyed the essays in this volume. The chapters reflect the diversity of views, approaches, and beliefs about which questions most need to be answered. By its very nature, a volume such as this one does not and cannot offer conclusive answers about the field; creativity research is ever-evolving. Indeed, many chapters focus on how the authors' own interests and emphases have evolved over the course of a career. What this book can do, we believe, is to clarify the big questions currently being asked in the field by the top scholars. It is our hope that young and rising researchers (and even senior researchers!) can use this volume as a base from which to ask themselves which questions are most worth asking. We now present what we believe are some of those big questions. We further will compare those questions with the questions that have dominated the field of intelligence, from which the field of creativity, through the work of Guilford (1950, 1968), partly originated (as discussed in the preface).

- What is creativity? It may seem odd that as basic a question as "What is creativity?" still would not have a clear-cut answer, but even in this volume, there is not a full consensus as to its exact definition. Most agree that a component of novelty is needed, but what else? Does creativity also need to be compelling (Sternberg, this volume), appropriate (Amabile, this volume), or valuable (Lubart, this volume)? Does it refer to the construction of original meaning (Runco, this volume)? Does it require a product (Baer, this volume; Plucker, this volume)? Silvia (this volume) has suggested that there is even a futility to trying to come up with a definition of creativity. There is also less than full agreement in the field of intelligence as well as to precisely what intelligence is, with some investigators believing that it is not much more than general intelligence, or g (Jensen, 1998), others believing that intellectual abilities are hierarchically arranged under general intelligence (Carroll, 1993), some viewing it in cognitive or "triarchic" terms (Sternberg, 1985a, 1985b,

1988a, 1988b; Sternberg and Grigorenko, 2004), and still others seeing it as comprising multiple intelligences rather than a single one (Gardner, 2011).

- How is creativity best measured? Once upon a time, psychometric divergent thinking tests of creativity, such as the Torrance Tests, were the generally accepted coin of the realm for measuring creativity. Today there is no such coin. Many still use divergent thinking assessments (Runco, this volume). Others use insight problems (Davidson and Sternberg, 2003; Sternberg and Davidson, 1982, 1983; Weisberg, this volume) or self-assessments (Furnham, this volume; Reiter-Palmon, Robinson-Morral, Kaufman, and Santo, 2012; Silvia, Wigert, Reiter-Palmon, and Kaufman, 2012). One method rising in popularity is the use of expert raters to judge creative products, an outgrowth of Amabile's (1996) consensual assessment technique (Amabile, this volume; Baer, this volume; Kaufman, this volume).

- Are there different kinds of creativity? Some investigators have focused upon different kinds of creativity, ranging from mini-c (Beghetto, this volume; Richards and Goslin-Jones, this volume) to Big-C (Simonton, this volume) levels of creative development (Kaufman and Beghetto, 2009). Others, like Runco (this volume), question whether such a hierarchy is valid. In the field of intelligence, there is more of a view that levels of intelligence are continuous, perhaps because of the long-standing existence of the bell curve of an IQ scale (Willis, Dumont, and Kaufman, 2011). But there is a raging dispute over whether there are different kinds of intelligence (e.g., Gardner, 2011; Sternberg, 1997; Sternberg and Hedlund, 2002) or just one basic kind, general intelligence and its subabilities (Carroll, 1993).

- How does creativity change with age? In the field of intelligence, there have been numerous attempts to relate the construct to age. Indeed, Binet and Simon's first notions about intelligence were validated on the basis of IQ increasing with age, at least in childhood. Other research since then suggests that intelligence can decrease in the later years, especially fluid intelligence (Kaufman, 2000, 2001). In the field of creativity, there is nothing like a consensus regarding the relation of age to creativity. Russ (this volume) suggests that young children develop creativity in large part through their imaginative play. Some (Simonton, 1977, this volume) have studied the issue in detail, looking at creative trajectories across the life-span. Indeed, as Simonton has noted, creativity may decrease with age, but the decrease may reflect reduced productivity rather than less ideation.

- Is creativity domain specific? Most (but not all) researchers believe that creativity is at least somewhat domain specific (e.g., Kaufman, Glăveanu, and Baer, forthcoming), but the question is still an open one. For example, Baer (this volume) and Gardner (this volume) are strong believers in domain specificity. Runco (this volume), Renzulli (this volume), and Plucker (this volume) take a more domain-general approach while also viewing creativity as having some domain-specific aspects. The field of intelligence, in contrast, is dominated by hierarchical models (Carroll, 1993; Johnson and Bouchard, 2005), with domain-general intelligence, or g, at the top of the hierarchy, and more domain-specific aspects of intelligence lower in the hierarchy.

- Does creativity involve special processes, and if so, what are they? The answer to this question is wide open. Ward (this volume) and colleagues (Finke, Ward, and Smith, 1992) have proposed a set of cognitive processes that can be particularly applied to creative work, whereas Weisberg (this volume) has suggested that the processes of creative thinking are no different from those processes used in ordinary thinking. Others look at different stages of the creative problem solving process, from problem construction to idea generation to idea evaluation (Mumford, Martin, Elliott, and McIntosh, this volume; Reiter-Palmon, this volume). Investigators even differ as to whether they emphasize, in their work, creative processes, or products. For example, Ward (this volume), Lubart (this volume), and Runco (this volume), have emphasized process in much of their work, whereas Baer (this volume), Reiter-Palmon (this volume), Cropley (this volume), and Amabile (this volume) have more emphasized products.

- Can people be taught to be more creative? There is a large literature on teaching for creativity (Beghetto, this volume; Renzulli, this volume), and the consensus seems to be that creativity can be developed (Beghetto, Kaufman, and Baer, 2014). In the field of intelligence, there is much more skepticism regarding whether intelligence can be taught or even developed in some degree (Sternberg, 1985b). Certainly, many researchers believe that creativity is an ability or set of abilities (Sternberg, 2005). There is also, however, a great deal of work that examines creativity as a trait, more comparable to personality (Feist, this volume) or beliefs.

- What is the role of culture in creativity? There seems to be widespread agreement that creativity is a cultural phenomenon, and that cultures often have different ideas about what creativity is (Lubart, this volume).

This topic continues to inspire extensive research that covers many different related issues, including how creativity is conceived by distinct cultures (Niu and Kaufman, 2013; Niu and Sternberg, 2002), how multicultural experience can enhance creativity (Tadmor, Galinsky, and Maddux, 2012), and the way in which one's cultural context shapes creative expression (Glăveanu, 2015). Cultures are equally likely to have different views of intelligence (Sternberg, 2004), but some investigators are less likely to care, with many of them believing that intelligence transcends culture (Jensen, 1998).

- Who decides what is creative? The consensus in the field of creativity is that society plays a major part in labeling behavior and products as more or less creative (Csikszentmihalyi, 2013), a point emphasized by Sternberg (this volume) and Amabile (this volume). The field of intelligence, with some exceptions (e.g., Sternberg, 1984), ignores societal conceptions of what is intelligent.
- What is the role of groups in creativity? There seems to be a consensus that creativity often can be an emergent phenomenon in groups (Lubart, this volume; Sawyer, this volume) but that individuals play a key role. Mumford, Martin, Elliott, and McIntosh (this volume), Reiter-Palmon (this volume), and Amabile (this volume) especially have studied creativity in the context of larger group and organizational settings. In the field of intelligence, investigators are just beginning to realize the importance of group or collective intelligence (Malone and Bernstein, 2013).
- To what extent is creativity traitlike versus statelike? Creativity seems to have aspects of both a trait and a state (Sawyer, this volume). Some people are clearly more creative in their performances than other people, but creativity is less stable than intelligence. There are days when the most creative person just does not best express his or her creativity. Intelligence is generally viewed in the field as traitlike, although some have argued for statelike properties (Sternberg, 2014).
- What are the roles of personality and motivation in creativity? The consensus seems to be that personality and motivation play a major role in creativity (Amabile, this volume; Feist, this volume; Hennessey, this volume), whereas there is much less consensus regarding their role in intelligence. In particular, intrinsic motivation and openness to experience seem especially important to sustained and meaningful creative performance. Personality and motivation have not played key roles in the study of intelligence. They are often studied in relationship to

achievement (such as GPA or work performance), with conscientiousness typically the personality factor most strongly tied to successful outcomes (DeYoung, 2015).

- What happens at the extremes of creativity? Some researchers specialize in the upper extreme, or Big-C creativity (Simonton, this volume). Other researchers are more interested in everyday creativity (mini-c and little-c creativity) (Baer, this volume; Kaufman, this volume; Richards and Goslin-Jones, this volume). There is a large literature on extremes of intelligence, and even the suggestion that people at the most upper end are the ones with the potential best to shape society.

These are, we believe, the dominating questions today in the field of creativity. What is interesting is that some of the dominating questions in the field of intelligence are not particularly prominent in the creativity literature, especially questions about group differences and heritability. Perhaps future investigators will be more interested in these questions, but we view it as salubrious that investigators do not have the same fixation on such questions that some intelligence researchers have.

It is daunting to predict the future, but one broad question that we hope will be more salient to the next generation of creativity researchers is to articulate how creativity can make the world a better place. Many chapter authors note that creativity underlies many of humanity's great accomplishments. Several note the potential for creativity to continue to improve the world. How can this happen? Plucker (this volume) calls for creativity researchers to better communicate with policy makers. Kaufman (this volume) argues that creativity can help improve issues of social justice and inequity. Sternberg (this volume) asks whether creativity will be used for good or evil in years to come.

If creativity as a field grew out of intelligence, we hope it will continue to embrace different constructs, such as wisdom, ethics, and kindness. Such tendencies will not only impact the science of creativity, but also the world.

REFERENCES

Amabile, T. (1996). *Creativity in context: Update to "The social psychology of creativity."* Boulder, CO: Westview Press.

Beghetto, R. A., Kaufman, J. C., and Baer, J. (2014). *Teaching for creativity in the Common Core classroom.* New York: Teachers College Press.

Carroll, J. B. (1993). *Human cognitive abilities: A survey of factor-analytic studies.* New York: Cambridge University Press.

Csikszentmihalyi, M. (2013). *Creativity: Flow and the psychology of discovery and invention.* New York: HarperCollins.

Davidson, J. E., and Sternberg, R. J. (Eds.). (2003). *The psychology of problem solving.* New York: Cambridge University Press.

DeYoung, C. G. (2015). Cybernetic Big Five Theory. *Journal of Research in Personality,* 56, 33–58.

Finke, R. A., Ward, T. B., and Smith, S. M. (1992). *Creative cognition: Theory, research, and applications.* Cambridge, MA: MIT Press.

Gardner, H. (2011). *The theory of multiple intelligences.* New York: Basic Books.

Glăveanu, V. P. (2015). Creativity as a sociocultural act. *Journal of Creative Behavior,* 49, 165–180.

Guilford, J. P. (1950). Creativity. *American Psychologist,* 5, 444–454.

(1967). *The nature of human intelligence.* New York: McGraw-Hill.

(1968). *Creativity, intelligence and their educational implications.* San Diego, CA: Knapp.

Jensen, A. R. (1998). *The g factor.* Westport, CT: Greenwood-Praeger.

Johnson, W., and Bouchard, T. J., Jr. (2005). The structure of human intelligence: It's verbal, perceptual, and image rotation (VPR), not fluid crystallized. *Intelligence,* 33, 393–416.

Kaufman, A. S. (2000). Seven questions about the WAIS-III regarding differences in abilities across the 16 to 89 year life span. *School Psychology Quarterly,* 15, 3–29.

(2001). WAIS-III IQs, Horn's theory, and generational changes from young adulthood to old age. *Intelligence,* 29, 131–167.

Kaufman, J. C., and Beghetto, R. A. (2009). Beyond big and little: The Four C model of creativity. *Review of General Psychology,* 13, 1–12.

Kaufman, J. C., Glăveanu, V., and Baer, J. (Eds.). (forthcoming). *The Cambridge handbook of creativity across domains.* New York: Cambridge University Press.

Malone, T. W., and Bernstein, M. S. (Eds.). (2013). *Handbook of collective intelligence.* Cambridge, MA: MIT Press.

Niu, W., and Kaufman, J. C. (2013). Creativity of Chinese and American cultures: A synthetic analysis. *Journal of Creative Behavior,* 47, 77–87.

Niu, W., and Sternberg, R. J. (2002). Contemporary studies on the concept of creativity: The East and the West. *Journal of Creative Behavior,* 36, 269–288.

Reiter-Palmon, R., Robinson-Morral, E., Kaufman, J. C., and Santo, J. (2012). Evaluation of self-perceptions of creativity: Is it a useful criterion? *Creativity Research Journal,* 24, 107–114.

Silvia, P. J., Wigert, B., Reiter-Palmon, R., and Kaufman, J. C. (2012). Assessing creativity with self-report scales: A review and empirical evaluation. *Psychology of Aesthetics, Creativity, and the Arts,* 6, 19–34.

Simonton, D. K. (1977). Creative productivity, age, and stress: A biographical time-series analysis of 10 classical composers. *Journal of Personality and Social Psychology,* 35, 791–804.

Sternberg, R. J. (1984). What should intelligence tests test? Implications of a tri-
    archic theory of intelligence for intelligence testing. *Educational Researcher*,
    13, 5–15.
    (Ed.). (1985a). *Human abilities: An information-processing approach.* San Fran-
    cisco: Freeman.
    (1985b). Teaching critical thinking, Part 1: Are we making critical mistakes? *The
    Phi Delta Kappan*, 67, 194–198.
    (Ed.). (1988a). *Advances in the psychology of human intelligence.* Vol. 4. Hillsdale,
    NJ: Lawrence Erlbaum Associates.
    (Ed.). (1988b). *The nature of creativity.* New York: Cambridge University Press.
    (1997). Managerial intelligence: Why IQ isn't enough. *Journal of Management*,
    23(3), 463–475.
    (Ed.). (1999). *Handbook of creativity.* New York: Cambridge University Press.
    (2004). Culture and intelligence. *American Psychologist*, 59(5), 325–338.
    (2005). Creativity or creativities? *International Journal of Human Computer Stud-
    ies*, 63, 370–382.
    (2014). Intelligence as trait – and state? *Journal of Intelligence*, 2, 4–5.
Sternberg, R. J., and Davidson, J. E. (1982). The mind of the puzzler. *Psychology
    Today*, 16, 37–44.
    (1983). Insight in the gifted. *Educational Psychologist*, 18, 51–57.
Sternberg, R. J., and Grigorenko, E. L. (2004). Successful intelligence in the class-
    room. *Theory into Practice*, 43, 274–280.
Sternberg, R. J., and Hedlund, J. (2002). Practical intelligence, g, and work psy-
    chology. *Human Performance*, 15(1/2), 143–160.
Tadmor, C. T., Galinsky, A. D., and Maddux, W. W. (2012). Getting the most out
    of living abroad: Biculturalism and integrative complexity as key drivers of
    creative and professional success. *Journal of Personality and Social Psychology*,
    103, 520–542.
Willis, J. O., Dumont, R., and Kaufman, A. S. (2011). Factor-analytic models of
    intelligence. In *Cambridge handbook of intelligence*, edited by R. J. Sternberg
    and S. B. Kaufman, 39–57. New York: Cambridge University Press.

Index

381